Wish The
World Away

Wish The
World Away

Mark Eitzel and
American Music Club

Sean Body

SAF Publishing Ltd

SAF Publishing Ltd

First published in 1999 by SAF Publishing Ltd.

SAF Publishing Ltd.
Unit 7, Shaftesbury Centre,
85 Barlby Road,
London.
W10 6BN

ENGLAND

ISBN 0 946719 20 9

Photo on page 8: Phil Nicholls,
Photo on page 236: Steve Gullick.

A CIP catalogue record for this book is available from the British Library.

Printed in England by Redwood Books, Trowbridge, Wiltshire.

To my father and mother

"The musical canon is not decided by majority opinion but by enthusiasm and passion, and a work that ten people love passionately is more important than one that ten thousand do not mind hearing."

Charles Rosen

"You'll have a good time with this story. Everyone you will talk to is an egomaniac – with a totally distorted version of events – and an alcoholic with no powers of recall."

Vudi

"We were just human beings. We made five good records, so what do you want? Most bands don't even make one."

Mark Eitzel

Prelude 15th April 1998

In a Victorian Hotel on the corner of 4th and Bryant in the South of Market district of San Francisco, two musicians are performing a selection of old and new songs. The stage is almost completely dark, and the musicians are barely visible in the dim red glow. Bruce Kaphan is hunched over a pedal steel guitar that looks like a cross between a knitting machine and a synthesiser, out of which comes a beautiful, sweeping unearthly sound. Mark Eitzel sits holding an acoustic guitar close to his chest and finger-picks haunting, unfamiliar chords as he sings with rare aching emotion. As each song climaxes, his back arches and his brow grows more twisted with anguish as he searches for the right phrasing – the right melody to communicate what he clearly feels strongly in his heart. After each song the small crowd applauds vigorously.

As they begin a song announced as "What Holds the World Together," Dan Pearson, who until now has been sitting on the side of the stage, stands up, straps on a bass guitar and starts playing. It is the most beautiful song yet.

Before they follow it, the singer calls out into the audience, "Tim Mooney? Tim do you want to play on this one?" Tim clambers on to the small stage and sits down behind the drum kit. Then the four musicians blend into one mesmerising sound as they play four heartbreak-strewn songs; "I've Been A Mess," "Why Won't You Stay," "Firefly" and "Apology for an Accident." Each one sets a wealth of emotion and drama to a heaven-sent melody. The songs are sad, but the atmosphere is one of celebration and the audience grows more rapturous with each song. The band's smiles are just visible through the darkness. It is the first time they have played together for four years.

Another musician sits at the bar throughout the show. People in the audience repeatedly shout his name – "Vudi!" – and entreat him to get up on to the stage and join the band, but he does not turn around.

Not one of the five anonymous-looking musicians would be recognised in the streets outside, but on and off for ten years they had played together in a band called American Music Club. Briefly the most critically acclaimed act in popular music, they were arguably for a short period, also the greatest band in the world.

Chapter One

United Kingdom

Gotta keep moving
Gotta keep moving
Blues falling down like hail
Blues falling down like hail.

Robert Johnson

Maybe it's time for me go away
I'll get a new name
Maybe I'll get a new face.
It's time to go away
I don't belong in this place.

Mark Eitzel, "Western Sky."

The singer-songwriter medium is a peculiarly confessional one, and yet few have worn their broken heart on their sleeve, or bared their tortured soul to the degree that Mark Eitzel has. His work, both with American Music Club and solo, has always been achingly personal.

Because of this it is not always easy to separate the artist's work from his life. His songs are not just his perspective on the world, they are packed with detailed reconstructions of his own experiences, and peopled by his friends, family and lovers – often without the names being changed or omitted.

Across two decades, one of the key themes that runs throughout Mark Eitzel's songs is that of dislocation. To an extent, it is the underlying text of everything he has done. There's a feeling that his protagonists don't belong, or that they have lost their way or not found their true home. The characters in his songs are constantly moving on – searching for a happiness and a stability that has so far eluded them – or simply moving to escape a past that has offered them very little. This theme of dislocation is often amplified by the plaintive unresolved chords in the musical accompaniment. The music hangs in suspension, waiting for some outside force to bring it home.

Considering this, it is perhaps not surprising to discover that Mark Eitzel had a relatively unhappy childhood. It wasn't that he was brought up in an atmosphere of violence or neglect, simply that there was an intangible coldness in the family home. It did not help that his father's job meant the family were always moving to a new town or country before they could put down any roots, did not help.

John Mark Eitzel was born on the 30th January, 1959 in the San Francisco suburb of Walnut Creek. His father came from Denver, Colorado, trained as a marine engineer, and at the time of Mark's birth was working for the army in a civilian capacity. His mother, a teacher, hailed from France, but had turned her back on any vestiges of her national identity, considering herself simply to be American. Mark had one sibling, an older sister, Renee.

Whilst reasonably affluent, they were not a particularly close or happy family. Eitzel-senior was distant and often absent, whilst Renee and her mother never really got along. As parents they had very high expectations of their children – expectations which both children found hard to live up to. "Our parents demanded perfection," Renee would remember years later, "and they were very vocal about it."

In 1967, when Mark was eight, they moved to Okinawa and lived on an army base. The family then settled for four years, in Taiwan, where they had their own house in the Taiwanese community. Eitzel remembers it as "a pretty nice house, but ... surrounded by slums."

In a later interview Eitzel would speak of his isolation there: "I lived in Taiwan for years and went to school there, but no-one spoke to me for years, I was a bit of a freak. I was a mess."

In spite of this, he made a few good friends in Taiwan, and revelled in the exoticism of the city, dazzled by its colour and the brightness of the fireworks at Chinese New Year. He also found a new freedom in Taiwan afforded by his US currency – at the age of ten he could get downtown in a cab for 25 cents, and as his mother was teaching English to local children, Mark was free to explore the city on his own, or with Renee when she was not at boarding school.

By now, Renee had discovered pop music and the two of them would go shopping downtown for records. The first album Mark bought was *Pisces, Aquarius, Capricorn and Jones* by The Monkees, and he'd also buy singles by The Archies.

Eitzel's first memory of anything musical was even earlier, when back in the States, he had gone to the mall with his sister to buy *Meet The Beatles* on the day it came out. He still remembers, "us sitting in front of the stereo, listening to that record for the first time, and totally loving it."

By the time the family left the US, Renee had already amassed a decent collection of records, but the only album that survived the trip from the US was the soundtrack to *Mary Poppins*, a film Eitzel has enigmatically claimed to have "marked [him] for life". In Okinawa, Mark and Renee soon wore the record out, memorising the words and inflections. One of their favourite aspects of life in

Taiwan was that you could buy pirate copies of any album you wanted for 25 cents. The only snag was that they'd only last about 30 plays. Despite the disposable nature of these records, many of them made a lasting impression on Mark. To this day, he can still remember the dance routine he and Renee had worked out to Arthur Brown's "Fire".

"The quality wasn't good," recalls Renee, "but who cared? I spent a lot of money on all sorts of different kinds of music – sometimes I bought albums just because I liked the title. I must have had hundreds by the time we left… Our parents weren't home very often so we could play everything as loud as we wanted and would dance or perform everything over and over again. We had set pieces for different songs and even perfected harmonies to sing in the car or when we were out walking. Because we moved from school to school almost every year, music became our retreat and, at least in my case, salvation."

Despite Mark and Renee's love of popular music of most kinds, their mother disdained any interest in music, although she'd listen to Edith Piaf when she thought she was alone. Their father was initially more enthusiastic.

"Dad had stuff like Mitch Miller, Dean Martin, Lamplighters, and The Lettermen," Renee recalls, "and he would play Burl Ives at Christmas. These were on reel-to-reel tapes … [and] dad taught me how to mix, splice and blend when I was a kid. We would put together tapes for his friends or remix conversations we had recorded. After a while, my dad quit listening to music – I never knew why."

In 1970, the Eitzel family returned to the US. For a couple of years they moved from state to state, never really putting down roots anywhere. Then in 1972 they relocated to the United Kingdom. Mark's father was to run a base shared by the USAF and the RAF at Hythe, on the outskirts of Southampton.

On arrival, Renee was sent off to a new boarding school, while Mark tried to fit into another new environment – this time as a day pupil at St Mary's Grammar School. Joining a new school can be a traumatic experience. Entering a class mid-term that had already been together for two years, would be hard enough for any kid. For Eitzel, an outsider by way of being an American, it was particularly hard. To make matters worse, the years of constantly moving from country to country, and all the time spent on his own, had left Eitzel with little confidence in social situations.

"I was a basket case," he recalls. "I could barely deal with people. I didn't know what to say; it took me years to learn." Eitzel was desperate to be sociable, but felt unnaturally withdrawn and prone to morbid preoccupations.

"I always wanted to be totally into life," he later told journalist Andrew Smith. "One of those kind of flowing kids that just wears a smile all the time. I think I've got it in me, but I've always been obsessed with death, always. Even when I was a kid, I don't know why."

With Mark's father in a senior position, the family did a lot of entertaining at home. It was a time of endless cocktail parties, which the shy teenage Eitzel found excruciating. His mother insisted that the family had to put up a good front to the local community. Eitzel would rebel by writing "Love and Peace" on his school notebook.

The image of an embarrassed child at his parents' cocktail parties would stay with him for years as an example of his estrangement. In 1989, when asked by writer Steve Connell to figure out why his band American Music Club worried so many people, Eitzel returned to this theme with a peculiarly graphic image:

"Maybe they [the record listening public] find [AMC] cloying – like an overweight twelve-year-old boy you meet at his parents' cocktail party. He has this lugubrious thing he wants to show you, like his science project – it's this boring clumsy model of a volcano. And after your patronising attitude towards it wears off, you're left confronting this stupid kid and his ugly volcano, and it's dark in the room, and you want to get back to the cocktail party…"

Throughout his life, Eitzel has always been at pains to stress how ugly he believes he is – a feeling that was inevitably acute during adolescence. But in truth, he was a fairly normal looking youth. And, as he grew older, he became reasonably handsome. But, for Eitzel there was no middle ground in this area – because he wasn't beautiful, he had to be completely ugly. His hatred of his appearance would give him a powerful sense of self-loathing that would frequently spill over into all aspects of his life.

From the age of fourteen onwards, like many teenagers, Eitzel began to hate his parents. He also hated the idea that he was American, partly because it was where his parents were from, and partly because it set him apart from his classmates who would call him "a yankee Irish Jewish bastard" – an oddly illogical insult considering he was neither Jewish nor Irish. He later realised that his place of birth was not his only problem.

"For a long time I thought they hated me because I was American," Eitzel recalls, "but I think they hated me because I was weird."

In spite of his unhappy memories of school, Eitzel did make a few friends at St Mary's, and he is remembered fondly by many of the staff.

"He was a very pleasant and friendly student," his English teacher Pat McCarthy would say. "And he was far more mature than most of the other boys." McCarthy also thinks Eitzel may have exaggerated his fellow students' antipathy. "If anybody was giving him a hard time," he muses, "it was not evident."

The key cause of Eitzel's social isolation during his time in Southampton was the fact that his parents lived miles from St Mary's, in uninspiring suburbs like Hythe or Dibden Purlieu. With buses only running every two hours, it was difficult to see friends out of school hours. So, with his sister away at boarding school, Eitzel would spend a lot of time in his own company, and would find solace in books and music. He also started a love affair with alcohol that would dominate his life for years to come.

With time at home on his hands, Eitzel soon became a voracious reader, and harboured ambitions of becoming a playwright. Harold Pinter was his role model, and he also loved Samuel Beckett. At age fourteen, he had acquired his first book of poetry – a Dylan Thomas collection he glanced at in a shop and bought on impulse. He would call this a fluke that changed his life. Thomas quickly became a favourite. A "life changing" performance of Strindberg's *Dreamplay* further strengthened his resolve to write plays. But in spite of his dramatic aspirations, Eitzel had no desire to act or perform, and would confess later, "I never really wanted to be on stage at all."

At school Eitzel channelled his creativity into verse rather than drama, show-ing a keen interest in words – influenced perhaps by Thomas. "He produced a lot of poetry at that time," Pat McCarthy recollects, "It was very adventurous and he obviously enjoyed writing, though I can't say I understood all of it – sometimes it was difficult to fathom out what he was driving at." Renee read some of this early work and found it powerful, if occasionally disturbing: "Sometimes a line or paragraph would leave me uncomfortable and I didn't realise why until I was older."

McCarthy was also quick to notice in Eitzel's approach to his work a trait that would stick with him. "Mark was very self-critical," he remembers. "He always thought he was doing worse than he was."

While he wrote a number of full-length plays during this time, Eitzel was never really satisfied with them, and would compare his best effort to *Peyton Place*. He dabbled with drawing too, but music was becoming an increasingly important part of his life.

After acquiring his first guitar at the age of fifteen, Eitzel found it surprisingly easy to write and play his own songs. He maintains he had always heard tunes in his head:

"I'm insane. When I was a little kid, I remember I'd hear songs in my head, and then I'd wake up the next day and turn on the radio, and I'd hear the same songs, and I'd think people were listening to my thoughts and recording them really quickly. I was really tied into music and songwriting from a very early age. All I could do was write songs, it was all I ever wanted to do."

Eitzel's initial tastes were influenced by the records that his English teacher and his fellow students would play during Friday lunch breaks – progressive rock acts like Yes and Genesis. Gradually though, he found himself drawn to singer-songwriters. On a night his date stood him up, he saw Joan Armatrading support-ing Supertramp, and decided that her songs spoke to him in a way that Supertramp's could not. "I remember that her songs didn't sing down to me," he explains. "They included me, … and she meant it." He bought her eponymous album and it convinced him that he could start writing proper songs, "Suddenly, it seemed that in songwriting anything was possible."

Eitzel's early songs were, in his own words, "very Jazz-like." He didn't learn chords formally – instead he would experiment with finger patterns on the frets. He would never venture out of his bedroom with his guitar, but unbeknown to him, when Renee came home on vacations she would sit on the stairs beneath his room and listen to him play. And while she didn't like all of his songs, she was immediately "in awe of his ability."

Against the flow of Eitzel's increasing interest in literature and left-field music, at the age of sixteen he briefly dabbled with born-again Christianity on a trip to Cornwall. As a former choirboy, Eitzel had been brought up in the catholic tradition and still went to church each week, so he was fairly suscepti-ble. But, Eitzel's "born-again" phase only lasted about a week. "It was a bore to go to church," he recalled later, explaining his complete rejection of the church. "It doesn't do any good, and organised religion is evil."

After his short flirtation with the church, Eitzel became captivated by the bur-geoning musical revolution that was punk rock. He was soon addicted to the "punk-championing" *New Musical Express*, and tuned in every night to the John Peel radio show to hear acts like the Sex Pistols, The Stranglers and X-Ray Spex. "Blank Generation" by Richard Hell and the Voidoids struck a particular nerve, he remembers, "because they were American punks, and I thought I'll be loyal to them."

Though, contrary to punk's year zero ethos, Eitzel's tastes remained wide ranging, and his love for acts like Richard Hell didn't stop him from enjoying David Bowie, Leonard Cohen, Joan Armatrading or John Martyn.

At about this time, Eitzel attended his first punk rock gig – The Damned and The Adverts at Southampton Polytechnic. It would change his whole approach to songwriting. "I imagined singing [my songs] for an audience," he explains. "Before I only imagined people listening to them on records, and then suddenly I saw that I could do this live, and have a direct effect on people."

In spite of this realisation, Eitzel was never in a real band while in England, although he did get an early taste of live performance:

"There was this punk rock band in Southampton who befriended me and I was going to be their opening act... But I only did two shows when I lived in England, and they were both really embarrassing displays. My hit song was called 'I Love To Masturbate to Gilbert and Sullivan'."

By now Eitzel was drinking regularly, and a large intake of beer helped him overcome his shyness for these performances.

In the autumn of 1977, just as punk was beginning to get a real hold on the nation, Eitzel's father got posted back to the US. Having failed all of his A-level exams, Eitzel went back with his family. Perversely for someone who loved literature and wanted to write creatively, Mark had taken A-levels in Chemistry, Biology and Physics. In another context, Eitzel has said that he doesn't trust his own choices. This would appear to have been a prime example. His choice of A-level subjects showed a self-destructive willingness to subordinate his own needs and desires to those of others – in this case his parents and teachers – that would manifest itself in many aspects of his later life.

On arrival back in America, Eitzel enrolled as an undeclared honours student at Ohio State University in Columbus. He also stopped reading the *NME*, deciding its peculiarly English perspective was irrelevant to his new circumstances. Eitzel now resolved to draw artistic inspiration from his immediate surroundings, considering it his duty to write only about Columbus. Bearing in mind the nature of Columbus life, this would not be an uplifting experience.

"I lived in the East Side of Columbus," he recalls, "which is all shopping malls and suburbia, ... those people have everything, but they're the most miserable people on earth," adding later that Columbus was the place to go if "you wanna see people who look like hell."

Located on North High Street, Ohio State University's huge population of students was so far untouched by punk rock. The campus and the Columbus radio stations were dominated at that time by the music of The Eagles, Journey and Bruce Springsteen. Having left a country with his appetite whetted by a new radical musical explosion, he had arrived in a State where rock music was still stuck in 1973.

There were a few punk acts including Joboxers [no relation to the UK 80's pop band] and Nowhere 80, but the punk scene was under-developed, which was extremely frustrating to Eitzel who was now desperate to get a band together. Eventually he formed a punk rock covers band called The Cowboys with some people he met in a local bar.

The Cowboys' initial set list comprised punk "classics" like Sham 69's "Borstal Breakout," The Dead Boys' "Catholic Boy" and "Sonic Reducer," and a collection of awkward reggae songs. Considering Eitzel always wanted to write plays rather than act, and was not especially extroverted, live performance was potentially daunting. He would get over his embarrassment at being on stage by getting so drunk that he didn't care what the audience thought of him – a habit that would stick! During the shows he'd fling himself so frantically around the stage that he would crash into amplifiers and other band members, "I reasoned to myself that [on stage] you just have to lose all sense of shame," Eitzel explains. "That was important to me as a really shy person."

Eitzel's stage persona helped the band develop a certain local notoriety, but they were more well-known for their offstage activities – living the rock 'n' roll lifestyle to the full. The band members shared a house in Columbus that was the setting for a frenetic pace of partying.

"The Cowboy house was famous," Eitzel would later recall, "Every week we had a party there Friday, Saturday, and Sunday. After the local bar shut it would be everyone back to the Cowboy House, and we'd party to five in the morning." After one long party, the house actually burnt down. No one was hurt, but the era of The Cowboys' parties had come to an end.

While The Cowboys were a fairly unambitious college bar band, they did manage to put out one single, "Teenage Life" on Tet Offensive Records in 1980. The A-side was written by a friend of the band, and weighing in at a mere two and a half minutes, it is a classic punk outburst of teenage angst and boredom. Eitzel says elliptically of his influences at the time of making the record, "I was into Althea and Donna – does it show?" In truth, the sound most resembles The Buzzcocks. The lyrics are fairly unsophisticated:

> *Sit at home watch TV,*
> *Wonder what will satisfy me.*
> *Teenage life. It's just an excuse.*
> *We are animals in a zoo*
> *Doesn't matter what we do.*
> *They say Teenage life is the best*
> *I look to the future I get depressed.*

While Eitzel's vocal style on "Teenage Life" is more like Johnny Rotten than anyone else – occasionally drifting into a Feargal Sharkey quaver – the primitive sound and lyrical nihilism is most redolent of Eitzel's early punk favourite, Richard Hell's "Blank Generation."

The B-side, "Supermarket," was the first recording of one of Eitzel's own songs. It has a quasi-Clash reggae beat complete with Clash-influenced "Oh oh" backing vocals. Eitzel's voice sounds like David Byrne on what is a much more arty take on punk. But as well as being another angst-ridden attack on the mundanity of life – shopping malls, piped muzak, growing up just so you can die – the song also seems strangely autobiographical. Many of the lines sound like a highly demanding parent berating a child. Renee's earlier description of their mother and father come to mind as he sings:

> *I'm stuck in a supermarket,*
> *Mommy please hold my hand.*
> *They're pushing me in a basket,*
> *I can't move, I don't understand.*
> *Put your hands on your head and stay in your place.*
> *Put your head upon her shoulder*
> *Cry cry I want to see you cry*
> *Grow up so you get older*
> *Grow up so you can die*
> *Now I'm running away*
> *From all the things you say...*
> *You can't learn until you listen*
> *But I can't sit still.*

The track also features a brief, slightly out of place, weird art rock guitar solo, not quite Robert Quine's riffing on "Blank Generation", but interesting nonetheless. Both A and B-sides were probably too weird for the Columbus scene and after one review which praised the guitar solo and nothing else, the single disappeared without trace. Eitzel would later consider it an embarrassment.

At the time though, The Cowboys weren't unduly worried about the record's lack of success. On the whole they just wanted to play live, but Eitzel was beginning to tire of doing cover versions, and his main gripe was that the other Cowboys refused to play any of his songs, considering them "too dark, too twisted, and maybe too Joy Division...." Eitzel also remembers a personality mismatch between himself and the rest of the band, "I was serious and into yoga, and I didn't do as many drugs as the other guys." Shortly after the single's release, The Cowboys broke up.

In retrospect, aside from the single, Eitzel looks back fondly on the band's early days.

"The thing that was good and different about The Cowboys was that it was before Hardcore became popular, so we would go and play mid-western cities before anyone even knew anything about punk, and people would think that we had written all of the songs. Of course we said we hadn't, but nobody had any idea what we were. So we'd play these towns and we'd blow people's minds. They'd get really into it, we were like a really upbeat dance band ... but they were shocked, because they had never heard anything about punk rock."

By the time the mid-West caught up, Eitzel wasn't interested anymore:

"I remember my last night with The Cowboys was in Dayton. The year before we'd played The Forest Lawn and the crowd was full of shocked and stunned long-haired people, and it was fun... But the next time we played Dayton there were two punk rock girls who pretended to have a fight while we were playing, and it just seemed stupid."

Before the end of The Cowboys' brief but eventful existence Eitzel met someone who would have a profound effect on his work and life, and whom he would later refer to as his "muse", Kathleen Burns.

Many years later, Kathleen would still vividly remember the first time she saw Eitzel:

"I'd seen him on his bike tucking his pants into his tennis shoes, and he had this big moustache and a lot of hair, he looked like Einstein. I thought, I want to meet him. Then I found out that he'd been following me. We finally met in the college library."

Kathleen and Mark knew a lot of the same people, but while she was a big fan of rock music, with extremely varied tastes – "I grew up in Cleveland, Ohio and there was nothing to do there except go to rock concerts, collect records, and read books" – she wasn't part of the small Columbus punk rock clique. The fact that Mark was a musician was initially a shock to her, "I thought 'Oh My God! He's in a rock band'." Shortly after they would embark on an intense relationship that would provide much of the subject matter for Eitzel's songs across a number of years.

After the break-up of The Cowboys, Eitzel's music took a sharp turn. As punk was finally starting to graze the American consciousness, and beginning to get a foothold in Ohio, Eitzel started to play post-punk folk music at open mike sessions in local bars – performing his own material solo on an acoustic guitar under the name Billy Lee Buckeye. He also had a regular folk slot at the deli where Kathleen worked.

With the "Cowboy House lifestyle" a thing of the past, Eitzel started hanging out with a group of local rockabillies who would have a lasting impact on him. The rockabilly scene was thriving in Columbus, much more so than punk at the time. This particular contingent took great pride in dressing immaculately, their drug of choice was heroin, and their preferred reading was surrealist literature. The Ohio rockabillies gave Eitzel a first-hand lesson in "how to be cool," but it was their choice of reading matter that would make the biggest impression. Through this scene Eitzel discovered Rimbaud, Lautreamont's *Chants de Maldoror*, and Georges Bataille, whose highly-charged transgressional, quasi-erotic *Story Of An Eye* was a particular favourite.

The key to surrealist writing was the unconscious, as revealed in automatic writing, dreams, everyday objects juxtaposed in unpremeditated ways and in artistic endeavour. Scholar, Franklin Rosemont later elaborated on the movement's intent:

"Surrealism aims to reduce, and ultimately to resolve, the contradictions between sleeping and waking, dream and action, reason and madness, the conscious and the unconscious, the individual and society and the subjective and the objective."

Surrealist writers saw themselves as "specialists in revolt," and refused to accept rigid definitions or conventional, rational boundaries. The key therefore was to suspend one's rational judgement and self-censorship, and let the unconscious part of the mind shine through the writing and art.

Surrealist ideas about creativity and communication would become integral to Eitzel's views on art, as well as a significant influence on his song-writing and his chaotic stage performances. His songs would often bring together disparate images, and on stage he would get so drunk or high that he would have little conscious control over his actions.

Eitzel would try to avoid taking the conventional path, and would ensure that there were no barriers in his approach to work. More problematic to a musician trying to operate in the "popular" field was the surrealist position of rejecting the commercial market-place. If he wanted to bring his music to a larger audience, he would have to deal with the record industry.

Surrealist literature would remain one of Eitzel's passions, but it could be argued that an adherence to the values of surrealism would ensure that the commercial failure of his later bands was inevitable.

Eitzel carried on playing folk-tinged acoustic music for a few months, but this was only catering to one aspect of what he wanted to do. Post-punk bands such as Joy Division now gripped him, and he started to look for a more musically eclectic outlet. John Hricko, a bassist he knew from the local bar Crazy Mommas, introduced him to Nancy Kangas, a Raincoats fan with a love of American folk art, who wanted to make naive traditional music, and the Naked Skinnies were born. Eitzel and Nancy shared the songwriting and singing, while the line-up was completed by Greg Bonnell on drums.

According to Eitzel, the Naked Skinnies were formed with the eclectic manifesto "that everything is good. We wanted to be everyone from *Metal Box* era PiL to The Raincoats to Joy Division. *Metal Box* at the time was such a revolutionary record for me, because it was so anti-musical and it really pushed the barriers of what music could be."

While Eitzel was later dismissive of the songs he wrote during his time with The Skinnies, he still found the experience of learning to express himself energising, and also in keeping with surrealist ideas of letting the unconscious speak:

"It wasn't real writing. [It was more] exploring how to talk, but it was somehow exciting because sometimes you reveal more by making glaring mistakes. I was just really saying I am alive, I am here. Look at me!"

After about a year of rehearsals and local gigs, the Naked Skinnies went into a local studio to record a nine-song demo tape. They sent the tape to a number of record labels and radio stations, and Ron House, of local Columbus label Magnolia Thunderpussy Records, agreed to put up half of the $500 needed for the band's first single, "All My Life."

That Eitzel had moved on from his days of straight punk is instantly clear from the first bars of the A-side. The chords are strummed rather than thrashed, the bass snakes in an English gothic fashion, and the vocals are crooned.

The lyrics are a series of almost surreal images of dislocation and alienation. Verse one begins:

> *1,000 poisons in the window*
> *A pointed face he looks right at you*
> *Abstract moves instigated*
> *Separated, assassinated...*

In the chorus, as he repeats the line "All my life for someone to talk to" four times, Eitzel lets rip. By the final line he is shrieking.

In spite of the Skinnies' eclectic intentions, "All My Life" is a fairly straight-forward melodic pop song. Still, while it may not have seemed out of place in early '80s London, Manchester or Liverpool, this was a radical sound for Ohio and the B-side took the more extreme elements even further. While "All My Life" follows a fairly conventional intro-verse-verse-chorus-verse pattern, the song at the heart of "This is the Beautiful Night" is merely a fragment, a few softly repeated circular phrases. It hints at the way forward for some of Eitzel's more haunting songs. With its Martin Hannett-style production, "Beautiful Night" could be an outtake from Joy Division's *Unknown Pleasures* or an early track from Leeds Goth pioneers, The Sisters of Mercy. Beginning slowly, the song grows from a tinny echoey distant guitar, accompanied by spaghetti western style whistling feedback, into a powerful panoramic gothic anthem, as Eitzel sings:

> *This is the beautiful night*
> *This is the beautiful night*
> *And it makes me so happy.*
> *And there is no-one there at all*
> *Why should anyone care at all.*

As the song continues, the Peter Hook-style high-fret-bass riff pulsates more and more manically. The drums reverberate and Eitzel's singing grows increasingly tortured.

The track is certainly derivative, and yet the power of Eitzel's voice, and the intensity of the other musicians' performance somehow lifts it above mere mimicry. When pushed, Eitzel would concede reluctantly that maybe it "wasn't such a bad song." Unfortunately, on release the single failed to garner any kind of attention. While some people in Columbus were catching up with punk and new wave, the two local radio stations stuck to a diet of FM rock bands like Foreigner and REO Speedwagon. They were never going to play the Naked Skinnies.

"We made 1,000 copies," Eitzel remembers wryly, "and I think I threw away 500 of them."

Although the Skinnies' vinyl debut was not a success, no-one but Eitzel really had expected it to be, and just having made the record was some mark of progress. Unfortunately, Eitzel didn't see it this way. As he spent more and more time with the Naked Skinnies, he started to have significant doubts about what he was doing, feeling that playing in a punk band was perhaps beneath him. These feelings were certainly influenced by his parents' attitude to his music. Aware that they disapproved strongly, even though he was in his second band, he would rarely discuss his musical activities with them:

"I was in The Cowboys and they didn't know. They didn't know I was into any music when I was in Columbus. I didn't tell them. They knew I played guitar but they didn't know I was in bands. They hated it."

Mark's sister Renee remembers things slightly differently:

"Our father was proud of Mark's creativity and would play his Naked Skinnies' single for their friends. Unfortunately this embarrassed our mother terribly."

According to Renee, their mother's definition of success was extremely rigid:

"Mark would become a 'professional' which meant a doctor or lawyer or CEO and I would marry well which meant a 'professional' and have children. She was bitterly disappointed when Mark's interests and passions were artistic and creative.... I don't think she ever forgave [him]."

Even Eitzel's delicate style of guitar playing had come about partly as a result of trying to avoid his mother hearing him practice in his bedroom:

"The reason I play songs so quietly is because my mother had fucking radar, and every time I'd play one note on the guitar, she'd say, 'Put that down and get on with something else'."

To add to his doubts about music as a career, Eitzel was increasingly pressured by many different demands on his time. In addition to the Skinnies, and his full-time course, he was working on a performance art piece. He was also managing somehow to hold down a 35-hour-a-week "day job" coding computer data – earning money he needed to survive in the absence of any grant. He also found time somehow to write a regular column in a local magazine called *The Offence Newsletter*.

Although interested in his studies, it was hardly surprising he found it difficult to find the time and motivation required for his college work. Torn between his job, his music and his performance art, he decided to drop out of college without completing his course.

The Skinnies carried on gigging, but after their single flopped so resoundingly, part of their impetus was gone. It seemed that they would never get anywhere if they stayed in Ohio, so towards the end of 1981 Nancy and Greg decided to move to San Francisco. Stuck in a dead-end job, without even his band to keep him going, Eitzel quickly followed them. Initially he wasn't sure where to go. He didn't want to go to New York, and while London held an attraction for him, he felt that he couldn't go back to England, believing that as he was American he should live in America. In the end he decided to go to San Francisco in order to keep the Naked Skinnies together.

In retrospect Eitzel views this move to a bigger more exciting environment as something of a "cop-out". Looking back he told one interviewer that New York was the happening place for music, but San Francisco by comparison was dead:

"In America there's a tradition that you either move to New York, Los Angeles or San Francisco, maybe Seattle now. If you wanted to work you'd go to New York; if you wanted to find yourself you'd go to San Francisco."

Much later Eitzel confessed that at the time he was simply "afraid of New York." Until then he had felt his music and writing was too influenced by other artists, and feared that his music might be diluted or somehow tainted by the New York or London scenes.

San Francisco had the attraction that its music scene was somehow fresher and less established. Also, Eitzel's parents were married in San Francisco, and he was born in the San Francisco suburbs. To have some background in the area was perhaps a measure of comfort.

Kathleen was supposed to go to San Francisco with Eitzel, but in the end she decided to go to Europe instead. She returned to Ohio six months later, to find "all kinds of letters" from Eitzel telling her why she should follow him to San Francisco. A month later she went.

Historically a beautiful sea-port with a warm climate, San Francisco was also the place where sailors and silver prospectors would come to blow their wages on booze and whores. It has always been a city of contrasting cultures. Below the quaint mansions on its hills lurked derelict Spanish Missions and waterfront dives – the earthquake that devastated much of the city in 1906 was seen by some as divine retribution for the city's gold-lust and sinfulness, its vice and violence. As a by-product of San Francisco's social diversity, the city has an atmosphere of tolerance to non-conformism that has always been attractive to bohemians and artists operating around the fringes.

Before San Francisco became the centre of the late 60s Summer of Love music scene dominated by the acid rock of Jefferson Airplane and the Grateful Dead, it was a pivotal city for the 50s Beats. Kerouac, Ginsberg and Neal Cassady would hang out in the bars on North Beach, near where Lawrence Ferlinghetti would later open the City Lights bookstore. In the 70s, after the decline of the Haight Ashbury scene, San Francisco saw the emergence of a hugely visible and vocal gay community.

Over time, the influence that San Francisco's history and geography would have on Eitzel's life and music would be immense. But it would take a while. On arrival he found San Francisco "intimidating." Unlike Columbus, where punk was a very minor fringe thing, San Francisco already had a huge thriving punk rock scene with Jello Biafra's Dead Kennedys and Flipper at the top of the pile. In addition to the bigger artists, there was a huge number of minor punk bands gigging regularly in the area. Oddly for such a bastion of hippiedom, San Francisco had become one of the key punk capitals in the US.

After a few weeks the Naked Skinnies settled in, bought a home studio and started to rehearse and record. Their initial demos were accomplished, but it soon became clear that the other Skinnies were less ambitious than Eitzel. "I wanted to be number one," he recalls, "they just wanted to be artists." His ambition didn't mean compromising the band's musical vision; he simply wanted to be successful on his own terms.

Eitzel's ambition was offset by the Skinnies' punk anti-commercialism – it simply would not have occurred to them to try to sign to a major label.

While the band had a punk attitude, their music did not comprise of two-minute sound barrages. Instead they were trying to produce melody and beauty from amongst a wall of noise.

"We just wanted to make music," Eitzel remembers. "I was always into making timeless music. Music that would be great forever. We just thought, let's make these beautiful recordings, and we did."

Then two months after arriving in San Francisco, Greg and Nancy's house was burgled, Nancy narrowly escaping injury in the process. The couple's resulting paranoia soon rubbed off on Eitzel. The band moved to another house in a better area, but within a few months they were robbed again. This time, tragically all of their tapes were stolen. They had no other copies, and Eitzel's first stab at 'timeless beautiful music' was lost forever.

Shortly after this blow to their recording ambitions, the Naked Skinnies' viability as a live act was severely dented when they were banned from playing the two largest punk rock clubs in town: the Mabuhay Gardens, and its sister club, On Broadway, located upstairs in the same building.

Owned by the notorious local impresario, Dirk Dirkson, nephew of Senator Everett Dirkson of Illinois, the Mabuhay Gardens had opened its doors to punk in 1976. It soon became the city's premier venue for punk and new wave, after a previous existence hosting supper shows featuring dancing girls and a Fillipino Elvis impersonator.

On the night of the Naked Skinnies' final show at the Gardens, a popular San Francisco band called Girls On Drugs were playing upstairs at On Broadway. Girls On Drugs were local heroes, but this was to be their last gig. In fact it was a memorial for one of their members who had taken the band name a little too literally and overdosed on heroin in the club's toilets.

So, while Girls On Drugs ran through an emotionally-charged set of their best songs in front of a packed and highly partisan crowd, the Naked Skinnies went full tilt to alienate the few punters who had strayed downstairs to see them.

"With the Naked Skinnies, our biggest thing was that if you drive people out, that is a reaction. It doesn't matter. Just get a reaction." Eitzel recalls. "For our first song that night, I played one note on a Moser guitar all the way through, with all the reverb on, the treble on full, and the treble boost on too... Nancy would sing this kind of sing-song thing over the top of it, and the drums and the bass would go on, and it was basically like that for 15 minutes."

Not surprisingly, most of the audience quickly abandoned the gig for the show upstairs. Dirkson was downstairs that night to witness the Naked Skinnies clear three-quarters of the Mabuhay Gardens' audience in just under five minutes, and was appalled. When the show finished, he told the band they would never play in either club again. Eitzel responded by telling Dirkson, "I hope you die." But in spite of his bravado, Dirkson's influence with other promoters meant that this was a disaster for an up-and-coming band.

Among the few punters who remained was a local musician called Mark Pankler, known later as Vudi. Pankler loved it, and after the show he approached Eitzel, telling him, "that was the most amazing thing I have seen in my entire life." Eitzel's response was to say simply "Fuck you." Vudi just laughed, told Eitzel he'd like to work with him, and left.

After the Mabuhay debacle, the Naked Skinnies continued to play small local clubs to audiences of less than ten people, but frustrated at their lack of progress, relationships within the band began to disintegrate – Eitzel in particular was becoming more and more tense. Back at the house the band shared, Eitzel would go from room to room, turning people's stereos off, yelling, "What the fuck are you listening to this fucking shit for?" in between bouts of door slamming.

Things came to a head when the band played the local Sound Of Music club in the sleazy Tenderloin district to an audience of about 40 people. After an intensely brutal version of "This is the Beautiful Night," during which a flailing Eitzel had managed to break every single string on his guitar, he completely lost control.

As the song finished, he noticed a kid in the front who was laughing and clapping at the same time, and got incensed at what he perceived to be ridicule.

"I guess [the kid] was enjoying it," he told Cary Tennis in a 1987 interview, "but … I smashed my guitar and I looked at him, and [I thought] so the song is over, and now you're happy, isn't that wonderful, you deserve to die … There was something in him that was evil … something that I wanted to destroy."

Overtaken by a Travis Bickell-type rage, he yelled at the kid, "What are you laughing at? What are you fucking laughing at?" then threw his guitar to the ground and dived from the stage onto the offending party, lashing into him with his fists.

The venue's security and the other band members intervened and pulled the two apart. Minutes later, his rage now dissipated, and with a growing sense of shame at his own behaviour, Eitzel left the venue without speaking to any of the other Skinnies and walked the streets until the sun came up.

When he got home Greg and Nancy told him that they'd had enough. Playing with Eitzel was just too unpredictable, they never knew what he would do next, and they could no longer handle it. After less than a year in San Francisco, and with only two tracks recorded for posterity on an impossible to find single, The Naked Skinnies broke up.

With hindsight Eitzel is philosophical about the band's demise:

"I don't like predictable … predictable is a bore. That's why I'm not success-ful. If I were predictable, I probably would be somewhere now."

Chapter Two

Restless Strangers

"We played this show in San Jose in like 1985, and it was filled with jocks, I called 'em Nazi fodder, ya know? One of the guys came up to us and said to Vudi, 'You guys gotta do two things – you gotta get rid of that stupid singer, and you gotta play pussy music'."

Mark Eitzel

"There's always a really big 'if'. It's always ready to break down every moment. What holds it together is everybody's frailness more than any dream."

Dan Pearson

Even though he had precipitated the split, Eitzel felt sad and betrayed after the final break-up of the Naked Skinnies. The various ex-members continued to share the same house for a short while, but there was no question of the band reforming. A few weeks after their last show he moved into an apartment in Park Beach with Kathleen Burns.

With no desire to start a new band, Eitzel got a job selling condo and car packages at a local travel agency called Creative Leisure, owned by a coke-snorting army veteran. Without the distraction of keeping a band gigging and rehearsing, and with the benefit of a steady salary, Eitzel could now concentrate on his real love – songwriting. Kathleen "never saw Mark without a notebook and a pen."

He didn't miss the attention of being in a band at all. He confesses that it was almost a relief, "because I'd already been a big fish in a small pool. And San Francisco was another small pool. I didn't care about being a big fish anymore. I just wanted to do my music, that's all."

Day to day, Eitzel enjoyed Creative Leisure, but the office conditions were not ideal. He coped with the stress of cold-calling by taking large quantities of speed, while his colleagues chain-smoked furiously. Eventually the huge amount of tobacco fumes caused him to contract a throat infection. It is a condition which continues to plague him to this day. It makes his voice weak and prone to give up completely if pushed too hard. As a result he can never play more than a couple of shows on consecutive nights without losing his voice – a handicap that effectively makes touring financially unviable.

Meanwhile, Kathleen got jobs at a market research company and a bakery, and the two of them settled into something akin to a domestic routine. Every day they would go to work, and every night they would go out and drink.

"We went to the local bars a lot..." Kathleen recalled. "Things were good and they weren't. Mark and I both have strong personalities, and as much as we could like each other, we could also hate each other."

Kathleen remembered Mark as being miserable but comfortable, though she added, "I can't say that Mark has ever seemed particularly happy."

While they weren't part of any local music scene, there would always be music playing on Kathleen's tinny portable cassette player in their flat. Eitzel's listening preferences were still rooted in punk rock, whereas Kathleen was a big fan of Nick Drake, Elvis Costello and Nico. Eitzel was initially uninterested in these people. Each evening, he would come in from work, turn off Kathleen's tape player and then disappear into the bedroom. Kathleen would then turn it straight back on again.

In the evenings, before they went to the local bar, Eitzel would work on his songs, and Kathleen would write poetry and stories, although she would not show her work to anyone, not even Mark. Eitzel could not resist peeking while she was out at work, "I'd come home sometimes and he'd be sitting back there reading [my] stuff and I'd get real mad."

A few months after the demise of the Skinnies, Eitzel bumped into a friend called Dave Paul who he'd met in Cincinatti when on tour with the band. When Eitzel explained that he was without a band, but still writing songs, Paul invited him to do some recording with his four track machine. The results, a seven song cassette entitled *Mean Mark Eitzel Gets Fat*, is an odd collection of feedback drenched, PiL-influenced, angular art-punk. It is dominated by tribal percussion, murmuring bass lines, and acoustic guitars which sound like they are being strummed by someone wearing boxing gloves. On one track, to a loud backing completely devoid of musical hooks, Eitzel yells over and over, *"I speak French very well... I don't speak French at all,"* on another he starts out singing the melody to the hymn "Swing Low Sweet Chariot," before a spoken rant over industrial percussion collapses into feedback and dog howls. The other tracks are more promising, and include lyrical and musical fragments of songs that would later be taken up by American Music Club. Eitzel's lyrics show more evidence of craft, and a clear talent for melody emerges on tracks like "Shadow of My Name," "You Can Be Beautiful," and "Keep This Dance For Me" – the latter a dark gothic surge, gilded with plucked Spanish guitar licks.

The stand-out track is a shimmering ballad, "Hold On To Your Love" – the first recorded example of the soft Eitzel vocals that would characterise the early AMC albums. Wracked with understated emotion, he repeats the tag line

"Something else, a finer pleasure, something else..." over aching, intertwined acoustic guitars.

Eitzel sold the cassette via mail order for the princely sum of $3.00 each. A local Rough Trade shop also sold a few copies. The cover was a primitive Eitzel line drawing of a stick man with a hugely inflated stomach. The self-deprecating sleeve notes explain that "This tape is the result of my forty hour a week job that helps me finance gross conceits of this sort." Typically, Eitzel would later say simply that it "sucked."

Towards the end of 1982, Eitzel started to perform some songs at a weekly acoustic new wave slot at a coffee bar called The Tattoo Rose. It was a small dank barely furnished place on Columbus, in a seedy part of the North of Market area, but Eitzel enjoyed playing his own material there. A lot of the same musicians would appear each week, and he made a lot of friends within the little scene that developed. The acoustic framework suited Eitzel's approach:

"I've always really loved acoustic music... Everything just boils down to that. That's what music is. Amps and [electric] guitars, or whatever, are just noise. I'm interested in songs."

After a few months of doing solo shows, Eitzel brought in Brad Johnson, a friend from the mail room at Creative Leisure and future room-mate, on upright bass. Johnson had grown up in Colorado and moved to Boston to study music at college. He had recently moved to Berkeley from the East Coast where he'd spent two years in a rockabilly band.

Johnson had seen a few of Eitzel's solo shows, and while it wasn't the type of music he had planned to get involved in, Eitzel was the only person he knew who was doing anything musically that excited him.

"Up until then," Johnson recalls, "I was interested in instrumental music and jazz, but I got out of that once I met Mark."

Pretty soon Eitzel and Johnson were performing as a duo at The Tattoo Rose and some other local cafes. They'd use a variety of self-mocking band names, including the prog-rock sounding "Wind Spirit" – the worst name Johnson could come up with. The material was mainly Eitzel's, but Johnson would have some input on composition. Rehearsals were kept to a minimum, and live shows were very spontaneous affairs.

"How we worked," Johnson remembers, "was Mark would ask me just to play a riff. He'd say, 'Play something, no matter what.' I'd start playing, and then he'd just start singing along. I'd often have no idea what he was going to sing."

One Thursday night, after the regular acoustic new wave night, Eitzel got talking to a guitarist called Scott Alexander, who'd moved up to San Francisco and needed a place to stay. Like Eitzel, Scott was from Ohio, and knew some of the same people. The two musicians immediately found common ground, and Eitzel offered him his couch until Scott could get settled somewhere.

Eitzel liked Scott's guitar playing, and after Scott moved in, Eitzel suggested he join himself and Brad for a few shows. After a few days of rehearsals, the augmented line-up started to perform under the name American Music Club.

The name at the time was a half-joke – utilising what Eitzel later called "the three worst words in the world for a band name." In spite of his English upbringing and the huge amount of his English musical influences, Eitzel was something of a cultural nationalist – still adamant that "if you live in America, you have to be American, and you have to express what it is to be American." His view was in part a reaction to the US charts, which at the time were packed with English and Australian acts, in spite of the huge number of great American bands, from The Gun Club through to The Cramps, that Eitzel felt were not getting enough exposure. So the seemingly innocuous name was Eitzel's "way of saying 'fuck you all!'"

With Alexander on guitar, the songs were more structured, and some even followed verse-chorus-verse patterns, but it was still a far from conventional sound. And, while the first line-up of American Music Club was all-acoustic, it was by no means a mellow or laid back affair. The music was very rhythmically angular, and Eitzel's live vocal style was still highly influenced by Public Image Ltd and Ian Curtis.

"He was really into Joy Division," Johnson remembers, "and he was into screaming, dropping to his knees and falling over, and having epileptic-type fits. AMC was much less sedate at that time. I'd make distortion sounds by hitting the double bass with the wooden part of the bow, while Mark would go nuts. He had some quiet sensitive songs, but his way of singing was not as soft. His throat infection was also bad for a long time, and he'd end these songs with a hacking fit and spit up a bunch of yellow bile, which added to the punk aspect."

"Also, when Mark would play guitar at that point he was kind of spastic. He didn't have the co-ordination of singing and playing at the same time. Some people dismissed him as too sloppy or too weird, because he wasn't too worried about the technical aspects of his playing. He'd also break lots of strings and drift out of tune, but that never really bothered me. I loved the way he played guitar in the early days. And you could tell right away that he was serious about what he was doing, and that he really had something."

Johnson loved these shows: it was exciting and spontaneous, and you never knew what would happen next. Eitzel would often stop songs in the middle and pretty much do anything he could to embarrass himself, but throughout all of this, Johnson remembers, Eitzel would maintain the image of "this suffering, intense, Ian Curtis-kind of guy."

This incarnation of American Music Club played small local gigs at cafes and art-shows for about a year, but this line-up came to an end when Scott Alexander quit to try his hand at computer music, and Brad Johnson took a job on a cruise ship. Johnson reasoned that Eitzel would keep going whether he stayed or not.

By now, Eitzel was enjoying being in a band again, and he soon formed a second line-up of American Music Club. He brought in Greg Bonnell from the Naked Skinnies on drums and the other instruments were covered by a floating combination of people from the new wave acoustic sessions, mixed in with some of Eitzel's friends from North Beach, including Jeanie Szudy on bass, Mark Elliot on guitar and Mona Fisher from local band Buck and Bubbles. The band also had a trombone player, and their line-up was completed with a model and part-time male prostitute who played an old car door by hitting it with an iron bar. American Music Club had metamorphosed from a trio into a rather bizarre big band.

NAKED SKINNIES

All My Life

This Is The Beautiful Night

NAKED HOUSE RECORDS

FARMERS

AMERICAN MUSIC CLUB

UGLY STICK

DEC.2 CHI-CHI

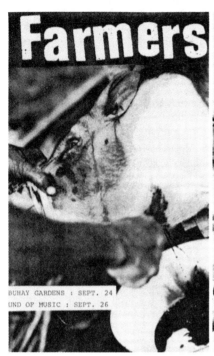

This line-up gradually developed a small local following. They even featured on a local live radio broadcast where they performed "Mr Lucky," – later to appear on the AMC debut album – and a manically deranged romp called "Terrorist City." The compere introduced AMC as a personal favourite and added, "They used to be acoustic, now they've gone electric. I think the lead vocalist is pretty wild."

Through the people Eitzel met at AMC's rehearsal studios, and the bands they shared club gigs with, Mark got to know a whole scene of San Francisco musicians beyond his previous contacts at The Tattoo Rose. One of the bands American Music Club mark II kept coming into contact with were a local cult act called The Farmers, which featured the guitarist Vudi, whom Eitzel had snubbed at the disastrous Naked Skinnies show at the Mabuhay Gardens. The Farmers had rehearsed in the same building as the Naked Skinnies, and Eitzel and Vudi had gradually become friends.

The "Vudi" moniker derived from an earlier nickname "Woody" – the origins of which are obscure – and was occasionally lengthened to the rather grand Vudicus Maximus. His band The Farmers had been part of the San Francisco music scene for years and were a much bigger draw than AMC. Their line-up included Vudi's brother Popeye on guitar, drummer Tim Vaughan, Brian Schindele on keyboards, plus a three piece horn section. Vudi was still impressed with Eitzel's work and enjoyed watching AMC mark II's bizarre shows. Over time Vudi convinced himself that he should get a new band together for Eitzel.

Eitzel saw The Farmers live on numerous occasions and was a firm admirer. He still vividly recalls their ramshackle spirit:

"They were an institution – the kind of bar band who every day would do mushrooms. They had a trumpet player, a trombone player, a six-string bass player, and a keyboard player who looked like Rick Wakeman. They were a punk rock bar band who also played progressive rock influenced by John Cale. Danny Thompson was their king. They were a strange amalgam of all these people who lived in the hills like hippies. Their parents were hippies, or people who lived with the hippies. Vudi lived in hippy communes all his life. He was kicked out of his house at eighteen, and lived in the woods with his best friends, taking drugs every day. The Farmers were at the centre of a whole world of tripped out people."

While the Farmers developed out of San Francisco's thriving punk scene, they were in fact very anti-punk. Their music was a strange Zappa-influenced, type of art rock fusion. They called it "agra-rock," imputing the agricultural as opposed to industrial, and would play at warehouse parties, their sets lasting for hours. They would add different instruments to the musical melange on an ad hoc basis – Vudi even played violin from time to time.

While Eitzel may have exaggerated his brief history of Vudi and The Farmers' dysfunctional upbringing, Vudi did have an unconventional childhood. Born in Chicago in 1952, he was considerably older than the other members of the first incarnation of American Music Club. His parents moved to the West Coast when he was still quite small. At the age of ten he met Mark Terrill at primary school. Terrill would remain a lifelong friend. He and Vudi gravitated toward each other because they were a little weird, both being the children of unreconstructed hippies who lived in the hills above Palo Alto.

Vudi and Terrill were separated when the latter was expelled for selling his father's LSD to some school friends. However, they continued to live in the same area and keep in touch. At secondary school, Vudi became more and more immersed in music, and started hanging out with another music obsessive, Bruce Kaphan. Kaphan was already an accomplished musician, having learned piano and drums at prep school. He also played bass, but was now concentrating on guitar, and collaborated with Vudi in "some really horrible rock bands." Even then they were playing their own compositions.

Kaphan was born in San Francisco in 1955, and grew up in the Bay Area. The Beatles made the biggest musical impression on him, but he was also profoundly influenced by the late 60s San Francisco music scene, as he explains: "One of the things that was great about growing up in San Francisco at that time, was that Bill Graham had come up with a brand new way to present music. It was a wonderful way to expand your musical tastes. He'd put on a show where Ali Akbar Khan, BB King, or Ravi Shankar would be on the same bill as the Grateful Dead or Jimi Hendrix. It was a fertile time for music because Graham was so open-minded."

Always keen to expand his musical horizons, a pivotal moment for Kaphan came when he was about 21 and working in a guitar store. One day the store took delivery of a pedal steel guitar, and thinking it looked cool, Kaphan started to monkey around with it. He enjoyed Pete Drake's pedal steel work on Dylan's *Nashville Skyline* and Jerry Garcia's playing, and gradually taught himself how to play the instrument. He would pick one song up, and then another, until eventually he considered himself to be a pedal steel player. As a freelance musician, Kaphan reasoned that he should get more work because guitar players are "a dime a dozen;" pedal steel was much rarer.

The late 70s saw Vudi, Kaphan and Terrill sharing an apartment together in a big beautiful house in Palo Alto, that was known as "Fat Cork." Built by eccentrics, and home to a whole series of musicians, one of the house's best features was a recording studio in its basement.

By 1977, when punk was beginning to get a grip on the UK and parts of the US, Vudi and Kaphan were enjoying a spell in an anachronistic outfit called Curtis Bunch and the Wild Bunch – playing traditional country and western standards in huge Stetson hats. They'd gig at honky tonks and country bars in Pescadero and Half Moon Bay. Curtis was from Louisiana, ten years older than Kaphan and had a huge knowledge of country music. He'd share lead vocals with a girl who looked like Linda Ronstadt and sounded like Tammy Wynette. This was not post-*Sweethearts Of The Rodeo* country rock, but the real thing. "It was the perfect vehicle for us," Kaphan explains. "Vudi had dabbled in country music but never really got into it hardcore. Curtis was an excuse to delve deeper."

In between day jobs and gigs, Kaphan and Vudi would record demos of their own material in the Fat Cork basement, collaborating with friend, Geoff Potter. Kaphan's songs were long and involved, with lots of twists and turns. His major influences were Ali Akbar Khan, Bob Wills, and Johann Sebastian Bach, but he was also capable of coming up with simple three-minute country rock songs like, "The Broken Dream Display," a lost Johnny Cash style gem with a rolling cowboy guitar rhythm and a sprinkling of saloon piano.

Vudi's own early music was much more in a British folk tradition. His demos from the era (on which he sings) conjure up images both of Irish folk revival outfits like Planxty and pre-"Harry's Game" Clannad, as well as '70s English acts like Fairport Convention and Steeleye Span. Uilleann pipes weave Celtic tunes in and out of songs with melodies that sound fresh from the Middle Ages.

After the decline of Curtis Bunch, Vudi put together the first line-up of The Farmers, and Kaphan sat in with them for a few months, but his pedal steel was perhaps one additional sound too far for the eclectic group. Being used to country and fusion, Kaphan found The Farmers sonic assault too much to bear, "It was so loud that my ears would be ringing for days after," he remembered. Also, Kaphan wasn't especially enamoured of the venues The Farmers played, as he recalled later: "the Mabuhay Gardens, The Sound of Music in the Tenderloin. A horrible environment. Urine-soaked, broken glass everywhere."

Keen to leave the guitar store, Kaphan was trying to make a living from playing music, and quit to join a country covers band. He would keep in touch with Vudi intermittently, but his new approach would take him out of the sphere of a lot of his old musician friends for a while. "I ended up not spending a lot of my time chasing the more eclectic and artistic end of things," Kaphan recalls. "I was trying to play gigs that actually paid money."

In 1979 The Farmers started working in a rehearsal studio on Market Street, upstairs from a Japanese delicatessen called The Dharma Sub, which had now become the centre of a burgeoning scene that would eventually include American Music Club mark II.

The Dharma Sub scene was highly incestuous and cross fertilised – members from a wide variety of acts were constantly collaborating and trying different projects. The Ironics included future American Music Club members, Dan Pearson and Matt Norelli. The Cubists featured Brian Schindele who had played with The Farmers, and who would go on to play on AMC's second album. Ugly Stick featured Mark Terrill, with The Farmers' Tim Vaughan, Wayne Newcomb and Eve Becker.

It was a very vibrant scene. Boundaries were ignored and the emphasis was on expression and creativity for its own sake. It was a time when creatively, everything really was up for grabs. The constantly shifting collaborations reflected another key thing about the Dharma Sub scene, which was how sociable and friendly it all was. Much of the music may have been avant-garde or angst-ridden, but the musicians were not tortured bedsitter poets suffering for their art. Neither were they icy cool and disdainful of each others efforts. The studio was the centre of a huge network of mutually supportive friends. Jenny Gonzalvez, later to be the subject of the Eitzel song "Jenny," remembers the era fondly: "We were a close bunch. Everybody would meet up on Friday night either at a bar or at the Dharma Sub, and we would more or less spend the weekend together. A lot of it was pretty platonic too, we were just friends hanging out together. People would sleep over at someone's house – sharing beds or sleeping on the floor…. It was a big group of pals…"

In direct opposition to their later image, Jenny recalls the musicians who would become American Music Club as "very sociable. I think you could say they were just basically happy people. Vudi has always been the most easy-going happy-go-lucky guy." Pearson and Norelli too were affable and friendly. "Eitzel though, was not really a part of that slumber party-ness," Jenny notes. "He was more on his own..."

In the early '80s, with money saved from more spells in the Merchant Navy, Mark Terrill set up a small record label, BFM records, and in 1982 put out a controversial EP by The Farmers entitled *Packed In An Urban Area*. "The EP made a big stir due to its artwork," Terrill recalls, "It was a photograph done in a veterinary school back East. Bobby Neal Adams [who would later contribute visual ideas and pictures to American Music Club's album covers] broke in to the school in the middle of the night and took photos in the cold storage cadaver room. There is one horse and one donkey both partly dismembered and hanging from meat hooks, and then there is a greyhound lying on the floor, stiff as a board, with his feet sticking straight up in the air. Artistically, it's a nice photograph, although the material is a bit weird. The main aim was to provoke, which this cover definitely did."

If the cover artwork was to push back the barriers of what was acceptable visually, the music on the EP was equally challenging. While they wore some of their influences on their sleeves, The Farmers' overall sound was indefinable – surreal even. Vudi's singing style had metamorphosed into a David Byrne-Captain Beefheart hybrid, with backing from a hugely heavy funk bass, crazy bar room piano, mathematical guitar and John Coltrane horns. It is an amazing melange: a salad bowl assimilation rather than a melting pot. As the instruments grow more and more frenzied, Vudi intones and growls impressionistic phrases, almost at random: *Boys will be boys/ Though the woods are full of bears...Flying Tigers. Chiang Kai-Shek/ ...Women make the best cigars.*

In 1983, they released a second EP, *Tragic Tales of Life*, also through BFM. More melodic and a little more straightforward, there were moments of sheer beauty on this record. It would be their last.

Without hearing the weird progressive jazz folk rock fusion of The Farmers, it is difficult to appreciate the true source of Vudi's guitar playing with American Music Club. The improvisational, improbable, and sheer unpredictable nature of his playing, both on record and live has its roots in The Farmers 'agra-rock.' The scales and chords that Vudi would play were from a tradition beyond American shores. While Coltrane was a huge influence, so clearly was music of a much more Eastern origin. For Vudi it was already established that there were no musical barriers; everything was "up for grabs."

In the summer of 1983, shortly after The Farmers split up, Vudi played a tape of acoustic songs to Mark Terrill and asked him who he thought it was. Terrill suggested Nick Drake, and Vudi told him it was actually a local guy called Mark Eitzel, and that he wanted to get a band together with him. "Mark Eitzel was the greatest songwriter I'd ever heard...," Vudi explained years later, "[and] I thought he should have a band."

Vudi then approached guitarist Dan Pearson and drummer Matt Norelli [known as "Sluggo"] who were both playing in The Ironics – a tight new wave band that would rehearse downstairs from The Farmers.

"Vudi just came down one day," Dan Pearson remembers, "and he said 'We're going to be a great band.' I was playing guitar at the time, and Vudi told me that in this new band I was going to play bass, Matt would play drums, and Vudi would play guitar... I said okay. [The Ironics] were pretty dead in the water anyway." Vudi also told Pearson that the singer would be Mark Eitzel.

Dan asked Vudi what the band was going to be about, but Vudi was non-committal, saying "he'd see". A couple of nights later he took Dan and Matt to a club called Rudy's up in the Berkeley hills, to see Eitzel perform in the final AMC mark II show.

Pearson was surprised by what he saw: "There was this band on stage, with a guy on trumpet, then two girl singers who looked kind of bored, a pretty wild guitar player, a drummer, a guy pounding a car door, and a couple of other people at the back. It was pretty vibrant."

Mark Terrill had agreed to give Eitzel a lift to the gig: "I picked him up in the van and drove him to the show. When he was on stage, some people were talking at the bar at the back where we were stood, and Eitzel got off the stage, and came and sang right in the faces of these people, without a mike, pointing his finger at them and berating them. Then he got back onto the stage and sat at the front, swinging his legs over the edge as he sang the next song. Then suddenly he threw his guitar down and walked straight out of the venue and disappeared. When the time came to leave, I asked Vudi what we should do about Mark, and he said, 'Oh, don't worry, he does this all the time.' Later I found that Mark had walked out of the club and carried on walking up into the hills. Eventually he got to this rundown group of farm buildings and climbed over a hedge, got under a tarpaulin and went to sleep. The next day he got up, caught a bus back into town, and just got on with things as normal!"

Within a few weeks American Music Club mark II had split up, and Eitzel agreed to work with Vudi but only on condition that it would be a serious undertaking.

"With the second line-up of American Music Club," Eitzel explains, "I used to book all the shows, I used to pay for the rehearsal space, I used to write all of the songs, I used to do everything. And when the band broke up, I decided that I didn't want to do music anymore unless I was in a band with musicians that were as ambitious as me, had their own rehearsal space, their own equipment, wanted to practice, and I didn't have to do all of this work myself. And Vudi formed a band for me."

By October, Vudi, Dan and Matt were rehearsing with Eitzel, who was delighted with the way the band gelled: "They were all great players. All of them." Eitzel would bring in his song ideas, and the band would work them up collectively. The band's initial setlist would also include new arrangements of Naked Skinnies' songs such as a revelatory take on "This Is The Beautiful Night," and revamped versions of tracks from the *Mean Mark Eitzel* tape, including the pretty awful avant-garde experiment, "I Speak French," which Vudi subsequently nixed, considering it too "art-school." Although Vudi had plenty of his own songs he didn't really like the way Eitzel sang them, so the band stuck to Eitzel compositions. Initially a disappointment – one of Eitzel's motives for hooking up with Vudi, was that he didn't want to write all of the songs – it didn't seem like a big problem at the time.

None of the band liked the American Music Club name, but no one came up with anything better, so it stuck. AMC mark III immediately adopted a more serious, career-minded approach, rehearsing most days and agreeing that they would only play clubs on Friday or Saturday nights. They also planned to tour. The intention was to do "band-like" things, as opposed to informal artistic experimentation.

Eitzel enjoyed this new seriousness, and was relieved not to be the band's leader. He remembers those early days with great affection: "It was all good, and it was nice to have these friends. Danny was so fucking cool. I was not used to dealing with people who had real jobs, and who were forthright, and that was what they were like."

American Music Club mark III was an ideal set up for Eitzel. Finally, in Vudi he had found someone who would take care of all the administration and organisation, while he was free to concentrate on writing songs and making music. The only problem was that Eitzel was used to being in charge. Because this incarnation of American Music Club had been put together by someone else, it would remain in Eitzel's view Vudi's band. This wasn't a problem for the moment, but like many things in the band's history, it would simmer.

Towards the end of the year AMC pooled their resources and recorded a demo with local producer Tom Mallon. Mallon was a key figure on the San Francisco music scene, having started out in the music industry in the late 70s recording live outdoor punk concerts featuring the likes of Flipper, Circle Jerks and Black Flag. He had his own 8-track recording studio where he would record local bands for rockbottom prices – if he liked something he would do it as cheaply as possible, or for no payment at all. Mallon explained his approach in a later interview with Alan Di Perna: "I just record what I like – people whose songs I enjoy. Songs and songwriters are my main focus. The music is important to me, sure, but when I listen to something, I tend to concentrate on the lyrics and the feeling that's being put across."

On the face of it, Mallon was the ideal producer for Eitzel's songs, and with his help AMC recorded versions of seven songs in their repertoire. Most of these would end up on their first two albums, although "Blind Girl," and "Where Are You?" never surfaced. The lyrics to "Blind Girl," were fairly corny – *"I fell in love with a blind girl, and the things she didn't see"* – but the song remained in AMC's set for another year; it was never properly recorded simply because the band could never get it to work in the studio. "Where Are You," while funky and immensely catchy, utilised a central riff that was perhaps too similar to Pigbag's "Papa's Got A Brand New Pig Bag." For some reason they chose not to record what was perhaps their best early song, the anthemic, "Maybe I'll Tell You Everything," which was subsequently dropped from their live set and then disappeared.

The demo also featured early versions of "Tell Yourself," "Broken Glass," "Big Night," "Heavenly Smile" and "Yvonne Gets Dumped." The sound may have been rooted in the early 80s sound of Joy Division, but Eitzel's singing was powerful throughout, and the chainsaw guitar-style was ferocious.

By now Eitzel and Pearson were both 24 years old and Vudi was 31, and all three had been in bands for years. As they had all made records, it is not surprising that the tapes sounded accomplished. But there was more to it than that. There was an instinctiveness in their playing and arrangements that would suggest they had been working together for years. The band was brimming with creativity and musical ideas. The main drawback was simply that they were still searching for the right sound – they hadn't yet found their own voice.

Shortly after this recording session, Brad Johnson returned from his cruise ship keen to hook up with Eitzel again. As Dan Pearson was now occupying the bassist's position, Johnson rejoined American Music Club as a somewhat reluctant keyboard player. He enjoyed playing with the band for a while, but immediately realised that this line-up had adopted a much more professional approach. The set lengths were standardised, and they would only play shows that paid upwards of $200. Also, Eitzel had set himself the challenge "to sing without falling down." AMC mark III were clearly a far more mainstream outfit than any previous Eitzel venture.

One of their early shows at the Graffiti Club was recorded for local radio, and it showcases a post-punk band with a sharp pop sensibility, although in an interview for the same radio station, prompted by Vudi, Eitzel proclaimed their main influence to be Waylon Jennings. In the same interview, Eitzel explained that AMC didn't have a manager, and requested any interested parties to phone in. They even gave out Vudi's home phone number, but did not receive a single call.

After more shows, AMC went back into Mallon's studio. Johnson's keyboards added a new dimension to the sound, and Eitzel had come up with two of his best songs yet, a manic *Unknown Pleasures*-style rocker called "Restless Stranger," and the melodic "Room Above The Club". The band sounded more confident, and the overall sound was less derivative than the previous sessions, although there was some tension between Johnson and his new bandmates. "Vudi and Danny were trying to get me to play like Simple Minds," Johnson remembers, "who I didn't like." Johnson wanted a more vintage sound, but was constricted by his cheap synthesiser.

The band sent the two demos to all of the usual places, but nobody showed much interest. As the year went on, in spite of a growing repertoire of songs and a much tighter and more sophisticated sound, nothing was happening for American Music Club. By the end of 1984, the lack of outside interest, the few poorly attended shows and the band's general failure to make any tangible progress was starting to grate. Then The Dharma Sub closed, and they were even left without a real rehearsal space of their own.

Drummer Matt Norelli became restless, and the others too, wondered if anything was ever going to happen. Then in April, without any previous history of illness, Eitzel's father died suddenly. By then he and his parents were on fairly distant terms, and he rarely saw his sister any more, but the shock still hit him hard. He had been trying to patch things up with his father, to the extent that they had booked a holiday in Hawaii that summer. Now there would be no chance of any future reconciliation.

Already of a fairly melancholy disposition, Eitzel was beset by morbid thoughts, and started to drink more heavily. In an attempt to get over his depression, at his mother's behest he went to Hawaii on his own, for the holiday that he was supposed to share with his father. Predictably, he had a truly horrible time. The tourist bars and beaches seemed hollow and meaningless, and the isolation and loneliness he was feeling didn't sit well on a tropical holiday island. When he returned to San Francisco he threw himself further into rehearsals and recording.

Morale among the band members was now pretty low. Additional tension was caused by Eitzel's disenchantment with Norelli's approach to the band. "Sluggo and I didn't get on, I didn't like his drumming – the way he played hi-hat would drive me crazy, and when I was trying to explain the way I felt about a song, he'd be busy tuning the snare drum. Also, he thought that when we played live, we should rehearse live – exactly the same tempo as we played live. I am completely the opposite... I feel like, when we play live, anything can happen. Sluggo had a little electric metronome, and he'd always play everything exactly the same way – the fills would always be the same, and he'd always play perfectly in rehearsal. He even got a pair of electronic Linn drums. So for a while American Music Club had Linn drums, which was so embarrassing.... I remember the day he had his $5,000 'brain' for the Linn drums stolen. I was so happy."

Being the most professional of the band, Norelli found it hardest to accept that after months of rehearsals, Eitzel would just get completely drunk at a gig and let everything fall apart. Eitzel remembers that Norelli would, "get really mad because I'd be falling over. I'd get so drunk I couldn't walk properly, and he'd be carrying on playing exactly... with this professional snap to the snare that I hated..." It wasn't just a personal thing, as Eitzel explains: "It was a time of transition. We were getting a sound, and Sluggo wasn't really part of it anymore. Sluggo was instrumental in getting us to play, but all this bullshit about always rehearsing the same song for hours and hours and never really knowing what it was going to be, killed the song. You'd lose the freshness of it."

Eventually Norelli decided to take a break and head for Hamburg to stay with old friend, Mark Terrill. He enjoyed the visit, and after a short trip back to the US, decided to settle in Hamburg for a while. After a number of long telephone conversations Terrill and Norelli had with Vudi, Eitzel and Pearson, the rest of American Music Club decided to head for Hamburg too. A San Francisco band called Tuxedo Moon had made it in big in Belgium and the Netherlands, so they thought that maybe they too would have more luck in Europe. As Tuxedo Moon's jazz-influenced synthesiser soundscapes were more in tune with the European electronic music scene, it wasn't a great precedent to base a decision on.

In the meantime, Tom Mallon was formulating plans to set up his own record label, Grifter, and was considering launching it with San Francisco band, Flying Color. When Eitzel told him that AMC were going to Germany for a while, Mallon convinced them they needed to have a record to sell. He booked them two weeks in his studio, and scheduled the album as Grifter's first release.

Eitzel's aim with the record that he would name *The Restless Stranger* was twofold: "I wanted it to sound like we did.... and I wanted it to be a big statement." The key problem was that their song arrangements were constantly in flux. Keen to avoid preconceived ideas of what each song should sound like, they had spent the previous few months trying their songs in different styles and tempos to ensure that each final arrangement was the best by a process of elimination. There were acoustic versions of all the rock songs, and rock versions of all the acoustic songs. As Eitzel explained later, nothing was simple with AMC: "We were a bunch of intellectuals, so everything was always in question all the time... Rehearsing a song, we had to try it in every way, we'd try it in a Flipper style, then like The Rolling Stones. Every tempo, guitar part and bass part was up to be explored."

Now that they had to quickly finalise all of their song arrangements, it was clear that the album could only be a snapshot of this wheel of change.

With so little time, Mallon drove the band hard in the studio and they recorded most of the basic tracks in a week. Mallon also came up with lots of musical suggestions and helped with arrangements. Occasionally his creative input would cross over into an overbearing mania for total control, resulting in clashes with Eitzel. He would even sometimes insist on lyric changes, and refused to let Eitzel sing the final half a line of the chorus to "Broken Glass," considering it too corny. The chorus originally read, *'I'll give you the future, I'll give you the past/ I'll give you diamonds, I'll give you broken glass."* Eitzel never did come up with something better to replace the offending line, so in the finished version he sings the chorus as far as "diamonds," and then the vocals just stop, with the music completing the final bar of the tune.

Eitzel remembers Mallon was particularly good with bass lines: "Danny [Pearson] is a great natural player, but he's really into country music and wouldn't really try strange musical ideas. Danny could play any rock and roll thing you imagine, but in terms of blue notes, he didn't have much idea, so Mallon would say 'Try a minor note instead,' and he'd try it. Tom would spend hours with a bass just trying different things to see if it would work."

Mallon would also redo a lot of Eitzel's guitar parts considering them not clean enough. His approach to keyboards was even more dictatorial. "I felt pretty useless," Brad Johnson recalls, "because I'd play my keyboard part and Tom would say, 'Well, that's okay Brad, but I'll come up with something better later...' and he'd just redo the whole part with something of his own."

All things considered, the final results were impressive considering the rushed nature of the project, but *The Restless Stranger* could not be described as a great album. There were too many keyboard parts and drum fills. The lyrics were occasionally naïve and some of the music still sounded too derivative. Having emerged from the idiosyncratic *Mean Mark Eitzel* track "You Can Be Beautiful," "Point of Desire," acquired a guitar sound that is a little too like Neil Young circa *Zuma*. "Heavenly Smile," having begun life as a frantic rock song became cod country/skiffle; and "Hold On To Your Love," the haunting acoustic highlight from the *Mean Mark Eitzel* cassette was so drenched in synthesisers that it veered towards soft rock territory. The record also featured a couple of unsuccessful art-rock experiments, throwbacks to Eitzel's earlier more anti-musical style before Vudi convinced him that it was better to sing than to yell. On "$1,000,000" Eitzel shrieks *"I'm a good man, I'm a good man/ I'm a bad man,*

I'm a bad man," over a churning rock groove; and the AMC mark II rant "Mr Lucky," where Eitzel shouts "Let's do the lucky dance," over funky bass and more tribal drumming.

For all this, at least half of the record is extremely strong. "Tell Yourself," "Goodbye (reprise #54)," and "Yvonne Gets Dumped," all transcend the record's generic restrictions, and in places really soar. "Room Above the Club," was Eitzel's first classic song. The club in question was Mr Brown's – the number one punk rock bar in Columbus, where Eitzel saw great shows by Pere Ubu and Niagara Falls. Upstairs he and his friends would hang out in a really disgusting room owned by the dislikeable Tom Brown, who was known to brandish a lead pipe if there was anyone present who was black or gay.

The song conjures up scenes and images from that time, and Eitzel would call it: "The first song I ever wrote that I thought was a real song."

While the music on *The Restless Stranger* is often up-tempo and in places even sounds pop, Eitzel's lyrical subject matter is fairly bleak. The songs' narrators are "lonely children," misfits and lost souls who seek solace in bars, dreams and escape. Events are mostly set in winter, and rain and tears are the recurring images. For all this, there is no self-pity. Indeed, few of the songs are set in the first person, and in many the tragic protagonists are women. As Eitzel surveys these unhappy characters, it is possible to see him projecting both anguish at his own weaknesses, and an awareness of his own guilt as a man in playing a role in the women's unhappiness.

In "Yvonne Gets Dumped," the central character's *"heart starts off brave, but it can't hide."* In the end she is only at ease, *"when she forgets the whole world."* In "Point of Desire," *"Mary was born in the funhouse/ She loves the hall of mirrors/ Because there, she can be beautiful."*

The only hope Eitzel sees for most of these characters is love. The album finishes on the simple, wistful "Hold On To Your Love." He is not talking about romance here; he is looking for salvation. Only love can *"keep out the clouds that sit on [his] shoulders."* Dissatisfied with everything he sees around him, in love he is looking for *"Something else, A finer pleasure."*

One surprising omission from the album was the [nearly] title song, "Restless Stranger," a furious, guitar-driven, peculiarly gothic look at birth, death and dreams, set to a frantic beat. Eitzel later claimed the song just sounded "too Joy Division," but it was pure American Music Club to drop the title track from the record, especially when it was not one of the weaker songs.

For the album cover the band chose a prussian blue monochrome shot of a wolf lying dead by a highway in the middle of a vast and inhospitable desert. The photo by Bobby Neal Adams hints at his earlier more controversial work on The Farmers' EPs.

While at the time he was fairly happy with the album, Eitzel would quickly come to view it with embarrassment. He didn't like some of the song-writing, and hated the way, "it sounds like a band that is failing miserably to be Joy Division..."

"I don't like to be in bands with influences," he explained, "and we had so many influences at the start."

The record would soon be deleted, but when it finally resurfaced in 1998, Eitzel had mellowed in his views, conceding "there are a lot of songs on that album that I love."

After *The Restless Stranger* was pressed, that August the band headed for what was initially planned as a short trip to Germany. Mark Terrill had married a German girl he met on a Hamburg train, and her family had a farm about an hour from town. On arrival, the band settled into one of the sheds behind the farmhouse, while Eitzel chose to find alternative accommodation.

"First I stayed in a tent, then I went crazy," he recalls, "then I got a flat in the centre of Hamburg. I thought, what the fuck, I don't want to sit out here with these dumb guys and drink beer and play cards all day. But it was fun really."

Dan Pearson agreed: "It *was* kind of fun. For some reason the Deutschmark had risen to four to the dollar. We'd been working our butts off saving all this money for the trip, and when we got there, because of the exchange rate, we were living like kings."

After a few days they decided they would stay a while, and went into town to hire some musical equipment. They then bought a van and went looking for somewhere to rehearse, finding a great space above a disused fire station. Most days they'd walk through the forest surrounding the farm, catch a bus to the railway station and then get a train into Hamburg where they'd practise for hours. Johnson would often sleep over in the studio, allowing himself extra time in the morning to try and get his keyboard to actually work: "I kept hoping that if I kept programming it and designing the wave sounds, then something would sound good." The rest of the time, Eitzel would write songs and roam the streets on his own, while Vudi tried unsuccessfully to get a German distribution deal for *The Restless Stranger*, and Mark Terrill pressed local promoters for gigs.

After a couple of months, Terrill got a local promoter called Joachim at the Jojo agency to take a chance on AMC for a prestigious slot supporting Sonic Youth at the Markethalle. For some reason, this show was billed as an East Coast vs West Coast show down.

Oddly, AMC had supported Sonic Youth back in San Francisco only a couple of months before, but the two bands did not hit it off. Sonic Youth weren't especially friendly, and aggravated Eitzel by snidely telling him he should give up his old style of conventional songwriting.

Realising that the Sonic Youth fans were expecting hardcore rock, AMC played their loudest, most rock 'n' roll set, but it made little impression on the crowd. Eitzel shudders at the memory, "I think we were forgotten within five minutes of them coming on stage."

"It was kind of an anti-climactic flop," Mark Terrill recalls, "because after all this waiting, all this work and all this anticipation, this was supposed to be the big show. Unfortunately, backstage afterwards Joachim's only comment was 'Well, not bad, but I think we should really send you guys on a tour of country towns, before we do anything else'."

The band played only one more show in Germany. In November a promoter Terrill knew at the Logo club, called to tell him he'd had a band cancel, and that AMC could go on the next night. Terrill remembers this show fondly, "They played and it was tremendous. The exact opposite of the Sonic Youth concert.

Everybody who was friends of the band came, as well as all the people they'd gotten to know while they were in Hamburg."

A group of Turkish immigrants who ran a local bar the band frequented also came to see the show, and afterwards everyone was invited back for a traditional Turkish night. The atmosphere was one of real celebration, and there was drinking, singing, shouting, dancing on the tables, glass breaking and general mayhem until well into the morning.

In spite of this triumph, Terrill could not get any more gigs and the band's money quickly ran out. It was fun being in a new country but frustrating not to have anywhere to play. While Eitzel roamed around Hamburg, the others would explore the countryside by day, and then in the evenings settle down in the farm house with a case of German beer and play poker. "It just fizzled out," Brad Johnson remembers. "The tour never materialised, and we were just in limbo for months."

Eventually it became clear that nothing was going to happen and that they'd all have to go home.

Matt Norelli was first. Missing his girlfriend, and worn out by the tension with Eitzel, he decided to quit before things got ugly. He headed off with Brad Johnson to explore a bit of Europe and then went home. Shortly after returning to the US, he quit music and moved to Alaska.

Johnson was the next to leave. He'd never really enjoyed playing keyboards, and was worried about the direction the band was taking, considering their more recent music to be a touch "bombastic," and lacking in humour. Johnson also found that playing in a "professional" band like this incarnation of AMC, was simply not as much fun as informal artistic experimentation. After Hamburg, he left to play upright bass in a lounge covers band.

After Pearson left too, Vudi and Eitzel held out for a few weeks. But by Christmas they were back in San Francisco.

On their return they found Mallon had had little success with their album. He still hadn't got a distribution deal, so it had only been available in a handful of stores around the Bay Area. It did manage to attract some critical attention, and in an end of year round-up, Californian rock writer Jackson Brian Griffith deemed *The Restless Stranger* "worth checking out," adding: "these guys write and play some pretty nice stuff." Kevin Berger, writing in the prestigious trade briefing, *The Western Association of Rock Disc Jockeys* ("The Ward Report") considered the "level of excellence" sustained throughout the album to be "truly a promising beginning."

It was a shame that for the moment American Music Club didn't exist anymore.

Chapter Three

Watch My Family Tree Burn Down

"When I started doing this punk rock thing my interpretation of being a punk rocker was, 'Okay, put everything on the line. Every moment, put it on the line'."

Mark Eitzel

"In all human experience, there are parallels which permit common understanding in the telling and hearing, and it is the frightening responsibility of an artist to make what is directly or allusively close to his own being, communicable and understandable, however disturbingly, to the hearts and minds of all whom he addresses."

Tennessee Williams, "Too Personal?"
Introduction to Small Craft Warnings, *26 March 1972*

After a Christmas recess, Eitzel, Pearson and Vudi reconvened in January and agreed to carry on working together. Their first job was to try to push radio stations into playing tracks off *The Restless Stranger*. Each day, they would sit in the small office at Tom Mallon's studio for hours on end, and take it in turns to call a list of stations. They didn't have much success, and Dan Pearson remembers that eventually Mallon took things into his own hands:

"Tom would tell us we were doing it all wrong, and then one day he came in and said, 'Just get outta here! I'll do it! It's the only way it'll be done right'."

Mallon didn't have any more luck, and the album remained a stranger to radio.

AMC's next priority was to flesh out their line-up. After Brad Johnson's departure, Eitzel decided that maybe they didn't need a keyboard player after all. "We just thought, 'fuck it!'" Eitzel remembers. "My ideas about synths at the time were pretty dumb, and the idea of dealing with another musician was pretty terrifying."

But, now that Matt Norelli had departed, there was no escaping the fact that the band needed a drummer. Eitzel approached Tim Mooney from local cult band, The Toiling Midgets.

Mooney had been drumming in San Francisco punk bands for years. He started out in Sleepers with cult hero, Ricky Williams, on vocals. Williams was a founder member of Flipper and rumour had it was also briefly considered by Joy Division as a replacement singer after the death of Ian Curtis. After two years and a couple of poorly distributed records, Williams departed, and Sleepers grew into Negative Trend, who gigged in the Bay Area for a year or so before more personnel changes transformed them into The Toiling Midgets.

The Midgets began as an instrumental band, but after a few months Williams was back in the fold as singer. In 1982 they put out the Tom Mallon-produced *Sea Of Unrest* on Rough Trade's Instant label, and started to attract a small following and some critical acclaim. The slow grungey, grinding punk of the record influenced a lot of local musicians, although it was best appreciated live. Williams was a highly talented and charismatic frontman, but was also unreliable, erratic and often drunk or strung out. His chaotic stage persona and intensity of vocal delivery would be a big influence on Eitzel who saw the band live a number of times, and loved the album. The Toiling Midgets came to a premature halt because of drug problems.

Mooney already knew Vudi and Pearson, liked the band's music and agreed to join. After a couple of months of rehearsals, they lined up their first show in the back of a local coffee shop. Tim Mooney remembers: "The first two bands played, then a girl at the front of the stage started to have a seizure, and the fire department arrived and closed the place down. We never got to play."

It would be some time before the band got another chance. Mark Eitzel's mother had contracted cancer the previous winter, and he now got word that she was in serious decline. He returned to Columbus, Ohio. She died a few weeks later.

Eitzel stayed there for about three months, and although he and his mother had not been close for some time, he found her death extremely hard to deal with, especially coming so soon after the death of his father. He and his sister Renee had drifted apart and now it felt like he had no family left. While Renee struggled with funeral arrangements, insurance, courts and lawyers, Eitzel started to drink heavily.

Without a job or band rehearsals to give some structure to his days, Eitzel would wake at noon, hit the bars at 6.00, and drink until the early hours. He was slipping downwards. After three months, somehow he managed to stay sober long enough to return to San Francisco. More than ever before, he needed his songwriting, and his band.

On his return, he moved with some friends into a new apartment on Filbert Street in the bohemian North Beach area. He was glad of the company. A few days later he met Vudi and Pearson at the rehearsal space. Sadly while Eitzel was away, Tim Mooney's drug problems had escalated and now proved a stumbling block. The drummer later admitted, "I was having a hard time making it to rehearsals. They were ready to go again, and I wasn't."

Eitzel loved Mooney's playing and really wanted him in the band, but recalls, "Tim was just too strung out on drugs at the time. He'd show up four hours late for rehearsals and then be great. He was so high and yet he would always be great. We almost did a show with him, but then we told him to clean up first."

They hoped Mooney would get himself together quickly, but it didn't happen and the band were again without a drummer. Tim Mooney's absence inadvertently had one positive effect on AMC. Vudi and Eitzel had been listening to Neil Young and Van Morrison, and lacking a replacement drummer, they started experimenting with acoustic music – working with guitar, accordion, mandolin and violin. This acoustic format brought a discipline that was previously lacking, as Eitzel explained to writer Andrea Freedman: "It's a lot harder to do than our regular set. You can't get drunk and get away with it. You have to sing, you can't scream."

Towards the end of the year, the depleted AMC line-up returned to Mallon's studio to record their second LP. First of all though, they had to help Mallon move. He was in the process of relocating his studio to a new and much larger space on Folsom Street, right under the Bay Bridge. The band helped him put the equipment together, and in between work would sit on the studio roof and look at the ocean.

When everything was set up and ready to go, Mallon caught Eitzel's hand in a car door, and the bulk of the recording was delayed until February and March of 1987.

For *Engine*, named after the disused fire station in which they had rehearsed in Hamburg, Eitzel adopted a new approach to writing, arranging and recording. Rather than bringing in half-finished lyrics and ideas, Eitzel presented the band with a batch of finished songs: "I discovered that I could write songs more and I got frustrated with collaborating with the band because they were not coming up with their own songs…. After *The Restless Stranger* where everyone changed my music, I thought I would take control."

The only exceptions were a band collaboration on "Electric Light," which dated back to Hamburg, and an Eitzel/Mooney co-composition on "Art of Love." Tim Mooney explains that he came up with the guitar part when he was briefly in the band: "That was at a time when things were less defined. It was one of those days in the studio when someone said, 'Hey, do you have any songs?'" Tim played his song idea and Eitzel liked it and later remembered it – adapting it to a set of lyrics he'd had since the earliest days of the band.

As their debut had been done in something of a rush, Vudi, Pearson, Eitzel and Mallon were determined to get things right on *Engine,* no matter how long it took. Mallon's increased input would have a dramatic effect, helping to develop and crystallise AMC's sound. He put hours and hours of time into the production for no charge.

"Tom Mallon is amazing really," Eitzel later reflected. "He is a great engineering presence, and he had a lot of good ideas… If Tom Mallon hadn't existed, there would have been no American Music Club."

Eitzel is not just being unduly modest here. Very few bands signed to a small independent label have ever been able to spend as long polishing and perfecting an album as AMC did with *Engine.* The only way a new band would have the luxury to spend so long on a record would be if they were signed to a major label for a huge sum, but that would bring pressures of its own.

Mallon's involvement did not come without a downside. He had a huge admiration for the talent within the band, yet would adopt a dictatorial approach to studio work, insisting that everything was done his way. Eitzel and the rest of the band had faith in Mallon's ability, but they found his negative attitude harder to accept. Eitzel remembers Tom Mallon's standard reply to virtually everything they played was: "This sucks! It's fucked!"

After a take, Mallon often said nothing at all. Eventually, feeling his silence intimated something was wrong, someone would suggest another take. Mallon would frown and ask grudgingly, "Do you really want to? Do you think that it'll be better?...Okay."

During the recording, American Music Club remained a three-piece. They augmented their sound by bringing in old friends like Brian Schindele from The Farmers to add some keyboards, and Carla Fabrizio, who had occasionally sung backing vocals for AMC live, to play cello on a couple of songs. Mallon would assist with guitar parts and they alternated between three different drummers. Dave Scheff from Translator played on some tracks, Tim Vaughan from The Farmers and Ugly Stick played on "Electric Light," and Matt Norelli played on the rest.

Just back from Alaska, Norelli was still on good terms with Vudi and Pearson, so they asked him to sit in. Wary of a return to the tension of the old days, he told them: "Okay! I'll record with you, but I am not in the band."

Later they persuaded him to do the odd local gig, but after each show he'd remind them, "It's time you guys got yourselves a drummer."

Brad Johnson also briefly returned to the fold for some of these sessions, and added upright bass to a few tracks, but his parts did not make the final mix. After sitting in for a couple of live shows, Johnson moved away from the AMC circle. Later he would forge a career as a comic book artist, and form the band Virginia Dare with his wife Mary O'Neill, and put out a number of fine low-key records in the nineties. At one point Eitzel briefly played drums for Johnson's band under the pseudonym "Cricket."

Throughout the recording process, AMC kept up a prodigious intake of alcohol. Eitzel was showing signs of a strong George Jones influence both in his vocal phrasing and his ability to drink. Tom Mallon told him one night as he surveyed a huge pile of empty cans, "you guys drink more than any band I've ever had in the studio." Eitzel confessed later, "I couldn't even do a vocal take until I'd had about five beers."

Towards the end of March the band broke off from recording to play a John Cale support slot at the I-Beam in Haight-Ashbury. It went pretty well, and garnered a review in San Francisco's *Calendar* magazine which praised them in peculiarly florid prose: "This band combines lyrical intensity and cleverness with the wide, wind-blown prairie spaces of sombre country and roots-flavoured American rock and folk idioms to create one of the best sounds in SF today." The reviewer described Eitzel as "like a German shepherd dog and the poet Rilke battling to the death inside one man," and compared his dancing during a guitar solo to that of "a shy Polish boy in the Armory on a Friday night."

Shortly after the show, the lease on Eitzel's North Beach apartment fell through. Without a home, short of money, and aware that he was spending most of his time in the South Park area – either rehearsing, recording or mixing at Tom Mallon's studio or hanging out in the surrounding bars – Eitzel's solution was to move into the storage room at the studio. For better or for worse, for the next nine months he and Mallon would see a great deal of each other. Mallon would teach Eitzel a lot about recording and arranging, and Eitzel's close proximity would also fuel Mallon's desire to play a bigger role in American Music Club.

When Mallon finished mixing *Engine*, he resumed his efforts at getting a licensing deal for his other band, the poppier and more accessible Flying Color. As you could actually dance to them, they were more obviously marketable than Eitzel and co. Mallon got a Flying Color tape to Redd Kross' manager John Silva, who in turn played it to Lisa Fancher at Frontier Records. Fancher loved it.

After a brief spell in the UK writing about music, and falling in love with punk, Fancher had spent the late 1970s working at Bomp Records, learning about the music business. She formed Frontier in 1980 and named it after her favourite place in the world, Disney's Frontierland. Fancher found success with Circle Jerks and then the huge-selling eponymous debut album by Suicidal Tendencies. By 1987 Frontier was a very successful independent label, whose roster included Thin White Rope, Redd Kross, and The Long Ryders.

Fancher went to see Mallon to discuss licensing the Flying Color debut. As the meeting drew to an amicable close, Mallon pressed a tape of *Engine* into her hands, and intimated that she would only get Flying Color if she took American Music Club too.

"He told me this was the best record that I'd ever hear," Fancher remembers. "I started rolling my eyes, thinking 'Oh great, now I'm going to get all the records this guy can't afford to put out,' and American Music Club was about the worst band name I'd ever heard. I took the tape of *Engine* home, and played it a couple of times, and it just didn't sink in. It didn't do anything for me at all. But for some reason I kept going back to it, and then on about the fourth listen, I realised that it was the best record ever made."

Frontier signed a deal with Mallon's label Grifter, and released both *Engine* and the Flying Color's debut record in September of that year, marking the occasion with a joint press launch at the I-Beam club.

Anyone expecting *Engine* to be a continuation of *The Restless Stranger* was going to be disappointed. It sounded like a completely different band. Eitzel would consider this to be "their first record that sounded like American Music Club." It was also a masterpiece.

All of the members of American Music Club had eclectic music tastes, and it might seem a simplification to dwell on one or two particular influences. But just as *The Restless Stranger* wore a love of Joy Division on its sleeve, the one artist whose work imbues the sound and spirit of *Engine*, is Nick Drake – the ill-fated English singer-songwriter who overdosed on anti-depressants at the age of 26 after years of frustration with the music industry. With the help of an acclaimed biography and a series of magazine articles, Drake has become a popular name for young musicians to drop. Back in 1985 and 1986 he was a much more obscure and unlikely reference point for a rock 'n' roll group.

The distinguishing characteristics of Drake's records are his fragile voice, his use of open guitar tunings, and his dextrous finger-picked style of guitar playing. There is also a deep-rooted bleakness running throughout his music, and his final album, *Pink Moon*, takes this to the extreme. Recorded by one man and a guitar, with practically no overdubs bar a hint of piano, *Pink Moon* is the chilling portrait of a man trailed by the intangible hell-hound of blues legend.

While American Music Club were in Germany, Vudi insisted that Eitzel listen to all of Nick Drake's records and showed him Drake's favoured open D guitar tuning. Vudi was already adept at this guitar style, and used to busk Drake songs in the street as a teenager. Eitzel was now smitten. He loved the songs and the haunting unresolved feeling of the guitar style. He adopted the D tuning on about half of the tracks on *Engine*, and experimented with different alternative tunings on a number of other songs. To Kathleen Burns, who had been trying to convert Eitzel to Drake for years, this was all rather ironic.

There is no doubt that *Engine* is a rock record, but in the Drake tradition. In many places it is stripped down and stark in sound, in keeping with its more sombre subject matter. *The Restless Stranger* was about loneliness and dislocation. *Engine* is about terror, horror and death. *The Restless Stranger* felt hurried in the way it was put together, but *Engine* is tightly structured; the order of the tracks is crucial.

The opener "Big Night" had been an Eitzel staple through various art-rock incarnations ever since its debut as the awkward "Shadow of My Name" that closed the *Mean Mark Eitzel* cassette, but here it is transformed into a melodic and organic elegy – an ominous opening to an unsettling album. The piano is fragmented, the bass lines brooding, and the guitar and vocals are portentious.

The foreboding atmosphere of "Big Night" is followed by the record's two anthems, "Outside This Bar" and "At My Mercy" – a pair of twisted Bukowski-esque tales of love gone wrong, with tunes most major bands would kill for, set to a big country rock beat. The former documents Eitzel's lifestyle with Kathleen – collapsing outside bars, and slumped on empty streets, like millstones around each other's necks. Together, they must *"destroy this world."*

Eitzel remembers, "We wanted a hit and 'Outside this Bar' was going to be the big rock song." Written in Hamburg, it is about Andy's Pub in Columbus, and features an angel dust addict friend of Eitzel's called Arlis. Andy's was where Kathleen's sister used to make Long Island Teas for her friends for free. She'd also try out new cocktail ideas on Eitzel and Kathleen on Sunday afternoons.

Eitzel continues: "So it's about leaving the bar on a Sunday afternoon, so drunk that I couldn't walk, in about 100 degrees and 90% humidity, and Arlis came into the picture because to me Arlis sums up what's best about Ohio and Columbus."

In spite of the glorious melodies and fluid country rock guitar hooks – indeed neither song would sound out of place on an REM album of the time – the subject matter of both "Outside This Bar," and "At My Mercy," maintains a strong sense of claustrophobia. Through the alcohol haze, something is wrong. There is the feeling of a bitter tale unravelling.

After *Engine's* two big rock tunes comes the twisted country waltz, "Gary's Song," – *"As we sit here, drinking our beer/ We'll be two inflatable dolls in a hooker's bad dream/ And I think I just came in my pants/ Oh Darling, do you want to dance"* – but this gallows humour only masks the fact that Eitzel's friend Gary is drinking himself to death. *"And the shame of my life is watching you drown."* The surreal imagery set to a straight country accompaniment is part of the joke too – to rock listeners' ears it sounds like a pastiche or parody. It's another way for Eitzel to say "fuck you all," just as he revels in the song's bad taste imagery. After "Gary's Song" *Engine* starts to take an even darker turn.

For a while, Eitzel's parents lived right next to the interstate ring-road that surrounds Columbus. "Nightwatchman," the next track was inspired by a revelation Eitzel had one night sitting on the front steps of their house.

"There was a stormy sky – the sky was beautiful," he told a journalist, "You look down from the sky and everything is stupid. Everything is a waste; everything is asleep and dead. And I looked up at the sky and it seemed like the sky was trying to say something to me. If nobody could hear the pain up there, if there was nobody to witness, then the world is completely and utterly desolate."

Midway in, Eitzel sings the heartbreaking and revealing lines: *"Once I knew the secret of happiness / I knew it once, but now it's gone."* But it is the refrain *"The nightwatchman, he's asleep,"* that contains the most pivotal image of both the song and the album. This is the idea that the one character who is trusted to watch over people does not care enough to stay awake – in effect, our night-time guardian has given up his post. It implies there is no witness to human suffering – a picture of hopelessness and despair that is inextricably tied up with the death of Eitzel's parents. Eitzel is not saying that God doesn't exist; just that God has turned his back, become indifferent, which is somehow more terrifying.

For the rest of the album, tales of broken relationships and dysfunctional families play out against this back-drop of a spiritual vacuum, while jagged-edged electric guitars continue to shift, murmur and rumble. Yet as Eitzel's sense of horror grows, so does his defiance. On "Clouds," far worse than skeletons in the closet, Eitzel has *"a wardrobe filled with blood."* Still, as he feels macabre strangers gather around his grave, he responds *"So come on in, you're welcome in."* On "Electric Light," he sings of some twisted love affair, *"I'm not afraid of it.../ but I ain't never going back,"* and he dares anyone to be *"his judge and jury."*

In "Mom's TV," Eitzel vividly mingles filial resentment and anger at his then lone-surviving parent, with sympathy as he notices the way his mother watches television to keep loneliness and bleak thoughts at bay.

> *God I hate you*
> *God I hate you*
> *Tellin' me what's gonna happen*
> *The rest of my life...*
>
> *It's read all off of your face*
> *It's in everything you say*
> *Echoes of the end*
> *And the fade of night or day.*

Engine's darkening mood is alleviated briefly by the grunge rock of "The Art of Love." Then things get altogether starker. Eitzel later would cite "Pink Moon," as his favourite Nick Drake song, and "Asleep," and "This Year," the album's closing two tracks, about sleep and death respectively, follow that song's bleak blueprint.

In "Asleep," co-credited to Kathleen Burns, over a slowly plucked, open tuned guitar, Eitzel slowly whispers one verse that circles around a pattern, while never quite following one. As the protagonist tosses and turns on his *"Bed of nails in the sky,"* he sees in his sleeping lover a happy peace. He doesn't say anything negative about the relationship, but implies that their only chance of happiness is to just stay like this: *"You sleepin' / I like to see you that way / I wish that you would just sleep all day."*

Gradually an undercurrent of bass is added, then more guitars. At each line the music become louder and more urgent. When Eitzel has breathed the last words, the drums, guitars and bass fight for ascendance in a brief instrumental coda.

On the final track, "This Year," a dark confession with a heaven-sent melody, Eitzel brings all of *Engine*'s subject matter back home. picking out a descending series of chord fragments in unfamiliar voicings, his singing remains just above a whisper. Slowly and quietly, the narrator draws back the curtain to reveal *Engine*'s source of foreboding. This is the revelation that we have been waiting for the whole record. Eitzel has been weaving in and out of the concentric circles of his own private hell, and now he is finally at the centre. This is Kurtz at the source of the river – the heart of Eitzel's darkness. Like Gram Parsons on the chilling "$1,000 Wedding" Eitzel's voice is matter of fact as he recounts the tragedy:

> *This year, This year*
> *What's the look this year?*
> *Is it the look of things to come?*
> *Has it all been said?*
> *Has it all been done?*
> *The sun upon the sea*
> *Did you dress that way for me?*
> *This year, this year*
> *Everyone just stood around and*
> *Watched my family tree burn down.*

Dan Pearson's voice mingles with Eitzel's on the final few lines, as Vudi's accordion adds a barely audible undercurrent of melancholy. Then it is over.

The ultimate difference between *Engine* and Nick Drake's records is that while Drake sounded doomed and resigned, Eitzel makes it clear that he will rage and rage against the dying of the light. Later records would see love and compassion as the only solace when faced with horror, pain and disappointment, but for now the redeeming theme of *Engine* is defiance. At times almost unbearably bleak, this is ultimately a life-affirming record in the black tradition of Neil Young's *Tonight's The Night* or REM's *Automatic For The People*. It is also quite simply one of the greatest American guitar albums ever produced.

Closer to home, *Engine* would help to heal the rift between Eitzel and his sister, Renee. Since the death of their parents, they'd rarely spoken, and Renee was still angry at the way Eitzel had left her to cope with the funeral arrangements and the aftermath. Renee remembers: "I couldn't get over my anger enough to realise how deeply their death affected Mark until I listened to his music about that year. His music hurt. His lyrics bit. He would sing thoughts that I felt and express emotions that I couldn't."

On its release, *Engine* was pretty much ignored by radio and the press. Fatally, even college radio failed to notice it. The few writers who did review it, didn't hear much that they liked. Alex Abey in the *California Aggie* was one of the least impressed, seeing only self-pity in Eitzel's lyrics and vocals, and dismissing the music as "a kind of mish mash of the 'sound' that has come to be known as 'American music'." Abey concluded: "This is by no means a bad record; however, it is pathetically interchangeable with so many other American discs of recent years. Not that I mind another country-tinged guitar record to drink to, but one doesn't want to hear some guy whining in existential pathos while you're sippin' Jim Beam. Buy a Green On Red record instead."

While the mainstream music press shunned them, fanzine writers took to AMC's cause like a noble crusade. *Your Flesh*'s Amy Gelman declared *Engine* "by far the best rock or 'rock' album of 1987," and *Scott's Tissue* proclaimed it "The LP of the year, period." A few fanzine reviews though would not be enough to influence the record buying public. Sales of *Engine* were poor.

Lisa Fancher was dismayed by the overall reaction: "No one got it. Critics, DJs, everybody – did not get it at all. They hated it. People said it was too slow... and said that Mark sounded like Bruce Springsteen. Whatever was popular in the fall of 1987, it was not a sound like that."

Although AMC were just one of many bands on Frontier, by now Fancher was obsessed with them, admitting later that, "If people said they didn't like them, even if they were my friends, I instantly hated them, and thought they were idiots." She was determined to keep pushing American Music Club until a breakthrough came. Her next step was to set up a US tour. But, even with a new album and licensing deal, Fancher could not get a booking agent to take them on. Maybe the record was just too quiet and too slow for prospective bookers. Considering an agent would often only listen to the first track on a band's album, *Engine*'s low key opener "Big Night" was not the big rock attention-grabber that would appeal to the trade. Without an agent it was difficult for them to get US shows outside their native Bay Area. Fancher's solution was to book AMC to play in record stores in the towns where they couldn't get club dates.

Before embarking on the tour AMC needed to finalise their line-up. After the problems of using three different drummers on *Engine*, Tom Mallon told them he'd play drums, just so that he wouldn't have to listen to them "whining about not having a goddamned drummer anymore."

"Tom Mallon had worked with Toiling Midgets a lot," Eitzel remembers, "so he knew Tim Mooney's style very well. He'd just play like Tim, which made us all happy."

Drums were not Mallon's instrument, as Dan Pearson explains, "Tom never would have played drums at all, if AMC had had a drummer." It was a move as extreme as if Martin Hannett had decided to play keyboards for Joy Division after working on *Unknown Pleasures*, or Steve Lillywhite had joined U2 after working on *War*. Becoming a fully-fledged member showed just how completely taken Mallon was with AMC.

For three weeks in October 1987, a four-piece American Music Club travelled across the United States playing independent record stores in 13 cities, sleeping in an old Dodge van each night. They would drive for two days straight, play a record store to 10 people, then drive another two days and play another store. They drove through snowstorms and up through the Rocky mountains with the van regularly breaking down and them having absolutely no money.

For the store dates they reverted to an acoustic format, with Vudi strapping on an accordion and occasionally playing fiddle, while Dan Pearson played mandolin. They also interspersed new arrangements of *Engine* material with embryonic versions of new songs like "Firefly," "Western Sky," "Blue And Grey Shirt," and "Kathleen." They even covered the occasional Carter Family song. Attendances at these shows were not great, and the audience reactions were varied. Lisa Fancher recalls that "they went down really well once people saw them and got charmed by Mark's whole trip, but I have photos from some of those stores and there were absolutely no people at them."

Dan Pearson told writer Ralph Traitor: "We played a shopping centre in Santa Rosa, a little town – pretty scary, but we moved people. They'd never heard anything like it in their lives... there were only four walk-outs, which was pretty good."

"We were playing rough," Dan Pearson continues, "and anything could happen at any moment. Bits of the music were totally astounding. The music was totally stripped down, and songs would just stop in the middle. Tom Mallon would be getting up a head of steam, and then if he sensed it wasn't right, he'd just suddenly stop. Then he'd have a big explosion like an epileptic seizure."

The high point of the tour was when they got to Minneapolis. Pete Jesperson, then manager of local heroes The Replacements, had liked *The Restless Stranger* and took a shine to the band. Whenever The Replacements played San Francisco, he would have AMC open for them, and when AMC came to Minneapolis, Jesperson would get them a good $500 club show, which Pearson remembers as all-time high: "It bought enough gas to get to New York."

Earlier in the day they had played a breathtaking acoustic show at the Minneapolis Garage D'Or record store, where the running order of the final two songs displayed a shift in Eitzel's perspective. The chilling closing track from *Engine*, "This Year" was followed by a beautiful acoustic revisiting of the early song, "Hold On To Your Love."

> Hold on to your love, because now when I walk,
> I never touch the ground.
> There must be something else
> We've got nothing else.

While *Engine* was an amazing record, playing live was American Music Club's real work. From day to day, Eitzel would alter song lyrics and shift the emphasis of lines, and the band would regularly change the musical arrangements, improvising new instrumental breaks and leads. Shows revealed their music as an exploration constantly in a state of flux.

The following night AMC were in Chicago, playing to 20 people at the Pravda Records store in the shadow of Wrigley Field – separated from the small audience by just a few record bins. After subsequent shows in Ohio and South Carolina, AMC eventually made it to New York, where they hooked up with Gerard Cosloy, then head of Homestead Records, and later Matador boss. Eitzel remembers it as pivotal in the band's growth:

"Our first show ever in NYC was at a record store. Most of the audience were there for the new wave art band support act and I had driven them all out. The crowd wouldn't shut up or leave, so I said, 'Look, if you're not here to see us, get the fuck out.' We then waited three quarters of an hour until they had all left. Only three people remained, one of whom was Cosloy, who subsequently wrote about us in *CMJ*, and helped get us an agent."

On their return to the West Coast, Lisa Fancher arranged a Saturday night showcase gig for the band at the Music Machine in Los Angeles. Because AMC were still unknown in LA, Fancher invited all of her friends to lend some support – an action she would later have some cause to regret. While Eitzel was quite restrained in the acoustic record store shows, on stage in a club, he was like a wild animal suddenly uncaged. He told a journalist, "a stage is a place where anything can happen," and would get so drunk that anything normally did.

Lisa Fancher recalls the impact of AMC's early club gigs:

"In that kind of setting, right in your face, it was incredible. If you heard *Engine*, you really were not expecting what they were like live. In those days, Mark was something else. He would just get so incredibly drunk that the other guys were very wary of what might happen. On stage he would jump up in the air, and if he didn't land on his own knees, he'd land on Vudi or do something terrible to Danny."

Dan Pearson would later admit that he was terrified all the time he was playing live with AMC, and for good reason, as Fancher explains:

"Mark's caused Danny some pretty serious injuries over the years. Not hospitalisations, but I've seen him push Danny off the stage, or smash him with the tuning pegs in the general mayhem."

Before the Music Machine show, Eitzel got particularly wasted, even by his own standards. By the time AMC took to the stage, he was literally falling-down drunk. While the band roared on, he careened wildly around the stage, repeatedly falling to his knees, dropping his microphone and bumping into things.

"Mark was so drunk"... Fancher remembers, "it was just horrible – just pathetic... Mark was knocking people over and pulling the leads from the other guys' guitars. It was just a fiasco. The sound guy actually cut their set in half so I went up and started trying to have a fist-fight with him. People were coming up to me at the end going 'God, have you already signed them? Can you get out of this?' My publicist was pretending she didn't know who they were. But I wasn't discouraged by it."

The press reaction was mixed. It was impossible not to be moved in some ways, but Eitzel's performance was not what the press had expected. One LA rock writer, while confessing to being "overwhelmed by AMC's sound," was "dismayed and astounded by the behaviour of their lead singer." Another journalist felt "it was quite overwhelming, but seemingly at odds with AMC's personal, brutally honest lyrics."

The morning after the high-profile Music Machine show AMC played an acoustic set at Texas Records on LA Broadway, and then headed back to San Francisco.

Ironically, after surviving a truly gruelling tour, AMC actually hit crisis point once they were back on home ground. The band were confirmed to play at a new San Francisco record store owned by Denise Sullivan, a local DJ and REM cohort. But, as building work was still continuing within the premises, it appeared unlikely that the store would be ready for AMC's appearance. With 24 hours to go, Sullivan telephoned to cancel.

Eitzel had found the whole touring experience stressful and exhausting. For him, this was the last straw, as he later explained to journalist Andrea Freedman: "[Sullivan] decided she was too tired and didn't want to put it together. All of a sudden that kind of tiredness was the root of all evil. She let me and everyone down at a time when I was feeling like I didn't want to have to depend on people like that."

From Los Angeles, Lisa Fancher spent two hours on the phone trying to convince Eitzel that this wasn't the end of the world. It was only one show, but something had gone off in his head, and there was no reaching him. Later that day at the studio, after a row with Vudi and Mallon, Eitzel quit the band and disappeared.

Fancher immediately feared that he might do something stupid – he had sounded terribly fragile to her on the phone. Determined to track him down before it was too late, she called everyone she could think of, but not even Kathleen Burns knew where he was. In a state of some agitation, Fancher persevered: "After more sleuthing I found out that he was staying at the YMCA. It had one depressing pay phone in the hallway but nobody would go knock on his door. I called a zillion times hoping he'd pick up the phone to make it stop ringing."

Nobody answered.

Vudi, Pearson and Mallon were extremely upset and concerned. Eitzel had threatened to quit many times, but no one ever thought he would. They figured that the band was now broken up for good. Though worried about Eitzel, they decided they should not pursue him if he wanted to be left alone. Fancher, however did not give up: "I spent about four hours writing him a letter that used up a whole pad of paper. I told him he was born to write songs, how much he affected people's lives and that he had to be in AMC... I reminded him of lots of things, and told him how much we all loved him."

When Eitzel called her to say he had got the letter, Fancher cried like a baby. AMC had a show booked in LA for the following week, and there was a huge sense of relief when Eitzel showed up in the club's foyer.

"When I walked into the soundcheck," Fancher remembers, "Mark ran over and practically broke my ribs hugging me.... He told me he was going to quit, but that he realised how much AMC meant to everyone, and that he didn't want to let us down."

Eitzel later admitted, "The band was the one thing that was holding me together."

Shortly after the LA show, Eitzel went back to the telesales department at Creative Leisure. Keen to move out of the storage room at Mallon's studio, and having spent most of the money his parents had left him, he now needed a weekly wage. "I was a good salesman, too," Eitzel later reflected with pride.

Engine was released in the UK in February 1988 without a fanfare. Only about 20 press copies of the album were dispatched, and the few reviews that did appear were mixed. In the late 1980s, the ultra-hip *NME* was never likely to rush to praise country-tinged American guitar rock and their reviewer pulled few punches, dwelling on the "naff" name, comparing them adversely with REM and summing them up as "possible pub rock for the future." *Sounds* was more positive though, and *Melody Maker*'s David Rothon praised "songs truly stunning in their range and power." He compared Eitzel to Jim Morrison, Gram Parsons and Springsteen, before concluding: "Melodic, understated, dark and disturbing, *Engine* is one of this year's unexpected pleasures."

Reviewing the proofs of the review section, *Melody Maker* editor Allan Jones was intrigued by what Rothon had written. Realising that a copy of this album had languished unplayed in his office for weeks, he dug it out, and then as the record played, leafed through the enclosed press clippings that documented Eitzel's erratic stage behaviour. "Eitzel seemed an interesting character from the off"... Jones remembers, "I played *Engine,* and although it wasn't an immediate Damascus-type conversion, I kept coming back to it and it just slowly sank in."

Jones was fascinated by Eitzel's driven, drunken barfly image and felt that, "there was something gritty and real about *Engine* – that it was the kind of record that really spoke to you, the more you listened to it." He saw traces of the influence of bands like The Replacements, REM, The Minutemen, and Hüsker Dü – all acts which had been revitalising a previously moribund US music scene – but what struck him most about *Engine* was that it was so unique. He explained later, "It didn't really conform to anything that was around at the time."

Still, other than in the *Melody Maker* offices, *Engine* did not make much impact in the UK. There was no press launch, no showcase gigs, no advertising and the band did not tour. The UK record company Zippo did little to push the album and it was quickly forgotten, until it eventually became obvious that Demon, Zippo's parent company, could, and should, do more to promote their imported new releases. Accordingly Spike Hyde was recruited to the Demon press office.

Hyde heard *Engine* prior to joining the company and had liked it. On arrival he listened to it again, and remembers: "I was just amazed how good it was, and how little Demon had done to promote American Music Club – I couldn't believe that there was this incredible record that nobody had done anything with". Hyde sent out another batch of review copies – targeting those journalists he considered the most discerning. But other than talk *Engine* up, there wasn't a great deal he could do, as he later explained, "Demon certainly were not going to go back to an album released the previous year just because a new press officer was keen."

Ten years later, Mark Eitzel would grin wryly, and explain through gritted teeth: "I thought *Engine* would sell millions and millions of records, I believed it would get to number one." When pressed if he was being sarcastic, Eitzel would insist, "I thought it was a good record and I thought it would be a hit."

Engine's US sales were negligible. In the UK, it sold fewer than 2,000 copies and then just sat gathering dust in a Demon cupboard.

Chapter Four

No-one Loves Anybody Here And That's The Truth

"What the public wants is the image of passion, not passion itself."
Roland Barthes, Mythologies *(1957)*

"If something terrible happens you drink to forget it; if something good happens you drink to celebrate and if nothing happens, you drink to make something happen."
Charles Bukowski, Women

By the time *Engine* was released in the UK, Eitzel had a new job and a new home. Tired of the increasingly bizarre demands of his boss at Creative Leisure, who was now insisting that employees look into a mirror on their terminals to ensure that they smiled as they pitched at all times, he quit to take a job doing data input at the St Francis Hospital. He also moved out of Mallon's studio into a small flat on Geary Street in the Tenderloin area.

About a mile north of the San Francisco Civic Centre, the Tenderloin is a pretty rough stretch. Its streets are strewn with litter and detritus, and lined with seedy bars, small hole-in-the-wall restaurants, porn shops, massage parlours, and large, grubby, run-down apartment blocks. Hispanic and Asian immigrants mingle uneasily with elderly native San Franciscans, an extremely high proportion of the local population are drug addicts, dealers, pimps, prostitutes and the homeless.

Though depressing in many ways, there was initially a poetic glamour in the Tenderloin's low life that would be attractive to a man whose favourite writer was now Charles Bukowski, the hard-drinking poet laureate of Los Angeles flophouses, barflies and lowlife. Bukowski's upbringing, though much harsher, shared key characteristics with Eitzel's. Whereas Eitzel has always believed himself to be ugly, Bukowski was actually hideously scarred, having contracted the worst case of acne his local health authority had ever recorded. Bukowski also grew up without any childhood companions because his overbearing father saw the local children as unworthy of his son. Though Eitzel's early isolation was rooted in his family's constant relocation, similar forces would drive the two men to pick up a pen. Eitzel loved the rough-hewn honesty of Bukowski's work, and he was drawn to the writer's uncompromising outsider's stance on life.

Because of the subject matter of Eitzel's songs, and his apparent self-destructive love affair with the bottle, press commentators would repeatedly draw the Bukowski comparison.

"I'm not Bukowski, but I love him..." Eitzel would say, "his art was very pure and very pop. And he's this great poet but women think he hated women, and gay people think he hated gay people, but he only really hated himself. I've read stories where he's with a beautiful woman and it is all beautiful, and then he just says, well 'fuck it.' I just love him and always have."

Though not the kind of person that would seek out his heroes, Eitzel did once nearly meet Bukowski: "Me and a friend went to a bar in LA, because I thought it looked a great bar – like a huge drawing room. And Bukowski was there, and he knew we recognised him. I was like [makes bowled over fan type gesture]. Immediately I started drinking scotch. To this day I regret not going to the bar and getting him a tab and just saying 'Get him whatever he wants'. I wish I had, but a lot of his writing is about people like me going up to him and talking to him and being nice, and he hated that. I didn't want to be like that."

AMC shows were even reminiscent of some of Bukowski's later poetry readings, where the audience would howl for request after request, while the poet laughed with them and berated them. Bukowski, like Eitzel, would ensure he got so drunk that anything could happen. Also, Bukowski didn't achieve any commercial success until the age of 50 – an encouraging fact for an acclaimed songwriter who had yet to receive a royalty cheque.

Dire and degrading as it was, the Tenderloin would give Eitzel plenty of food for his creativity. It was a setting that would inspire many of his songs of the period. It was also only about a mile from Tom Mallon's studio. Vudi lived nearby in the South of Market area and for most of the duration of the next two American Music Club albums, the band's lives revolved around this part of town. Eitzel recalls that "every night during *California* and *United Kingdom*, we'd record at Tom's and then go to the Hotel Utah to drink or play."

Another key development for the band between the release of *Engine,* and work on its follow-up was the recruitment of a new manager. Dan Pearson's girlfriend Mary had been managing the band for a while, but now Tom Mallon's new girlfriend, Leslie Rule, wanted to try her hand at managing American Music Club. Leslie had played bass in some local bands and according to Mark Terrill, she "understood the band's mentality, and she was good at what she did."

A change of management at this point was a good move for American Music Club as they now needed to capitalise on their growing cult following. They also needed to build on their relationship with their record company. The best way of doing this was to nurture the talent of their singer-songwriter, whose writing was getting better all the time.

There were just three problems: Leslie Rule had no experience of manage-ment, and she didn't get on with either Mark Eitzel, or their record company boss, Lisa Fancher, neither of whom thought she should manage the band.

Lisa Fancher is quite clear on the latter two points: "Leslie and I never got on in the slightest, as far as I could tell, she hated my guts from the minute she set eyes on me. It was a pretty big problem. She didn't know what she was doing, and I don't think she respected Mark. I think she thought Mark was a clown... But we had no say in this decision – it was just one of those done deals."

It seems bizarre that Eitzel, by now the main creative force in the band, would not have a say in the choice of manager. He may have been overruled, but his attitude to the recruitment of Leslie appears symptomatic of a wider problem. At various stages in American Music Club's career, when faced with a band deci-sion that he didn't like, rather than argue his case, Eitzel would repeatedly shrug, go along with it, and then rail against it subsequently when the damage was already done.

After Leslie's recruitment, the band started on the follow-up to *Engine* at Mallon's studio. Breaking off for local live shows, and the occasional trip to Minneapolis, Columbus, or anywhere else they could get a gig, the band would work continually on the new album until the summer.

Even before they entered the studio, the band had spent hours discussing how they wanted the album to sound. Eitzel and Mallon in particular were conscious of wanting to move in a new direction. Eitzel had been immersing himself fur-ther in the music of Nick Drake, and in his own words, was now "trying to strip all of the rock out of the songs..." He wanted to create something more subtle and fragile, as he explains: "Tom's and my conception of the album had a lot to do with the power of something you hear coming from the other room – suggest-ing something different from the blatant and obvious."

According to Eitzel, this transformation was partly a reaction to all of the "indie" guitar rock that was dominating the "alternative" scene at the time, and partly a pragmatic response to his belief that AMC "never really rocked that well." It was a conscious attempt at finding a unique voice, "because we were trying to forge an identity and get people to listen to us, and not play things that are big and bombastic."

Though hampered by Eitzel's difficulty in expressing some of his musical ideas in musician's terms – for example, telling Dan Pearson that he wanted one track to "sound like a sunny day" – the band had gradually developed arrange-ments that they were happy with. The initial demos for the album were astound-ing. Eitzel would rarely sing the lyrics the same way twice, and would repeatedly improvise new melodies and words. Lisa Fancher remembers: "Mark would do three takes of a song, and except for the chorus line, he'd come up with com-pletely new stuff each take."

Not surprisingly, this approach didn't make it easy for the band to record their parts, but they were keen to keep things fresh, and Eitzel's takes were raw and passionate. All of the band were keen to avoid a repeat of the *Engine* recording process where Mallon spent hundreds of hours erasing, re-recording and mixing. This time, they wanted to make a simpler record in a much shorter time. Whether or not an album as unpolished and spontaneous as the demos would have been acceptable to Frontier in the end is difficult to say, but Tom Mallon was not going to allow the tapes out of his studio until each track passed his own extremely exacting standards.

It got so that Eitzel dreaded going back into the studio, because Mallon was so demanding in his insistence that every single part of every recording had to sound just right. Occasionally, Eitzel would try to put his foot down and refuse to redo a vocal part again, but Mallon would still make him sing until his throat bled.

According to Fancher, "the band were even talking about using an outside producer, but they figured Tom wouldn't go for that. They just wanted a buffer so that Tom wasn't completely in control."

But as the only person who knew how the studio worked, Mallon truly was in control. If the band played something he didn't like, and couldn't or wouldn't redo it, he would simply redo the offending part himself after they had gone. Lisa Fancher remembers that "the band would go into the playback and Tom would have added stuff that he thought would be cool without even asking them." Not surprisingly, this drove the band crazy. Eitzel and the others had a lot of faith in Mallon's judgement, but that didn't mean they liked the way he worked. Every time they came back to find Mallon had tampered with their work in their absence, the simmering tension got worse.

Gradually, Mallon's perfectionism got more and more out of control. One evening Eitzel arrived in the studio control room to find Tom sat on the floor surrounded by hundreds of tiny strips of tape. Frustrated by the band's musical time-keeping on one track, Mallon had cut out millimetre widths of tape from between every single drum beat in order to bring the recording into perfect time. When the shocked singer asked Tom what he was doing, Mallon replied defiantly: "You can't fucking play it, so I'm gonna cut it up. Fuck you!"

Whether or not Mallon was taking things too far, in spite of what Fancher and Eitzel would say, it is clear that the band did need a strong outside presence to help shape what they were doing. To keep changing his part on every single take was interesting experimentally and in keeping with Eitzel's cherished surrealist ideas of freeing the imagination, it was also an approach that would make AMC consistently revelatory as a live band – but it was just not suited to record-making. Mallon may have made himself unpopular, but it was his job to try and harness the radical, intellectual experimentation into a permanent statement. As the band enjoyed trying every song in many different styles, someone had to pin them down, and get them to settle on finished versions of each track.

For all his criticisms, Eitzel is keen to stress the value of Mallon's contribution: "Mallon is probably more important to American Music Club than I am. With his manipulative negativity, he whipped us into what he wanted to hear. And that was more or less what we wanted to hear."

In spite of, or because of, Mallon's overbearing perfectionism, it quickly became clear that this was going to be a very fine album. As work progressed, even Tom Mallon appeared reasonably happy. The band's playing perfectly complemented Eitzel's strongest batch of songs to date, and Vudi, Mallon and Pearson found new shades of musical colour to bring out the beauty of Eitzel's melodies without resorting to anything obvious or hackneyed. In particular,

Eitzel wanted a different sound for one of the most upbeat new songs, and one of the last to be recorded, "Firefly." He felt the bass should sound more like Jack Bruce, and saw Danny's playing as lacking in "swing." Eventually Eitzel called Lisa Davis, a former dancer who was then bass player with local band Naked Into. Davis came over the next day and on the second take, they got it. Davis remembers, "It was natural, and it clicked."

After Davis had given the song a much looser feel, Eitzel felt it still needed some additional colour and suggested that staple of country music, the pedal steel guitar. This wasn't a conscious move in a country direction, and contrary to what some might believe, Eitzel was not a big Gram Parsons fan.

"I [just] wanted something that was different from a synthesiser or string arrangement," Eitzel explains, "but that had a symphonic feel to it. I asked Vudi and he said 'I know a great pedal steel player, Scary Larry'."

Larry's moniker came from nothing more terrifying than his ability to play every single instrument. His real name was Bruce Kaphan.

Kaphan was aware of Eitzel and American Music Club, but didn't really like either of their albums, and had never seen them live. He was now an established session player, fresh from engineering John Lee Hooker's *Jealous* album, and his initial reaction was "Okay, how much are you paying me?" It wasn't a lucrative offer, but as it was Vudi, he agreed to do it anyway.

By now Kaphan was used to working in extremely professional set-ups. On arrival at the studio, he was immediately struck by how disorganised it all seemed. Tom Mallon was at the helm, but there was a very odd atmosphere and palpable tension between Mallon and other members of the band.

Kaphan wasn't sent a tape before the sessions, and neither Mallon nor the band gave him any idea of what they wanted. "Just play," they told him. Bruce quickly improvised a shiny joyful opening signature riff. When he was finished, Eitzel asked him to add some pedal steel to another song, "Blue And Grey Shirt." At the end of the session, Vudi asked him if he wanted to join the band, but Kaphan didn't think he was serious and made light of it. After just a couple of hours Kaphan headed for home.

When Mallon had finished refining the tapes, what remained was still very much in keeping with what the band wanted. It may have been less raw than the original demos – for instance the power of Vudi's menacing electric guitar on early versions of songs like "Highway 5" had been severely tempered – but the desolate spirit of the original takes remained. In keeping with Eitzel's intention to strip all of the rock out of the band's sound, there was a sparseness on *California* that had only been previously hinted at in a tracks such as "Asleep" or "This Year" from *Engine*.

After the tension in the studio, it was a relief to have the album completed, and ready to be pressed. There was however one final complication. Shortly before the album sleeves were due to be printed, Lisa Fancher sent the cover artwork to Eitzel for his approval – at this stage a simple rubber stamping process. But as Eitzel looked it over, he noticed that some of the songwriting credits were not what he'd expected. There were multiple credits to songs that he was sure he'd written on his own. Maybe the other band members had helped in realising the song's potential, but he'd written the lyrics, the chords and the melody. And more importantly: why hadn't he been consulted?

With the offending album cover still in front of him, Eitzel immediately called Mallon to protest. Eitzel maintained that he'd give the band a fair share of any publishing money, and that he'd given the band arrangement credits, but he was adamant that he'd written the songs. The response was not sympathetic. Mallon told him, "Yeah Eitzel, well fuck you, man. Okay we'll change the name of the album to 'Eitzel'. In big letters it'll just say 'Eitzel.' And we'll put your fucking ugly face on the cover too."

But for all his perceived compromises, songwriting credit was the one area in which Eitzel would not back down. It was then, as it is now, his craft. He sees himself as a songwriter before he is a singer or a musician. And to him, credit for his work equalled respect. It is a subject that still rankles: "I'd written all of the songs on *California*, and somewhere they'd taken my song, they moved a chorus, added a middle eight, and that was it. They didn't change the lyrics and they didn't change the chorus melody. There was a song that Mallon said was written by all of us, and I went to Mallon, and he said, 'Hey Eitzel, you weren't fucking there, I asked Danny, and Danny said we all wrote it,' and I said, 'Well, Tom I have a phone number, I could have told you', but Tom never returned calls. Never!"

Eitzel believes this was a pivotal moment. He'd remained silent as they had recruited a manager he disapproved of, and had gone along with many other band decisions, just for an easy life. But this area was sacrosanct: "For me, it was the first time I ever stood up for myself and said, 'You know what, I do a lot of work. The other members of the band don't stay up all night writing songs... If you have a painter, and somebody who frames the painting, you don't say that the framer and the painter share credit for the painting."

After speaking to Mallon, Eitzel was even more upset. So, he called Lisa at Frontier and told her the album was not coming out. Then he called Vudi and Danny and told them the album credits were "bullshit."

They were defensive, adopting an argument Eitzel believed had come from Mallon: "Well, Eitzel. We won't have a pot to piss in, and you're going to take all our money all the way to the bank, and we're going to go broke."

To which Eitzel replied, "Well, write your own songs."

It was a serious point. Both Vudi and Pearson had written songs of their own in previous bands, but now nobody other than Eitzel was coming up with new material.

Eitzel would maintain: "My biggest frustration with American Music Club, in fact it nearly made me quit the band, was about a year into it, when the other members told me, 'Well, you're the freak, you're gonna jump around, fall over and sing, you write the songs and you write the lyrics, don't worry about us.' And I said 'Come on! You write songs too.' And they were like, 'No. We don't do that. We're the journeyman rock musicians. We're the back-up group'."

An earlier band meeting had ended up with Eitzel shouting at the rest of the band: "I want you to play with soul, and I want you to write songs." When he got no response, he just thought, "fuck it, I'll write them all."

However, as Dan Pearson points out, even by the time they were working on their second album, it was becoming clear that Eitzel's songwriting vision was totally central to the band. Eitzel didn't use conventional song structures, or traditional guitar chords, and rarely adopted the conventional guitar tuning, so by the time they were recording *California,* songs by any other member would probably have felt out of place, unless they had consciously mimicked Eitzel's style, in which case what was the point? Vudi had asked for a couple of his songs to go on the new album, but when pushed he did not produce anything, and that was that.

Pearson and Vudi saw their role as creating music around Eitzel's songs. It would inevitably rankle that they got neither credit nor financial reward for it, as Pearson explains: "I would work and try to create and come up with ideas and force things in directions. We would all rehearse and compose Mark's songs into a band setting for free. We were never paid, ever."

In the end the cover artwork was changed to credit Eitzel as sole songwriter, and the album came out as planned. But Eitzel believes that these events changed the rest of the band's perception of him: "I became 'that asshole Eitzel'. And whenever I got sensitive about any issue, they would go 'fuck you, you write all the songs'."

As an additional complication, Eitzel was beginning to realise what the implications were of having Tom Mallon's Grifter Records as his publisher. Without even the most minimal advance on royalties, he had signed over to Mallon the rights to, and a quarter of the income from, some of his finest songs. This was not uncommon practice in the US, where small record companies would often use song publishing as a way of hedging against a record failing to recoup its costs. However, in the context of the wider picture this only caused to further muddy an already unsatisfactory business situation.

It appears Mallon's Grifter Records had an informal arrangement whereby income from the first three American Music Club albums would go against all of Mallon's so far unspecified and non-itemised recording and production costs – although to what level remained unclear. Tom Mallon had spent literally thousands of hours of his own time on *Engine* and *California,* but on the other hand, the band had neither asked him nor wanted him to work on the records for so long. American Music Club were now faced with a ledger of almost unlimited costs, against which any income earned from sales of the albums would be set, before they would receive any payment for their recorded performances. Eitzel now realised that any song-writing income would also be lumped in the same pot, even though where the songs were recorded, and who produced them, had no impact on their composition.

"Eitzel always had publishing beefs with Tom," Lisa Fancher remembers, "because Tom had decided he was co-publishing the band's songs. At the time, Eitzel didn't really know what publishing was, and when I explained it to him, he was pretty unhappy that the stuff was published by Grifter, and he was really shocked that he'd given his publishing away for nothing."

It is important to point out that while Mallon was an extremely demanding producer, he did not have a reputation for sharp business practice. Part of the reason he'd taken care of the publishing was that someone had to do it, and Eitzel was initially too drunk or too uninterested to care. Indeed, when Frontier Records commissioned Mallon to produce Thin White Rope's *Sackful Of Silver* album, at three times the usual fee, he would not consider accepting the sum and insisted on his standard low rate. With American Music Club he was perhaps too close to the band to see clearly.

Before *California* was released, a number of record industry people started taking an interest in American Music Club. They had been playing highly acclaimed shows in San Francisco, and their reputation was spreading by word of mouth. Elektra were the first company to come forward and discuss a distribution deal through Frontier, whereby the band would retain full artistic control. (Eitzel suggested in an interview that $300,000 was mooted for the deal, although Fancher believes numbers were never discussed.)

"I had a meeting with Howard Thompson of Elektra," Fancher remembers, "who was very interested in AMC. Howard had liked *Engine* a lot. I was in New York for a trade convention and we had a meeting, and I showed him the video press kit I'd made, where Mark was doing his rap, 'blah, blah, blah, we suck, we're the worst band ever.' And he started saying to me, 'You must tell Mark this. You must tell him to dress like this. You must tell him not to say that they suck.' We just started screaming at each other. A crowd gathered outside his office as a result. I was saying, 'No-one is going to tell him what to do, or what to say.' He was saying, 'No band of mine would ever give an interview like that'."

Eitzel would be repeatedly criticised for denigrating himself, his band and his music. When an outtake from the *California* sessions, "I'm In Heaven Now," appeared on *Human Music*, a double album compilation of left-field US bands released by Gerard Colsoy's Homestead Records, Eitzel used the sleevenotes to continue apologising:

"There's thousands and thousands of rock bands better than American Music Club. [We're] just four passive aggressive dullards slipping quietly into middle age with no clue how to make it in Today's Rock Market."

For all his self-criticism, it was clear that Eitzel strongly believed in what he was doing. Indeed back in 1985 he told a radio interviewer, that he had an attitude problem, in that he considered AMC to be "the best band in town." Later he attempted to explain this contradiction: "This famous American band came on the radio and they were saying 'We're the best band around.' And the music was absolutely crap, and you know what? They became the biggest band around.

But I was always wary of being like that... I didn't want to be the kind of person who sat there and ballyhooed himself, and had nothing to show for himself. I'd rather make really quality things, and let that speak for me, than sit there and brag about it. So that is why everyone said I was self-deprecating in interviews... I wasn't really. People would say to me, 'Do you know how great you are?' And I'd be like 'what? no, no, there are lots of people better than me."

After Fancher and Thompson's meeting, Elektra declined to pursue American Music Club. The next AMC album would come out under the same distribution arrangements as *Engine,* but it was hoped that something would be put in place with a major label in time for its follow-up.

The working title for this new album had been "Meet the American Music Club." When it was completed, Eitzel decided to call it *California*. At the time, he said this was because that was the "stupidest" title he could think of, and yet it is a title imbued with meaning. Calling the album *California* drew attention to Eitzel and the band's love-hate relationship with their home – one of the sunniest states in the Union, and in some ways, one of the harshest. Few other albums have such an all-pervading sense of place as this. While it would be a later album that would bring AMC to international recognition, it is *California* that is the touchstone of their work. Both in the skill and radiance of the musical and lyrical craftsmanship, and in the way all of the key themes of Eitzel's writing are crystallised in its twelve songs, *California* is the definitive American Music Club album.

For someone with no real home or an unhappy past, the old notion of America as a haven, the chance to start afresh after leaving the Old World is an attractive idea. In these circumstances the American idea of Manifest Destiny, which defined and justified in spiritual terms the pioneers' settling of the West and their constant pushing forward of the frontier until they finally reached the Californian coast, has a deep and quasi-religious resonance. Eitzel told journalist Simon Williams, "I even go so far with these songs as to imagine that I'm destined to say these things, which is actually a Californian thing."

California is the ultimate destination for those moving on in search of something better. The West stops there. Kerouac's *On The Road* has San Francisco as its final destination. And for Eitzel too, the most western state of America is such a powerful metaphor because it is both physically and spiritually the ultimate last resort. Indeed when he first arrived in San Francisco and walked around the streets he felt like he was in "the last city on earth." He told Simon Reynolds: "My idea was that California has long been the best hope of a new beginning for disillusioned Americans, the last frontier, a final chance for the dream."

Dan Pearson concurred: "People still move to California to get away from somewhere else. I'm a native Californian and I remember my school teacher asking the class how many kids were born in the state. There were only two."

The tragic aspect of Eitzel's vision is that for most people this push forward to the West in search of something better, normally ends without redemption. His music is imbued with loss, disappointment and tragedy – the same underbelly that came with the gold rush that created San Francisco, the empty pot at the end of the rainbow. The cruelty of the West Coast is that its failure as last place of opportunity, is ultimate. There is nowhere else to go.

On release, the album would be compared to Neil Young, Alex Chilton, John Cale, and most obviously Nick Drake. The atmosphere of tracks such as "Jenny" and "Last Harbor," is reminiscent of parts of Drake's *Pink Moon* and *Bryter Later*. Neil Young's *On The Beach* also has something of the same spirit. *California*'s closest antecedent however is the much less well known Australian band The Triffids, who covered similar territory on their classic 1984 album, *Born Sandy Devotional*, which like *California* employed pedal steel guitar to conjure up the desolate sound of wide open spaces.

In Eitzel's songs, California's endless highways are roads to get lost on, the desert is as barren as the spirits of his protagonists, and all the while, like Dr

Eckelberg's spectacles in *The Great Gatsby*, the sun shines down cruelly exposing their failings. Later, on the last American Music Club album, Eitzel would sing that California's *"blue blue skies are made of butcher knives."* On "Highway 5," all of these ideas come together:

> *It takes so much to make us feel alive*
> *Weary traveller at a smooth 75*
> *Make pretend that the landscape ain't so dry*
> *Do anything to maintain a lie*
> *To the left, the beautiful California scenery dead-ends in the sky*
> *To the right, beautiful mountains rise high and dry*
> *Another futile expression of bitterness*
> *Another overwhelming sensation of uselessness...*
> *Let's pretend that the lover ain't so barren...*

"The first time I'd ever been on Highway 5 (on our first trip to LA)," Eitzel recalled, "I just fell in love with it. A lot of classic American art has talked about America's empty spaces; about places of spiritual sense. Highway 5 took me back to biblical times; to Sodom and Gomorrah, to Gilgamesh and to Hollywood."

As the tone of "Highway 5" suggests, the album is bleak. But, although sombre and forlorn in places, it is tender too. There is less evidence of the misanthropic disgust and terror that runs through certain of the tracks on *Engine*. Here the bleakness is accompanied by sympathy for the lonelier characters that inhabit the songs. And throughout all of it, there is a search for redemption whether through love or through escape.

The most impressive thing about *California* is simply the quality of the songs. On "Blue and Grey Shirt," "Last Harbor," and "Western Sky," Eitzel weds some of his most affecting lyrics to the most alluring melodies. "Western Sky," both in band or solo performance, would become the quintessential Eitzel song. Tom Mallon's role in the musical development of this track was fundamental, starting with Eitzel's solo demo he spent a whole night working out parts for all of the other instruments, committing them to tape himself.

"Western Sky" has been described as Eitzel's attempt to rewrite Nick Drake's "Northern Sky," and while that is an over-simplification, "Northern Sky" did play a major role in the song's genesis. "I was staying in this cabin in the middle of the country," he explains, "and I hadn't talked to anyone in about two weeks, and I only had three tapes to listen to, one of which was a Nick Drake compilation. I was writing this song, and I had everything except for the chorus.

"I heard the song 'Northern Sky' – it's a beautiful song – and I listened to it maybe 1,000 times, and I kept thinking about what that meant. How he looks towards the Northern polar wastes as a vision of a future in a way. And I thought about how that pertained to my own life. And I thought about what the song [I was writing at the time] meant. Later, I was sitting on a cliff, on acid, watching the sun set.... There was an unusually colourful sunset that night and kids were letting off fireworks on the beach.... Basically, the West is the place where transitions happen. It's where the sun goes down, and where things change. There is always this idea of going west. It's not a death reference, it's more of a change.

So I was just really thinking of the Western Sky. 'Northern Sky' was part of the songwriting process, but I don't know why people think the two songs are so similar."

Though on the sleeve notes to his later live solo acoustic album, Eitzel confessed, "I had no chorus and had been listening to 'Northern Sky' so I stole the idea. 'Why not?' I say, no one will ever know."

Later Eitzel would tell a journalist that the song was in part about a friend dying of AIDS, emphasising the line, *"hate to see you look that way/ All the beauty has left your face."* On another occasion he would tell Demon press officer Spike Hyde that it was just a love song: "It is what everyone thinks it is." In the end though, Eitzel captured the essence of the song in one short line, "'Western Sky' is basically about God putting messages up in the clouds for us all to see."

The delicate, acoustic "Jenny" would also become a crowd favourite. Eitzel got to know Jenny Gonzalvez through Vudi, who met her in the late 70s when she waitressed at a restaurant bar managed by Ugly Stick's Wayne Newcomb. When the place was quiet, Jenny would sit at the bar while Newcomb poured pitcher after pitcher of beer for Vudi, Mark Terrill and his other musician friends. Gradually Jenny got to know most of the Dharma Sub crowd. She'd hang out at Farmers' rehearsals, and take naps while they played, finding a pleasure in sleeping amid their strange noise.

The first time she met Eitzel, he was rude about the boots she was wearing. She was immediately moved by his music, but it took a while for them to become friends. "We slowly got to know each other," Jenny remembers. "We were never super-super close, but we did develop a mutual attraction."

When Eitzel presented her with the song he'd titled with her name, she was initially surprised. Although they'd had some moments of "real connection," it still was not the kind of thing she was expecting. But she loved the song, and was "flattered, and touched... I thought it was a little bit sad, but I liked it very much. [Hearing it live] was wonderful, ...amazing. It felt like a real honour."

In addition to the more crafted conventional songs, *California* is also remarkable for the unearthly fragments that show the band discovering a wholly original sound.

The album's opening two tracks, "Firefly," and "Somewhere," have straightforward time signatures and a verse-chorus structure, while "Laughing Stock" is the album's first curious Eitzel anti-song. Like many of American Music Club's best recordings it is a haunting ebb and flow. A few concise images and ideas are set to a fractured tune with no structure. As the track builds, the power is in the intensity of Eitzel's vocal delivery, as his voice grapples with the different emphasis of lines and half-lines. And all the while Vudi's guitar rumbles and rages like a thunderstorm in a distant town, occasionally moving nearer, before fading from earshot.

The band expand on this new musical territory on the mesmerising "Pale Skinny Girl." The song itself is simply two short verses, and in between are shards of twisted guitar that evoke the broken "wasteland" of this girl's surroundings as she looks out from beyond a desolate parking lot. It is a chilling sound that has no real precedent.

Ultimately, *California* is compelling listening because it shows Eitzel coming to terms with his own demons, and offering solace to others with theirs. The album's subtitle might as well be "Everybody Hurts." Vudi would comment at the time of its release: "All the songs are of a different spirit to the previous album. They might sound dark and brooding but when you get into them they seem more about looking for a way to live. To me, these songs represent the germ of hope."

Eitzel told Ralph Traitor from *Sounds:* "I wanted to write songs to give people hope, to make them want to live. Basically, my whole goal now is to give people a balm, to put in their pockets and take like aspirins."

Eitzel's more optimistic outlook is most prominent on the album's upbeat, pedal steel-assisted opening track, "Firefly." It may be fatalistic, but it is celebratory nonetheless. For the song's narrator, human lives may be as short and pointless as those of fireflies, but that doesn't mean we can't try and burn as brightly as we can for this brief span – wringing the most pleasure and beauty out of our apparently futile existences. Similarly, just because love may be transient and doomed, doesn't mean we can't enjoy it while it lasts.

As Kaphan's incandescent pedal steel weaves a heavenly melody, Eitzel sings,

> *So come on beautiful, let's go sit on the front lawn*
> *Watch the fireflies as the sun goes down.*
> *They don't live too long, just a flash and then they're gone*
> *We'll laugh at them, and watch the sun go down.*
> *You're so pretty baby,*
> *You're the prettiest thing I know*
> *You're so pretty baby, where did you go?*

The shadow of mortality is present, but there is no bitterness here. Whereas on *Engine,* Eitzel would sing, *"Outside this bar, there is no one alive,"* on *California* he wants to leave the bar and go *"somewhere where there's people living."*

For all the attempts to find the cohesion on *California*, one track defies analysis. As if to avoid things getting too precious, or simply to purposefully destroy the record's hauntingly beautiful mood, "Bad Liquor" is a no-nonsense heads-down boogie, allowing the band to let rip. Indeed, Eitzel blew his voice out screaming his vocals through a guitar amp. The song is as out of place here as "Motorcycle Mama," on Neil Young's *Comes A Time*. Inspired by a huge Bourbon and Coke session at the North Beach bar Vesuvio's on Jack Kerouac Street (a favourite watering hole of Eitzel's childhood hero Dylan Thomas), "Bad Liquor" is a basic rock song that Eitzel would come to loathe playing. It symbolised what was dumb about rock music, and was the opposite pole from the more fragile acoustic songs he loved. Dan Pearson said of the recorded version, "That was us trying to get a radio hit."

Finally, if not a conscious decision, it is no coincidence that Eitzel would close an album called *California* with the song, "Last Harbor." Both titles refer to physical destinations in his search for happiness, and both are places of escape. On another unreleased song from the same sessions, Eitzel would ask, *"How many nickels quarters, dimes / Do I need to pave my way from here?"* Now he has gone as far west as he can, and he still has not found respite – there must be somewhere else – some final resting place. Eitzel originally planned to call the song "Safe Harbor" after a local bar of the same name, but settled on "Last Harbor" after reading Eugene O'Neill's *Darkness At The Edge of Night*. Inspired by a Christmas Day Eitzel spent alone, walking around in the rain, he would consider this his "best song."

Eitzel softly finger-picks arpeggios that descend along the frets of a guitar set to a haunting tuning that seems to suspend every single note between major and minor. As the guitar strings delicately hover and echo, Eitzel whispers, and croons, always on the verge, but never actually letting his voice break into a scream, wringing every drop of meaning from the deceptively simple words:

> *Some of them are kind, but it's phony*
> *Some of them are kind but it's ok...*
> *Some of them smile but it's phony,*
> *Some of them smile but it's ok.*

Eitzel may ask *"Are you going to be my last harbor?"* in a tone that suggests that you probably won't be, but he does not dismiss the possibility that, against his better judgement, maybe you will.

***

Prior to the album's release, Frontier had the opportunity to place an American Music Club track on a widely distributed Tower records promotional compilation. At that point, recording was still in progress and Tom Mallon felt "Bad Liquor," to be the only track that was complete enough to be released. Considering this was one of their weaker songs, completely unrepresentative of the rest of the album, and at this stage even sloppier than the ramshackle finished version, this was a questionable method of paving the way for the new album, but Mallon was adamant.

California was released in the US in November 1988, and though not widely reviewed, the press it did garner was extremely enthusiastic. *Cashbox* proclaimed it "a masterpiece of understated intelligence cloaked in roots-folk music." *The Daily Californian* ranked it "with the very best of this year." And *Spin*'s Karen Schoermer concluded: "For somebody who claims to be so lonely, the guy's got something worthwhile to say, and I figure, if I had a club, I'd probably ask him to join." Nonetheless, it would be in the UK where things would really start to gather momentum.

When the tapes of *California* arrived at Demon Records, press officer Spike Hyde instantly knew they had an extraordinary album on their hands, "I can remember hearing them for the first time and thinking that is probably the best record I had ever heard."

Hyde had a flexible brief to push any Demon act he wanted to, and he was determined to make up for Demon's lack of effort in promoting *Engine*. The label just wanted to put *California* out and leave it at that, but Hyde saw that so much more could be done with this record, and sent out review copies to pretty much every "discerning" writer he knew of.

Melody Maker's Andrew Smith remembers hearing a cassette copy of *California* for the first time, and just thinking it was "magnificent. I really did think they were better than anyone around at the time." He called up editor Allan Jones to ask if he could review it, only to find that Jones was already in the middle of penning his own rave review.

"By then my ear was attuned to what they were doing," recalls Jones, "When I played it I couldn't believe it...A bolt between the eyes. Especially the last three songs: 'Highway 5,' 'Western Sky,' and 'Last Harbor,' It was the album that everyone picked up on. There was something so singular about it."

NME's Edwin Pouncey found the album "both beautiful and, at times, terrifying." *Sounds'* Roy Wilkinson felt, "American Music Club revitalise a traditional music with the kind of nuances you'd dearly love to read into Springsteen." Mat Snow, writing in the new, conservative, adult-oriented monthly magazine, *Q* concluded a four-star review with the words, "In these intriguingly opiated moods I suspect remarkably durable music dwells." Finally, Allan Jones concluded an in-depth essay in *Melody Maker*, "Technicians of critical language like ourselves have a word for records like this. We call them classics and we're rarely wrong."

Lisa Fancher was delighted with the UK press, and took out full page trade adverts in the US combining the best American and British press comments under the heading "Some records are more important than others." Unfortunately in the UK, the press fervour completely failed to impress the sceptics at Demon, who were still wary of risking money on promoting a new act, and if anything the critical response only hardened the internal view that AMC were an uncommercial band that appealed only to critics.

Hyde did not give up. His next step was to bring Mark Eitzel and Dan Pearson to Britain. As the budget for this trip was non-existent, Mark stayed in Hyde's flat and Dan stayed at a friend's. Hyde took Mark and Dan to London's Capital Radio and GLR before embarking on a well-received whistle-stop tour of the UK's regional radio stations, doing interviews and sessions wherever they could. To Hyde's frustration, though despite his repeated efforts, Radio One, and John Peel in particular as champion of intelligent alternative music, failed to pick up on the band.

But by now AMC had won another highly influential fan. Hyde had sent a cassette of *California* to the UK booking agent, Mick Griffiths of Asgard. Griffiths was bowled over by what he heard: "Spike sent me the album, and I remember, I put it on straight away and I immediately started writing a fax to their manager [while 'Firefly' was still playing] saying I'd really like to be AMC's agent. I put in the fax that I thought the album was 'really good', the second track started, and I changed 'really good' to 'brilliant', and then by the fourth track I changed it to 'fucking brilliant'."

Eager to see the band play live, Griffiths organised a mini UK tour for March, 1989. This would follow on from a brief US tour that would involve the band's first New York dates.

While this was a great break, finding time to tour was not easy because the band all had day jobs. Dan Pearson was a restaurant chef and when he asked his boss for time off to go on tour, he was told, "Okay, but don't come back." The other members had similar difficulties.

By now American Music Club were again a five-piece. After the *California* recording sessions, they asked Lisa Davis, who had played bass on "Firefly," to join the band. The rhythm section had been finding it difficult to keep time with Eitzel's increasingly erratic guitar playing, and the recruitment of a new bassist was to change all that, as Dan Pearson explains: "We got Lisa in because we were having so much trouble with Mark not knowing his tunings, breaking his strings and throwing his guitar down. It was always chaos, which was the charm of it in hindsight. But we had the idea that we should try and be a bit more professional because we really weren't getting anywhere, so I said I'd play guitar."

The idea was that Lisa Davis would help the band develop a more professional presence, in keeping with their attempts at building a larger audience. As her friend Lisa Fancher points out, she also improved the visual image of a band that weren't especially photogenic, "She gave it a different focal point, she was a real cute blonde girl." Davis was certainly extremely attractive, and she dressed and played bass with a real punk attitude. There was also an instant on-stage rapport between her and Eitzel, who would often go over to her and share some private joke.

But Davis had her own demons. Mark Terrill remembers that, "The chemistry was a little more volatile with Lisa in the band." He adds: "She was a good personality – a good person to have on the road – very entertaining. But she had some problems."

Davis was already friends with American Music Club through her band, Naked Into. They had shared the same bills at various local clubs. But, in many ways Davis was a diametric opposite to the other band members. She was a championship diver at college, and in her spare time liked to cycle, run and fish.

Initially things went extremely well though, and Davis quickly realised that she was part of something unique: "What was good about that band was that everyone had a really strong unity about the music. It wasn't like other bands where people go on tour and are worried about getting laid, getting fucked up on drugs, and impressing people and walking around like prima donnas. AMC cared about who played with them, and anyone who opened for them, or who played on any tour date, was treated with great respect. They were very warm, and they cared about the music. There was a rapport between each player, so no matter what everyone's problems were, we all knew that it had to be a certain way."

Davis was surprised by how much AMC were like a family. The sense of belonging the band gave each member was almost as important as the music. "You have Danny who had a twin brother who died. You had Vudi who had a hard time with his dad. You had Mark who didn't have much of a relationship with his father. This was very much about wanting to belong with men," Lisa explains.

The initial shows with Davis on board were no less intense than before. With Pearson on extra guitar, and Davis on bass, the music had even more of an edge. Also, Eitzel's drinking had got worse, and on stage he would go crazy, jumping into the audience and regularly injuring himself. At a show in Oregon, both he and Lisa Davis fell off the stage at the same time, collapsing onto a bunch of tables and chairs, and knocking them over in the process. The rest of the band kept on playing, as Davis and Eitzel clambered back up and carried on as normal.

Another drunken night at the Hotel Utah, Eitzel was hurling himself around so chaotically that he slammed against a stage door which gave way, catapulting him through it.

"Mark fell head first down a flight of stairs into a giant crate of tomatoes," Lisa Fancher remembers, "he came back upstairs encrusted with tomatoes, and just carried on singing. I think the audience thought he had cut his head off or something, since he was covered in red, they thought he was dying. Meanwhile, the rest of the band just kept on playing."

After another show, a girl gave Eitzel a St Christopher medallion to wear. She felt he needed something to protect himself.

One night at The Covered Wagon, Eitzel took to the stage so drunk that while the band worked their way through the set list, he sang the same song over and over again, convinced he was a singing different song each time. "Crowds seem to expect the show to sound as good as the record," Eitzel explains, "Bullshit! I think the band has to sound 3,000 times worse than the goddamn record, and the audience has to give the band the chance to sound human."

At the end of a number of these shows, with the final note still ringing in the air, Eitzel would just walk straight off the stage, out through the auditorium, and off down the street until out of sight, without saying a word to anyone. When a journalist one night asked Vudi what this was all about, Vudi just laughed, and said, "he's the real deal."

In Salt Lake City, while having dinner before the show, the band were shaken down by cops who accused them of being drug dealers. That night on stage, Eitzel smashed his microphone, and dived into his monitor, slashing his arm and cutting his head open. Another night he smashed a glass against the side of his own head.

"He would hurt himself," says Davis, "and sometimes it was hard to watch. But it wasn't because he was a rock star, it was just a reaction, 'If you treat me like shit...'"

At a show with Thin White Rope in Davis, California, AMC played for ten minutes and then left. Lisa Davis remembers: "Some people in the audience pissed Mark off, and it sounded like shit. Mark just said, 'Fuck you!'" and after ten minutes we were gone." The scene was repeated later in Long Beach. On other nights, they'd play for three hours. "After one show Mark was in such a rage," Dan Pearson remembers, "that when we loaded the equipment back at Mallon's, he smashed his Mosrite guitar to pieces and told me to do the same to his Fender which I was borrowing at the time." Pearson demurred.

In addition to the on-stage tension, as they continued playing, it became clear that Lisa Davis and Tom Mallon were not going to get on. The new bassist found Mallon's moodiness and inflexibility frustrating, and resented the fact that no one in the band would argue with him. "I think Mallon wanted me out," Davis explains, "I grew up with two brothers and I have always been around men, whereas Mallon was the kind of guy who was used to treating women in a certain way. When he pulled his stupid little stunts, I'd be like, 'What the fuck are you doing?' And I don't think anyone had ever said anything like that to him before. When you walk into Tom's studio, he's the king. He controls everything. Now he was in the band and he wanted to control it too. Also, the band I was in before had a great fucking drummer, and in AMC I would have to drag Tom along."

Lisa also felt that the band's new manager was just making everything worse: "Any time anyone had a problem with Tom, and tried to ask him something, Leslie would answer. She would never, ever let him talk. To have a conversation with Tom, you'd talk to him, and Leslie would respond...."

Davis remembers an on-stage accident at the band's New Year's Eve show in San Francisco, "The area behind the stage was covered with all these crosses and lights and stuff. Tom was up to playing like an idiot, and one of the crosses fell off and hit him right in the bass pedal foot. I was so fucking happy."

Even by AMC's standards, their prestigious February CBGBs show in New York was particularly chaotic. The venue's management treated the band badly, and as Lisa Davis reiterates, "When Mark gets treated like shit, he treats the club like shit." That night, Eitzel outdid himself in terms of self-destruction: repeatedly falling to his knees, pouring beer over himself and the front rows of the audience, and generally disrupting the band before they could gather any semblance of cohesion. In his brief review of the show, critic Tony Fletcher commented, "If Eitzel wasn't drunk, he should be certified." After a supporting slot with Nick Cave in San Francisco, the band then headed for the UK.

On March 29th, 1989, American Music Club made their live UK debut at a small country and western club in Birmingham called The Breedon Bar. It was to be a very inauspicious start. The venue had a very traditional country feel – even featuring full-size wagon wheels on the walls. The whole set-up was pretty grim, but determined to triumph over adversity, AMC played a good show, and went down fairly well with the small crowd. Eitzel had made an effort not to get drunk beforehand, and the band were trying to be more professional. However, as soon as they finished their set, the promoter, an ageing rock 'n' roll type, climbed on stage and stepped up to the microphone: "Ladies and gentlemen, I'd just like to apologise for that. I know that's not up to the usual standard of the Breedon Bar. So if anyone would like a refund, please ask on the way out, and I will totally understand." No one did.

When road manager Mark Terrill went to collect the money, the promoter commented, "Good band! Shame about the singer." He paid the band their £500 anyway, but the incident only exacerbated Mark's insecurities. The band took consolation by stealing all of the venue's Guinness towels and ashtrays.

The next night in Sheffield, Eitzel's relative sobriety was making him nervous and tense, and his mood was made worse by the venue's unprofessional set-up. As a result, the band went on late, by which time the small audience was noisy and impatient. Eitzel's response was to tell them, "fuck you." This drove Lisa Davis mad: "The tickets were not cheap, and all these people had been waiting ages in the rain to get in. And Tom always copies everything Mark does. So as Mark had said, 'Fuck you!' Tom goes, 'Well, I'm going to play with my brushes tonight.' It was that kind of shit."

Eitzel remained in such a bad mood, that after half an hour the band took a break. Davis remembers: "I walked off stage and said to them, 'How the fuck can you do this? We're here to play.' They were all like spoiled brats." Meanwhile, Leslie was going mad, telling them all, "There are important press people here. How can you go back stage and start yelling at each other in the middle of the show?" Finally, Eitzel shamefacedly went back out and the band played for another two hours.

After a few more regional British dates, the band played their first London show at the Mean Fiddler. While the venue was reasonably full, many of the audience were local club regulars there just to drink. The people actually there for AMC were mainly press, record store people, and a few actual fans.

"There weren't that many people there," Allan Jones recalls, "and there wasn't a feeling of a huge occasion. But everybody present, if they weren't converted before, were immediately won over by the power of it. It started off normally, with one song after the other. But suddenly you were aware of all these dramatic undercurrents. And you realised that Eitzel was living out all the impressions you got of him from the songs. You just didn't know what he would do next. The band were great too. Vudi was such a great guitarist, and the whole set was electrifying. Eitzel was like a ticking bomb."

Andrew Smith was also there that night: "They were just so good. It was partly the chemistry of the band, the musicians were fantastic, but it wasn't just that, it was this performer who would get up in front of them and just gradually dissolve throughout the show, he was just so revealing in what he did, and quite often, just on a whim in the middle of a song, he'd just lose confidence in a song in the middle and just stop…you never really knew what was going to happen. A song would break down completely, and then the next song would take off completely, and would just be swirling about your head …They could be so powerful, and then just disintegrate the next minute."

The set featured the best songs from *Engine* and most of *California* and finished with a manic howl through "Bad Liquor." By then Eitzel was drenched in sweat, his body almost unhinged by the manic flailing and jolting he had put it through. Afterwards, people were aware that they had seen something extraordinary. The music press reviews were rapturous.

Roy Wilkinson in *Sounds* saw the gig as "a fantastically uplifting resolution of melancholy." *Melody Maker* editor Allan Jones gave the gig the best part of a page, and concluded, "American Music Club are a ghastly fascination, driven and damned: a singular constellation. You should discover them."

The day after the Mean Fiddler show, the band went off to Europe where AMC's reception was more mixed. In Hamburg, they enthralled The Star Club audience, while the following night they were in France playing to a small crowd who were practically catatonic with boredom. In Amsterdam an entire Dutch first division soccer team turned up, and most of them knew all of the songs. The next night, as a result of a booking blunder, they found themselves in a Norwegian hard rock club.

"We weren't giving the audience what they wanted," Eitzel told *NME*'s Simon Williams, "right next door was this huge disco playing Michael Jackson and lots of bad rap music. Every time we finished a song, one person would clap sarcastically and there'd be nothing but '*I'm bad, I'm bad,*' coming from next door. It was horrifying."

"All these Vikings were drinking, stone-faced and unemotional," Lisa Davis remembers, "then they cracked and wanted to beat the shit out of us." The

Norwegians wanted the band to rock out, but Eitzel refused, "because every time I hear a one-two-three-four rock beat I get really sad. I mean, why bother? You're not communicating anything…We just don't play rock."

As the mainland European leg of the tour went on, the tension between Lisa Davis and Tom Mallon started to have an impact on the rest of the band. Also, while some of the band were trying to reduce their alcohol intake, Davis was drinking even more heavily.

"After a show Lisa would go to clubs and find out who had the most booze," Eitzel recalls. "Then she'd get high, and start shouting at everyone."

Things came to a head in Berlin. The show finished late and after a couple of drinks the rest of the band wanted to go to off to bed. In order to make the next show they had to be back in the van at 5.00 am the next morning. Davis decided she wanted to party.

"She came up to us," Eitzel continues, "and she started shouting, 'I hate you, you pussy-assed mother fuckers,' and so I jumped on her back saying 'don't break up my band, bitch,' and some other horrible stuff. That night nobody could get to sleep for hours, and the next morning we woke up and Lisa had forgotten the whole thing. She was like 'How are you all doing? Alright?'"

For Davis, this row had been building up for some time, and she was not afraid of confrontation, "I was just really tired of Tom saying, 'I'm not gonna to play that song,' or 'I'm gonna play with brushes tonight.' I just said, 'What is up with you?' I'd try and talk to Tom, and the others would say, 'Come on, leave him alone.' I'd say, 'Tom, fucking talk! Say what you think. What is going on? Do you hate this?'

I was also just tired of everyone complaining to me about Tom. I'd say, 'Why don't you go and talk to him?' But everyone was too afraid to say anything. Tom was like the little baby. You had to baby him through everything. When you're on the road, it's like, 'Why? I mean, the guy can't even play drums well.'

So, that night, I did say, 'Come on! You guys are all fucking pussies, you know. You're putting up with someone who is just dragging it all down.' But I would drink too, and it just got a little out of hand."

That morning, as Davis tried to make conversation, the rest of the band sat in stony silence. Then, after only a few miles, a huge pigeon hit the windscreen head on. They stopped and pulled over. The bird was dead and had left a large crack in the glass. It was an ill omen.

On their return to San Francisco, Davis was diagnosed with hepatitis B and C, and minor cirrhosis of the liver. Unsympathetic to her condition, Tom Mallon had had enough. He was also keen to switch from drums to bass and gave the rest of the band a her-or-me ultimatum. By now Mallon was such an integral part of American Music Club, that the band's viability would have been almost unthinkable without him. Mallon owned their rehearsal studio, the place they recorded and their record company. He was their drummer and their producer and his girlfriend was their manager. While some of the band found Mallon increasingly difficult to deal with personally, they could not think of parting company with him. Also, now that Eitzel was trying to reduce his alcohol consumption, in order to maintain his on-stage edginess, it was important to have something to rage against. The unspoken conflict between Mallon and himself would fuel his performance.

Aware that she "was just the bass player," Lisa Davis was not surprised to be sacked. By now she was so ill that she could not have toured anyway, so it didn't make much difference. But, regardless of her own situation, Davis was concerned for the rest of her friends in American Music Club: "If you are in a band with a bunch of guys who don't say how they feel; but instead their intensity comes out in the playing, fine. Play with it – ride with it, but eventually, it will explode in your face."

Footnote

When asked to contribute his perspective to this book on a number of issues concerning arrangements, publishing and royalties, Mr Mallon's only response was a one word email to the author. Echoing General MacArthur in the Battle of the Bulge, it said simply: "nuts."

Chapter Five

Never Mind

"They drove us out to a graveyard to take out pictures today and I was, like, really dubious! I thought, Hey, c'mon! We're trying to smile, get out of it somehow but … look, if you're gonna set me up as an Ian Curtis clone at least make me 23, alright?"

Mark Eitzel

On AMC's return to San Francisco, there was inevitably a sense of anti-climax. *California* had been highly acclaimed in the UK, and parts of the European tour were well received. The press attention that accompanied the tour had helped their local reputation, and they were now playing regularly to audiences of 200 people in packed clubs in San Francisco and Los Angeles. They were also starting to get more press notices in the US. But, none of this acclaim had translated into sales. Record stores and the record-buying public alike had still not heard of them. Worse still, radio programmers gave them an even wider berth – wary of a bunch of middle-aged men playing country-tinged rock.

Steve Granados was Frontier Records' East Coast field representative at the time and it was his job to persuade American radio stations to playlist tracks from *Engine* and *California*. In spite of his love of the band, he found it hard-going: "To get a record played on American radio – even on small college stations – a record company typically has to contact the station's music director each week and attempt to push their albums by building relationships with the station's staff or 'influencing' them with free records, concert tickets, and so on. College stations were the only ones that would even consider an AMC record.

"While I could usually get the music directors of college stations to add Frontier bands like The Young Fresh Fellows and Thin White Rope to their playlists, there seemed to be little interest in AMC. The usual response from music directors was, 'Well, it's a little too bland for our station.' Granted, AMC had yet to receive any significant American press and it is not the kind of music that immediately jumps out at a listener. When a music director would audition a record, they would cue up an AMC record, hear the soft acoustic guitars and pedal steel and immediately move onto the next record, not even giving Eitzel's words and melodies a chance to cast their spell."

AMC were falling unnoticed through a gap – too alternative for mainstream radio, and too mainstream for the alternative stations. Granados feels that Frontier's decision to promote the uncharacteristic "Bad Liquor" as a radio track, only made matters worse: "No one I spoke to at the stations had a kind word to say about that song and it was a difficult first impression to live down."

In his role as record company boss, Tom Mallon was becoming pessimistic about AMC's commercial prospects, as he confessed to Alan Di Perna shortly after the tour: "Flying Color could do it, but AMC probably isn't going to make any money. People don't understand them. When we went on tour, it was evident that college kids weren't into it, because it's not like rock music. It's more like the blues."

In the UK, Demon's Spike Hyde was convinced that American Music Club's breakthrough would eventually come. In the meantime, he needed to somehow maintain their profile and momentum. The fact that AMC were merely one of a number of licensed foreign acts on Demon Records' books made this difficult. Demon had no investment tied up in the band, and wanted to keep AMC on terms that guaranteed an acceptable return at very low risk. They were happy to ship a couple of thousand copies of AMC albums to the retail trade, despatch two dozen or so review copies to the specialist music press, and leave it at that. Demon's management was hostile to the more risky idea of funding attempts at winning the press and public over to AMC's cause.

In the middle of Hyde's efforts at breaking *California*, a senior Demon executive took Hyde, Eitzel and Pearson out to dinner. The executive spent the entire evening pointing out how few records AMC had sold to date, and how few they would sell in the future. When the bill finally arrived, as the executive reached for his gold credit card, he pointed to the total and told the incredulous Eitzel and Pearson that the sum was in excess of any revenue that AMC would ever generate for Demon. The two musicians were shocked both by the man's rudeness, and his lack of faith in one of his own bands. The only exception amongst the Demon sceptics was Andy Childs who set up the Frontier deal in the first place ("Saint Andy," as Lisa Fancher would call him).

Ironically, part of the reason for AMC's low sales in the UK was the poor distribution of their albums. *Engine* was virtually impossible to find in UK record stores at this time and two weeks after release, *California* was still not even listed on the computers of large London record stores such as Tower or HMV. The situation outside of the capital was far worse. Demon's fear that AMC would be a critical success without commercial sales was becoming a self-fulfilling prophecy.

It would be missing the point to blame the distributor. Distributors are not able to create demand, they merely fulfil it. They will push records by name artists that retail outlets already want, and they will also push records that they know have a lot of record company support, and will have a high profile in terms of reviews, interviews and radio airplay – thus creating automatic customer demand on release.

"But, if pressure is not exerted from the record company," Spike Hyde explains, "then the record will easily get put further and further down the rep's list."

A large UK tour would have helped the situation, but because AMC were based in San Francisco, without major financial support from their record company, they could not afford to play many British shows. This was something Eitzel's persistent throat problems made hazardous anyway.

For all these problems, AMC's biggest barrier to success in the UK, was exactly the same as in the US. In both territories, all of their obstacles could have been overcome by one thing. Hyde reiterates, "the missing ingredient was always radio."

"We'd tell people that the press really loved us, and they'd say 'Oh really'," Dan Pearson remembers. Eitzel was starting to sound resigned to cult success as he told *Musician*'s Duncan Strauss: "I do fantasise about [my songs] being played on the radio, and I actually think through videos that could be made about them. But when push comes to shove, I realise that probably won't happen, 'cause the stuff I write is just too weird. It's really not weird at all, but it just seems too morose."

After Lisa Davis' departure, AMC had more line-up issues to resolve. Tom Mallon now had the bass player's role he had coveted, which considering Eitzel's faith in Mallon's ability to come up with interesting basslines, appeared a good move. Eitzel found a replacement drummer when he met Mike Simms at a party. Simms had a background in St Louis skate punk bands, and fitted in quickly, although he too occasionally found Mallon difficult to deal with.

AMC also started augmenting their live sound with occasional appearances from Bruce Kaphan on pedal steel guitar. After his brief involvement in the *California* sessions, Kaphan hadn't given a thought to the idea of joining American Music Club until Vudi gave him a copy of the record. Kaphan remembers that he, "listened to it and just fell in love with it." Kaphan was tiring of playing with covers bands and approached Vudi about performing with AMC on an ad-hoc basis.

Unsure of what to do next, AMC continued to build a cult following by gigging regularly in the Bay Area, and Eitzel carried on writing prolifically. In April, he recorded a number of his new songs in his kitchen on a four-track tape machine. The idea was the band could then listen to these solo "demos" and work the songs up into full arrangements. For a number of reasons, only four of the nine ever surfaced. "Here They Roll Down" and "When No-one Cares For You," would appear on their next album, and the slow and embryonic "Royal Café," and "Day to Day Life," would grace its follow up, the latter song re-titled as "Ex-Girlfriend."

Eitzel was disappointed that the band never really got to grips with some of the material: "I remember that I liked all those songs but I knew that AMC would never be able to play them. They were 'too easy'. That was always the thing that drove me crazy about AMC – certain things were too easy to do. I think we could have been a successful band if the median IQ was dropped about 20 points."

But, with one or two exceptions, the released songs were the best of this selection. "Citizens of the True World," a ballad reminiscent of parts of *California*, was one of the better discarded songs. It was even part of the band's live set for a while, where over deftly plucked acoustic guitar, Eitzel would croon:

> *On good days we pretend the chill hasn't reached our bones;*
> *On good days we pretend we can lead a normal life*
> *On good days we pretend we're just like them.*

"If I Can't Get In" – *"If I can't get in here, I don't know where I'll go"* – was less successful, and "Frivolous Children," and "Hidden Camera," were beautiful, but perhaps just a little too gentle. There is one song from these home recordings that does merit further discussion, and that is Eitzel's lost touchstone, "Mrs Wright."

It is often easy to exaggerate the brilliance of unreleased songs, because they have a mystique missing from released material. Also, they are judged against much weaker yardsticks than an artist's best released work, set against which they might often be found wanting. It would be difficult to sustain an argument that "Mrs Wright," in its demo-ed version is a better piece of work than finished Eitzel tracks such as "Western Sky," or "Blue And Grey Shirt." Nonetheless, it is somehow strangely more compelling than many of his better-known songs. The introduction lasts only four bars, before Eitzel begins singing, and the performance itself is less than two minutes. The entire lyrics are as follows:

> *Mrs Wright,*
> *Bids her children goodnight,*
> *With her back to the shore,*
> *She stares at the horizon.*
> *All the grey women*
> *Stare at the horizon line*
> *All the grey women*
> *At the horizon.*
> *All the sea trapped in the barrel.*
> *Mrs Wright launches her children into flight,*
> *Mrs Wright stares over the horizon line.*

The opening guitar melody incorporated into a rolling arpeggio is not repeated and the verses are implied rather than fully drawn out. When the final passage turns out only as a half-verse, the effect is startling. What we are left with is a mystical, beautiful fragment – the shadow of a ghost or a fading dream. Because of the technological and commercial processes involved in making a record, there is often very little mystery in pop, but this home recording of "Mrs Wright" remains inscrutable, undocumented and frozen in time – untainted by either artistic or commercial compromise.

The subject matter was extremely different to any of Eitzel's previous songs. Until then, he had written almost exclusively about his own experiences and those of his friends. Mrs Wright is clearly someone from beyond Eitzel's circle and as she *"launches her children into flight"* she is depicted with greater compassion than the "Mom" of his previous songs who ignored her children or who held them back. This is the first time Eitzel looked at anything to do with the idea of family in a positive manner, and as such is a turning point. In singing positively about another mother figure without a shudder, he appears to be coming to terms with his own family relationships.

It would be difficult to imagine this fragile performance worked into a full band arrangement, without taking something more pure away. And in this, the song is representative of some of Eitzel's fundamental problems in bringing his music to a wider audience, both in terms of the double-edged sword of musical collaboration, and with regard to commercial considerations. Nonetheless, with "Mrs Wright" Mark Eitzel realised his quest to make timeless, beautiful music. In terms of his artistic achievement alone, it may not really matter that the song was never released. In AS Byatt's novel *Possession*, the narrator comments:

"There are things which happen and leave no discernible trace, are not spoken or written of, though it would be very wrong to say that subsequent events go on indifferently, all the same, as though such things had never been."

***

Towards the middle of May 1989, Spike Hyde called to say that Demon needed another record to keep the band's momentum and profile going in the UK. He was keen to bring the band back to Britain, and so Demon needed an album to promote. If necessary, he said, the album could be a UK-only release.

Even though it was just over six months since the release of *California*, Eitzel was excited by the plan. He'd been writing steadily since the previous summer, and had stockpiled a lot of songs. However, without consulting Demon, their manager Leslie and Tom Mallon who had recently married, decided the new record should be a "greatest hits" album of old songs. The band would record their best songs live in San Francisco, in front of their regular crowd, acting as an introduction for European audiences. Also, as the previous two albums had been fairly restrained, the live record would feature all of AMC's louder electric songs. It would be quick, cheap and simple and Tom and Leslie were convinced Demon would love it. It is possible that there were other factors at play too. Lisa Fancher was convinced Leslie had ulterior motives: "I had one album left on our deal, and Leslie was just trying to give me some piece of shit that would fulfil the contract so they could walk. I don't think the band were of that mind, I think that was just something Leslie cooked up. It was just a really stupid decision that didn't make any sense at all. What's the point in a new band putting out a live record?"

Fancher was not alone. "I was always against this," Eitzel maintains, "because I had all these fucking songs. I thought, why can't we just do the new songs?" Tom and Leslie were adamant that they should do a live album though, and Eitzel reluctantly gave in. Leslie promptly booked AMC for four nights at the Hotel Utah, a Victorian building on the corner of 4th and Bryant Street. They would record each show and select the best material.

The first live recording session took place on 10th June 1989. It was a humid, close evening, and as the fans filed in, there was no mention of any recording on the posters. Tom Mallon set up his 8-track recorder in the toilets directly stage right which, as he was also playing bass, meant the band would have to take a couple of breaks while he changed the tape reels.

The band took to the stage in near darkness. The only illumination came from a skinny string of predominantly red Christmas lights strung across the back wall. Barely visible within the blood-red glow, Eitzel announced their intention of recording an album and said that if anyone had anything to say they could come up on stage and "be on the record." Then, after a curt "Fuck you!" from Eitzel in response to an audience request for Joy Division's "Love Will Tear Us Apart," AMC launched into a searing, intense set of their best material with Bruce Kaphan's pedal steel, drenched in guitar effects and making an unearthly noise, taking their sound to a whole new level.

In spite of the proposed album's format, they interspersed this material with a number of as yet unreleased songs including, "Heaven of Your Hands," "The Right Thing," and "Miracle on 8th Street." They also tried the never-to-be released, "If You Won't Let Me In."

The night's many highlights included a full-on country take of "Gary's Song," a truly epic version of "Laughing Stock", and two versions of "Bad Liquor", one fast and then one slow. It was one of AMC's greatest ever shows, and the band, and Eitzel in particular, appeared to be really enjoying themselves. The one exception was Tom Mallon. Now on bass, he had much more freedom to express himself. Throughout this and most future shows, he would maintain a fixed frown, barely move his body at all, and keep his back to the audience at all times.

The band reconvened at the Utah on the 27th July and played for three consecutive nights. For these shows, Eitzel's mood was much darker, and each night he appeared extremely drunk. There was also visible tension between the band members. When the band discussed doing a Beatles cover as a jokey encore, Mallon refused to take part, and Simms pushed him right off the stage, causing a serious row. But the bad feeling only seemed to fuel the intensity of the music. Simms' powerful drumming helped push their sound to new levels, and Eitzel would repeatedly flail around the stage, or drop down on his knees, as he howled with emotion.

The momentum of the final show was interrupted mid-set, when Eitzel threw a full pitcher of beer down onto the stage. The pitcher shattered, sending beer and shards of broken glass all over two girls at the front tables by the stage. Both girls ran out of the room screaming. Eitzel was horrified. He immediately clambered down off the stage and ran out after them to say sorry. When he eventually caught up and offered his apology, one of the girls explained that the glass incident was not the only reason they left. She told him, "Mark, you're singing like shit and not giving me the show I came to see, you're an asshole." Chastened, Eitzel returned to the stage and tried to sober up for the last few songs, but it was not a great way to round things off. When the band listened back to the tapes, in spite of the mixed quality of the shows, they were reasonably happy with the results.

A few weeks after the last Hotel Utah show, Spike Hyde arrived in San Francisco. He'd been visiting relatives, and now showed up at Mallon's studio to listen to the new album. As the tape continued to roll, Hyde listened with increasing dismay. Instead of a record that might finally break the band in the UK, what he heard, in his own words, was "just a mess. Dreadful! I was horrified."

Lisa Fancher was not surprised. She had already made it clear that she would not put out an AMC live album on Frontier: "Unless you do a live recording with a mobile truck, and do it 24-track, it's going to sound like shit. The Hotel Utah doesn't have good sound, period".

Hyde told Eitzel what he thought of the record and immediately called Demon to tell them that the album was unfit for release. As the record wasn't going to come out in the US anyway, Demon had the full power of veto, and got the proposed album stopped. Eitzel was initially angry that their work had been rejected, but on further listening, all of the band members conceded that the tapes were simply not good enough. Some tracks appeared fine initially, but even on these, the snare was inaudible or the voice "EQ" was out.

Sitting on a stockpile of new songs, Eitzel proposed they record an album of this material from scratch. Hyde and the rest of American Music Club agreed. Nobody, except for Tom and Leslie, really liked the live album idea that much. But, considering it was now August and Demon wanted finished copies of an album to tie in with another European mini-tour in October, AMC were going to have to work quickly. Mallon was used to spending months honing and polishing AMC records; now he had two weeks.

He started by salvaging three of the previously unreleased songs from the live recordings: "Kathleen" ("When No-one Cares For You" from Eitzel's Spring 4-track demo), live staple "Hula Maiden" and a newer song, "Never Mind." The band, augmented by Kaphan's pedal steel, then rehearsed and recorded basic tracks to another batch of Eitzel's new songs. Charlie Gillingham, who would later find success with Counting Crows, was brought in to add piano on a couple of tracks.

These recordings were in a low-key, acoustic vein. The live album experience had made the band recoil from the idea of a full-on rock approach. Eitzel also felt that the rock songs "Somewhere" and "Bad Liquor" didn't really fit on *California,* and was now keen to make this a more coherent and less obvious record. He told writer Steve Connell: "We do have new rock songs, but we just got bored with [them]. Unless you're drunk or fucked up, or just young, with lots of hormones going – which we're not – rock is just boring."

One of the most startling things about AMC's fourth album is how bare it sounds. In many cases instruments are implied rather than present, and there are fragments of chords and echoes of notes rather than conventional guitar sounds. This was not entirely intentional. "If you were to ask Tom why the record is so stripped down," Eitzel claims, "he would say, 'Because they couldn't fucking play. ... And because there wasn't any fucking time'." As the tight deadline prevented Mallon from insisting that everything was redone over and over until it met with his satisfaction, he simply erased anything he didn't like.

Eitzel arrived at the studio one evening to find that in the course of mixing one of the songs, Mallon had wiped all of the guitar tracks and all of the bass tracks leaving only the drums and vocals.

In a state of mild shock, he asked Mallon: "Where are the instruments?"

Mallon: "They sucked."

Eitzel: "But…"

Mallon: "They sounded like fake jazz. Sucked!"

This hurried experience was torture for Mallon. He worked around the clock to try to get the album into what he considered was a reasonable state. But, all the while, he felt he needed much more time, and was not happy with the end result. Eitzel, however, loved the finished record and gives a lot of the credit to Mallon: "Tom did a really good job on some of the tracks. If you listen to 'The Dream is Gone,' without any reverb on it – just the eight tracks – it is mind-blowingly great. Tom did a beautiful job on that. He was such a pain in the arse to work with, but he did great work when he was inspired."

Some of the other band members were less keen on the album, which is not surprising. In many places, it sounds like an Eitzel solo album. Much of the other band members' contributions have been removed completely. Eitzel had told an English journalist back in 1988 that he'd "rather not have a band at all. I'd rather just sit there with a guitar," and on many parts of this record, Eitzel and his guitar are the only things that are really audible.

On 6th November, 1989, just as San Francisco was reeling from its worst earthquake in years, American Music Club released their fourth album. It was a UK-only release, so they called it *United Kingdom*, but as with its predecessor, this title had a far deeper resonance. This record dwells on bitter memories of his childhood in Southampton, England, and exudes a fatal resignation, as he sees the pattern of his life unavoidably mapped out by his upbringing. In spite of its bleak, pared-down sound – reminiscent in places of Big Star's third album, Lennon's *Plastic Ono Band*, and again, Nick Drake's *Pink Moon* – *United Kingdom* is not a pessimistic album, simply a fatalistic one. It is the sound of Eitzel arriving at an accommodation.

The title track is Eitzel's most explicit exercise in conjuring images of a dysfunctional upbringing, and specifically of a child who feels unloved by his mother:

> *Child keeps its toys hid away*
> *Until it wants to break them*
> *Take your share and go away*
> *Make sure you get the last word.*
> *United Kingdom….*
> *When you held me in your arms*
> *Why didn't you want me?*

Now, he has gone beyond the reach of his family and accepts himself for what he is, *"happier now, in my shame."*

On this record, instead of searching for escape from his problems, Eitzel is coming to terms with them. The discarded but contemporaneous song "Citizens of the True World," with its refrain: *"On good days we pretend we can lead a normal life"*, makes explicit the belief that while he will never be like normal people, the differences are not always unmanageable.

In "Kathleen" one of the live favourites from the record, Eitzel distills down to two verses the essence of the relationship that has dominated his life and – along with his family – underpinned his music across the three previous American Music Club albums. A bare and haunting virtually solo acoustic track, this double-edged take on a doomed love affair is as much about the narrator as his subject. When he sings, *"Your love Kathleen is for someone/ I swear I could have been"* he bemoans his own failure rather than hers. The refrain *"When no one cares for you / You're made of straw,"* appears to be about Kathleen, but Eitzel told writer Andrew Smith that line was "what I experienced. ... You're like a matchstick ready to burn, you're like a shadow. I feel that way sometimes."

When asked about the song Kathleen Burns would only say, "In a way it's very complimentary and in a way it's not at all. That is just that." She did find listening to the song more difficult live, and would often leave a club if Eitzel played it.

She was always ambivalent to her role as Eitzel's muse. "I told him once to quit living vicariously through me," Kathleen remembered, "and he replied that he'd never write another song about me. I said, 'Good!'" Regardless, Kathleen Burns would remain Eitzel's closest friend and confidante. The nature of their intensely close relationship was such that few who were close to Eitzel would make any stab at fully understanding it.

Though both songs are hugely resonant, the pivotal moment on *United Kingdom*, is neither "Kathleen" nor the title track. The point where the narrator explains the link between past and present is the hauntingly beautiful, "Heaven of Your Hands."

With a gorgeous melody and some mesmerising finger-picked guitar lines, this is one of the few surviving full band arrangements on the record. It is also one of Eitzel's most moving vocal performances, as his gently intoned words trace an inability to sustain love, back to a mother's neglect of her child.

> *There was so much that I had to offer*
> *But now I'm all alone at four a.m....*
> *Mother, don't you hear your baby crying?*
> *Why don't you reach down and pick it up?*
> *Mother, all your baby's toys are broken*
> *But I know heaven's not for me*
> *Yeah' that's something I understand.*

Previous Eitzel songs saw the narrator escaping an unsatisfactory reality through physical departure – heading West or wherever – or through the forgetful oblivion of a drunken stupor. The narrator of these songs finds that while he is without love or true happiness, his life is mainly bearable – and he will settle for this. The one harbour in which he could transcend this condition is no longer equated with a person or place – instead it is seen only in dreams:

> *Finish the dream*
> *That brought you so much bliss*
> *Sails filled with wind*
> *And the joy deep within*
> *Finish with the light*
> *That holds you to the floor*

You don't need it anymore. ("Dream Is Gone")

This dream-like quality pervades *United Kingdom.* The songs are a series of memories and reveries – scattered with images, scenes and snatches of dialogue from the writer's life. The music shares the same qualities, ethereal and drifting, with the odd flashes of the full band. The sense of 'something heard from the next room' that Mallon and Eitzel discussed at the time of *California* is realised – whether intentionally or not. Eitzel happily told friends at the time that AMC band were starting to sound like the Cocteau Twins – purveyors of multi-layered sonic dreamscapes – something that was only really apparent on the final record's opening track "Here They Roll Down."

Previously known as "The Miracle Was Over," the song begins with traffic noise – sounding like waves on a distant beach. The effect is not mere embellishment, as Eitzel wrote the song on the ramp outside Mallon's studio, and that traffic noise was its nucleus. It also has the effect of framing the record – like a fade into a cinematic dream sequence. The wave upon wave of traffic, also emphasises the fatalism inherent in "Here They Roll Down," which would have made an equally effective title for the album. Its sub-title could be "So it goes," or taking a title from another of the songs within, and pre-dating another American rock group, "Never mind."

On reflection, while *United Kingdom* is a beautiful record, its most striking aspect is an anorexic sparseness. Just as the music has been stripped bare, so Eitzel's lyrics are dramatically honed – shorn of any sense of place or person. Even "Kathleen," rather than a full portrait of the title character, boils down to one idea, that *"when no-one cares for you, you're made of straw."*

United Kingdom marks the culmination of a number of different forces in American Music Club's work. Lyrically, Eitzel now seemed to have laid to rest the ghosts of recent years. He had even finally given a recorded airing to "Hula Maiden", the dark journal of the Hawaiian nightmare holiday he took alone shortly after his father's death. It's as if he has now said everything he had to say about his family. He'd also vowed to never write another song about his lover, best-friend and muse, Kathleen Burns. Eitzel's future songs would draw inspiration from a wealth of different sources, but the searing feelings burning a hole in his soul had been exorcised for a while.

On the musical side, the process of paring down that had begun on *Engine* had been completed on *United Kingdom.* There was no rock left on this record at all. For their next album, to avoid repeating themselves, they would have to start reversing the process. In many ways, *United Kingdom* would be the end of an era.

On completion, Hyde was happy to accept the new record. Frontier's Lisa Fancher decided to pass and wait for the next completely new work:

"I didn't want to put that out, because it was basically just a live in the studio album. I did like it, and thought some of the songs were really great... But it was a short album, and some of the songs were old staples of their set that were not my favourites. And I knew Mark was writing better and better songs, so I didn't want it as my final record."

When Leslie Mallon insisted that *United Kingdom* was the third AMC record in Frontier's three-album deal with Grifter, relations between her and Fancher started to get distinctly ugly. In the meantime, without a US release, *United Kingdom* would have to be judged by British critics alone. Already attuned to what AMC were doing, the British music press rose to the occasion.

Melody Maker's Bob Stanley concluded that, "*United Kingdom* isn't the greatest record ever made, but it serves notice that AMC are capable of scaling mountains. Buy this." *NME*'s Edwin Pouncey compared Eitzel favourably with Morrissey, and *Sounds*' David Cavanagh gave the album the maximum five stars. Cavanagh had clearly fallen in love both with the band's music, and Eitzel's lifestyle, real or imagined: "[SF] is the place where Mark Eitzel drinks, in Mission Area bars where the real action only starts around 2am when all the people who have gone there to enjoy themselves go home and leave people like Eitzel there all night with their heads on the bar, six inches away from a bottle."

The portrait was compelling, if romantically exaggerated. In terms of the quality of the art, it probably didn't matter too much that Eitzel would often have cycled home before midnight, having to get up the next day for work. If he was drinking, his evening may well have involved a large group of friends swigging a few beers around a barbecue in the park. Regardless, Cavanagh concluded: "It's difficult to find a record to compare to this; all I can think of are the last two albums by American Music Club, and Gram Parsons on '$1,000 Wedding' holding back tears as he's singing, 'Supposed to be a funeral ... it's been a bad, bad day.' The world must surely now stand in awe and horrified admiration of Mark Eitzel and American Music Club."

The positive press vindicated Hyde's decision to scrap the original album. The likelihood that a rough and ready live record would have kept AMC's critical momentum going is remote. The transformation of *United Kingdom* was one of AMC's best career decisions. But even on its release Leslie was not placated. Hyde remembers: "She was very unimpressed. She wanted to keep the [new] material for someone else."

Who was actually in control of American Music Club was becoming a potentially harmful issue. It appeared their manager was willing to risk sacrificing AMC's glowing critical standing in the UK in order to keep back Eitzel's new material for the purpose of getting the band a deal with a major US label. That was possibly the only way that her husband would ever recoup the huge amount of time and resources he had put into the band's early records. It would also take the band away from Spike Hyde and Demon Records in the UK. To complicate matters further, Lisa Fancher was in the process of setting up a major distribution deal for Frontier through RCA. AMC would be one of the key acts to benefit. Things were starting to get extremely messy.

In the meantime American Music Club came to Europe to promote *United Kingdom*. After a festival appearance in Belgium, they played a series of low-key European dates before returning to London's Mean Fiddler.

Booking agent Mick Griffiths remembers "Vince Power [Mean Fiddler organisation supremo] booked them personally because he liked them."

For their second Mean Fiddler show, there were more people in the audience, and in spite of the background noise of the club's regular drinkers, the atmosphere was even more expectant than before.

At about 10.00 pm Eitzel walked onstage in a navy velvet jacket that drew Engelbert Humperdinck comparisons from one reviewer. With Pearson stood to one side, Eitzel held up a copy of the previous week's *Sounds*, that contained a photo of his features contorted with emotion into what the caption called a "rictus of pain."

"I wouldn't come to a show by someone who looked like this," he told the audience. While the nervous laughter was still ringing, Eitzel warned the audience they were in for a bad evening, before beginning an acoustic version of "Outside This Bar," augmented by haunting vocal harmonies by Pearson. After acoustic versions of "Citizens of the True World," and "Gary's Song," the rest of the band took to the stage.

As they moved into 'Pale Skinny Girl' with Dan Pearson's ominous buzz-saw guitar crashing and reverberating, the crowd sensed that they were witnessing a very special event. Mallon's bass rumbled, Eitzel's voice burst into an anguished howl, and Simm's drums shuffled in awkward fits and starts, echoing like the footsteps of a guilty man walking down a corridor away from a crime. Finally all the disparate elements merged into one, a wall of beautiful noise more powerful than anything they had recorded. Eitzel would say: "It's the physicality of the singing that really gets to me. It's sort of like a gymnast spinning around on ropes or something. I don't have any melodies that are confirmed ... I try to make the moment give me a melody. I'm always searching for what the melody is."

Andrew Smith tried to capture the song's visceral force in his *Melody Maker* review: "When the whole band ripped into 'Pale Skinny Girl' the power was overwhelming, gut-churning, something we haven't heard before... Pearson's razor-edged guitar lurching off the front of the stage and spinning out over our heads like a blade through a field of wheat. The feeling was indescribable, overwhelming even."

Far more so than on any album, this performance was what American Music Club were all about. Using the song as a template, the band spontaneously created something new. This was not a studied experiment in improvisation, though it had links in the surrealist idea of just letting go in order to see what happens. As each band member went beyond the song's remit, eventually all of the disparate elements forged together in the moment.

At the end, the crowd's roar was deafening, and the clapping went on and on. Taking strength from the audience response, the band powered on through their best songs with increasing intensity, as Eitzel wailed, slobbered and contorted, crashing occasionally to his knees. "Laughing Stock" was a crazy frenetic workout climaxing with Eitzel staggering around the stage spitting over and again the tag line *"Hey baby that's hard for some."*

After a twisted fragmentary "Highway 5" Eitzel was alone on stage singing "Last Harbor."

Half-way through, gradually becoming drowned out by the background noises of clinking glasses and after-hours chatter, Eitzel tugged loose his guitar, drifted away from the mike, and tried to finish the song without the PA. It took the song away from any remnants of performance, and onto a different, more fragile plain. It was as if Eitzel could not bear the idea of finishing his set with a rock flourish of any kind. It could only end in collapse.

In the following week's *Melody Maker*, Andrew Smith took his praise to new levels of hyperbole: "I wouldn't have swapped a note for all the gigs I've seen this year.... It is only a matter of time before Mark Eitzel is recognised as one of the best songwriters operating anywhere, and AMC as one of the most consistently dangerous live bands you can see. Because they are dangerous. They confront us not with violence or volume, but with what we are and what we might be. Dreamers of the Dream."

The *NME*'s Simon Williams started out sceptical of Hyde's comment that

"AMC are the best band in the entire world," but concluded "I'm buggered if I can recall any performance as overwhelming, as condemning, as bitterly benign as this before. Genius incarnate."

Keith Cameron reviewed the show very sympathetically in *Sounds* emphasising the pain and anguish Eitzel went through during the performance, even going so far as to imply that he was bearing on his shoulders the audience's collective pain like some kind of creative scapegoat. Cameron was especially moved by what he saw as the impenetrable gulf between Eitzel and his audience. When the biggest cheer of the night goes up for what Cameron calls "the worst AMC song," 'Bad Liquor,' the journalist concluded: "Mark laughs. It's enough to make you cry."

At the time though, Mark Eitzel and American Music Club had plenty more to cry about. Their album and UK show couldn't have met with a better press reception, but it was already clear that they were not making any commercial headway. *United Kingdom* sold no more copies than *California,* and they had still failed to get any radio airplay. As 1989 drew to a close the "greatest band in the world" were back playing in the same small San Francisco clubs, squeezing time for rehearsals in between the grind of their day jobs.

Chapter Six

Sadder Than The Songs Themselves

"[I'm] doomed to sing, that's all I can do. Which is a shame, 'cause most of the time I hate it like I hate an orgasm, same thing."

Mark Eitzel

Interviewer: "How much do artists now know about the sort of deals you're offering them?"
"The artists and 80% of their managers still have no idea whatsoever."
Muff Winwood, senior director A&R, CBS.

"The Gulf [War] pisses me off so much. The American government is so corrupt. It's like Nero playing the fiddle while the world burns... I just fucking resent this stupid war so much. But let's talk about me and my career – that's a fucking disaster too."

Mark Eitzel

By the middle of November, 1989, it appeared that Lisa Fancher had succeeded in hooking her Frontier label up with a distribution deal through RCA Records, which was part of the huge BMG group. However the differences between Fancher and AMC's manager Leslie, meant that this process would not run smoothly. Fancher felt that Leslie was trying to take a Frontier deal and commandeer it exclusively for AMC on her own terms. Fancher explains: "It was a licensing arrangement through Frontier Records, not a deal with the band. RCA didn't want to sign AMC, they wanted to license some bands from me – a typical deal. RCA just wanted two bands, and they told me to pick which two. I had other bands that were doing better, but because of my total AMC psychosis, I thought that if RCA would pay for the [next AMC] record, it would take a lot of stress off Tom."

RCA's contractual arrangement would be with Frontier only. They would give Frontier a cheque to cover recording production costs for two artists, and would also help with the promotion and distribution of the bands. They were paying for Frontier's A&R expertise rather than signing the two acts. The other band Fancher selected was Thin White Rope.

American Music Club's record company arrangements were becoming extremely complicated. Nobody in the band seemed to understand the precise nature of the relationship between Tom Mallon's Grifter label and Frontier Records, never mind how this would be affected by any arrangement with RCA.

Mallon's Grifter were AMC's actual record label, and accordingly bore the costs of recording and manufacturing their albums. Lisa Fancher's Frontier label had a three-album licensing deal with Grifter. Frontier would distribute and promote the AMC records that Grifter presented them with; for this service they would retain 30% of the wholesale value. Frontier would pay the balance over to Mallon, who was then responsible for accounting to the band for royalties and any other income. Frontier would pay Mallon an advance on these earnings of $5,000 per album.

Fancher was now contracting with RCA to take care of the physical distribution of AMC's next album. RCA would even pay her a large sum for the privilege, knowing that they could make significant amounts of money if provided with the right bands. With the RCA money, Fancher could now cover the full cost of AMC's next album, but as she had no contractual relationship with AMC, this was a risky strategy.

Leslie's main dispute was that she wanted Fancher to give her RCA's cheque. She and the band would take care of all the money, make their record and return it to RCA. As it was Frontier that had the contractual obligation to provide RCA with the album they had paid for, Fancher would not allow this.

"I never had any problem with the creative control, but if you hand over the money and they don't make the record, or if Leslie goes and buys a Lamborghini with it, I'm responsible. So I said that RCA would put the money in my account, and I would write the cheques. Leslie would not have any of it. The next thing was that she wanted the band to go on salary. I tried to explain that this was not that kind of a record deal, that RCA were not signing the band, and that they didn't care about her problems. If she didn't want to be part of it, they'd just take another Frontier band."

To try and square things up, Lisa Fancher met with Tom, Leslie and the band at Mark's apartment. Tom and Leslie had gone through Fancher's draft agreement concerning the RCA deal, and had come up with pages of notes and queries. The negotiations did not proceed smoothly as Fancher recalls:

"Tom was adamant that he wouldn't get an attorney and was going to negotiate himself. It certainly isn't wise and I don't know if it's legal to sign an agreement with a band that hasn't at least shown it to a lawyer."

The upshot of the meeting was that Tom and Leslie felt that Frontier should not make any money out of AMC's part of the RCA deal, and would not agree to the deal as it stood. As AMC and Grifter still owed Fancher one album as part of their contract for a mere $5,000 advance, the alternative of making a $50,000 album which would be sure of nationwide distribution for Frontier via RCA would seem preferable. Nonetheless Leslie continued to contest virtually every other part of the deal. In the meantime, Thin White Rope signed the RCA deal and put out their Tom Mallon-produced *Sackful Of Silver* album under this arrangement without a hitch, though it was not a commercial success.

While the business disagreements between Leslie Mallon and Lisa Fancher continued, the band started to rehearse material for their next proper album. Bruce Kaphan would sit in on some of these sessions. Kaphan was still earning a living playing pedal steel in country bands, but on his nights off he would some-times join AMC as a sideman for gigs around the Bay area. "But I knew I wasn't a member of the band," he later explained, "I was still considered to be kind of auxiliary."

When it came time to discuss recording the next album, Eitzel wanted to get a different sound from its predecessors, and specifically did not want Tom Mallon to produce it. He envisaged a major change of direction, as he recalls: "I wanted to make something more lively and upbeat. And frankly, I was tired of every gig being these simple arrangements. Personally for me, AMC albums sound too vanilla – too MOR… too nice. I like to hear big mistakes."

Eitzel was highly aware of Mallon's strengths. He was great at making things sound moody and he'd ensure that every single moment of every single song sounded just right. But Eitzel was now tired of all the pain and tension involved in working with Mallon: "I didn't want that negative, manipulative thing that Tom has. So, I said 'I'm sorry, but I can't do this again'."

Eitzel was also looking for a more expansive sound on the next record, and wanted it to sound spontaneous and "sonically big":

"I heard 'If I Have To Be This Lonely' on the radio [a rare appearance]. Right after it came some awful Bon Jovi thing. But the thing I heard was that the Bon Jovi song sounded huge on the radio, and our song was barely audible. It just wasn't interesting sounding: it sounded dull. It wasn't that I didn't like the song, or the playing or the recording. It just had a cheap sound. So I wanted to go into a real studio and do a big album, like a pop record. Something that would sound good on the radio."

Mallon on the other hand was keen to produce the next AMC album, and wanted to start recording it at his studio. Eitzel was adamant that this would not be the case, but while they waited for the RCA deal to be sorted out, he agreed to do some preliminary demos with Mallon.

"I said, 'Well, we can do demos for the album, but I really don't want to do the album here, …Tom said, 'Okay, okay, let's just work, let's start'."

Eitzel believes Mallon was convinced the RCA deal would never happen and that they would have to record the whole album at his place again.

Before they went into the studio, AMC played their first show at the 350 capacity Great American Music Hall in San Francisco – a beautiful room with a balcony, an ornate stage, mirrors, red velvet upholstery and a gold painted ceil-ing. Although reputedly a former brothel, the hall marked a step up from the smaller clubs they were used to playing in their home town. It would be the last time they would ever play with Tom Mallon.

Even during the initial demo sessions, it was clear that there had been a major shift in the band's working practices. Eitzel was starting to take more of an interest in the actual recording process. Bruce Kaphan had opened Eitzel's eyes to alternative ways of doing things in the studio, consequently Eitzel got less tolerant of Tom's demanding and stressful recording techniques. Kaphan was horrified by the acoustics in Mallon's place and the calibre of the equipment. Used to working in 24-track professional studios, he found it difficult to accept that not only was Mallon's place only 16-track, but that Mallon actually preferred the sound of his old 8-track machine. Kaphan's misgivings were not lost on Eitzel; regardless of how the demos turned out, he was even more convinced that the album itself must not be recorded at Tom's studio.

In the past, Eitzel had spent a lot of time defending Mallon, but now he no longer had the patience or strength of mind. Eitzel often felt that his role in the group was to provide a template to enable the band and producer to do their work. Now he didn't feel like enabling anybody. He just wanted this record to be made the way he wanted. "I was like the girl of the group," Eitzel explains. "I'd go to people, 'Well, you're great, and it's going to be great'. So, whenever Tom got flustered, I'd say, 'You know what Tom, this is cool. Don't worry about it, we'll just work through it, blah, blah, blah'. But when we were working in his studio on the *Everclear* demos, I would just go, 'whatever'. I just didn't care."

About a week or so into recording, during a discussion with Tom in a room adjacent to the studio, Eitzel got especially surly, and the producer decided he had had enough. "Ok, that's it," he yelled, throwing Eitzel a look of defiance, "Everybody get the fuck out of my studio."

The band packed up their equipment, and Mallon then literally kicked them out on to the street. Mallon refused to hand over the tapes of that week of recording, and Eitzel claims Mallon told him on his way out:

"Fuck you, Eitzel. You are never getting any fucking royalties from me."

It was the end of Mallon's working relationship with American Music Club. Eitzel was now free to record anywhere he chose, but in every other respect AMC's situation was disastrous. Not only had they lost their bassist and producer, they also no longer had a working relationship with the owner of the record label on which their first three albums had been released. The fact that Mallon was married to their manager was an even bigger complication.

The situation was arguably more tragic for Tom Mallon. For four years he had given his life to AMC and he was now out of the picture. It would be easy to criticise Mallon for his dictatorial and negative approach, but he was essential in the development of AMC's sound. "I have a lot of respect for Tom," Lisa Fancher confesses, "I think he probably loved Mark and AMC more than anyone else ever did, or will."

In spite of the split with Tom, Leslie continued to manage the band, but the rift between AMC and her husband made her even more belligerent. She still wouldn't accept the proposed RCA deal so AMC were left in a state of limbo. Now that they had parted company with Tom Mallon, they had nowhere to demo their new songs. They couldn't afford to go into a studio until the RCA money came through, unless they signed with a new record company.

Fancher too was in a difficult position. She had scheduled AMC along with Thin White Rope to play at a Frontier Records showcase for the Gavin Report Tip Sheet at the I-Beam on 16th February 1990. The idea was to show off to the music industry the two Frontier acts that RCA would be pushing through the new distribution deal. A large number of RCA executives were invited on the basis that the deal would be done and dusted by then.

As the date approached, Leslie made it clear that she was not going to sign the deal. Frontier would thus be showcasing a band they had not signed, and at the same time giving AMC an ideal industry platform from which to attract another record deal.

A few days before the show, Fancher got wind that Leslie was talking to Silvertone and Fiction with a view to getting AMC a new deal. Fancher hit the roof and on the 13th February she faxed Leslie to tell her AMC would no longer be playing the I-Beam on Friday. "It'll be embarrassing no doubt," Fancher admitted, "but since you seem to be under the impression that the band is free to go and have no qualms telling A&R the same, I'm not going to enable them to showcase for other labels."

When Leslie got the fax, the real fireworks started and angry phone calls and faxes were exchanged for the next 24 hours. Leslie was turning fierce, but Fancher was used to playing rough – in a recent spat with a promoter over Young Fresh Fellows, she had Fedex'd a pig's head to the opposing side.

As the dispute intensified between Fancher and Leslie, the bad feeling started to spread to the band. They began to ask Fancher how come she had never paid them any royalties on their previous albums, even though she had paid her license fees to Tom Mallon, who was responsible for all royalty payments.

Events culminated when Frontier's publicist faxed a note to Leslie on a Young Fresh Fellows promotional 10x8 photograph of a monkey wrench. Leslie Mallon was pregnant by now and she allegedly told the band that Fancher had faxed her a picture of a coat hanger – an infamous instrument in self-administered back-street abortions.

In the end Fancher relented and she allowed them to play the gig. But at the show, after hearing the "coathanger" story, none of the band would have any-thing to do with her. It was a turning point in her relationship with AMC: "Normally no matter what happened between Leslie and me, Mark always stayed neutral. That night he gave me the dirtiest look ever, after they played, so I start-ed power-drinking Bushmills whiskey…"

Fancher got drunk, then broke down, crying hysterically, and left the I-Beam before the final band went on.

This was AMC's first show since they had been once again reduced to a four-piece. In Mallon's absence, Eitzel strapped on an electric guitar and Pearson reverted back to bass. They had barely rehearsed any of their new material at all with this line-up. But, rather than revert to a set of their best-known songs – which at least Dan Pearson had played bass on – they chose to play a completely new set. Instead of distracting the band, the background tension with Tom, Leslie and Fancher, appeared to give them an added sense of purpose – something to rage against – and that night they played one of their most intense shows.

Eitzel introduced the band somewhat ironically: "Hi .. uh .. we're a four-piece now, so ... uh, this is kind of a little experiment ...a jazz odyssey. Every song is going to be a jazz odyssey. We're going to do all new stuff because we're trying to re-group."

Most of the new material would eventually surface on their next album, while some of it was destined to be "lost" forever. Ditching the setlist's opening track "Act of Devotion," the band began with "Confidential Agent," then "A Summer Place," where Eitzel howls *A summer place, I think I'm going to stay / The lies I told, to save her face,*" as the band stop and start, their guitars grated menacingly.

"Why Won't You Stay" was breathtaking. Eitzel muttered some of the words, catterwauling others, and then crooned beautifully for long stretches, while the chorus became a screech of pain. Vudi's guitar raged and scraped. Without a pause they were into "Sick of Food," and the playing became even more ferocious: feedback, overdrive echo, Pearson's rumbling bass and Simms' drumstick whispering on one cymbal as Eitzel spat the final refrain.

In a brief pause, Eitzel joked that they are now "focused." After "Jesus' Hands," and "Miracle on 8th" Dan Pearson called their performance "a symphony in D," referring to the dominant key of the new batch of songs. But it could easily be a potential greatest hits set: every single one of the new songs was breathtaking.

AMC were doing something no other band would or could. Faced with a wall of adversity, unrehearsed and without a record label, they had simply produced from nowhere a whole set of totally new songs and played one of their most powerful shows.

As the band shuffled back on stage for an encore Eitzel addressed the audience: "We're called the Average Mid-age Crisis ... yeah, that's what we're called ... Any Mediocre Combo ... It doesn't matter ... We lost everything this week, this will probably be our last show..."

AMC then lurched into "Firefly" but each member of the band started off playing a different song. They stopped except for the bass, and Eitzel muttered an inaudible few phrases to a new melody. It was a mess, but it was something eerily beyond just a mistake. They stumbled on the only old song, as if they were so set on a move forward that they literally could not turn back.

Then they started again, and the full version of "Firefly" was amazing. When it finished, Eitzel tells the crowd, "Thanks a lot for coming everybody; We'll probably never see you again..."

But the applause was so strong that Eitzel finally came back for a solo encore, flanked by Vudi, who now clutched a bottle of Heineken instead of a guitar. Eitzel introduced "Act of Devotion" with the line, "Yeah, how bad can it get." When the song finished, like a trainer with a battered prize fighter, Vudi threw a coat over Eitzel's shoulders and dragged him off stage.

Melody Maker's Everett True was blown away by the set: "The room is on fire.... I guess this is what you call a happening. Some happening."

It was an impressive artistic event. But it was not a performance guaranteed to win over major label executives. Their show was beautiful and spontaneous, but it was also ramshackle and chaotic. All in all, with AMC's performance, and

Fancher's tears, RCA's people did not leave the I-Beam with a great deal of confidence.

After the show Fancher straightened things out with RCA and tried to tie up the loose ends of the contract, but Leslie fought her every step of the way. Fancher recalls: "Leslie was writing these wild letters straight to the RCA Business Affairs guy, and he'd call me up and say, 'What the fuck is this woman's problem?' Then I'd call her up and scream at her. We got in some unbelievable fights – really nasty stuff."

RCA's original budget for the next AMC album was $50,000. When Leslie presented her own revised budget to RCA it came to $100,000. RCA agreed to go as far as $82,500, but by then Leslie had other issues which prevented the band from signing.

Eventually the band and Fancher stopped communicating, as Leslie apparently insisted that they keep a unified front against Frontier. "Mark and I even put our friendship on hold, as it created more problems if we talked to each other. If we remained on friendly terms, it would piss the band off. I had no idea what anyone was thinking at this time... It was killing me. It ruined my life – I had the worst insomnia ever – I was depressed, and I really thought I would die if I didn't keep working with American Music Club."

Weeks quickly turned into months. By late Spring 1990, AMC still had no label and consequently no money to record. They couldn't even afford to tour. They'd play the odd San Francisco show with Bruce Kaphan, but as the summer drew on, AMC barely existed.

In the interim, Eitzel got a new job working in children's services at a local library. He also moved into a new apartment on the top floor of a three storey Victorian apartment building just on Capp Street at 19th, just over from Mission Street in the Mission District of San Francisco.

The Mission is the Hispanic quarter. Back in the 30s it was an Irish ghetto, but the only remnants of that era are a few bars like McCarthy's. Now Spanish alternates with English on the shop signs, and the balance of the ethnic population comprises Mexicans and Filipinos. It was a busy colourful neighbourhood, and there were always plenty of people on the streets, loud music playing and the smell of different ethnic foods cooking. There were also a lot of drugs, gangs and whores. Jenny Gonzalvez lived on nearby Shotwell Street, and a Hispanic gang would stand outside her house and drink noisily all through the night. Vudi was nearly beaten up on one visit merely for speaking English.

The area was named after and dominated by the Mission Dolores – an 18th century church built by the Spanish Franciscan Monks, and named in honour of Our Lady of Sorrows: "Nuestra Senora de los Dolores." Around the Mission grounds in unmarked graves lie the remains of 5,000 Native American Indians – over half of the Bay Area population before the Spanish arrived. No other part of town was so steeped in guilt and death. Even the Mission's big annual festival is the ghoulish Day of the Dead – a Halloween-style candlelit parade.

The Mission is a sunny part of San Francisco, and Eitzel's flat was usually flooded in sunlight. But, in every other respect, this was a dark corner of town, as a former resident of the same block explains: "Capp [Street] is a narrow, sleepy street by day, and a very dark, creepy street by night. People just appear out of the darkness. When the police department cracked down on drug dealing and prostitution on Mission St, it came over to Capp St... At night-time there's this procession of cars slowly going up Capp St. to pick up dope, crack or whores. Several times I came home late and there would be some woman doing drugs at the entrance to the flat or passed out ... it was that sort of street..."

The street itself was strewn with detritus, excrement, soiled mattresses, used condoms and litter. In its physical degradation, Capp Street was reminiscent of the stinking, derelict kingdom of Eitzel's favourite Lautreamont text, *Maldoror*.

The living-room window of Eitzel's flat commanded great views of the Capp Street nightlife. With the band apparently on hold, Eitzel would hang out at the Uptown bar on the corner of 17th and Capp and watch the drug dealers and prostitutes ply their trade. A dealer sold drugs directly in front of Eitzel's building, while skinny, washed out women would lounge on the street corner waiting for cars to slow down or stop. He'd often come home to find some poor prostitute spread-eagled on the road with an ambulance attendant shoving a tube down her throat.

"The ugliest whores in town used to work in front of my house," Eitzel remembers. "Every morning there would be something. You'd get up in the morning and there'd be some junkie in the backyard with a huge slash on his wrist, or somebody would be shooting up in their leg on the front step, or there'd be a whore hiding behind the letterbox. There were always ambulances, and there was always gunfire."

The people in the flat below Eitzel's would fight all the time, and there would be screaming for hours, all through the night. He would often hear the woman being picked up and thrown across the room. "The week before I moved in," Eitzel recalls, "one of the women who lived there went downstairs and told these people that she was going to call the police if they didn't sort themselves out. They threatened to kill her if she ever came down to their apartment again. But you know what, they ended up being really sweet people. We ended up becoming friends with them. They were a nice Filipino family, but there were problems."

In fact their problems were more serious than most. Shortly after Eitzel left the apartment, a typical domestic argument downstairs led to the Filipino woman shooting her husband. He was only wounded and he then stabbed her to death. As Eitzel explains, "It was a very violent little nexus."

Like the Tenderloin before, the Mission area in all its bleakness would become the setting for many of Eitzel's new songs. But this was not just a case of writing about the surroundings he found himself in. Eitzel was always drawn to the weak, the desperate and the downtrodden. It was what interested him, and he could only understand it enough to write about, if he lived at its heart. Like Bukowski, or Orwell or Jack London, to be a writer as Eitzel understood it, was to live a writer's life. In order to write about the underbelly, you had to immerse yourself in it. This was not a recipe for a happy life.

As AMC's record company difficulties remained unresolved throughout Spring and the Summer the band drifted apart, though one of their demos "Crystal Always Knows" came out on a flexi-disc given away with the *Breakfast Without Meat* fanzine. Recorded on a 4-track machine in Eitzel's flat, it wasn't one of his better songs, and the band could never agree on an arrangement for it, so this was the only time the song surfaced.

Although they continued to rehearse sporadically and play shows at the Great American Music Hall every couple of months, without a new album to focus on, a lot of their impetus had gone. Eitzel was starting to feel artistically lost and frustrated, so when his old friend Tim Mooney, now back from a drug-induced wilderness, started rehearsing with a reformed Toiling Midgets, Eitzel agreed to try singing with them. The line-up also included Lisa Davis on bass, whose liver problems had now cleared up.

The Midgets' songs were already constructed instrumentally, so as lyricist and singer Eitzel had a completely free rein. Mooney remembers that, "the writing of the songs was really easy. Mark would just come in with his notebooks and sing over whatever we were playing."

On 5th August 1990 at the San Francisco Paradise Lounge, Eitzel made his live debut as the Toiling Midgets' singer. As the gigs with the Midgets were much louder and rockier than AMC, it was hard for Eitzel to be heard so he'd have to sing really loud and he'd jump around a lot more. Also, he'd often make up half of his lyrics on the day, or actually on stage during the show. It was a physically and mentally hard experience. Eitzel told one interviewer that he would "Take on the role of a mass murderer, a very American role."

Eitzel found it rewarding to be on stage with Mooney and Davis again, and at times some of the original AMC chemistry returned. "It was good while it lasted," Mooney remembers. For Eitzel, it was also a welcome change from the tensions of American Music Club.

But, other than Mooney, the rest of the Midgets were not really the same kind of people as AMC. With the Midgets, being a rock star – even if just a local rock star – was always more important than the music.

"Those people were fucked up," Davis believes, "They were not good-hearted people. Craig and Paul had just been such bad junkies. They kept all the rock 'n' roll antics and they were in it for the wrong reasons. AMC was a necessity. With Danny and Vudi the music is always a necessity for them."

For a year or so, Eitzel would sing with the Midgets in San Francisco clubs. In spite of the enjoyment it gave him, he was always at pains during this period to remind people that he was not a member of the Toiling Midgets, insisting he just turned up for the odd show. The rest of AMC didn't mind this extra curricular activity, as the band always had an open policy about people playing with anyone they wanted.

Meanwhile, Lisa Fancher tried to finalise the RCA deal, although Leslie Mallon did her best to sabotage progress. Fancher remembers that: "When we finally resolved our problems with RCA and decided to do it, they realised that Leslie was calling other major labels. I found out about this and would call up the labels she had got interested, and tell them, 'You know they owe me one more record, and if you touch them, I'll sue your ass off.' I put out any fires she got going, so she finally had to give in and accept the RCA deal…"

Finally, in August 1990, Fancher and Leslie arrived at a compromise. AMC signed to Frontier Records on the understanding that they were about to sign with RCA. Frontier would underwrite the studio costs until RCA's cheque came through. After a year of bitter wrangling, AMC could get back to work.

The band convened at the Music Annex in Menlo Park, and started work on their new album, with Bruce Kaphan informally ensconced in the producer's chair. With his extensive experience in modern studios with state-of-the-art consoles and tape machines, he was in a good position to help the band make the transition from an indie-record feel, to a much bigger sound.

But, after less than a week in the studio, the RCA President Bob Buziak was fired, and RCA's new boss showed AMC the door. They would never get a record distributed by BMG. Worse, without anyone to pick up their recording costs, they had to immediately stop work.

Their career was back in a state of impasse. Leslie Mallon's attitude of complete resignation in the face of this new crisis exacerbated relations between her and Eitzel. He was tired of her negative outlook. "Leslie walked into the studio," he remembers, "and she said 'It's up. It's fucked. RCA just dropped Frontier so it's not going to fuckin' happen. I guess we can get some money from them, but fuck it, it's bad'." This was simply not what Eitzel wanted to hear. He continued to play live shows with the Toiling Midgets, keen to maintain a creative outlet, but he was getting extremely frustrated with his own band's lack of progress.

Then, just as it appeared that AMC would never actually get back in a recording studio, Lisa Fancher gave the band a break. RCA had paid Frontier $40,000 as compensation for breaking their agreement, and Fancher offered to pay for *Everclear* to be completed. AMC would have to sign a new contract with Frontier in the light of the changed circumstances, but Fancher was willing to advance all of the RCA money, without cross-collaterising the new record against the substantial losses she'd incurred on the previous two AMC albums. The band did not want to remain on an independent label any longer. But, Fancher's offer at least meant they could get straight back to work. Though the new recording budget of $40,000 was less than half that scheduled for the RCA deal, it meant they could pay Bruce Kaphan, book 17 lock-out days at the Music Annex and still have some living expenses for each member. They agreed to sign for just one more record, and went back into the studio.

The sessions started off well. Bruce Kaphan's approach to working was less demanding, less confrontational and less negative. Kaphan had heard all the stories about Mallon's demanding work practices, and was determined to take a very different course.

"My aim as a producer, was to let Mark be Mark," explains Kaphan. "I felt my job was to make sure we stayed in budget, and that we got good solid takes on tape. But, rather than force my own personal agenda on Mark and the rest of the band, my idea was that this was the band's fifth album now, they've been around the studio a lot, so, let them make their own fucking record.

"I'd loved the direction of *California*, but I didn't like it sonically! I thought if we could do *California* with deeper textures and more varied instruments, and more than anything else with good sound and better quality recording, that was the record I wanted to make."

The long hiatus between the start and finish of the album also had one extremely positive effect. For *United Kingdom*, there wasn't any time to reflect on the work in hand, whereas this time they had time in spades. As with *Engine,* the long recess had given Eitzel and AMC a chance to hone the new material live – both solo and as a group – reject songs, add songs, and then redo the whole thing from a different perspective. Bruce Kaphan explains:

"We'd been approaching the tracks in a certain way, and when we came back together, Mark had had a chance to listen to the work in progress a lot... Any song that was pretty, we put a whole bunch of ugly stuff on it, and any song that was ugly, we put a whole bunch of pretty stuff on it."

In spite of Kaphan's designation as producer, the rest of the band were given a much greater say in the studio than with previous AMC records. "It was our first stab at trying to make our own record and not have somebody lording over the controls and the arrangements," Vudi later told a journalist. "We just did it democratically." The exception was drummer Mike Simms who not really a part of this democracy. Simms would just come to the studio, play his parts and then leave.

After three weeks, the band had good basic tracks laid down for about ten songs. They had also racked up recording costs approaching the $30,000 mark, but this did not seem a problem. Then the contracts from Frontier arrived, and everything started to disintegrate again. According to Eitzel, the band had made it quite clear to Lisa Fancher that they would sign for one record only: "We thought she'd said OK, so we went in the studio and spent an awful lot of money. Then her lawyer sent the papers, and the deal wasn't what we thought, it was that we agreed to six records for Frontier."

AMC continued to record, but refused to sign the new contract. They also started to avoid Fancher, who got increasingly anxious as to what was going on. The band had spent more than half of the money she had got from RCA, and the costs were continuing to climb, while she still had nothing in writing.

Her worst fears appeared to be realised when she went to see AMC play The Great American Music Hall, only to find the audience packed with A&R men and outside producers. Fancher explains sadly: "I felt that I could no longer trust Leslie. I was freaked that she was going to take the tapes, and ... I didn't know what she was going to do really. I'd spent this money [from RCA], and I didn't really have any contract with them."

The gig was a turning point for Fancher. It was now clear that AMC were not going to sign. The next day, she called the studio and told there was no more money and that they had to stop. In the meantime, taking no chances, she caught a flight from LA to San Francisco and rushed to the studio to pick up the tapes. But, before Fancher could get to Menlo Park, Vudi kidnapped the tapes and the band fled the studio.

Eitzel was in New York for a few days, so Fancher traded angry phone calls with Vudi across the weekend. She felt betrayed, but there wasn't much she could do. "At long last, I realised there was no point in trying to get things back on track, and told them if they could find a new label fast, then I was all for it... I only asked for my out-of-pocket expenses." With AMC back in a state of limbo, over in London Spike Hyde was getting worried that all the good work that had been done in building their reputation in the UK was now going to waste.

Without a new album, and without any money to tour, it was difficult to keep the band's momentum going.

Hyde's stop-gap plan was to re-release *Engine* in the UK. Sure enough, the UK press went crazy for it once again. In *Melody Maker* Allan Jones called it a "masterpiece," while *Sounds*' Ralph Traitor felt it contended "seriously as perhaps the greatest American album of the late '80s." Traitor concluded, "Whatever you do, get this." But nobody did. Sales of the re-released record barely made an impression. While on the West Coast of America record company contractual matters continued to keep AMC out of a recording studio, in the UK, Mark Eitzel and American Music Club were sinking back into obscurity. Hyde also realised that in order to have the time to keep writing songs, Eitzel desperately needed some money. Struggling to come up with something that would maintain their profile within Demon's modest budget, Hyde hit upon a singular idea.

On 14th November, after liaising with booking agent Mick Griffiths, Hyde invited Eitzel to play a solo acoustic show in London the following January, which Demon would record for a Mark Eitzel live album. As Eitzel and AMC were between labels, there would be no contractual issues to overcome. Eitzel would have 100% control over what would go on the record, and he could even veto the whole thing if he wasn't happy with the tapes. Demon would advance him $5,000 plus his expenses. Not surprisingly, Eitzel jumped at the chance.

While the exercise would help American Music Club in the long run, initially the rest of the band were quite cool to the idea, and when Leslie Mallon heard the plan, she was outraged. Hyde had mooted the idea of the gig with her a few weeks earlier, and she'd made it clear that she did not want it to happen. When she heard that Eitzel was going ahead anyway, she flipped.

"How dare you do this?" she yelled at him. "If you do this Eitzel, you are just an egotistical prick. And, you'll never be successful anyway." Leslie accused him of betrayal and called him a crazy alcoholic. She even told him she didn't like his music solo.

"Of course I'm an egotist," Eitzel later admitted, "of course I want an audience to applaud, of course I want to go to England for a free trip." But that was by no means the main reason for going. In the face of his manager's rage, he told her:

"Well, you know Leslie, I've got nothing else going on, and the idea of a free trip to England, and being paid for the show, seems a really good idea. If I sit around doing nothing forever, I'll be worse off than if I do something." In the face of Leslie's pessimism, Eitzel was also keen to prove to her that he was getting offers to do things.

Leslie then claimed that Tom Mallon's Grifter label owned the re-recording rights to all of Eitzel's songs, and threatened to sue him if he went ahead with the live album. Next she sent an angry fax to Spike Hyde's boss at Demon claiming that the promotions man was undermining her role, "Spike absolutely must be reined in," she insisted. Eitzel also felt that Leslie used the opportunity to alienate him from the rest of the band by stressing that Eitzel had no right to take all the money from the trip. Eitzel was torn – he didn't want the band to feel he was deserting them. But there was no budget for anyone else to fly to London. Either he went alone and did the show and album, or he just stayed at home and did nothing at all.

Things went back and forth for a while, and in the end Eitzel just thought, "fuck it", and flew to London on 15th January, the day of the Gulf crisis. "I kind of decided my loyalties were towards myself, towards my music." Eitzel reflects, "Because nobody else gave a shit."

On the 17th January 1991 at the Borderline, just off London's Charing Cross Road, Mark Eitzel walked on stage with a borrowed guitar. Unshaven and awkward in an old red shirt and jeans, he looked a wreck. He was nervous, not having played many solo gigs in recent years. Regardless, the welcome was rapturous. People called out for requests constantly, mouthed the words to songs, and generally revelled in what felt like a semi-religious event; part stand-up comedy, part theatre, part concert and part revivalist meeting. In their stripped down form, many of Eitzel's best songs took on a whole new life. Some of the subtleties may have been lost, but Eitzel made up for it with the intensity of his delivery. He previewed a number of songs from the unreleased AMC album, including "Jesus Hands," "Why Won't You Stay," "Miracle on 7th Street," "Ex-Girlfriend," and "Royal Café." All were well received, but it was the solo versions of AMC classics that got by far the biggest roars. "Western Sky" and "Blue And Grey Shirt" were heart-stopping. Eitzel performed "Room Above The Club" as a defiant a capella, and for "Last Harbor" he brought the haunting guitar arpeggios from the recorded version dramatically to the foreground, and the effect was gut-wrenchingly mesmerising.

Whereas some performers, when faced with the solo acoustic spotlight, merely reduce their songs to one man strum-alongs, Eitzel was an accomplished enough guitarist to fill out the missing instrument parts with intricate finger-picking as well as powerful rhythm playing. The way he twisted his voice this way and that in search of the perfect spontaneous heartfelt melody was positively acrobatic. It was as gripping as watching a clown doing a circus high wire act and the audience alternated between laughter at Eitzel's self-deprecating banter and awestruck silence at the power of his performance. He sang and played as if his life depended on it.

The reviews were rapturous once more, and this show marked the point at which Mark Eitzel was officially canonised by the UK music press. *NME*'s Bobby Surf described the show as "remarkable," but it was Andrew Smith of *Melody Maker* who took the praise to a new level:

"That Eitzel is one of the greatest living songwriters is beyond question. If a choice had to be made between the release of a new AMC album and the entire remaining output of the record industry, I wouldn't have to think about which I'd go for. It'd be AMC every time...

In the face of all this praise, interviews of this time saw Eitzel growing more and more eccentric. The image he was projecting was not the expected tortured poet. "I dreamt about my underwear last night and it turned into this plant," he told *Melody Maker*'s Bob Stanley. To *Vox*'s Max Bell, he professed to "hate all [rock] shows, apart from a San Francisco band called The Grateful Dead Kennedys – total white trash with go-go girls in fur bras and pebbles costumes."

After the London trip, Eitzel played a solo show in Switzerland and then returned to San Francisco to record an album with the Toiling Midgets. In the meantime, a small independent label called Alias had approached Leslie with a view to signing AMC immediately. By the time Lisa Fancher heard about Alias' interest, she was well and truly ready to quit. "Fine," she told Leslie, "just pay me back my recording costs on *Everclear* and I'm out of here'."

Alias Records was a tiny independent label owned by San Francisco million-airess, Delight Jenkins. As the only "name" act on the label was The Sneetches, it was an odd choice for a band with four albums already under their belt. But, Leslie Mallon got on with Delight and Alias did have the money to pay for *Everclear*'s recording costs. Lisa Fancher bowed out battered and disappointed. It would take her years to recover from the loss of American Music Club.

While Leslie and Delight worked through the terms of the Alias deal, Eitzel and Spike Hyde concentrated on finalising the solo live album. Hyde and Paul Riley edited it in London while Hyde and Eitzel exchanged tapes and notes about each others' preferences. In order to whittle the setlist down to a single album, Eitzel gave each track a mark out of ten. In Eitzel's trademark style, only two songs scored above the average mark of five and old AMC favorites "Western Sky," and "Kathleen" came in at two out of ten, although he still put them on the record. Once the grading process was completed, Eitzel felt there was not enough good quality material. Accordingly, he recorded "live" versions of two brand new songs, "Take Courage" and "Nothing Can Bring You Down" in a small backroom facility at Demon's head office. Hyde set a DAT machine running and left Eitzel alone for a few hours. When he returned later that afternoon, Eitzel had finished.

The live album's working title was "Challenger", and at one time, Eitzel would refer to it, perhaps jokingly, as "From Chernobyl to Challenger". The cover was originally planned to feature a photobooth shot of an plain-looking old woman that Eitzel found in the street, and the title was to be the then heavily ironic "Love Songs". In the end the photo could not be cleared for copyright purposes and a live shot of Eitzel at the Borderline was substituted. When Demon released the album in the UK in April 1991, it was called *Songs of Love Live*. "Essentially," Eitzel would insist, "my songs are love songs."

A slightly revised version of Andrew Smith's *Melody Maker* review of the Borderline show formed the album's back cover. Smith was so convinced of the record's importance that he refused to accept any payment.

As with the startling live show from which the bulk of the album was taken, there was a beautiful directness to *SOLL*. While the role of Mallon and the other members of the band cannot be underestimated in producing the American Music Club sound, this was the first time the listener would get to hear Eitzel performing his hauntingly personal songs as they'd actually been written, solo with just an acoustic guitar. There was none of the compromise associated with allowing others to arrange, produce or mix his work. The "live in the studio" version of "Take Courage" is particularly striking.

Courage is an English beer that was popular until the mid-1970s, and during its heyday, the advertising slogan "Take Courage" appeared on storefronts and billboards all over the country. As a child back in Southampton, Eitzel would take the number fourteen bus to school each morning and stare out of the window waiting for the sign. Presumably for someone who had difficulty fitting in with his classmates, and dreaded the social interaction that each day would bring, the words held a deep resonance. Eitzel vowed to write his own jingle for the beer and later expressed his hope that the beer company would buy this song for use in a promotional campaign – though admitting that he now finds Courage beer "undrinkable."

Though it has a beautiful, haunting melody, and features some of Eitzel's best finger-picked guitar to date, this slow, rolling solo acoustic song would certainly make an unlikely advertising soundtrack. The song revisits the mood of *United Kingdom* as Eitzel looks back to the school bus ride. *"If we could walk without our crutches,"* Eitzel softly sings, *"would we have anything to offer them..."* – accepting with defiance his earlier failings and anxieties. Eitzel would later release a reverb-drenched version of "Take Courage" as a one-off single for Gerard Cosloy's Matador label, under the title "On the Emblematic Use of Jewelry as a Metaphor for the Disolution [sic] of Our Hopes and Dreams." The cover would be a Brad Johnson cartoon of Eitzel soaking his feet near an old shack bearing the word "Drink" on its roof in huge letters.

By the time of its release, Eitzel was quick to dismiss the single. "You don't want to hear that," he would tell the editor of US fanzine *Cream Puff War*, "it's a piece of shit. I'm trying to sell enough of 'em to get my money back".

In addition to a selection of previously released Eitzel favourites, *Songs of Love* featured "Crabwalk," an up-tempo romp with deceptively crafted lyrics that would be reworked on the next AMC record, the ironically titled "Nothing Can Bring Me Down," – an embryonic version of a song that would appear on the album after *Everclear,* and another haunting new gem, "Chanel No 5." Later to surface on the "Rise EP," slowed down and doused in studio effects, this solo live version is one of the high points of Eitzel's career. Told in matter-of-fact tones that are tinged both with sympathy, curiosity and a touch of admiration, it is the story of a scene he witnessed from his window in the Tenderloin involving a prostitute who lived down the hallway. The shouting from her apartment would often keep Eitzel awake:

"I always think of this as a light on Geary Street near Levenworth, when it gets to be about five in the afternoon when it's really beautiful 'cause there's this blue light that descends over everything and there's lots of working women and their friends.

"She was running. He was following. She wasn't smiling. Neither was he. She had one black eye. And he looked like he was about to give her another one."

In an interview with *Melody Maker*'s Simon Reynolds, Eitzel was quick to criticise himself for impotently watching such a scene and then "very crassly, ... think[ing], 'Oh, I'll write a song about this'." But the song is not exploitative or voyeuristic, what shines out from it is the woman's pride. As she stands in the grim glare of a kerb-crawler's headlamps, she walks, *"holding her head upright; she wants to show she's got some pride to the headlights/..She's got her Walkman on / She's got, Chanel Number 5..."* While Eitzel may romanticise the downtrodden and the defeated, the true heroes and heroines of his songs are those who manage to retain their dignity in the face of adversity.

On release, Eitzel quickly became *SOLL*'s worst critic. "I can't listen to it," he complained. "It got reviewed in *The Guardian* as 'tuneless bellowing,' and that's what it was. Bellowing. Like a cow in a field." Eitzel quotes his source accurately, but it is typical that this is the only review he would remember and use it to negate his most pure work to date. Especially considering *The Guardian*'s writer was truly on his own. *Songs of Love Live*'s release was another chance for the UK press to shower Eitzel in superlatives.

Everett True in *Melody Maker* compared the album to Lennon without the Beatles, and signed off: "Treasure him now… God I wish I'd been there." *NME* called Eitzel a "master storyteller," and *Select* gave *SOLL* a two page spread as its album of the month. "To fail to be moved by Mark Eitzel," *Select*'s Nick Griffiths opined, "is to have your heart in a blender." Griffiths concluded by referring to the new material on display as "a tantalising taster of tracks from an American Music Club album that may never see the light of day. And that is sadder than the songs themselves."

Like *United Kingdom*, *Songs of Love* was a UK only release. Lisa Fancher had opposed the project, and felt it would harm AMC by diluting their profile. It was never licensed to any other territory or label, which is surprising because it was Eitzel's bestselling album to date. Capitalising on the quality of the music, and the fact that most of the media interest was in Eitzel himself, *SOLL* sold 5,000 copies very quickly, and went on to sell about 10,000 copies within a year. By the late 1990s sales were approaching the 20,000 unit mark. *Songs of Love* was the first album to produce a royalty cheque for Eitzel.

When Leslie Mallon still didn't have a good word to say about what was clearly an extremely successful exercise, Eitzel's patience with her ran out. With the Demon deal, he'd seen how easily agreements could be completed and was beginning to realise that Leslie's overtly aggressive business stance was not always the most productive approach. His reception in London had convinced him that he and AMC did have prospects, and he was tired of his manager's habitual negativity.

"The last meeting I had with Leslie really convinced me that I didn't want to work with her any more. She said 'Well you know AMC is really not going to do very well.' And I thought 'Fuck that! I'm tired of hearing that, and I don't want to hear it from our manager."

A few days later the band fired her. Leslie promptly threatened legal action against AMC. "She wanted $40,000 compensation against lost future earnings," Eitzel recalls through gritted teeth. "She also said that we couldn't use *Everclear*, because we'd started to record it at Mallon's studio, and Mallon intended to release it on Grifter."

But, Leslie's writ was the least of AMC's worries. They had no money to give her, and Mallon's claim to the album appeared fairly weak. More critical was the fact that they had signed over their new album to a small label with no track record and poor distribution, and now that they needed advice the most, they were without a manager. For too long Eitzel and AMC had underestimated the value of professional management. To take their career up to the next level – even to make enough money to give up their day jobs – the band needed a loyal and committed manager with industry clout and expertise. Someone who believed in them fully and who had a business track record. A person who could be taken seriously by major record labels. But Leslie wasn't the only reason American Music Club had failed to make progress in industry terms. As Eitzel later reflected:

"A manager represents you, and how do you get someone to represent you when you're four guys who don't give a fuck?"

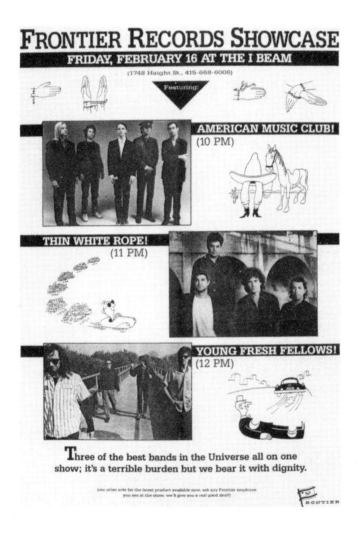

Chapter Seven

Your Basic, Sell-out, 24 track Album

"In matters of grave importance, style, not sincerity, is the vital thing."

Oscar Wilde

"AMC have always managed to snatch defeat from the jaws of victory with tremendous regularity…"

Spike Hyde

Though signing to Alias was a move AMC would later regret, the deal did allow them to complete their album in the record label's in-house studio. However, when they finished recording, Eitzel still wasn't satisfied. During the final sessions, he had written two new songs, "Rise" and "Dead Part of You," – the latter intended originally for Al Stewart! – which he insisted belonged on the record. He felt the record needed them, but Delight at Alias told him there was no budget, and that the album was finished. Eitzel persevered, and eventually hooked up with Norman Kerner at Brilliant Studios who agreed to record a few tracks for free. AMC recorded both new songs in one night together with a version of "The Right Thing." The next day they started mixing. Again, this process would not go smoothly.

Bruce Kaphan did some rough mixes, but Eitzel found them "too plain sounding". It still hadn't quite got the big sound he was looking for. At a loss, he called up Joe Chicarelli, an old friend of Lisa Fancher's, to see if he could help. Fancher had originally tried to get Chicarelli to produce the band, but schedules had never allowed it. Kaphan was furious at this undermining of his work. But Eitzel was adamant about making a "record that could be played on the radio", and thought Chicarelli's experience would help.

Chicarelli had built up an impressive CV, working as engineer on records as varied as Zappa's *Joe's Garage: Acts 1-3*, The *Rocky 4* Soundtrack, *Recently* by

Joan Baez and albums by Poco and Pat Benatar. He'd also produced a number of records including Stan Ridgeway's classic *Mosquitos*.

When Lisa Fancher first mooted the idea of Chicarelli collaborating with AMC, she sent him copies of *Engine* and *California*.

"I listened to them," Chicarelli remembers, "and I just didn't get it initially! I couldn't really hear the songs through the home recording method. Then one day I put on *California*, and I was just blown away by a couple of the songs. I heard through the shoestring recording sound, and, I went, "Oh my God, this guy's songwriting is just fantastic. I called Lisa up and told her, 'I get it. This stuff is really great! I would love to do something with them'."

By now AMC had actually started recording their album themselves. Nonetheless, Chicarelli stressed how keen he was to help the band out in any way he could. Fancher introduced him to Eitzel over cocktails, and they seemed to hit it off. Eitzel subsequently invited Chicarelli to drop into the studio and listen to their initial recordings. "I visited them at The Music Annex," Chicarelli remembers. "It all sounded great, and I made a couple of small suggestions and left it at that."

A month later, on his way to Vancouver, Chicarelli got a call from Mark saying that the band were stuck at the mixing process, and asked him to come and help out.

Chicarelli rapidly rearranged his schedule, and rushed to the studio. He was encouraged by what he heard. "I thought the stuff overall that they had put on tape was really great. It was just a matter of rounding things out. I wanted to put some more stuff in the background of the record, more of a soundscape. I wanted to add some mood and some atmosphere. For me the thing that made AMC work the most, was when there was some degree of tension behind the vocals, whether that comes in Vudi's guitar playing, or some other twisted sound or weird dissonance. When some sound is fighting Mark's vocals, that heightens the emotions for me. So that was something I went for in the mixing."

"Joe completely changed the sound of the record," Eitzel muses, "and mostly he did a great job. What he did with 'Sick of Food' and 'Rise' was great, but he totally fucked up 'Confidential Agent'. He couldn't understand that song at all."

For "Confidential Agent," and "What the Pillar of Salt Held Up," Bruce Kaphan's mixes were retained. Chicarelli's mixes of everything else ended up on the album. Not surprisingly this drove Bruce Kaphan crazy. He'd taken the recording this far, and in his own opinion, he was quite capable of mixing the album himself. Still, Kaphan felt *Everclear*'s production values were a major improvement on previous albums.

As soon as work on *Everclear* was finally completed, Eitzel flew to London to promote the recently released *Songs of Love Live* album. As well as doing more press, he played the Mean Fiddler on May 11th. It was an acoustic show, but this time Eitzel performed as a duo with Dan Pearson on guitar, mandolin and backing vocals.

Again the noise of the Mean Fiddler's drunken regulars started to impinge on the music, and so once more Eitzel tugged the lead from his guitar and sang the last song without his microphone.

"I just hated the audience," Eitzel remembers. "They wouldn't shut up, so I thought, well then, I'm not going to let you hear it, I'm only going to let the people at the front hear it, because they are the only people listening anyway."

The *NME*'s reviewer was especially taken with this moment:

"Eitzel's whole oeuvre is captured in that exposed minute; he's reaching out by retracting himself and at the same time allowing the clamour of the bar to enter his song. His voice is drowned. Real life is providing the soundtrack to his performance. Usually it's the other way round."

On arrival back in San Francisco, Eitzel started to try to straighten out American Music Club. After all the months spent in limbo, he wanted to get their career back on track. The first thing he did was fire Mike Simms and replace him with Tim Mooney. Dan Pearson was initially upset, having grown close to his fellow rhythm section member, but Eitzel was adamant that Mooney was the right drummer for AMC.

Mooney's first show was supporting The Feelies at The Warfield. There had been little time to rehearse the new material.

"It was fun to do," Mooney remembers. "Mark would call out a song that I knew but had never played, and we'd just play it. That was always fun."

AMC followed this show with a short tour that finished at the CMJ seminar in New York.

While things were finally beginning to shape up for the band, they were still without management. When their lawyer Deena Zacharin got a call from her old friend Wally Brill out of the blue, she thought he might be a possible candidate for the job and invited him to come and see AMC play later that night.

Wally Brill had been in the record industry as an engineer, producer and A&R man for nearly 20 years, cutting his teeth as an office assistant for Morris Levy at Roulette records. Levy was one of the major players in the post-War US record business and was also one of the business's most controversial figures. By the 1980s his empire was allegedly worth some $75 million. He was also known to have a lifelong association with the mafia, including the Genovese family. He had put a policeman's eye out in a 1975 brawl, was accused regularly of royalty accounting irregularities and payola, and finally in 1988 was convicted of extortion. In spite of all of this, the industry revered him.

Working for Morris who Wally viewed as his "adopted uncle" was almost an appropriate apprenticeship for the chaos of American Music Club.

When Deena invited him to his first AMC gig, Wally had already heard most of their albums, and liked them, but didn't know anything about the band. Deena insisted he really should see them, and told him they were desperately looking for a manager. Wally wasn't convinced. It was a cold wet day and by the evening it was raining heavily, and he simply didn't want to go out at all. In the end he decided to drop in for an hour, but by the time he arrived, the band were already leaving the stage. Then Eitzel came back on with an acoustic guitar and performed a couple of solo songs.

"Mark played 'Ex-Girlfriend' solo, and I was absolutely devastated," Wally recalls. "I just started to cry. I had never been so touched by anything in my life. It was just extraordinary. Then the band came back on and finished the set. At the end, I turned to Deena and said, 'I have to work with these people.' There was no doubt in my mind, I had to do it."

A week later, Deena set up a meeting between Wally and the band. Wally was horrified at how few albums AMC had sold and how little money they had. He talked about major labels and his contacts in the industry, and told them to give him three months; then they'd see what he was capable of.

The band gave him a bit of a grilling, and while it went fairly well, Wally left convinced that they wanted to go with someone else. After all he didn't have much high profile management experience. However, the next day Deena called him to say he had the job.

"We thought, 'Okay, if you can do, what you say you can do, that is great'," Tim Mooney recalls.

Wally was delighted, but pretty soon he realised the extent of his task.

"AMC had a total miasma of legal paper trails," he remembers with horror. "For nearly ten years, any time anyone shoved a piece of paper in front of the band, they had signed it. So there were all these contracts floating around, and all these involvements, and entanglements. The band's position was always, 'Oh no, we're not tied to anybody.' Except I'd go, 'Well, what about what this says here?' and they'd say, 'Oh, [pause] yeah. Does that mean...? Oh, ok... Well, we're fucked.'"

In an attempt to sort out the legal problems, Wally called his friend Ross Schwarz – a well-known music industry lawyer. Schwarz had a number of big name clients, including Richard Marx, and some members of The Beach Boys. Schwarz already knew the band and liked them.

Considering the level of legal untangling required, and the almost certainly exorbitant fees involved, Wally thought it would be better to have a lawyer on a commission rather than fee basis. He knew Ross was an excellent lawyer, and so invited him to co-manage the band in partnership.

The first thing Wally and Ross did was try and stop *Everclear* from coming out on Alias. He knew Alias had very poor distribution. "Our belief was that it could do a lot better with a different label," Wally explains. Delight Jenkins didn't want to know, and insisted on putting it out. It was a personal thing to her – she loved AMC and wanted to keep them. Wally and Ross were even more horrified to discover that AMC had signed to Alias for at least two albums; as with Frontier, they were convinced they had only signed for one. In the end, even with the considerable help of Ross Schwarz, unravelling the legal tangle surrounding Alias and Grifter would cost AMC in the region of $100,000. But, although they knew they couldn't avoid Alias putting *Everclear* out, they were willing to pay this in order to escape the world of independent labels. The longer AMC spent in record company limbo, the more adamant they had become that they didn't want to carry on the way they had. They decided they would only do a record if they could afford to make it properly, and if it would be supported. Also they decided they wouldn't tour again unless they had enough money to buy a motel room every night. They were just tired of roughing it for endless hours in a ramshackle van and then dossing on people's floors.

In the meantime, while Wally and Ross started courting the major record companies in the US and Europe, AMC flew to the UK to play the Reading Festival.

After warm-up dates in London and Northampton, they headlined the Festival's acoustic tent on the 23rd of August, going on straight after another former Frontier act Thin White Rope. Though it was one of their most important shows to date, the band appeared very much at ease. Eitzel introduced the opening song, "Mom's TV" as "Now I Wanna Be Your Dog," in acknowledgement of Iggy Pop who was playing the main stage. Later he would thank the audience "for missing Iggy." New song "Gratitude Walks," with an opening riff so fragile it sounded like it must be out of tune but wasn't, was the highlight of a majestic set that was rapturously received. "AMC are the highlight of the whole weekend," *Melody Maker*'s reporter concluded. "Total strangers turn to us and tell us so."

"A tent full of Big Black fans are nearly moved to tears by classics like 'Blue and Grey Shirt,' and 'Mom's TV'," a fanzine editor noted, gripped by the oddness of the spectacle.

"It was one of those really scary shows where it's over in about a minute," Eitzel recalls. "Then I went out and saw Sonic Youth, and it was beautiful."

Reading was certainly one of the highlights of AMC's career so far. It was also a weekend where Tim Mooney bumped into an old girlfriend, as Eitzel recalls:

"I was walking around with Tim who used to date Courtney Love, and we came across Courtney, Sonic Youth's bass player, and a couple of other hot rock chicks. Courtney says 'So Tim, how are you doing?' and Tim says, 'I'm fine. I'm playing with American Music Club.' And she goes 'er, oh great'. Then Courtney looked at one of the other girls and laughed, and made Tim feel *that* big."

"That was just strange," Mooney acknowledges. "because Courtney was standing there with Kim from Sonic Youth and Kjat from Babes in Toyland, and it was a weird moment. I felt like the reverse of when guys talk about girls."

The following night AMC played a Dutch festival, and then returned to the US.

Shortly afterwards, the first fruit of the much prolonged *Everclear* sessions were finally revealed to the public with the release of American Music Club's first ever single, "Rise." It was also their most obviously commercial effort to date, featuring an anthemic chorus in a major key, although the circumstances surrounding its conception were far from uplifting.

"I had a friend dying of AIDS," Eitzel explains, "who didn't like any of my songs, and so I said 'OK I'll write a pop song for you'... I wrote it because I thought I'd love to bring in my guitar and play him some songs, but then I found myself wondering what the fuck he was going to get out of that, me coming in and playing him all these quiet, sad songs. He was sick, he already knew that. So I wrote 'Rise' because I was really, really angry about the fact that he was sick."

Eitzel's friend preferred Barbara Streisand. He later died because his health insurance ran out. Aware of the problems in producing an uplifting song for someone in impossible circumstances, Eitzel was quick to question his own motives.

"This song is like me being a complete jerk to somebody who's really sick. It's me saying, 'Go on, rise, maybe what you need is food for your eyes.' But who am I to fucking say that?"

Initially Eitzel felt "Rise" might even be a hit, though he would later dismiss it for being too obvious, having too many choruses, and for sounding like U2. It wasn't one of AMC's better tracks, but it could have fitted comfortably on to a daytime radio playlist.

Excluding a no-budget effort shot by a friend for "Electric Light," "Rise" marked AMC's first foray into rock video. The rarely shown footage features Eitzel in a dunking booth, surrounded by dancing girls in mermaid costumes. As if in penance for having penned such a conventional chorus, every time the word "rise" is sung, he is ducked in the water. The single also featured a slowed down version of "Crabwalk," and Music Annex takes of "Chanel #5" and the pedal steel-laced country rock gem, "The Right Thing." *Melody Maker* made it single of the week.

Two weeks later, after the gestation period of a pachyderm, *Everclear* was finally released. It was immediately clear that the money spent at the Music Annex had not been wasted. AMC had acquired a big sound. Arrangements were richer and much more varied, and, drenched in reverb as it was, it had an atmospheric warmth missing from the Mallon productions. And, in addition to the deeper production, a whole new layer of musical texture is present in the panoramic sound of Bruce Kaphan's other-worldly pedal steel guitar.

"It's your basic, sell-out, 24-track album which costs a lot of money," Eitzel explained to Max Bell. "It isn't doomy or claustrophobic and doesn't have any three-syllable words." It was also American Music Club's third masterpiece.

In press interviews at the time, Eitzel claimed that *Everclear* also marked a change in his approach to songwriting. He was keen to move away from his tragic poet image, and would go out of his way to distance himself from the protagonists of his songs, stressing the artifice involved in his work.

"My new songs aren't about me so much," he told Bob Stanley, "they're funnier, they're more self-consciously 'songwriting' songs. So hopefully nobody will review our next album and say, 'The shocking confessions of Mark Eitzel!' again. That really got on my nerves after a while."

Although later Eitzel confided that this was something of a red herring.

"You just say this kind of shit for interviews. You do interviews, and you sit there for eight hours, and just reel off the first thing that comes into your head.

"I just wanted to avoid analysing the songs for people. They want to know what the song is about, and then they want to psychoanalyse you. They want you to talk you about your problems, and they want to make the interview into some big cathartic event. So I would say, 'These songs are not really about anything real. They are songwriting songs about weird things.' But in fact they were pretty personal songs."

While there is nothing on this new album that is as obviously achingly confessional as the songs on its three predecessors, it is still a record born out of Eitzel's life experiences, rather than a studied exercise in songcraft.

What distinguishes *Everclear* lyrically is that it is set wholeheartedly in the present. A scenario where Eitzel's relationships are disastrous, his hangovers are getting worse, his friends are dying, and he is sick of it all, but can't seem to change a thing. And as he guides the listener through these tales of sickness, heartache and bad luck, drink is the holy fool that comforts and taunts him.

While this record certainly exists in the shadow of the AIDS epidemic which had claimed a number of Eitzel's friends, and is strewn with tales of love lost, alcohol is its dominant thread. Eitzel may be concentrating his art on what WB Yeats called, that murky place "where all the ladders start/ In the foul rag and bone shop of the heart," but, he is still watching from the bar. The album was even named after a horribly potent clear spirit favoured by winos.

But for all this, as with *California*, what is most impressive about *Everclear* is the quality of the songwriting and the playing. From the angry clamour of "Dead Part of You," to the joyous country rock of "Royal Café," and from the haunting, aching sweep of "Why Won't You Stay," to the romp and roll of "Crabwalk," this is a band on a creative roll musically and lyrically. Even the apparently throwaway "Crabwalk" contains some of Eitzel's most deceptively crafted couplets underneath its rollicking humour: *"He reels around the night club like the hub caps of a car / That just crashed into a sign that said, 'This way to the nightclub!'"*

Incidentally, this song's image of a $5,000 country guitar that *"sits at home sad and lonely"* is a riposte to a prolonged heckling AMC got while soundchecking at a bar in Kentucky. The band played a country tune as a sop to the assembled redneck throng, one of whom kept ridiculing Vudi's Stetson hat, and repeatedly yelled "You ain't worth ten cents."

The consolation to a heart-broken friend, "Ex-Girlfriend" and the frighteningly bereft, unresolved and chorus-free "Confidential Agent" are among Eitzel's most moving songs to date. "Ex-Girlfriend" was so close to the bone that the friend who was the subject of the song refused to speak to Eitzel again once it appeared on the album. But, although the opening line, *"your ex-girlfriend told me you were having a bad time,"* lays out the plot, the following lines appear to revert to the narrator's own feelings:

> *Day to day life shouldn't be what it's all about*
> *Day to day life is something we all know too much about*
> *I guess you got no one to take care of you.*

The implication is that the narrator too is still reeling from a similar experience. In this approach, "Ex-Girlfriend" may be more songwriterly than a simple first person exposition, but the honest anguish is no less powerful for it.

Eitzel himself is all too aware that *"bad habits make our decisions for us,"* but it is the line *"You gotta do something, I'll help you try,"* that lies at the song's heart. Like many of *Everclear*'s tales, it is a story of survival.

Like "Ex-Girlfriend," "Royal Café" is a series of extracts from a one-way conversation giving comfort to a friend. But, there the similarity ends. "Royal Café" proves to be AMC's most uplifting moment since "Firefly" – a fact that is particularly interesting considering Eitzel's original solo demo was an extremely slow dirge. Now speeded up and completed with a sparkling guitar riff, it is one of *Everclear*'s high points, and a rebuke to those who would dismiss AMC as doom-mongerers. In concert, Eitzel would rather oddly refer to this as "an early Guns 'n' Roses song," claiming to have heard stolen copies of Axl's early demos. In its subject matter, again it offers solace to someone worried and in pain, but like "Firefly" its spirit is that of carpe dium. While the narrator invites his friend to leave their worries behind and join him in the Royal Café, it is not as a permanent escape into a drunken stupor, simply a break from day to day problems. Drink here is a celebration and solace rather than a permanent escape.

> *Don't worry about anything*
> *Hurry, hurry make sure there's no time*
> *For them to get their claws in us*
> *We'll raise a toast...*
> *At the Royal Café*
> *At the heart of your pain, you got to find a way to survive*
> *At the heart of your pain, you got to find a way to keep alive*
> *Don't worry about the magic kingdom*
> *They wouldn't even let us through the gates...*

Have a drink, the narrator, is saying, it's alright, it's alright, it's alright.

While musically, "Royal Café" is typical of the *Everclear* sessions, in that it has evolved steadily over a two-year period into this final flawless version, "Why Won't You Stay" by contrast was somewhat diminished on its way to the album. Lyrically, the song is another despatch from the frontline of Eitzel's tortured love life.

"It's about this ex-lover of mine," he explains, "crossing the street in traffic, higher than you can believe, and in the CD player was one of my stupid records." Musically, it's also possibly the only track that was better in demo form that on the final album. Somewhere along its evolution a breathtaking Dan Pearson mandolin line was ditched, and its time signature altered for the worse. The song's progress was a cautionary tale in the way it showed that a prolonged period of tinkering would not always produce improvements. It was something they would have done well to bear in mind for the following year.

For all of *Everclear*'s tales of love gone bad, its two pivotal songs return to the central motif of alcohol consumption. Liquor here is a comfort and a taunt. "*Everclear* is underscored with the moods of habitual drinking," critic Nick Johnstone muses, "and whether it's a celebration of rediscovering that giddy drunk recklessness after days of bleak alcoholic maintenance ('Royal Café') or alcohol soaked self-pity ('Jesus' Hands'), Eitzel's lyrics are obviously written within the merry go round of alcohol dependence."

While "Royal Café" offered hope at the bottom of the bottle, "Sick of Food," is *Everclear*'s most powerful evocation of a doomed love affair with bad liquor, as the narrator attempts to come to terms with an inner emptiness he just can't fill: *"I'm sick of food,"* he sings,

> *So why am I so hungry?...*
> *I was sick of love so I just stopped feeling*
> *But I couldn't find anything to take its place...*
> *I'm sick of drink, so why am I so thirsty?*

The protagonist knows that love is the thing that should alleviate these pains, but he feels himself drawn to the alternative of alcoholic oblivion instead. "Sick of Food"'s imagery alludes to the wasting condition of AIDS sufferers, but Eitzel would describe the song as "a tribute" to the tragic anorexic Karen Carpenter.

Still, the image of an unquenchable thirst is the one that remains in this chilling paeon to a self-destructive addiction that cannot be kicked.

"Sick of Food"'s notional sequel is *Everclear*'s closing song, "Jesus' Hands." For all his talk of these songs being "song-writerly," this is the nearest we get to a portrait of the artist in the present as over a swaying, circular shanty-like rhythm, Eitzel croons,

> *Well, I'd like to hang out*
> *But I can tell that you're not a drinking crowd*
> *I got places to go, people to see*
> *I got a thirst that would make the ocean proud....*
> *I'm walking in circles in a waiting room*
> *For a welcome I don't feel in my soul*
> *I watch the time pass, it pours in my glass*
> *I drink it down, blood from a stone...*
> *Looking for love in all the wrong places*
> *The sidewalks and the sky*
> *Looking for something that no one can give me*
> *And no one can help me buy...*
> *Oh brother, oh sister*
> *Don't you see a crack form in the dam?*
> *For a loser, no one can touch him*
> *He's out slipping through Jesus' hands.*

These spine-shivering words have a crisp poetic simplicity rarely seen in popular music. The structure and cadence emphasising how the narrator is trying to walk forward with a metaphorical ball and chain attached to his leg, dragging him around in circles against his will.

Musically, it is interesting that the lushness of *Everclear* followed so quickly on the heels of Eitzel's solo record. On *Songs of Love Live*, the audience could admire the intense clarity of Eitzel's music delivered in all its raw glory straight from the horse's mouth. On songs like "Royal Cafe," "Sick of Food," "Confidential Agent," and "Dead Part of You," we are reminded of what an extraordinary band of musicians made up American Music Club. Eitzel may have honed his writing craft significantly, but the band are playing for their lives.

Both in terms of AMC's career, and Eitzel's end-of-his-tether mental and spiritual state, *Everclear* is the work of a band giving the game one last throw of the dice. "Few albums bristle," Johnstone would conclude, "with this 'last chance' desperation." It was a relief to discover that shortly after *Everclear*'s release, Eitzel temporarily stopped drinking. But, it was even more gratifying to realise that out of the eighteen months of bad tempered adversity, setbacks and disappointments, AMC had produced such an artistic triumph.

As if to underline the fact that *Everclear* was a step away from the dark Mallon era, it came housed in a brightly coloured sleeve featuring an expressionistic Jean Lowe painting of a tiger grasping a small alligator. Lowe was one of Jenny Gonzalvez' oldest friends and Vudi gave her carte blanche with the design.

The other notable factor of the *Everclear* artwork was that Bruce Kaphan was listed as the fifth member of AMC. Even though he had produced the sessions, it was only when he saw the sleeve that Kaphan realised he was actually a member of the band.

On its release, *Everclear* received more praise than any other AMC album in the US. But once again, it was in the UK where the critics would go completely overboard. First of all though, a UK record label had to be found to put the record out. If *Everclear* had been released by Frontier in the US, it would have automatically gone to Demon in the UK. But Delight Jenkins decided the album was worth more than Demon were willing to pay. No one else came in with a better bid and so the responsibility for selling what was arguably American Music Club's most commercial and important album to date, came down to a mixed assortment of small independent distributors and importers.

It is difficult to overstate what a disaster this would be for the band. In the short term, it would also mark the end of AMC's business association with Spike Hyde, thus ridding them off any continuity in the UK. Hyde would have paid whatever price Alias asked to keep American Music Club on Demon, but it was not his decision. He was frustrated by the end of his involvement, but also because he knew it was a bad move for AMC.

Distribution and radio-play were the key factors that Spike Hyde had been working on since the days of *Engine*. Now, to a degree, the band would have to start again. Though not entirely – Hyde's friends in the British music press were still primed and ready, and as soon as they got the chance, praised *Everclear* to the rafters, with nearly all the reviewers noting a more accessible strain.

"*Everclear* is perhaps AMC's finest achievement," Keith Cameron wrote in *NME*, "although that is really like saying which of the Seven Wonders of the World was the most wonderful … Listen and gasp at the awful loveliness of it all." *Q* magazine's four star review saw in the album "a new-found aggression and commercialism that should broaden the growing fan base." *Select*'s reviewer concurred: "*Everclear* is their best work since the truly excellent *California*," and for Andrew Smith it was another "masterpiece."

Predictably, it was early champion Allan Jones, in a near full-page review in *Melody Maker*, who waxed most lyrical. While he acknowledged that "there are definite attempts on *Everclear* to let in a little more light than we may previously have been used to," his closing paragraph, as he quoted from the album's closing track was chilling:

"And finally, this: '*I'm walking in circles in a waiting room for a welcome I don't feel in my soul,*' Eitzel sings on the closing mandolin gloom of 'Jesus' Hands,' and we are back where we began. With a desperate man in search of love. One of us; all of us. Battered, maybe, but eventually fucking heroic."

As soon as *Everclear* was released, AMC prepared for a US and European tour. But Eitzel was determined that this time things would be done differently. Still concerned at the overlap between his artistic image and his actual life, he gave up alcohol – "it changed my life, it was the best thing I ever did" – and made up his mind to distance himself from his work. The songs on *Everclear* may have been personal after all, but he was determined to separate the man from the myth. Ironically considering this, Eitzel's eventual reasons for kicking the bottle were pretty much prefigured in "Sick of Food."

"I'm an alcoholic," he would tell writer Michael Goldberg. "You stop drinking 'cause it stops working for you. It's a drug that stops working for you." Eitzel would promote AMC's liquor-drenched masterpiece, while proclaiming to all and sundry how without alcohol "life is so much better."

But Eitzel was also keen to stop drinking in order to put on a more professional show. It was a pivotal time for AMC, and he began to realise how much of a mixed blessing his truly drunken performances could be: "A lot of people hate that whole thing, and the band kind of think that that is pretty weird too. It was so messy and chaotic. It was just really unsatisfying. There was no support from the band. How can you get that, when you're just this drunken asshole, singing your guts out."

Still, after years of revelling in his drunken, tortured barfly persona, it would not be easy for Eitzel to change overnight. For a significant minority of their fans, Eitzel's stage act was AMC's main attraction. This point was made clear to Eitzel when the band played their second Amsterdam show within the space of a year. At the first show, Eitzel was so drunk and high that he was crawling across the stage, knocking over monitors and mike stands.

"Shameful bullshit," Eitzel admits, cringing at the memory. "Half of it was like an average child, falling over and wanting people to look at you, and half of it was just alcohol abuse."

When Eitzel returned with AMC about twelve months later, completely sober, it was a shock for some members of the audience.

"This huge Dutch football team used to love us," Eitzel says, "and after the show, this seven foot footballer confronted me saying [affects thick Dutch accent] 'You are a fake. You don't care anymore. You come here and you don't sing like you supposed to. You just an asshole, and I fucking hate you.' But the only thing that was different was that I wasn't drunk."

The drink wasn't the only reason for Eitzel's change in his onstage behaviour. The lines between his art and his life were just getting too blurred, and he realised that if night after night, you give your all to the audience, there is very little left for yourself. "People don't understand, that you play these shows and you are so out of your mind, and so high that you can't think anymore, and you get home and spend the whole night staring at the ceiling, going 'What is my life about?'. So, I'd think, who am I doing this for. I don't need to be a rock 'n' roll martyr."

Eitzel told *Melody Maker*'s Andrew Smith shortly after *Everclear*'s release: "I'm not Judy Garland. My songs you can have, but you can't have me... If you lived these songs, they could devastate you, so yeah, I do look for ways out of them. I'm afraid that I'm going to live my songs. It could happen so easily."

The English poet Philip Larkin wrote in 1956, that "I came to the conclusion that to write a poem was to construct a verbal device that would preserve an experience indefinitely by reproducing it in whoever read the poem."

Eitzel had recently reached the same conclusion. "These songs are not easy to sing," he explains. "They are traps. I write them so that every time you sing them, you are invested with the same energy – with the same feeling. Otherwise you are not doing your job."

But, lying in bed after a gig, staring at the ceiling for hours on end, Eitzel started to ask himself, "Is it worth it just to sing a song?" He discovered that Bob Mould would refuse to sing the Hüsker Dü track "Too Far Down" in concert, because in singing it, he would literally get too far down.

It became a huge dilemma for Eitzel, because he saw the toll that his strength of feeling was taking on him, but on the other hand this emotional honesty was what he liked to see in other performers..

This whole issue prompted writer Andrew Smith to recall a conversation he had with Greil Marcus:

"We were talking about Kurt Cobain and Richey James, and Greil had this theory, about what he calls 'The Folk Virus.' He told me the difference between folk and pop is that in folk when you say 'I really mean it, man,' you do mean it, and the audience know you mean it. Whereas in pop when someone says 'I really mean it, man,' like the Sex Pistols for instance, the audience think, 'No you don't, you're being ironic.' Greil had this theory that every now and again, this Folk Virus comes into pop and infects it. The artists start to think that they need to feel what they are singing all the time. And the audience come to feel that the artists have to mean it, and have to be real. Otherwise they are fakes and we shouldn't give them the time of day. Mark is like that.... Most performers have some armour, some kind of protective shell, and Mark doesn't have it, and he doesn't want it."

But now Eitzel was beginning to appreciate the need for protection.

"I'd rather be capable of writing songs about dying in bars," he confessed to Ralph Traitor, "rather than actually dying in a bar."

On *Everclear*'s release, in spite of the rave reviews, initial sales were no improvement on the Mallon albums. Very few stores had the record in stock due to slipshod UK distribution, and outside of the review pages in the music press, it did not make much of a splash in the media. The mainstream national press all but ignored it, and radio-play was once again non-existent.

Also, for all the ballyhooing in their album reviews, the music press would not commit to put AMC on their cover. An *NME* or *MM* cover may have forced a wider audience to pay attention, but the editors were worried about the effect of leading with someone so unhip. Even super fan Allan Jones could not get them an all important cover feature. Andrew Smith had to fight to get space in *Melody Maker* for a reasonably sized editorial interview.

"I know Allan [Jones] was the editor," Smith explains, "but at the weekly Tuesday editorial we had to reach an element of consensus [about what we would feature], and particularly about what went on the cover. And above all Allan Jones and Steve Sutherland had to agree. Sutherland never had any time for AMC, and while he didn't say that we couldn't write about them, he would never have allowed them to go on the cover...

"When we allocated space for a two-page spread at the time of *Everclear*, I can remember Sutherland saying in the editorial meeting, 'Why are we giving this band so much space? It's only Jones and Andrew Smith that cares about this band?' Then Everett True said 'Well, actually I really like American Music

Club,' and then Matt Smith said, 'I really care about them too,' and then every-one else round the table said that they liked the band, so we got the feature. But they could never have gone on the cover. Steve Sutherland would not have allowed it."

Ross and Wally took the rave reviews to all of the major labels in the US, and managed to entice a number of executives to see the band in concert, but initially they had no luck. Ross Schwarz told a journalist later, "They basically all said, 'This is maybe the most brilliant act we've seen in years, but we don't know what to do with them. We got passes everywhere." The feedback from major labels in the UK was initially more positive, but still no one seemed willing to put their money where their mouth was.

After a few US shows, AMC spent the rest of the year doing press and rehears-ing in Jellyfish's Indian Basin studio in between holding down their day jobs. The Alias deal had left little money over for living expenses. Their last show of the year was supporting Billy Bragg at an AIDS charity event in San Francisco.

Come December 1991, *Melody Maker* voted *Everclear* its eighth best album of the year, and *Hot Press* in Ireland made it ninth. But as AMC prepared for their next tour, they still hadn't managed to get a major label to make them an offer. Eitzel was starting to tell journalists that if Ross and Wally couldn't get AMC a major deal, he'd quit the band. Somehow, from somewhere, they badly needed a break.

Chapter Eight

Then It Really Happens

As 1991 drew to an end, Wally and Ross continued courting the major labels. In direct contrast to Leslie Mallon's aggressive hit and miss tactics, AMC's new management were at least given a hearing by the record companies' senior executives.

Mick Griffiths, AMC's UK booking agent explains, "The thing Wally was good at was schmoozing senior record company people in America – this is an art form. He had Irving Azoff's ear. People of Azoff's level would call him back. He got a lot of respect because he was a producer, and because he'd worked for A&M for a long time too…. He was chatting to all of the major US players – Azoff's Giant Records, Warners, David Geffen and the rest."

Oddly it was Irving Azoff, one of the record industry's most controversial power brokers who would prove pivotal. To say that Azoff's reputation came before him, is a huge understatement. Fredric Dannen, in his excellent study of money, power and corruption in the US record industry, *Hitmen*, described Azoff as "more ruthless than [David] Geffen, probably more powerful, and even shorter."

Known in the industry as the "poison dwarf," the five foot Azoff made his first fortune managing The Eagles, Jackson Browne, Steely Dan and Heart. In 1983 he took command of MCA records, turned it around, and went on to become one of the industry's top label bosses. A loud and fast-talking dealmaker who liked to trade favours with friends and humiliate and abuse his enemies, according to Dannen, Azoff was, "easily one of the most loathed men in the music business." Famous for his intimidatory tactics, Azoff once sent an industry rival a birthday present of a gift-wrapped live boa constrictor, and when dissatisfied with the speed of waiter service was known to set light to his menu to get attention.

By now Azoff was president of his own Giant label. Wally Brill got a tape of *Everclear* to him through some A&R contacts at the company, and Azoff took it on a skiing holiday that January. Azoff put it on his walkman out on the slopes and fell in love with it. He listened to it every day for the rest of the trip. As Ross would later tell a *Rolling Stone* reporter, this was "the crack in the dam." The mere fact that Azoff was interested immediately pushed up the value of American Music Club overnight. On Azoff's return, things started to finally happen.

"I also had a relationship with Azoff's co-president at Giant, Charlie Minor." Wally Brill recalls, "Charlie was an ex-head of promotions at A&M US, who was later shot dead by a prostitute."

"I hadn't seen Charlie in five years, and he called me up and went, [Wally affects Jive-style accent] 'Hi, … it's Chaaarlieee. Listen, I'm, sitting here with Irving, and we're listening to this American Music Club stuff, and we just want you to know we're going to write any numbers you want on this here cheque. We just gonna put any ole goddamn numbers you want. We gonna give you so much fuckin' money, you just gonna be swimmin' in fuckin' money.' And I was like, 'Ok… but ….'

"Both Ross and I knew Irving from before, and Irving was wonderful. He said to us, 'Whether or not you come along with me, I will at least drive the price up for the other people, and fuck 'em that way'."

Wally and Ross were ecstatic that they had finally made a breakthrough. The only problem was that they knew Eitzel was going to have difficulty dealing with some of Giant's more gung-ho record men. Wally explains,

"We knew Mark wasn't going to get along with Charlie, although he did like Irving, and one of the A&R guys. But Giant also made one fatal mistake. They took Mark out to lunch at the Royalton in New York, and the A&R guy insisted on showing Mark his room because he was so thrilled by the Jacuzzi and how cool all the stuff was. It was entirely the wrong vibe for Mark Eitzel. Mark just went, 'God, do I really have to deal with these people?'"

In spite of these misgivings, Wally and Ross vigorously pursued the Giant deal. AMC had made it clear they wanted to escape the indie treadmill – they were sick of not being able to pay rent, and tired of making records that would not be properly distributed. Giant may not have been the perfect fit, but Azoff was bandying about huge sums of money, and his label had excellent nationwide distribution.

Wally, Ross and the band flew up to Los Angeles at Giant's expense to try and finalise the deal. Azoff's label ensured that the party were met by limousines and given the full VIP treatment..

"Hollywood is Hollywood," Bruce Kaphan muses, "but it was a new level of oddity… It was almost a caricature of itself."

On arrival the AMC party were greeted by a multitude of effusive besuited executives who repeatedly enquired after the quality of their flights. After hand shakes and more small talk, the band were ushered into a vast boardroom, with blotters and water tumblers at each place setting. Azoff arrived last and fixed each member of the band in his gaze for a few seconds before beginning his pitch:

"I love you guys and I love your record," he intoned with missionary zeal. Then he asked them, "Do you want to be number one? Do you want to be number one? Because if you do, I'm gonna make you number one." Azoff offered the band their own label within Giant, and was in the process of displaying other tantalising riches, when there was an interruption at the door. Azoff's son was outside, and only ten minutes into the meeting, Irving excused himself to go and play tennis with the boy, handing over the proceedings to a junior executive. Tim Mooney remembers: "It was strange, Azoff was nice enough to us, but there was that feeling that this could get scary. But, it wasn't so much Azoff. The other people in the meeting didn't seem very enthusiastic about us. They were just there for the meeting."

Still, Wally and Ross made it clear to Azoff's deputy that AMC were keen, and as the band flew out to the UK to prepare for a European tour, it appeared that all that remained was to go through the contracts and then sign on the dotted line. But now that Azoff had shown a firm interest, Wally and Ross started to get enthusiastic approaches from a number of other major US labels. Finally the critics' favourites were getting noticed by the commercial world.

In direct contrast to the champagne and limousine lifestyle glimpsed at Giant's Hollywood headquarters, by the second week of 1992, AMC were rehearsing in a small damp studio in the north England city of Leeds, sharing two rooms in their engineer's house. It was a cold winter, and the set-up was exactly the kind of indie arrangement the band were trying to leave behind, so morale was not good.

"I have memories of being up in the third-floor room with no heat and a terrible migraine," Tim Mooney recalls with a shudder, "It was bleak." Mooney had lost his day job at the *San Francisco Bay Guardian* after repeated prolonged periods of absence. For his employers, AMC's forthcoming tour was a tour too far. In Leeds, Mooney was cold, tired and stressed. Throughout the tour his migraines would recur when he was least able to deal with them.

On 21st January 1992 at Reading University, AMC began what was arguably their most important European tour to date. With Bruce Kaphan augmenting their live sound, and Giant's interest giving them a new confidence, it was one of their best shows during their most accomplished series of dates yet. Britain had waited a long time to see AMC's full line up again, and for a year or so it appeared that the band might never return to these shores. Eitzel's solo album and its surrounding publicity had helped add to the AMC myth – the best band in the world who somehow had lost their record deal, and were on the verge of tragically splitting up. Even in the quiet Berkshire town of Reading, AMC were greeted like returning heroes.

That night and throughout the UK leg of the tour, the audiences were primed and receptive. Night after night they would call out for songs from across the breadth of the AMC back catalogue, and every time Eitzel would smile, shrug and then come out with a derogatory quip at the expense of his song, nod to the band and in spite of the set list at his feet, launch into the request. He seemed incapable of ignoring any audience comment, whether heckle or encouragement, and seemed genuinely to be thriving off the audience's fervour.

"[Playing live] is a reactive process," Eitzel would say, "you react to the crowd. You stand there and you try to bring the moment to them."

"The music was about communication," Pearson explains, "about give and take with the audience. I think the audience gave us as much as we gave them. There was real interchange.

"You'd go and see a regular show and people would move around a bit. Then at our shows there would be girls down the front weeping. It was fascinating, but how could you explain that to someone like your parents. 'Our shows are great. There were 20 girls crying last night'."

But for all the heartrending moments, it is difficult to overstress how uplifting and joyous these shows actually were. The band were at the top of their game, and the crowds revelled in it.

At Reading, as the band took to the stage to a huge round of applause, Eitzel chided the audience jokily, "Don't clap. You haven't heard the new songs yet."

But the new songs, even scattered amongst a set of highlights from *Engine, California,* and *Everclear,* were stunning. It appeared that the next album would be AMC's finest work.

In between nearly every song, Eitzel told jokes about his balding pate, his mountain bike, and his band's unhip appearance. Pointing to his new guitar amp, he claimed to be now targeting the youth market. Going with the early 90s zeitgeist look, Eitzel had also now grown himself a goatee beard. It would later give him plenty of comedy potential.

Of the new songs, the highlights were the surreally named, "What Godzilla Said to God When He Found That His Name Was Not in the Book of Life," – an expanded take on "Nothing Can Bring Me Down" from *Songs of Love Live* – and the magical "Gratitude Walks," complete with spine-tingling guitar and pedal steel riffs and powerful Dan Pearson backing vocals.

Other great new songs included the rumbustious "Keep Me Around," – Eitzel: "we have a rock song now" – and the fragile "The Hopes and Dreams of Heaven's 10,000 Whores." "Apology for an Accident," was an overwhelming tour de force that allowed Eitzel to let go all restraint. As the song's ebb and flow reached a climax, he was screaming, spitting and shaking, his feet tangled up in his guitar lead and microphone cables. He clutched the mike stand for dear life as Bruce's pedal steel reached overdrive and Vudi's guitar went mental. It was a level of intensity, reminiscent of early versions of "Pale Skinny Girl," that could never be captured on record.

In the lull that followed, Eitzel introduced "Ex-Girlfriend" as their "big '70s number" and reminisced mendaciously about hanging out backstage with Steely Dan and Status Quo. As with all of AMC's best shows, the crowd didn't know whether to laugh or cry. Then a crowd-pleasing "Firefly" swung like never before, with the pedal steel, much higher in the mix than on record, really lifting off.

It was immediately clear that Bruce Kaphan's full time presence had changed the band. His pedal steel glued the disparate elements together, and when things fell apart, they didn't fall apart as much as they used to. The relatively free and easy nature of the band was good for Kaphan too. "It was a tailor made opportunity for me," he explains, "to explore a whole bunch of stuff with the pedal steel, that I'd never have had the opportunity to do otherwise." Kaphan would play

Midi from his pedal steel, and add electronic treatments that would add to the maelstrom effect of Vudi's guitar work.

During the Reading show Eitzel regularly interrupted the band's set to apologise for some imagined error or imperfection. This annoyed *Melody Maker*'s Caren Myers enough to take Eitzel to task on the issue. The apologetic singer promised rather unconvincingly that he would not apologise again.

"I just don't understand why you do it," Dan Pearson complained. "Why say 'Sorry' when 'thank you' would suffice?"

"But I'm not thankful; I'm sorry," Eitzel replied.

Wally and Ross caught up with the tour at Birmingham and brought the band up to date with the British record deal situation. The buzz about AMC generated by Azoff's Giant label had spread to the UK, and a number of labels were now vying for the signature of a previously unsignable band. With the shows garnering rave reviews everywhere, it felt like things were taking shape. The only problems were Tim Mooney's worsening migraines, and the total absence of *Everclear* in record stores in the towns AMC were playing.

One of the tour's odd treats came at the Psychic Pig in Bath, when after a bravura performance, Eitzel made it clear that he was not coming back for a second encore, in spite of unabating calls from an insistent crowd. Enjoying the reception, Vudi stepped up to the mike and sang a country and western number that was either the Merle Haggard song he said it is, or one of his own more country-tinged songs. Inspite of what *Select* magazine said later about a makeshift under-rehearsed finale, this informal performance was warm and engaging, and it felt like AMC were making an effort to thank the audience somehow while revelling in the pleasure of playing together in front of such a receptive crowd.

The UK leg of the tour climaxed on the 31st of January at the University of London Students' Union in front of a sold-out audience of 1,000. That night the crowd included nearly every rock journalist and record company A&R man in town. It was a crucial gig for the band, but by the time of the soundcheck, Eitzel's longstanding throat infection was back with a vengeance, and he started to lose his voice. By the evening, his throat was giving him a lot of pain, and he was rushed to a specialist just an hour before showtime.

When he finally went out on stage with the band, Eitzel explained that he had just come back from an emergency clinic because he had contracted laryngitis.

"So if any gobs of pus come up," he added smiling, "it's just part of the show." After suggesting that his Flowers Balsam throat remedy might make a suitable tour sponsor for AMC, he went straight into a softly crooned "What The Pillar Of Salt," and his voice sounded fine. While Eitzel never really stretched his voice to the limit throughout the performance, it was a good set, and the crowd – which included a lot of first-time witnesses to the AMC live experience – were rapturous. At one point a girl at the front even fainted and had to be lifted up onto the stage – a rock and roll moment that one would not normally associate with American Music Club.

Later during a moving rendition of "Last Harbor," Eitzel suddenly stopped in mid-verse in order to hack a deep long cough, before spitting a big gobbet of phlegm across the stage. He laughed, traded quips with the audience, and then resumed the unbearably moving song as if he'd never stopped.

Because of his throat problems, AMC restricted the number of encores they played that night. After departing once, they returned to the stage, picked up their instruments and Eitzel, while strapping on his guitar, walked to the front and addressed the crowd.

"What's dumber than rock music?" he asked them, and without a pause, answered his own question. "Rock musicians! What's dumber than rock musicians? Rock singers! What's dumber than rock singers? Rock song-writers! This is the dumbest song I ever wrote." A truly visceral surge through "Bad Liquor" followed. Then they were gone. "By the end, I had no voice," Eitzel remembers, "I couldn't even talk."

In spite of the problems, it was a winning performance, though not one of AMC's most transcendent. Still, the press reaction was again extremely positive, with *Melody Maker*'s Paul Mathur pronouncing that "the AMC experience is curiously uplifting, a spiritual purge that somehow lifts the heart."

The record company interest continued to grow. Throughout January, Wally and Ross had meetings with Warners Brothers UK, China, London, Phonogram, and EMI. But, by the time of the ULU show, they had decided that they would sign to Virgin – joining a roster that included Janet Jackson and the Rolling Stones. Wally had a longstanding good relationship with Ashley Newton, Virgin's head of A&R and also with Paul Conroy, Virgin's overall president who Wally knew from the days when Conroy was at Stiff Records.

The band met the Virgin team, and they were impressed with their knowledge and genuine enthusiasm. While some might say AMC would have been better on a good UK indie like 4AD, Wally was adamant that the band signed to a label that, in addition to knowledge and good relationships, were sufficiently international in outlook to liase with whoever AMC signed to in the US.

Only Bruce Kaphan experienced mixed feelings when he first met Virgin's A&R team: "Paul Conroy took me to one side and put his arm around me, and said, 'Ah, pedal steel. The kiss of death'."

There was a sense of unreality about the band's new found popularity. Within a couple of months, AMC had gone from indie hopefuls, to within a few negotiating points of signing to Virgin in the UK and Giant in the US. As they headed off for the European leg of the tour, they left Wally and Ross happily sorting through the finer detail of these deals. Then after low key shows in Denmark, AMC's progress took another bizarre turn.

The band were sitting in their hotel rooms in Hamburg, killing time before sound checking at the Markethalle, when Mark Terrill, their road manager for this tour, came in waving a copy of *Rolling Stone*. The best-selling rock magazine in the world had voted Mark Eitzel Songwriter of the Year for 1991 and singled out *Everclear* as one of the year's best five albums. AMC's rarely heard commercial failure was lined up next to Nirvana's era-defining grunge masterpiece *Nevermind*, REM's major breakthrough *Out of Time*, U2's *Achtung Baby* and Guns 'n' Roses' twin releases, *Use Your Illusion 1 and 2*. *Everclear* was the only album in the list that was not yet multi-platinum. To date it had sold approximately 10,000 copies.

While *Rolling Stone* is the world's best-known rock journal, by the 1990s it had become more of a lifestyle magazine. When it did cover music, it was seen as a mouthpiece for the mainstream. It was not a magazine that Eitzel respected, and now almost immune to critical acclaim, he was not initially very impressed.

"It's a drag," he explained to a journalist at the time. "Yeah I'm songwriter of the year for 1991; a month later I'm still songwriter of the year and still no-one comes to see us play".

"It made me feel really good," Eitzel admitted to Michael Goldberg. "But for the next show there were about 20 people in the audience. And they were army guys and they thought American Music Club were some righteous American freedom-fighting, cool ass Springsteen-influenced Guns 'n' Roses kind of guys. And we did not rock".

"They didn't know we'd made 'one of the best records of the year'," Tim Mooney added, "and that he was the 'best songwriter'."

"They couldn't give a fuck about that shit" Eitzel concluded, "and they certainly didn't agree."

But Eitzel completely underestimated the power of *Rolling Stone*. Bruce Kaphan was more familiar with the commercial workings of the industry. "As far as I am concerned," he opines, "that was the one pivotal event in the history of that band."

Record company interest in the band had continued to grow ever since Irving Azoff's brush with *Everclear* on the ski slopes, but once the *Rolling Stone* poll hit the newsstands, things went ballistic. Every record company executive who read the best album list would notice that AMC were the only band featured on an independent label, and thus ripe for picking. Also, the profile of AMC's Tom Mallon-era albums was so low, that for all intents and purposes, *Everclear* was their debut record. They were a hot new attraction. Suddenly, the phone at the band's hotel started ringing, and for days it barely stopped. In the end Bruce Kaphan took it off the hook.

"Things happened very fast for us right around then," Tim Mooney recalls with a smile.

The only foreseeable complication was that Alias wanted to keep the band and had a contract for at least one more AMC album. But as if they were in any doubt about leaving, the performance of Alias with *Everclear* after the *Rolling Stone* poll made things extremely clear.

A lot of labels would have immediately printed another 100,000 copies and put them out with stickers listing the *Rolling Stone* plaudits – even if they had to borrow money to do so. Alias could have also immediately released another single. Radio may have been receptive to the band because of the *Rolling Stone* interest, and there were songs on *Everclear* that radio could have played. But the album was just not out in the stores in any real quantities. In most stores it wasn't there at all.

Ironically when AMC did sign a major label deal, Alias got $110,000 for their troubles. Alias claimed this was the amount they were out of pocket on the band, but as the album actually only cost $50,000, it was far from clear to the band- where the rest of the money went. In spite of its huge acclaim, *Everclear* was yet another AMC album that would fail to produce a royalty cheque.

In retrospect Wally believed they should have buried the *Everclear* record. It should have been re-worked slightly, and then been released as the first Virgin and Warners release. "I believe 'Ex-Girlfriend' would have been the hit single," he explains. "It would have done the job. That record was there and ready to go, and it was the bloody mindedness of Delight Jenkins that she wouldn't let it go to a company that could do something with it."

At the time though, things were moving forward so quickly, that the band were much busier thinking about the next album, and the label it would come out on.

Desperate to avoid being outbid at the last minute, Virgin's executives flew out with their lawyers to meet the band at the next stop on their tour in Italy. The deal was signed then and there.

"It was good timing," Tim Mooney recalls, "because a lot of us didn't have dayjobs to go back to." The tour was nearing an end, and though huge sums were being discussed daily for the band's signature, none of the band had any money whatsoever.

"We were ecstatic," Dan Pearson remembers. "After ten years playing in a band and doing day jobs, you suddenly didn't have to go to work the next day. How exciting is that? It was amazing."

Virgin even came up with a small immediate cash advance.

"The managers got us £100 each from Virgin," Mooney laughs, "so we all got to go shoe shopping."

After one more date in mainland Europe, AMC came back to play a sold-out show at the 600-capacity Clapham Grand theatre in South London. Most of Virgin Records' London office turned out to witness the company's hot new signing.

"The atmosphere was great," Orla Lee from Virgin remembers, "We were really filled with hope. A lot of the people really believed in them." But, *Melody Maker*'s Allan Jones had reservations:

"Paul Conroy brought everyone from Virgin down by coach, from marketing people to office girls. It was great to see Conroy so enthused, but you could see that the people at Virgin didn't have a clue what to do with a band like AMC."

Virgin also invited every music journalist in town, and as word of AMC's Virgin deal had not yet filtered out to the industry, the theatre was also packed with hopeful A&R men.

"Derek Green from China Records came up to me at the Clapham Grand show," Wally recalls, "and said, 'Wal, if some fucker could put a bomb in here tonight, they could eliminate every cunt in the record business.' It was true."

In spite of a problematic stage sound, it was a good show. In between the songs, Eitzel had a tremendous rapport with the crowd, who were constantly calling out requests. The Grand Theatre had a huge stage, and Eitzel repeatedly joked how next time AMC would make full use of it like a proper rock band:

"We'll have ramps around the stage. I'll wear a track suit and I'll run back and forwards. I'll be full of passion and I'll really mean it. I just need a long frock overcoat." Every so often, he'd fall down on one knee holding his guitar out to one side, and contorting his face into a look of anguish – pulling what he would call "a rock shape." The show could easily have descended into a tiresome paro-

Top: AMC's first photo shoot, 1984.
(l-r) Vudi, Brad Johnson, Mark Eitzel,
Dan Pearson, Matt Norelli.
Photo: courtesy of Mark Terrill

Bottom left: Opening for Sonic Youth in
Hamburg 1985. *Photo: Mark Terrill*

Bottom right: Eitzel and Vudi back-
stage at the Markthalle, after the Sonic
Youth show, Hamburg, 1985.
Photo: Mark Terrill

Rehearsing in Hamburg, 1985. Clockwise from top left:
Mark Eitzel, Matt "Sluggo" Norelli, Vudi, Brad Johnson, Dan Pearson. *Photos: Mark Terrill*

Top left: Dan Pearson, circa 1985.
Photo: Mark Terrill

Top right: Eitzel and Brad Johnson in Hamburg, 1985.
Photo: Mark Terrill

Middle left: Tom Mallon and Dan Pearson on tour in the US, 1986.
Photo: Mark Terrill

Middle right: AMC in San Francisco, 1987.
Photo: Mark Terrill

Bottom: Mark Eitzel, 1985/86.
Photo: Tom Erikson

Opposite page:
Top: On tour in Holland, 1989.
Photo: Mark Terrill
Middle: In Copenhagen, 1989. (l-r)
Tom Mallon, Mark Eitzel, Mike Simms,
Dan Pearson, Vudi. *Photo: Mark Terrill*
Bottom: Broken down in Norway,
1989. *Photo: Mark Terrill*

This page, left: Somewhere in
Denmark 1988/89 (l-r) Tom Mallon,
Lisa Davis, Vudi, Dan Pearson, Mark
Eitzel. *Photo: Mark Terrill*
Below: MarkEitzel, 1989.
Photo: Lisa Fancher
Bottom: (l-r) Mark Eitzel, Tom Mallon
(now on bass), Vudi.
Photo: Tom Erikson

ANAL
ANIMAL
BI-LOVE
BIG BUST

BONDAGE
CANING
ENEMA
FAUST

FLOGGING
HE-SHE
KAVIAR
LEATHER

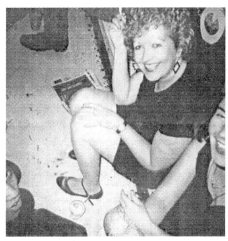

Top left: Mark Eitzel and Spike Hyde, Brentford, Oct 1989.
Photo: Bleddyn Butcher

Top right: Lisa Fancher. *Photo: MCA*

Bottom left: Eitzel at the time of *United Kingdom,* 1989.
Photo: Phil Nicholls

Bottom right: Mark Terrill on tour in the US.
(Courtesy of Mark Terrill)

Opposite page: *Everclear* UK tour, Jan 1992. (l-r) Bruce Kaphan, Dan Pearson, Tim Mooney, Mark Eitzel, Vudi. *Photo: Phil Nicholls*

Top: Mark Eitzel and Vudi in London's Hyde Park, 1994. *Photo: Phil Nicholls*

Middle: Clodhopper (l-r) Tim Mooney, JC Hopkins, Dan Pearson, Joe Goldring, Tim Bierman. *Photo: courtesy of Dan Pearson.*

Bottom: Mark Eitzel and Peter Buck. *Photo: Tom Erikson.*

dy, but while the audience was still laughing at some quip or joke, the band would move straight into an AMC classic.

Afterwards, the band were optimistic about their future, and it showed. Eitzel, embarrassed at literally talking down to his fans from the elevation of the stage, clambered down into the crowd. But, shocked at being instantly engulfed by enthusiastic fans with pressing questions, he upped and ran to the safety of the venue's toilets. He re-appeared later, but it was clear that he was going to have problems adjusting to the band's rising status.

The next day, Virgin's A&R team took Wally, Ross and the whole band out to dinner at a local Indian restaurant. The restaurant had the BBC Top 40 countdown playing in the background, and all of the Virgin staff were listening attentively and making comments on this and that artist. The band started to realise what they had got into.

"I just remember listening to the Top 40," Bruce Kaphan remembers, "and hearing these folks from Virgin talk about us having a hit, while thinking, 'What in the world is going on here? How do they think what we do is going to fit into what I'm hearing here?' It was not that I didn't think Mark was capable of writing a hit song. But, hits have to do with timeliness – doing the right thing at the right time – and what we were doing was not part of the hit fabric of the time. That was the first time that the expectation of us trying to get a hit reared its ugly head."

But the upside of the Virgin deal also became immediately apparent. On their way back to the States, AMC flew with Virgin Airlines, and on embarkation found themselves upgraded to business class. On AMC's return to San Francisco, the band and their management set out to finalise their US record deal. Wally and Ross were happy with Giant, but the band had misgivings. Warner Brothers were now keen to sign AMC, so Wally and Ross set up a meeting.

When AMC arrived at Warners HQ, it was immediately clear that this was a different set-up from Giant. The whole thing had a much better "vibe." All of the Warners senior management showed up – including industry legends Lenny Waronker and Michael Ostin. Eitzel and the other AMC members were impressed that not only had these people heard every single AMC album, they had also attended a number of their recent shows.

The band also quickly warmed to the easygoing, informal approach of the Warners executives. Waronker himself was sitting sideways in his chair with his legs hanging under the arm. For a while, the two parties just talked music – mulling over the wonders of Van Morrison and Smokey Robinson. It was much less industry-like than Giant, and in Bruce Kaphan's words, it felt "really homey and nice." Eitzel also loved the fact that "there was no bullshit," and they were all impressed by how much Warners appeared to want to sign American Music Club.

"Warners has such a long history of supporting artists," Tim Mooney explains, "so just to be sitting there, realising that Neil Young had been on this same label forever, and that Van Morrison was also there – people who didn't always sell a lot of records, but who were allowed to do their best work."

Even after this meeting, the management still favoured Giant. Azoff after all had been the first label executive to go out on a limb for AMC, and Ross and Wally had made it clear to him that the band were going to sign to Giant. But, the band had made up their minds to got to Warners.

The band then braced themselves for an angry reaction from Azoff, who they had effectively "betrayed." Oddly considering his reputation, nothing happened.

"Irving was one of those guys that plays the game," Wally explains. "Totally professional. He was like, 'Well, what the fuck. Whatever. Next One.' He said, 'Well I helped drive the price up. If I can't get the act, at least I can make some-one else pay too much money for them'."

Azoff was probably right. The deal being discussed for the US alone was now in the region of $500,000. AMC would have to sell a lot of records to recoup.

Having mistakenly lumped his publishing in with everything else back in the Grifter Records era, Eitzel made sure that song publishing was excluded from the terms of both the Virgin and Warners deals. He wanted to negotiate an independent deal for his writing. Now that his songwriting had been specifically singled out by *Rolling Stone*, the value of Eitzel's publishing went through the roof.

A number of offers were made, and after some discussions Eitzel favoured a worldwide arrangement with Polygram. Eitzel, Wally and AMC's UK lawyer, music industry specialist Nick Pedgrift travelled to Polygram's West London head quarters to thrash out the terms.

After handshakes and small talk, Eitzel's party took their seats opposite Polygram's senior management in the main boardroom. Polygram's senior executive then confirmed their offer of a six-figure sum. Eitzel and Wally were impressed. Then out of the blue, Pedgrift announced, "Of course Mark will be co-writing Bob Dylan's next album." At which point Eitzel did his best not to spit his coffee across the table. This was news to him. He exchanged nervous glances with Wally. There had been rumours that Dylan's people wanted him to do a song, but it was only a rumour. Still Pedgrift appeared supremely confident, and as discussions between him and the Polygram executives continued, the offer on the table got larger and larger. Eventually the meeting broke for a brief recess.

Outside in the corridor, Eitzel collared Wally:

"What do we do? What do we do?" Wally didn't know, and asked Eitzel what he thought. Eitzel said he didn't know either. They discussed coming clean about the Dylan thing, but there had been a huge increase in the offer. This was a lot of money. In the end they agreed to keep quiet, and the deal was done at the much higher sum.

As far as Wally was concerned, Pedgrift simply made the most of a bona fide position.

"It was one of those things that Nick would say tongue in cheek," he explains. "Someone had suggested that maybe Mark should co-write something with Bob Dylan and Nick just took this the next step up. That's the way these things are done. Nick is a master at that…

"I think it was in everyone's best interests to keep schtum. If I were Polygram, and someone was to tell me Mark Eitzel is writing Bob Dylan's next album, I would certainly check before making that deal. But I think that Nick had whipped up such a frenzy, and there was so much fear that the deal would go somewhere else that people didn't make the requisite checks." When the dust later settled, it became obvious that, regardless of his potential, Eitzel had been signed for an exorbitantly inflated sum. A couple of weeks later Eitzel was back at Polygram HQ to go through a number of unrelated issues when he bumped into one of the senior executives in the foyer.

Executive: "Hey, Mark. How are you doing? How's Bob."

Mark: "Bob who?"

Executive [walking off]: "Exactly. Bob fucking who?"

But, by the time Polygram realised how flimsy the Dylan rumour had been, the deal was already signed. Eitzel would be still living off his publishing advance five years later.

Once the publishing deal was done, Eitzel had to decide how much of the money to share with the other members of AMC. Unsure of his ground, he asked the only person he knew well who had experience of these matters – Tom Mallon.

According to Eitzel, Mallon told him he could do anything he wanted with the money, he could keep it all, but that the normal approach was to split it 50:50 into a songwriter's share and a band's share. The band's share would then be divided up equally between all the band members, including Eitzel. This all seemed fine.

"So I did the normal thing," Eitzel explains. "I always do the normal thing. Controversy then arose when Eitzel divided the money only between current band members. He'd tried to sort things out so that Mallon would get some bene-fit, but had found it impossible to negotiate with Tom and Leslie. So, Tom Mallon received nothing. Eitzel believes Mallon then proceeded to bad mouth him to the other band members. "I never did rip him off," he protests. "All he had to do was return some phonecalls, which he never did. He never returns calls. That's why, to this day, Tom has at least 30 reels of tape from the early *Everclear* sessions that no one will ever hear."

Eitzel believes Mallon's criticism of him as "That asshole Eitzel who took everyone's money" really harmed the band – especially once some money finally started to roll in – but he is adamant that he did nothing wrong.

"When we first got the publishing deal, just because ... I gave Vudi and Danny $30,000 each, in cash, of my advance, as a gift. I don't think I was ungenerous."

Not surprisingly, Pearson and Vudi believed this was no more than they deserved.

After all the struggles to take things up to the next level, it quickly became clear that the transition from indie losers to successful rock 'n' roll band on a major label, was not going to be an easy one.

Chapter Nine

Somewhere Along The Line I Lost My Nerve

"I could have imagined them doing something like REM, up to a point. But they were always different because of Eitzel. He has got a self-destruct button that is very easy to press. And when he gets in a situation when he feels insecure, his first impulse is to run, or to think, 'Fuck it then, I'm gonna destroy it.' Then he's got security that he doesn't have to deal with it anymore."

Andrew Smith

In April 1992, during the calm that followed the storm of the *Rolling Stone* acclaim and resultant industry bidding war, AMC set to work on the follow-up to *Everclear*. The fact that for the first time they could work on music full time, would be a mixed blessing. Without the sense of urgency caused by having only a short period of studio time available and without the discipline that came with Tom Mallon's dictatorial practices, AMC started to lose their way.

The band started demoing tracks with Irishman Kevin Killen, a young engineer who had worked on U2's breakthrough *War* album. But like schoolchildren with a temporary student teacher, the band appeared resolutely determined to do the minimum amount of work they could get away with.

"We spent the first two hours each day talking about the last *Star Trek: The Next Generation* episode we saw," Eitzel confesses, "not drum sounds or guitar sounds."

The band's initial failure to get to grips with the songs and sound unsettled the engineer, but AMC's difficulties were not all tied up with Killen. The band were having difficulty striking a balance between Eitzel's conception of the songs, and the band's own independent musical contributions. Their attempts at Eitzel's new song "Love Connection NYC" were symptomatic. It was a good song, but AMC never got a satisfactory version of it on tape. "That was impossible to get the band to play on," Eitzel says sadly. "The band had to know their parts, and wouldn't just jam. It was really frustrating for me, because we had to keep playing and playing and playing it, just to get back to where we started. We'd do the song 1,000 times until I couldn't feel it anymore, so that you can feel that you've got a part that you actually like, even thought the part you end up with is the part I originally showed you, because I know that's what fits. I wrote the fucking song, and I worked on this for days."

"Love Connection" would eventually be relegated to one appearance on a free CD with *Volume* magazine.

Now that he had the time and money to record his own 4-track arrangements, Eitzel was getting more hostile to the idea of using his songs as a basic template around which the band could improvise their own musical parts. He wanted the songs to come out as he envisaged them, and wanted the other musicians to play exactly what he wanted. Not surprisingly, the other band members were hostile to simply replicating Eitzel's arrangements.

Eitzel's other bugbear, and one which the other band members all deny, was that he felt they never listened to his songs properly before starting work on them. He wanted them to listen hard to the tapes he gave them and get an understanding of the lyrics before starting to play. This new approach would lead to a series of clashes with the other band members.

"Usually, I'd start playing the song," he bemoans, "and they'd immediately jam with me. I'd go, 'No! Listen to the song – hear what I'm doing. They'd go, 'Well, you're going from E minor to D to G, to one of your stupid weird chords.' And I'd go, 'No! Listen to the song. The song's about like you know, there's a river of life, and you're a turd floating in this reclining position, you're like in a poem by Beckett where you're born astride the grave...' I'd give the songs these great descriptions, and they'd go, 'Great Mark. That's really great.'

As time passed, AMC did gradually got to grips with the material, but by then relations between band and engineer had deteriorated further.

"We didn't really hit it off with Kevin," Tim Mooney reflects. "He was trying to get us to work in a way that he was used to, which didn't work for AMC. Click-tracks and things like that are not the thing for that band. That band really needed time to find out how each song should go."

Late one night Eitzel overheard Killen having a huge row down the phone, at one point shouting, "What the fuck am I doing with these losers?"

Against all the odds, the band assembled an encouraging series of demos which would work as a good starting point for the actual recording of the next album.

Highlights of the sessions included a visceral early take on "Heaven's 10,000 Whores", featuring a great Neil Young-style Vudi guitar solo. "What God Said to Godzilla," was also unique and compelling, "If I Had A Hammer" had a huge chorus in the tradition of "Outside This Bar," and "Gratitude Walks" was breathtaking. Featuring a gossamer-fragile opening acoustic guitar riff, the haunting tale of Mission life was caressed by chord fragments and ripples of notes by both Vudi and Kaphan.

At the start of May, AMC broke off from their studio work to play two shows at The Warfield Theatre in San Francisco supporting Bob Dylan.

Ironically considering the Polygram publishing deal negotiations, shortly after the "songwriter of the year" accolade, Dylan's people had contacted Eitzel via AMC's management. Apparently the great man wanted to come on stage and jam with AMC at their upcoming New York Knitting Factory date. Wally and Ross thought it a great opportunity for some high profile publicity but Eitzel's reaction was characteristically unpredictable.

"No fucking way!" He told Wally. "I'm not making this a big Dylan ego trip. This is our fucking show!" Wally and Ross protested, but Eitzel was adamant. Later that evening, as he stood out in the street taking in some fresh air, Eitzel watched a large limousine pull up in front of the Knitting Factory. After a few minutes, the limousine drove on. If it was Bob, he was quick to take no for an answer. The next morning Eitzel, who of course has always been a huge Dylan fan, instantly regretted his decision, and still does to this day. Back in May 1992, the Warfield shows would give him a chance to make up for the Knitting Factory debacle. But, driven by a surrealist's sense of the absurd, and keen always to provoke a reaction, Eitzel was incapable of letting the shows pass without incident.

AMC were not advertised as the support at the Warfield shows, and each evening they came on to an auditorium that was only two-thirds full. On the first night, Eitzel introduced his first song with a preamble about how "Visions of Johanna" was one of the most beautiful songs he'd ever heard about two lesbians. The Dylan camp was not amused. When AMC got back to their dressing room, angry instructions came round that none of the support acts were allowed to mention Dylan at all during their sets.

The next night Eitzel sang "In My Role As The Most Hated Singer in the Local Underground Scene," with added feeling, and as if in response to some imagined gauntlet, Vudi's guitar playing was at its wildest.

While Eitzel continued working on the next AMC album, some of the fruits of his earlier fringe projects appeared. The "Take Courage" single finally surfaced, to low key acclaim but was still majestic in spite of being drowned under swathes of reverb. Following hotly on its heels came a single and album from Eitzel's spell with The Toiling Midgets – though neither would be released in the UK until January of the following year.

The single, "Golden Frog" augured well. It was the best of the tracks recorded with the full Toiling Midgets line-up. Essentially "Golden Frog" is one long wail of defiance set to churning guitars and thundering drumming that just manages to leave space for Eitzel's to rage,

> You're a ... *marked card shit out of luck*
> *I don't need to apologise for anything I see*
> *I don't need to apologise, you just come right up to me.*
> *You were weak...*

The vocals are among the most ragged and piercing Eitzel has ever committed to tape. It sounds like a live take and conjures an image of the singer flailing drunk around the studio, clattering into the mixing disc and knocking over mike stands. The contrast with *Everclear*'s polished sheen could not have been stronger. Eitzel would consider the Midgets to be "360 degrees" (sic) away from American Music Club.

The single's B-side marked the high point of Eitzel's involvement with the Midgets – a stripped down version of the album track "Mr Foster's Shoes," featuring Eitzel backed only by Carla Fabrizio's cello. The subject matter recalls "Pale Skinny Girl," as Eitzel gets inside the heart and mind of a woman at the end of her tether.

> *She's checking in her pocket*
> *For something to make her feel good*
> *She's checking in her pocket*
> *For a reason...*
> *She's just trying to find a friend to call*
> *But she can't seem to find anyone at all.*

When the album appeared, housed in a distasteful sleeve featuring bad line drawings of naked "babes," snakes, skulls and playing cards, it was refreshing to hear Eitzel singing so freely and spontaneously throughout. Instead of detailed portraits, the lyrics are really just a series of images, pleas and exhortations like, *"It seem like the good things in life just cause me pain..."* or *"A little sleep, why don't you give me what I want."*

The music continues the piledriving pace of "Golden Frog," throughout guitar work-outs like "Slaughter on Sumner St." and "Fabric," though the tempo slows on "Process Words," where Eitzel sings much more softly.

While Eitzel enjoyed the collaboration initially, his own music had moved on from where the Midgets were aiming. By the time the record was out, he'd stopped appearing with them. Later, he felt that the Midgets had taken advantage of him.

"I got them their Matador recording deal by being in the band," he explains. "But then they never paid me the $600 that I was due, because they were like 'That asshole Eitzel, what does he need $600 for?' For me the money just equalled respect. I had wanted a fifth of a share [of the royalties] of all of the songs I sang on, and I didn't get that. All I got from them was, 'Well we don't really need a singer, and you're not as good as Ricky anyway, and you're really not very cool.' So I never felt that comfortable with it, except because I played with Tim [Mooney] and he was great."

Eitzel's final view of his collaboration with The Toiling Midgets would remain contradictory.

"They're fucking assholes," he would say. "They're like these ex-junkie rock stars who expect to be driven around in limousines all the time and they're getting older and they're not doing anything. Fuck 'em."

Though later he would reflect, "I thought it was a good experience. They are good people. Basically, I was just a guy who sang on the record. They should not even have had a singer. They don't need one."

Now that Eitzel had signed to a major label, he put a line under another era when he left his shared apartment on Capp Street in the Mission, and bought a house in the more salubrious area of Bernal Heights. He was fed up of the violence, the noise and the relentless misery of the place. He had served his time, and wanted a quieter place where he could write.

"I live in a nice house now," he told Julene Snyder shortly afterwards, "in a pretty good neighbourhood. You see, at some point you're not asking questions; it's just bringing you down. You're not scared anymore, just bored and pissed off."

But while the influx of money was making life easier in some ways, most of Eitzel's day was now spent doing interviews or promotional work of some kind. The rest of the time he was on the phone to the record company, his publisher, Wally, Ross or his lawyer. What he wanted was a few months of just watching television, hanging out with friends, and most importantly, writing songs. But, there was no time for anything. Somewhere in the middle of the flesh-pressing and meeting and greeting Eitzel had to write the rest of the new album.

Before recording work could commence, AMC had to appoint a producer. Considering the mixed experiences of working with Kevin Killen, this decision was absolutely key. *Everclear* was the AMC album that had attracted all of the attention, and though it was later re-mixed by Joe Chicarelli, the initial production work was by Bruce Kaphan. Not surprisingly Kaphan wanted to produce the next album, but he was still only a newcomer in the band and outside the main decision making process.

Eitzel later claimed that he had wanted the band to produce the album themselves under the supervision of Bruce Kaphan, but was overruled by Warners. Eitzel would blame Wally and Ross for not making a stand against the record company on this issue, which would be the start of a series of major disagreements between the band and their management.

"I don't believe Mark wanted Bruce to produce the record," Wally Brill later argued. "And I don't believe he wanted to produce the record [himself] although I know he wanted involvement... I think Bruce producing American Music Club [at that stage] was more something that Bruce wanted to have happen than something that was going to happen."

Considering the album had a six-figure recording budget and, bearing in mind the amount of money Warners and Virgin had already invested in the band, there was no way the job could have gone to anyone other than a name producer with a successful track record.

Interviews were held at London's Columbia Hotel. Wally's preferences were T-Bone Burnett and Gil Norton. Gil Norton in particular was an inspired choice. He'd worked on some of the greatest alternative rock albums of the era, including The Pixies' *Surfer Rosa*, The Triffids' majestic, sweeping *Born Sandy Devotional* and *Calenture*, and The Blue Aeroplanes' *Swagger*. But Norton was not interested.

"Gil had heard their early albums," Wally explains. "He really liked the band and was very excited. Then he got the *Mercury* demos and said 'These guys are taking the piss. Tell them to fucking get a life. Tell them to fucking cheer up!'

Another candidate was Mitchell Froom who had produced a series of hit albums by Crowded House, as well as working with a wide range of name acts that included Elvis Costello, Richard Thompson and Suzanne Vega – who he later married. Froom had also helped on Paul McCartney's acclaimed *Flowers in the Dirt* album and added keyboards to Bob Dylan's "Down in the Groove". It was a heavyweight CV.

Eitzel warmed to Froom because, unlike most of the prospective producers, he "was dour and uncool." Froom clinched the deal by telling Eitzel, "I'm not the guy for the job." Considering Eitzel's wariness of insincerity and fawning, this was probably the best way of securing the role. No sooner had Froom said he was not the guy, than Eitzel had decided he was the guy. Vudi was quick to agree.

The only dissenting voice was Bruce Kaphan's. He may have been biased having been passed over for the job, but he more than anyone else knew what production actually involved. "For whatever reason," he would later reflect, "The worst producer was always picked."

With Froom on board, AMC relocated to Los Angeles to record at the Sunset Sound Factory in Hollywood. Vudi later told a reporter LA was "like the manhole cover to hell," but he felt it had a positive effect on the album. It kept AMC in the studio and away from distractions. Conversely, Eitzel felt the location had a detrimental effect, because he "really wanted the whole thing to be over and done so [he] could get home." A few months before recording commenced, Eitzel had attended a Los Angeles party that he would later document in a song on the new album, "Hollywood 4/5/92." The party was packed with Hollywood types, and an American rock star who Eitzel declines to name decided he'd really get the party going by putting on some upbeat music. The star then put on his own record, which killed the party dead. For Eitzel, it summed up what was worst about LA. He considered it a "desperately sad" place.

Before actual recording, AMC spent a few weeks with Mitchell Froom in pre-production. This was the first time they had ever rehearsed for whole days at a stretch. Previously they would play together for an hour and a half and then go eat or drink.

Used to grafting with session musicians, Bruce Kaphan was impressed by Froom's work ethic, and retained respect for his musical ability. But, as Froom was a keyboard player, and until now Kaphan's pedal steel had fulfilled the role of keyboards in AMC, there was bound to be a clash.

"One of the most horrific moments I had with Mitchell," Kaphan remembers, "Was when we were still in pre-production. He came to me one day, and said, 'You know, I just don't know what to do with you in this scenario... He didn't get the pedal steel. He thought it was a country and western instrument, and he didn't have a place for it, in his concept of how to put the record together."

One of the most striking aspects of AMC's breakthrough album *Everclear* was the warm, unearthly swathes of Kaphan's pedal steel guitar. But, now Froom was consciously removing this distinctive sound to make way for his own keyboards.

"I felt a bit trodden on by Mitchell," Kaphan complains. "Simply because a lot of what I did in the band, he took over – making textures and that kind of thing. He would ultimately play his Chamberlain or mellotron parts."

Froom would repeatedly tell Kaphan not to play on certain tracks. The pedal steel man would spend a lot of time not playing on the album.

But Kaphan was the only band member to find fault with Froom. The rest of AMC loved him, and were enjoying the freedom of a different approach from that of Tom Mallon. In place of Mallon's relentless negativity, Froom brought encouragement, creativity and pragmatism.

"Mitchell Froom's greatest talent was for the arrangements," Eitzel reflects. "I really love Mitchell, he knows how to create a good vibe in the studio. He doesn't belabour everything. He'll take three takes and cut 'em together and make a song out of that."

"Working with Mitchell was great," Dan Pearson agrees, "because he fitted in so well with us. He was full of ideas and they were all really strange. He wasn't interested in making a commercial record and neither were we. We were like, 'Alright! This guy isn't going to push us around'."

In many ways this disregard for business factors is entirely admirable, but for a band with hundreds of thousands of dollars in unearned advances sitting on their record companies' books, it would soon spell trouble. Though initially, neither Virgin nor Warners put any visible pressure on the band to come up with a commercial product, there were still expectations of success. Normally the producer would, to some extent help ensure the record company got what they wanted. But at the time, Mitchell Froom was going through a divorce and was apparently too disillusioned to care.

"Mitchell's humour was incredibly dark and sarcastic all of the time," Kaphan recalls. "He got really into Mark's music because the sentiments were paralleling a lot of Mitchell's own personal problems at the time. He just got into how dark it was. I don't think he gave the record company what they wanted on that record."

The new album was in danger of getting stuck in one melancholy vein. The combination of Mitchell's divorce, the LA setting and the band's fear of appearing to sell out, was producing something much bleaker and more self-consciously clever than previous AMC records.

As time went on, Mitchell Froom and his engineer Tchad Blake added different sounds, quirks and layers almost for the sake of it. While sometimes this created a startling effect, on the whole, the songs themselves were getting lost. And as Froom continued tampering with the percussion sound, and removed more and more of Kaphan's pedal steel, Vudi's guitar and Pearson's mandolin playing, gradually the things that people loved about AMC became more scarce. On "Johnny Mathis' Feet" Kaphan only got to add an acoustic guitar track that failed to make the final mix.

The songs were so strong that the album could not fail to be good, but it was starting to sound like a Mitchell Froom and Mark Eitzel collaboration featuring guest musicians.

"Actually, I think Mitchell is a fine producer," Kaphan maintains. "But Mitchell produces Mitchell Froom records, and you hear it in everything he has done. They all sound like Mitchell Froom records, just like Daniel Lanois records all sound like Daniel Lanois. It was a phenomenon of Hollywood producers at the time, that you had to make every record you produced, sound like your record."

Warners appeared happy to trust Froom to do his job, but Wally Brill was also getting worried.

"I believe Mitchell over-influenced Mark," he bemoaned. "Mitchell convinced Mark that he had to do an arty record: he couldn't do a pop record... But Mark is a songwriter. It is in the writing, the chords, and the way the voice works. The songs don't have to be any cleverer than they are. To try and overproduce an American Music Club record is just stupidity."

Wally knew the album was not completely ruined, but he listened in dismay to the tapes as he heard how the full potential of some of Eitzel's most promising material had failed to be realised.

"I have one very specific problem with Mitchell Froom's job on that album," he complains. "He took a really great 6/8 song, 'If I Had A Hammer,' and rammed it into 4/4 time. It was a magical stunning thing, a beautiful waltz, and Mitchell flattened it out, and put a spooky bit in the middle that had nothing to do with anything except what I believe is Mitchell's ego. But there were a lot of things like that.

"The other disaster was 'Over and Done'. Mark did a demo of this and it is a huge, slamming punk rock anthem. It was the hit single. It had amazing guitar lines. Mitchell in the midst of his sadness and divorce convinced Eitzel not to do it in the most obvious way. And Mark went along with it."

Representatives from Warners did occasionally visit the studio, and according to Eitzel there were only two issues they wanted to discuss.

"The biggest problem was the gap in 'If I Had a Hammer' where there is no music. Because, if there had been drums all the way through, it would have been a hit, or so they were saying. The other thing was that Tchad Blake, the engineer, didn't want to put reverb anywhere on the record, but 'Johnny Mathis' Feet' kind of demanded it, so we just did it. He said, 'This is the best track on the record and it's ruined'."

Warners were confused but willing to put their faith in their golden boy producer.

"I think there was such a mystique around Mitchell Froom at the time," Wally muses, "That no one would say anything. It was the emperor's new clothes, everybody just went, 'this is a masterpiece, it's art, it's clever'."

Neither Kaphan nor Wally had enough sway with Eitzel to persuade him that things were going awry. So the process continued. More and more overdubs were added, and Froom and Blake kept on searching for weird new sounds, until finally they were done. Then Froom and Blake moved on to the next project, leaving Warners to puzzle over their new signing's expensive work of art, and AMC to sit tight and hope for the best.

"Warners told us that it was a great record," Dan Pearson maintains. "It was a notch in the belt for Reprise that they were still able to produce good art, no matter whether it would sell or not... The only problem when it was done, was 'What was going to be the single?'... That's when things started to degenerate a little bit."

Virgin too were initially happy with what was presented.

"Everyone [at Virgin] loved it," Orla Lee from their A&R department remembers. "It was a great album with many stand-out tracks... But then it was the sort of music that we all liked..."

But, in spite of Lee's enthusiasm, things had changed at Virgin since AMC were signed.

"We talked with Virgin and we talked with EMI," Eitzel explains. "And we didn't want to sign with EMI at all. So we signed with this guy at Virgin [Willy

Richardson, the band's original A&R point of contact], and a few weeks later EMI bought the company and he was fired. A whole new bunch of people came in and they had more of a pop sensibility and also Virgin became more corporate."

"Even with the change of A&R people," Orla Lee insists, "AMC were still really pushed."

But the bigger picture had changed. Although Virgin Records' main objective was to make money from its artists, as a privately owned company, they could afford to be reasonably patient in awaiting a return. EMI on the other hand was part of a group that was quoted on the Stock Exchange. Its shareholders would expect a good return on its investments each year. Accordingly, if a high profile act was losing money for the company, action would have to be taken as quickly as possible.

When the album was completed, Warners came back to the band with a request for more tracks. They were planning multi-format single releases and needed additional material for the B-sides. This was a rare opportunity for Vudi and Dan Pearson to give some of their songs a low-key outing, and the band agreed that some non-Eitzel compositions should be recorded. Eitzel admired the proposed material, but refused to take part.

"I must say that I did not distinguish myself," he confesses. "They recorded those tracks around a barbecue at Danny's house, way out in the country, and I thought, 'I'm not going to a fucking barbecue. I'm staying in San Francisco, you guys do it, you don't need me.' I was really jealous, and unctuous."

As a result the rest of the band had a fun time swapping instruments and cross collaborating. They even recorded a Vudi composition from an old Farmers' EP, "Green Borders," that unfortunately was never released.

"We did it in a day," Mooney recalls, "It was just fun noodling." Kaphan, who produced the sessions, even played drums on one track.

The songs came out well, and afterwards Eitzel felt ashamed at his behaviour. Nonetheless, he would never have considered letting one of the other members have a song on an actual AMC album, "I wouldn't do it. I write so many songs, that I said, 'Well, I have all my songs, if you write better songs, bring them and we'll see.' I write so many songs, and I want them all on the record."

While none of the B-side tracks was as good as Eitzel's songs on *Mercury*, Vudi and Mooney's plaintive "Memo From Bernal Heights," and Pearson's country-tinged "Walking Tune" were highly accomplished in their own right. Eitzel's attitude to the whole affair was symptomatic of the strains and pressures beginning to affect the band. Cracks were appearing.

After their Spring live shows, AMC spent most of the rest of 1992 away from public view. During this relatively prolonged absence, a new band appeared who were seen as carrying forward the AMC torch, Red House Painters. Essentially a vehicle for the demon-haunted songs of Mark Kozelek, the RHPs played majestic, introspective and melancholy music, predominantly based around major 7th guitar chords. They were also based in San Francisco.

As if this wasn't enough, Red House Painters were described regularly as Eitzel's favourite band, and Eitzel and other members of American Music Club were instrumental in them getting a record deal. Not surprisingly, few Red House

Painters reviews or interviews would appear without some mention of or comparison to AMC.

Kozelek grew up in Ohio. During a difficult early adolescence he developed drug problems, and entered rehab at a very young age. By the age of 18, Kozelek had moved to Atlanta, Georgia, where he formed the first line-up of Red House Painters with drummer Anthony Koutsos. In 1988, Kozelek and Koutsos moved to San Francisco, where they recruited guitarist Gorden Mack and bassist Jerry Vessel through adverts in local papers. After gigging around the Bay Area for about a year, the band crossed paths with American Music Club.

"Anthony saw AMC open for Bob Mould at the I-Beam on Haight Street some time in 1989 or 1990," Kozelek recalls.

"He liked them a lot and we went to see them at The Blue Lamp about a month later. I was really impressed with Mark. The band seemed really shy and uncomfortable and awkward on stage, but Mark seemed relaxed and natural in front of the audience. At one point a girl jumped up on to the stage and Mark danced with her during 'Gary's Song.' Mark was having fun, and his voice was great in spite of being drunk."

Some time after this show, Anthony bumped into Vudi, and gave him a copy of the Red House Painters' demo tape. Vudi passed it on to Eitzel, who immediately fell in love with it, especially "Michael," the tale of a lost golden-haired boy – "the oldest juvenile delinquent."

"From my understanding," Kozelek explains, "The way it [then] went was that Mark had our demo with him in England, and journalist Martin Aston asked him what he had been listening to lately. When Mark told him one of the things was the Red House Painters' demo, Aston asked to hear it, and liked it. Aston told Mark to have me send him a tape, which I did, and he passed it on to Ivo [Watts-Russell] at 4AD. Six months later Ivo called me, and three months after that *Down Colorful Hill* came out."

Down Colorful Hill was released pretty much in its unaltered demo form. It was bleak, shockingly confessional and achingly beautiful. The eponymous follow up album was even better. Reviews of each drew attention to the Eitzel connection, and found similarities in the subject matter and the nature of its bittersweet delivery.

The similarities of mood and lyrical concerns are undeniable – "Michael" was probably the greatest Eitzel song he never wrote – but while much of the Red House Painters' more bereft material calls to mind songs from *California* and *United Kingdom*, AMC's work was always more varied musically.

"The Red House Painters do pretty much that one style..." Eitzel would argue. "They never did country, they never did stupid loud rock, they always did that one thing. So when anybody says they were like AMC, it's like, well, we were pretty eclectic and we had a really good sense of humor about what we did."

Because of the mutual admiration between the two Marks, it seemed likely to outsiders that they were close friends. The UK music press would even refer to Kozelek as an Eitzel protégé. Oddly, they never really hit it off on a personal level. Kozelek remembers their first actual meeting, which was when AMC were in the studio finishing *Everclear.*

"Mark showed up at our show at Morty's bar with Vudi and some other friends, and invited us to join them in Specs on North Beach when we were finished. I ended up sitting away from them at a small table with my girlfriend at the time. They insisted that we moved to their table, and a seat was made available for me next to Mark. We didn't look at each other or talk. He had seen us a few times before and I knew he was a huge fan. Sitting next to him I felt some strange pressure, and felt that he felt that also. It seemed as if all eyes at the table were on us, to see if we would connect or to see what would happen. I felt self-conscious and I felt that he did too. We didn't speak more than a few words. He had a paper bag with some used books in it. I may have asked him what was in the bag."

Nonetheless, Eitzel continued to do everything he could to help the Red House Painters, including lining up AMC support slots for them at the Great American Music Hall. He also made more attempts to socialise with Kozelek. But, when Kozelek finally agreed to attend a party at Eitzel's invitation, it was not a success.

"At one point," Kozelek remembers, "[Eitzel] and Kathleen and some friends gathered around a table in the kitchen and started asking me questions. Kathleen told me she really liked [the Red House Painters' song] 'Uncle Joe'. Eitzel talked about Jonathan Richman and he was really disappointed that I didn't know who he was. Eitzel seemed disappointed in me somehow. He never invited me to a party after that."

Whatever the reasons, the two songwriters' mutual admiration cooled. In the long run this could only be a good thing for both bands. The Red House Painters began life so much under the shadow of AMC that their patronage could only keep drawing attention to the similarities. Also, The Red House Painters were the first in a wave of bands that followed in AMC's wake, making slow, bleak music that the press would later dub "sadcore."

Even with a decrease in AMC's patronage, Red House Painters career continued to blossom. "It seemed like as RHP started to get critical acclaim," Kozelek explains. "– getting press, going on tours – that Eitzel's excitement about us went away."

In the end Kozelek became more friendly with Dan Pearson and Bruce Kaphan. Both musicians were better equipped to deal with someone of Kozelek's temperament than Eitzel himself.

Eitzel would bump into Kozelek from time to time and they would say "Hi" but their paths were moving in different directions. The Red House Painters continued to steadily build a career in the indie rock sphere, following previous 4AD acts like The Pixies and the Cocteau Twins. Eitzel and AMC were now battling it out in an arena where U2, REM and Nirvana were the yardsticks of success – and anything less than sales of half a million would be seen as a failure. This was the way Eitzel wanted it. But, even for outsiders with unlimited faith in his genius, it was obvious that AMC were going to find this a painful struggle.

Chapter Ten

All The Pestilence That Sudden Pleasure Brings

"He had come a long way... And his dream must have seemed so close that he could hardly fail to grasp it. He did not know that it was already behind him, somewhere back in that vast obscurity beyond the city...

So we beat on, boats against the current, borne back ceaselessly into the past".

F Scott Fitzgerald, The Great Gatsby

"The dude's way sensitive"

Vudi on Eitzel, 1993

AMC began 1993 with a new sense of hope. People kept telling them their new album was a classic and that it would mark their commercial breakthrough. They also felt that they had record companies behind them who would ensure their album would be in the shops and their songs played on the radio. It was the dawn of a bright new era.

"Eight months ago nobody would pee on us, and now people are walking up to me and saying, 'Hey Rock Star'," Eitzel told journalist Michael Goldberg, back in a San Francisco venue's dressing room, in between sips of red wine. He and Vudi were taking time out to be interviewed during a break in the shoot for a $20,000 video for "Over and Done" they hoped would be shown on MTV.

"I feel it. We're successful. Even though we haven't toured, we haven't got any more new fans or sold any more records, but if feels different."

Towards the end of January Eitzel and Vudi flew to London to start preparing the ground for *Mercury*. Taking a break from press interviews, they caused a slight stir at a Bark Psychosis show at Ronnie Scott's when Vudi, frustrated at how worthy and precious he felt the performance, repeatedly heckled the band, yelling among other things, "Can You Play 'Wipeout'?"

143

After a short spell back in San Francisco, Eitzel returned to London in February to play two solo acoustic shows at the tiny Camden Falcon. The shows were timed to pave the way for the release of *Mercury*.

For the first night, Eitzel was nervous but in good spirits. He sparred with hecklers, joked with photographers, and performed stunning acoustic excerpts from *Mercury* such as a bravado "Johnny Mathis' Feet" and a jawdropping "Gratitude Walks." During "I've Been a Mess" he stunned the audience with his own personalised brand of self-deprecation. After singing the song's first line, "Lazarus wasn't grateful for his second wind," he burst out laughing, saying, "You all think I'm singing about farting don't you." The audience were temporarily shell-shocked at the typically inappropriate outburst. He followed with a heart-stopping "What God Said To Godzilla When His Name Wasn't Found in the Book of Life," – "You have to take it literally," he laughed, adding, "I'm Godzilla…"

"We really don't deserve him," Keith Cameron would conclude in the next week's *NME*. *Melody Maker*'s Peter Paphides started out sceptical of all the Eitzel brouhaha, but was quickly won over, concluding, "So there you have it. Hero. Genius. Saint. One man and his guitar. Between them, everything."

"It was kind of fun," was all Eitzel would say.

Before the second show Eitzel got extremely drunk. After eight months on the wagon, he'd recently taken to the bottle again. Later that Spring on stage in New York, he would quip, "I just went to see the doctor. He told me I had to quit drinking. So I said, 'Where am I going to get another personality?'"

During Eitzel's second Falcon set, he kept the jokes coming, but his mood was fractious. When after a series of self-deprecating one-liners, he started to introduce "Western Sky" as a song dedicated to those with AIDS, the audience laughed nervously, waiting for a vicious punch line. They had not realised his tone had shifted. Eitzel was convinced the crowd were making fun of him and his song, and started berating them as "assholes." He finished his set as quickly as possible and left in a black mood.

In a letter to *Melody Maker* published shortly afterwards, Eitzel attempted to explain his behaviour, "I've got to get this off my chest," he began. He was sorry that he had overreacted and maintained he was sure the people who laughed were "cool people" really. But it was important for him to prove he was not jumping on a trendy bandwagon. To underline his commitment to the issue, he stressed the number of his friends who had had died of the disease. *Melody Maker* made light of the issue by headlining the letter, "A serious artist writes."

Mercury was released on 21st March 1993. Warners and Virgin were primed and ready. All the hard work by the band, Spike Hyde, Lisa Fancher, Mick Griffiths, Wally and Ross had got American Music Club into this fierce spotlight. It was the culmination of ten years of momentum. Whether they liked it or not, AMC's future as a band would stand or fall on their major label debut.

For such a high profile release, the album cover was extremely unprepossessing – especially following on from the bright and dramatic *Everclear* sleeve. Similar in mood to *The Restless Stranger* artwork, the main image was a prussian blue tinted unearthly Eastern landscape taken by old cohort Bobby Neal Adams.

Without comment, the CD inlay artwork also featured a full-page photo of Jenny Gonzalvez.

The songs on *Mercury* were yet more evidence that Mark Eitzel was an extraordinarily gifted writer at the peak of his talents. "Gratitude Walks," "If I Had a Hammer," "I've Been A Mess," and "Johnny Mathis' Feet," married memorable melodies to some of Eitzel's most mature lyrics to date. Eitzel wrote most of the material during the period when he'd given up drinking.

"That made me a lot less self-absorbed," he told writer Andrew Mueller. "When you drink as much as I used to drink, you always think the world revolves around you. And I decided I had to write different kinds of songs, because what I wrote basically related to one person and the consumption of alcohol, and what can be said about that? Not much. So I changed."

Eitzel had started to move away from obviously autobiographical material and on *Mercury*, he takes this one step further. While the songs still evoke a bleak landscape and are peopled with the lost, the dying and the heartbroken, Eitzel is a much more detached observer. He empathises, but he is less involved.

The songs may often be in the first person, but Eitzel chooses to "internalise" events when describing another person's life, thus appearing to make that life his own,

"I think this helps to draw the listener in," he would say. "I'm not necessarily always documenting my own little miseries."

These are certainly more consciously "song-writerly" songs – packed as they are with poetic conceits, like "Hammer"'s *"I'm as priceless as a brass ring losing the heat from your hand"* – but they are no less powerful for it.

Part of the reasons for Eitzel's new detached stance was his continuing desire to escape the tragic, tortured poet's mantle. But, because many of the songs were for or about those suffering from AIDS, Eitzel was bound to feel powerless. Neither his help, his sympathy, nor his love, could save these people.

While the shadow of AIDS looms large, Eitzel tries to confront the disease in less obvious ways. If he was to tackle the issue head on, it would be easy to fall into the trap of appearing patronising or worthy, so fragments of images and oblique references conjure up the plague years instead. Whether asking to go *"back to the leper colony,"* or *"feel[ing] time pass like a joy no medicine can preserve,"* "If I Had A Hammer" is drenched in images that evoke a helpless diseased sinking. The folk standard of the same name was a joyous, idealistic call to arms for the American Left. Here all observers are helpless, as the protagonists contemplate whether or not they've reached the bottom yet. The chorus line *"Maybe, I'm almost there,"* could be a triumph, but it sounds like a tragedy.

Though Eitzel punctures any possible pomposity with the humourous image of the women of the title on a "party line to his big toe," "The Hopes and Dreams of Heaven's 10,000 Whores," is a horrifyingly vivid picture of an AIDS sufferer:

> *Forgive me if you can said the sad cashier*
> *for the dollars and cents our love has become*
> *No I didn't sell you anything my dear*
> *You are like a scarecrow looking for a bonfire to sleep on.*
> *Believe me if you can said the pile of bones*

> *I think that this is all there is left to see*
> *Just waiting for my prescription to come*
> *'cause every second hell dissolves more of me.*

In addition to his obvious compassion for all those suffering from the disease, the fact that AIDS is linked inescapably in the public mind with carnal behaviour makes it a compelling subject for Eitzel. Though he is a libertarian, there is a streak of self-hatred that runs through his work which appears inextricably tied up with a fear and loathing of his own flesh. In a tale of failed love, Eitzel's image of "a scarecrow looking for a bonfire to sleep on" could easily be a self-portrait. On the awesomely intense "Apology for an Accident," as he conjures images of Bataille and Lautreaumont, this idea is vividly revisited. *"Well I'm an expert in all things that nature abhors / the look of disgust when I touched your skin."*

On *Mercury*, even when Eitzel revisits his old haunts, he maintains his observer's status. "Gratitude Walks," the stunning opening song is a third-party despatch from the red light district Eitzel used to inhabit. As he watches and relays the scenes of the streets, he concludes, *"It's never what you want/ It's just the kind of thing that always happens here."*

"Over and Done" specifically evokes his old Mission home, but though these were scenes that would keep him up all night, again he is watching rather than soul bearing.

> *Capp Street is an underwater cave*
> *That's filled with crutches and canes*
> *And faces that were washed away*
> *From innocence and pain*
> *They don't care who lost and won*
> *They just wanna get the whole thing over and done.*

Eitzel's recurring preoccupation with AIDS sufferers, coupled with the fact that from *United Kingdom* onwards, his love songs were not gender specific, led to some speculation about his sexuality. He would still write heartbreaking love songs, but the object of his desire was always "you" rather than "she." Eitzel was also by now sporting the short cropped hair and extended goatee beard that was fashionable among gay circles, and San Francisco was after all the gay capital of the world. The self-loathing that is a constant in Eitzel's life and work is also a common trait in those having difficulty coming to terms with their sexuality, but it was an issue on which he refused to be drawn in public, and as far as Eitzel concerned, his sexuality was irrelevant to his role of songwriter – a fact he proved by his gender-neutral writing.

For all the imagery of disease, death and decay, *Mercury* does have moments of relief. The subject matter is less introspective than previous outings and a few traces of humour remain.

In "Challenger" the narrator, though anxious, describes himself as "the happiest hot potato on the plane," and "Johnny Mathis' Feet," is one long glorious joke at Eitzel's own expense. Eitzel lays all his songs down at Mathis' feet and waits for the great man's opinion. Though Mathis would tell him he was "on the right track," there was still plenty of room for improvement. Eitzel would discuss the song's genesis during live shows,

"A friend told me, 'Mark, if you took all of your songs and put them together, they wouldn't equal one tenth of the syrup that is Johnny Mathis.' And you know what? She's right." Eitzel was not a Mathis fan – the best thing he could say about him was that he's "not as evil as Neil Diamond." But, he told Keith Cameron, he wrote the song for a friend with AIDS, "I wanted to make him happy. I wanted to make him laugh…"

Mercury's long and often ironic song titles like "The Hopes and Dreams of Heaven's 10,000 Whores" and "What Godzilla Said To God When His Name Wasn't Found in the Book of Life," would lead a reporter from the staid English broadsheet *The Daily Telegraph* to puzzle over why Eitzel's titles bore no resemblance to the actual songs.

"Oh, but they do," he would insist. " It's just that when I'm finished whittling down a lyric, I have stuff left over, and I sometimes take the title from what I don't use. It's a way of making a song seem, umm larger. Also, I guess, I like funny song titles."

The new album's one absolute oddity is "More Hopes and Dreams." Without any overdubs, this track was the sound of a San Francisco power station. Eitzel and Vudi were out there one night taking photos and became hypnotised by its noise. They both thought it should go on the record. "I think there's a lot of suspense in that melody," Vudi would explain.

While many of the best songs on *Mercury* had been played live for nearly a year by the time the album arrived, the absolute highlight, and one of the definitive Eitzel songs, "I've Been A Mess," was relatively unheard. Turning the Biblical tale of Lazarus on its head, in three concise verses, Eitzel produces an extremely moving and world-weary twist on the love song staple that the protagonist cannot live without his lover.

> *Lazarus wasn't grateful for his second wind*
> *Another chance to watch his chances fade like the dawn*
> *And me, I can barely tell you*
> *Just how pale I get without you*
> *I've been a mess since you've been gone.*
> *What were the first words that the crowd heard him speak*
> *Bet he was cursing at the sky*
> *Bet he wasn't turning no other cheek…*

It is a perfect example of how Eitzel's writing had become more crafted and self-conscious without losing any of its emotional impact. The track also sounds like a classic American Music Club performance. Opening with just Eitzel's voice, Pearson's fragile mandolin and Kaphan's eerie pedal steel, it gathers momentum with haunting, almost out of kilter guitar work from Vudi and Tim Mooney's percussive drumming, adding weight to Eitzel's words without intruding on them. It also features Pearson's best, and simplest bass line on the album.

The fact that "I've Been A Mess" stands out so conspicuously on such a good album, points to *Mercury*'s main weakness. Most of the other arrangements simply don't sound like American Music Club. A simple Froom action like substituting the beautifully fragile guitar riff at the beginning of the demo and live versions of "Gratitude Walks" with a simplified piano arrangement took away part of the AMC signature sound, while detracting from the song's emotional impact. In the end a song that was a true band collaboration on stage, ended up a skeleton of its former self. On the album version Vudi's and Pearson's contributions can barely be heard.

On most of *Mercury*'s other songs, the production is just too cluttered and busy, and downright weird in places, for the beauty of the writing to shine through. "Godzilla" sounds like the backing tracks have been assembled from an almost random selection of tapes. Each verse was given a completely different musical character, and only someone already familiar with its previous incarnations could glimpse the beautiful song within. One of the more promising songs from the Killen sessions, "The Amyl Nitrate Dreams of Pat Robertson," was so submerged in studio effects that, sounding like a bad outtake from Suzanne Vega's Froom-produced nadir, *Days of Future Hand*, it was consigned to a cassette single only B-side.

"Be clever," Wally Brill reflects with despair. "That is the sin. It could have been the big record. The songs were there, and the demos were there, and I believe frankly with hindsight, they should have just gone in with an engineer and had somebody else mix it."

But Froom appeared to enjoy being clever. "Mitchell hates very simple pop songs," Eitzel would say. "Nothing could be done in a simple or obvious way."

While AMC's best albums have often had an organic ebb and flow, Froom was keen to give each song a distinct personality. Froom's engineer Tchad Blake, was so desperate to find a different percussion sound for each track that on "Godzilla" he even ran a bamboo tube between the snare drum and a microphone to get the drum sound he wanted.

"We had a philosophy of how it should sound," Eitzel sighs, "we wanted a live recording, with very simple arrangements. But when you have five people who all want to play at once, it gets difficult to make arrangements. Mitchell came in and totally changed our way of arranging."

Also, no matter how much Warners emphasised their belief in the band as artists, there was inevitably pressure on them – even if it was often implied rather than expressed – to produce a sellable product to a strict timetable. According to Eitzel, instead of sticking up for the band and fighting Warners on this issue, Wally and Ross would merely increase the pressure on the band to follow the record company's dictates, which inevitably caused more bad feeling and tension.

For all the criticisms of his approach to production, the problems with *Mercury* can't be entirely laid at Mitchell Froom's door. Some of AMC's problems arose from their new circumstances.

"What we should have done was say we need six months to do demos," Eitzel reflects. "Instead we agreed to do the complete record in two months...."

Wally Brill maintains that this issue was not raised at the time. "There may be issues of communication here. I don't ever remember Mark saying he didn't have enough time."

It may simply have been that the whole band were swept up in the excitement of being on a major label, and only later considered alternative ways of proceeding. But there were other issues too. Eitzel was undoubtedly worried about being seen to become just another group on a big record label with a name producer. For all his desire for success, he was wary of being seen to "sell out," and worried that if he made a commercial record, it would be interpreted "in the wrong way."

"Mitchell Froom did what we wanted," Eitzel insists. "We told him we wanted to make a non-commercial record. We were worried that it would be perceived in the wrong way – if we'd produced it ourselves, it would have been OK."

For someone who had yearned for success for so long, it seems odd that at the first chance Eitzel would instruct his producer to help him make a "non-commercial" work. The temptation to do the unpredictable must have been strong. Similarly the whole Bukowski instinct of destroying something good almost for the sake of it would have had some appeal. But overall, Eitzel's desire for success and recognition were stronger. An alternative explanation is that if AMC had gone all out with a major label's backing and name producer to make a commercial hit and failed, Eitzel would have found the rejection hard to accept. Undoubtedly Eitzel wanted *Mercury* to be a hit, but he ensured the album was just weird and arty enough to have something to fall back on if it wasn't.

For all this speculation, and notwithstanding what Eitzel and his cohorts would say in Mitchell Froom's defence, it is difficult to listen to *Mercury* without picturing a group of musicians sat in the control room of a lavish Hollywood studio, wondering where the hell all their music has gone. They hope against hope that maybe the producer did know what he was doing after all, and that this record would get them the audience they yearned for. They don't want to go back to their crummy day jobs, and are tired of getting nowhere. But as Eitzel listens back to an album that will have his band's name on it, deep down, in a place beneath his sense of irony, and beyond his relish for the absurd, a part of him is absolutely devastated.

***

Whatever its flaws, when *Mercury* was released, the press went absolutely crazy over it. Not only did they praise the record itself, some writers also predicted it might be the album to take AMC into the mainstream.

"We can start chiselling that tablet marked Album of the Year," Paul Mathur gushed in *Melody Maker*. "Just superglue the record to the deck and have done with it. I have."

"*Mercury* is another extraordinary collection of songs," Ann Scanlon enthused in *Vox* "perhaps the band's finest yet, and given that fellow miserabilists like Bob Mould and Paul Westerberg are now on daytime radio, maybe AMC's worth is about to be measured in record sales rather than just critical respect."

But for all the praise in the niche music press, the mainstream media were more wary. *The Times* concluded that "For all its intellectual clout, on a more basic level, this album lacks charm."

Ross Fortune in London's style bible, *Time Out* was even more telling:

"Indeed, Eitzel has the undoubted potential to emulate Evan Dando's recent success, [Dando's Lemonheads had recently broken though to major sales through a Simon and Garfunkel cover coupled with a full media onslaught] though whether he'd compromise as willingly, and give and promote as incessantly is less sure."

Still, the odd cautious review apart, AMC were on a roll. *Mercury*'s acclaim was widespread, and industry insiders were tipping the band for greatness. *Rolling Stone* ran a four-page interview with Vudi and Eitzel that named AMC their "hot band." But what should have been a triumphant feature took a macabre turn when, sat in a dark corner of the Tosca Bar up by San Francisco's Fisherman's Wharf, Eitzel started talking to the writer about suicide. "I should just kill myself," he said. "I should just do it!" It was a subject best left alone, but there was a terrifying honesty in the low-key way Eitzel raised the matter that made one fear for his survival in the world of *Rolling Stone*.

Flushed with praise, AMC set off on a UK tour to promote *Mercury* backed by the full might of Virgin Records, and finally, they had tour support. Their budget meant they could stay in reasonable accommodation, their shows were trailed in advance in local and national media, and record company representatives attended nearly every show. It would be the first tour where they didn't have to take it in turns to sleep in the van to keep an eye on their gear. Now they could sleep two to a room – previously they would have to decide whether to book one or two rooms for the entire party. The tour was certainly not the height of luxury, but as Tim Mooney puts it, things were "less gruelling."

The tour would take them from late March into Easter. The band named it ironically, "The bringing people together tour." Tim Mooney remembers it as, "the everyone wearing suits tour." It would be a strange trip.

"There was definitely a lot of pressure on everyone during that tour," road manager Mark Terrill remembers. "There was a lot of strange chemistry. They'd been building up to this for eight years, and they were all willing to go through with it all, and they were hoping it would go the way it should, but there were still times in the middle of it that were quite intimidating..."

They kicked off on the 24th March with a well-received show at the relatively small Duchess of York bar in Leeds. "You observe AMC for the first time," *NME*'s Northern correspondent averred, "And you fully understand why they inspire and deserve reverence. You know the all-important global breakthrough is on the horizon..."

The next day AMC moved on to Glasgow and then Edinburgh, where Eitzel introduced them as the "Gene Simmons Band." That same night in response to audience banter, AMC played a spontaneous cover version of the surf-guitar classic "Pipeline." Later, Eitzel would claim to have been listening to the new Ice-T album, and re-introduced himself and Danny as "Mark Motherfuckin' Eitzel" and "D. Motherfuckin' Pearson." The next morning, as they were in Scotland, Vudi bought tartan trousers, and wore them with pink socks and Jesus sandals – an ensemble that few other than Vudi could get away with.

The following night AMC were at Manchester University. Outside the hall, there was a huge queue of pre-pubescent girls. But, though it seemed initially that Eitzel had improbably won over the *Smash Hits* teen fanbase, it turned out the girls were waiting for the East 17 show at the much larger Academy next door.

In addition to the pin-stripe suit and tie, he sported throughout the UK dates, Eitzel walked on stage at Manchester wearing a very odd hat. Proceedings stalled briefly as he rather shambolically couldn't find anywhere to put his bottle of wine and then an electrical fault caused all of the venue's lights to fail.

Dan Pearson looked out into the auditorium and said, "It's kinda dark in here."

"Yeah, Dan, but we make dark music," Eitzel replied.

After a revelatory set packed with Eitzel quips and an extended rant about his hatred of cellphones, the show climaxed with a hard rocking version of Joy Division's "Isolation" in tribute to Eitzel's Mancunian heroes.

Andrew Smith in *Melody Maker* stressed how the show was much more enjoyable and jolly than one would expect. It certainly was a triumphant performance, but backstage in Manchester things were falling apart.

Eitzel was growing dissatisfied with his management, who he felt were not giving the band enough support or guidance. He considered that since the major deals had been signed, Wally and Ross hadn't done a great deal for the huge chunks of AMC's money they were getting.

The aspect of Wally and Ross's contract with AMC that Eitzel found most irritating was that they could invoice a 15% commission on all of the band's income, before the deduction of any expenses. While this was not an unusual arrangement, it meant that the managers could technically get rich while the band made no money whatsoever. For instance if the band made $20,000 income from a tour, Ross and Wally would invoice $3,000. From the remaining $17,000, the band would have to pay for all of the hotel rooms and meals, including Ross and Wally's if they came along, the transport, equipment, road manager, crew and other miscellaneous expenses. Even with record company tour support to ensure they didn't lose money, it is unlikely that at the end of such a tour, the band would have done anything more than cover their expenses. So after a few months on the road, Eitzel, Vudi, Pearson, Mooney and Kaphan might have nothing to show for it, while Ross and Wally could share $3,000 without any corresponding expenses.

The financial issue that rankled Eitzel the most was that when AMC signed to Warners, the company gave the band an additional $110,000 specifically to buy out their remaining contract with Alias. This money was immediately put in a separate bank account, and never considered to be band money. However, as the cheque was payable from Warners to AMC, Ross and Wally felt this was still band income, and invoiced them $16,500 commission accordingly. The band thought that Warners had paid off Alias, and then suddenly had to cough up another $3,300 each. There was certainly plenty of money around but certain members of the band were beginning to wonder where it was all going.

Even this current tour, the band's most lucrative trek to date, would not have left the musicians any the richer. AMC might gross £4,000 from their one London date,

"But of course, the band don't see any of that," their booking agent Mick Griffiths explains. "They were over for a three-week tour, and the other shows averaged way less money, and they had a bigger crew, and had to hire equipment – it's a very expensive process: they certainly wouldn't have made any money."

Paying significant sums of money to Ross and Wally after a breakeven tour such as this would hurt.

Also, coming from a left-field indie background, Eitzel felt that Wally, in his fondness for lavish lifestyle trappings – which of course were paid for by AMC – symbolised aspects of the record industry that he found distasteful. Eitzel had never had any money before in his life, and now he had some he didn't want to fritter it away on taxis, limousines and flash hotels. When it sank in that he was paying for Wally's high living out of his own pocket, Eitzel became exceedingly disillusioned.

"It was like because we suddenly had all this money," he would bemoan, "We had to spend it. And everybody had to have a chunk."

But Wally is adamant that money wasn't squandered, he just thinks the band, having come from a level just above the poverty line, were overly concerned with the way it was spent. As far as he was concerned, managers of rock bands signed to major labels took cabs and stayed in good hotels. Money was rolling in, so Wally couldn't see what the problem was. As for criticisms of his working methods, Wally maintains he told the band when they first met that he would not run errands for the band, act as tour manager, or generally participate on the level of the kid who manages his friends and drives the van.

"From day one I made it clear that I didn't do those kinds of things," he insists. "I told them I'd make them lots of money – enough money to hire a personal day to day person. I told them 'I won't do those things, and don't ever think I will!' And I think that became a problem."

Wally was right; it did. The band didn't see why they had to hire a day to day person out of income that their management had already commissioned by 15% just to do work that they felt their management should be doing in the first place.

"Wally was supposed to be our day-to-day person," Eitzel insists. "But he didn't do anything day-to-day. I had to organise the photos shoots, the flights and everything else." This was especially annoying as the management didn't seem to be overly busy anyway.

Bruce Kaphan had much more experience of the industry than the other band members. Unlike the rest of American Music Club who had had day jobs, Kaphan had been making a living as a musician and engineer for some time. He hadn't had any say when the new management were appointed, and did not consider Wally to be either a shrewd or effective manager. Also, Kaphan still felt he should have been allowed to produce *Mercury* and blamed Wally for not insisting to Warners that he did.

All of these issues had been festering since the *Mercury* sessions, and culminated during the middle of the UK tour.

"When we stayed at Leeds," Eitzel complains, "Wally stayed at the Intercontinental, while we stayed in a bed and breakfast. His reasoning was that he had to be near a fax. We thought, 'What?' We made such a big stink that in Glasgow the next night he stayed in the same shitty hotel as us. Wally Brill doesn't remember any of this, but it was the next night in Manchester where things turned irrevocably sour.

Wally wanted to follow each night of the tour, considering it to be an important time for the band. But, as AMC already had their old friend Mark Terrill along as road manager, there wasn't a lot of day to day work for Wally to actually do. This led to more questions about what it was exactly that Wally did for his money. In an effort to improve his relations with the singer and to show some goodwill, Wally took over some of the more mundane duties for this leg of the tour, including booking some of the hotel rooms – something that was previously Terrill's responsibility.

In Manchester, Eitzel and Vudi were booked to do a local radio interview after the show. They had an early start the next morning, so at the last minute Wally organised for them to switch to a hotel nearer the radio station. It was all done in a huge hurry and Wally somehow forgot to book a room for Bruce Kaphan, who ended up sleeping on a temporary bed in a room shared with one of the guys from the road crew. Considering Kaphan has always felt insecure about his standing in the band, this was more serious than it sounds.

"My memory was that it wasn't that big a deal at the time," Wally recalls. "Everybody shared… [But] that night Bruce went ballistic. He said, 'What am I? A roadie?' He felt he was not respected."

Kaphan threatened to quit the band, but though he was eventually placated, Eitzel was outraged by Wally's insensitive error. The singer refused to talk to his manager for weeks afterwards, and would walk out of any room if Wally walked in. For the tour's duration, Eitzel would even refuse to travel in the same car or van with Wally. Mark Terrill would end up interfacing between them. Wally would ask him to ask Eitzel a question, and Eitzel would ask Terrill to tell Wally to "Get fucked."

For relations to have deteriorated so dramatically over such a small thing as one hotel reservation, seems an absurd state of events, but for Eitzel it brought to the surface all of his anger and resentment over Wally's behaviour. Still, it was the kind of incident that, with the right will, could easily have been avoided or quickly defused, but Wally was perhaps too much in awe of Eitzel to have a go at properly clearing the air.

"This one event catapulted the whole thing out of control," Terrill sighs. "Bruce ended up sleeping on some rolled up cot or something, and rather than come and bother me, because he thought it was a problem with Wally, he just slept there and ate his sour grapes or whatever. These things went on and everyone just stored them away…"

In the meantime, the behind-the-scenes bad feeling did nothing to harm the band's live performances. On stage the band were playing great shows, and Eitzel – whatever his true mood – managed to play the raconteur and clown as well as the tortured singer.

At the Bristol Fleece and Firkin, he even performed two acoustic songs rather surreally wearing a piece of ham featuring a teddy bear pattern hanging from his nose.

"No other country in the world would make smoked ham with a picture of a teddy bear on it," he would comment afterwards. He might have added, that no singer-songwriter in the world would play a song while wearing the stuff.

On the penultimate night of the UK leg of the tour, AMC were in the Northern England town of Sheffield. It was a Saturday night at the Leadmill, and the crowd was packed with students, talking noisily through every track as they waited impatiently for the post-gig disco. Only a fraction of the crowd were there to see American Music Club. In spite of the band's new major label backing, it was a sharp reminder of their relative cult status. During a pause between songs, while the background chatter grew louder and louder, a fan from Birmingham shouted as loud as he could:

"American Music Club, the best fucking band in the world." The fifty or sixty people gathered around the stage that were actually listening, nodded and murmured their approval. Eitzel smiled and dedicated a song to this fan. But considering this was the night before their biggest London show to date, the gig was an unsettling experience.

After their set, the band lingered amongst the students, talking to fans and trying to forget the whole experience. The next morning they drove the 200 miles south to London, and prepared for the most important show of their lives – a sold-out show headlining the 1,600-capacity Astoria Theatre.

AMC rose to the occasion, and put on one of their finest performances in front of a rapt audience.

"It was the best I've ever seen them," Mick Griffiths remembers. "A great night – a real buzz – a major achievement, and a step up. They really delivered."

Backstage though things were not so clear.

"The one thing I do remember," Mark Terrill says, "Is that after the show, there was not a consensus as to what had happened. We were all milling around backstage, not saying anything – just looking at each other, wondering. There was no real feeling that 'Yes! We've done it,' or 'We failed,' though the Virgin people there were very positive."

But, as Tim Mooney confesses, "there was never a lot of euphoria in that band."

Eventually, AMC decamped to the Columbia Hotel, where they got extremely drunk. Gradually it sunk in that the show had been a triumph, Dan Pearson would consider it the highlight of their career. Later though, their celebrations were overwhelmed by an encroaching exuberant wedding party, and then Eitzel suddenly got depressed and went to bed.

After a last minute trip back to Glasgow to perform three songs on former Fairground Attraction singer Eddi Reader's BBC Scotland TV show, AMC headed off to mainland Europe for the next leg of their tour. They had left the country by the time *The Guardian* pronounced their Astoria show "damn fine." *The Times* would go even further and concluded a rave review thus, "This was apparently the biggest audience AMC had played to; not for long."

The press consensus was that AMC were about to become massively successful; and yet, even as AMC boarded their flights to the continent, it was a dream that was already behind them. For all the ballyhoo, the band were not getting noticed by the mainstream. In spite of the heaped praise, AMC didn't appear on a single magazine cover, and even with a host of pluggers at their disposal, Virgin could not get AMC more than a few cursory plays on the radio.

The positive press and improved distribution helped *Mercury* enter the UK album charts at number 41, but two weeks later it had fallen out of the top 100.

Still, at least the album had charted. But when AMC's debut UK single "Johnny Mathis' Feet," stalled at number 58 and the album sales showed no upturn, things started to look more problematic. The hugely expensive, self-mocking karaoke-spoof video for "Johnny Mathis' Feet" was shown only once on British TV. Two other videos were made at equally vast expense, but would never be completed or broadcast.

"It was just money down the drain," Dan Pearson admits.

For the follow-up to "Mathis," Virgin released "Keep Me Around" on the 27th June. It charted for one week at number 88, then disappeared.

Wally put more pressure on Virgin to get the band some airplay, but even though they worked as hard as they could, nothing was happening.

Without a hit single or any airplay, *Mercury* quickly faded from view, and the press went on to the next big thing. Worldwide sales of the album eventually approached the 60,000 mark, which was a big improvement on *Everclear*, but considering the money tied up in *Mercury*, and the huge promotional push it received, this was not a good result.

According to Wally, Virgin were not discouraged by this performance.

"Ashley Newton believed that there should be a really slow build," he recalls. "And that it didn't matter. Ashley thought that there would be time... The problem was that the band had clearly been launched now, this momentum would not go on forever."

It was hard to avoid wondering, if AMC did not succeed now – with ten years' momentum, the best reviews imaginable and a host of highly motivated pluggers working on their behalf – would they ever?

The band's UK agent Mick Griffiths believed the only reason AMC failed to make that all-important breakthrough was the difficult nature of the *Mercury* album itself; but he also doubted the band would get another opportunity.

"Had *Mercury* been a commercial record AMC could quite easily have been a big band, because everyone was ready for them. Every band has one window of opportunity in their career, where everything has built up for them. And when it is right, everything goes on from there, you suddenly start an irreversible momentum that will take them onto a new level. [The release of *Mercury*] was that point for AMC, and they failed to deliver an album that a major label could use."

Though weird, *Mercury* was a good album, but all the great rock album artists who have fostered long and interesting careers have always had more of a handle on the timing of the difficult, inaccessible record. When a successful artist makes an uncompromising album, it is nearly always a reaction to a more accessible work that was also a huge commercial success. With *Mercury*, AMC reacted against the relative accessibility of *Everclear*, but their profile was so low that nobody noticed. Instead all people heard was a strange multi-layered, intriguing but non-commercial record.

"We fucked it up really," Eitzel admits. "I should have told Mitchell that I wanted to make a big pop record. I remember Spike Hyde told me when *Mercury* came out, 'Mark, all you had to do to become a huge success was to make

California again. The songs are there, but why does it sound so fucking weird?' I said, 'Well, we're making art.' He said, 'You didn't have to make art, you had to make another *California*, and you'd have done it.' And he was right... Looking back, I wish we had made that big pop record..."

He would redress the balance, if he got another chance.

Chapter Eleven

It's Not Funny But It's A Joke

"But when a band is going up, the audience, the public or whatever, senses that and people want to hitch a ride. Once they sense that the band is never going to get any bigger, or is on the way down, they are not interested."

Peter Buck

"The entire business is run on bullshit ... But you don't have to fucking go up to your neck and eat it as well. With a bit of thought, you can sort of paddle across it."

Billy Bragg in Spin *1985*

"If you're not successful and there are five people to pay, it's better if you're not successful and there is one person to pay."

Mark Eitzel

Since AMC's first real stab at commercial success with *Everclear*, the rock and roll playing field had changed dramatically. When they first came to the attention of the music press, as a bunch of ordinary-looking guys playing guitar music with introspective lyrics, AMC were an anachronism. But the emergence of the Seattle grunge sound pioneered by Nirvana and Pearl Jam, had brought guitar rock back to the mainstream. Though the singers of both bands were literate, melancholy and prone to bouts of self-loathing, their relatively uncommercial sounding albums had gone on to become multi-million sellers. It was ironic considering AMC were regularly told they could not sell records because their lyrics were too depressing, but then Nirvana and Pearl Jam's music was such a fierce punk-hard rock amalgam that many of their fans were less concerned with what Kurt or Eddie were yowling about.

While the connection wasn't noticed at the time, *Melody Maker*'s Allan Jones is convinced that AMC were precursors of the grunge movement, in that "They were among the first to evoke that sense of a lonely, dispossessed and disenfranchised voice that ran through Nirvana and Pearl Jam's lyrics."

Interestingly, the ill-fated Cobain was said to be a great admirer of *Everclear*, and Pearl Jam's Eddie Vedder had been a fan of American Music Club for years.

"Pearl Jam's song 'Black'," Jones maintains, "Couldn't have been written without AMC's songs as an example. 'Black' doesn't quote directly from 'Western Sky,' but it paraphrases the line 'Please be happy baby' where Vedder sings in a very Eitzel way, 'I hope you have a beautiful life'."

Vedder confirmed Jones' interpretation when they first met. "Oh yes, nobody ever picked up on that," the singer told him. "It is American Music Club, but I'm surprised that anyone here has even heard of them."

In the spring of 1993, Pearl Jam were recording in the San Francisco area, and through mutual acquaintances got to know AMC. As a result of this burgeoning friendship, in May 1993 Eddie Vedder and bassist Jeff Ament, joined AMC on stage at Slim's for an impromptu version of AC/DC's "Highway to Hell" and a stab at "Bad Liquor."

Eitzel admitted to *Rolling Stone* that the impromptu jam "was really fun," and Vedder and Ament enjoyed it so much that they approached AMC about filling some support slots on the forthcoming Pearl Jam tour.

These dates would be in large venues, and it was a good chance for AMC to reach a whole new audience, but Eitzel had serious misgivings. The band had a packed schedule already and they never performed well in support slots. Also Pearl Jam were after all a hard rock band; their audience would not be receptive to AMC's more fragile sound. Wally and Ross persevered, convinced it was a golden opportunity, and so AMC cancelled a scheduled appearance at the prestigious French *Les Incorruptibles* festival in order to join Pearl Jam for a short West Coast tour towards the end of October 1993.

AMC were not advertised as the support band for any of these shows, so there were not many of their fans there, and for all Pearl Jam's enthusiasm, their fans did not take to American Music Club. Even though the band consciously played a louder and more rock 'n' roll set than usual, at gig after gig they were booed, jeered and pelted with rubbish.

"They were hard shows," Tim Mooney recalls, "We were not a rock band. I think it was hard for the guys in Pearl Jam too. To see that the bulk of their audience did not want to sit down and listen to us."

While at the occasional show the audience gave AMC some respite, their problems came to a climax at Berkeley's Greek Theatre – a 5,000-seat open air amphitheatre – where they were third on the bill below Pearl Jam and Henry Rollins.

"That was the worst one," Mooney remembers with a shudder. "Because the Henry Rollins people just wanted to see Henry Rollins – I'm not sure that they even wanted to see Pearl Jam. And it was scary. They threw things at us – sandwiches, apples…" AMC had to put up with salvos of coins, beer cans, bottles full of piss, and even a few shoes.

With a sense of horror, Eitzel surveyed the audience around the front of the stage,

"It was five mosh pits, like an inferno kind of dream with bodies coming up and coming down. It was not a good sight."

During the band's set, the young "jock" crowd was bored and belligerent; they wanted to rock and AMC were not giving them what they wanted. It was another reminder that for all their acclaim, AMC were still very far down the rock 'n' roll ladder. But, faced with a mixture of indifference and hostility, Eitzel was determined to get a reaction.

After "Keep Me Around" Eitzel responded to the crowd noise with a curt "Yeah, thanks. Fuck off." They later followed a vicious "Dead Part of You" with an unrehearsed romp through the garage classic, "Louie, Louie" that Eitzel dedicated sarcastically to "these guys here" at the front of the stage. By the time they reached "Heaven's 10,000 Whores," AMC had started to thrive on the negative energy, turning it back at the crowd.

"You'll hate this one too..." Eitzel sneered as he introduced "Sick of Food." "Good! Good! ... hate it... c'mon..."

Afterwards he thanked the crowd with bitter sarcasm, "It's so nice to meet a crowd that loves you, you know ... a nice polite Berkeley crowd..."

When the singer announced that his band only had two more songs left, the crowd let out a huge cheer, and some kids in the front give him the finger. Full of rage and frustration, Eitzel yelled out "Sieg Heil to you!" and gave the crowd a nazi salute.

He would later call the Pearl Jam experience "incredibly depressing." The only thing AMC learnt from the mini-tour was how to hone down their set to its bare rock 'n' roll essentials; which was not necessarily a good thing.

When they had completed their last Pearl Jam support slot, the band started to plan the next album. The Pearl Jam debacle did however leave a few lingering thoughts in the minds of band members and management. While they didn't want to be an out and out rock band, it did give them a chance to see what riches were available for a band that crossed over into mainstream rock success. All kinds of left-field rock newcomers were appearing from nowhere and selling millions of albums while AMC had yet to shift 100,000. At the same time, for Eitzel at least, the experience reinforced how far away AMC's music was from the sounds which could captivate these kinds of audiences. He would later confide in journalist Caitlin Moran,

"We got signed to Virgin. But the other members of the band became like dazed cows when we got the money. They were like, 'Mark, write pop. Write pop songs. We're gonna be the next REM.' And I'm not the next REM. Nowhere near. I write these little songs."

Tim Mooney is sceptical of Eitzel's charge, "I think he may have felt that, but I don't think anyone was [pressing him to write pop songs]." Though Eitzel dismisses the idea of wanting to become the next REM, he more than anyone else in the band wanted the success that he felt AMC deserved. He'd learned from the commercial suicide of *Mercury*, and though he didn't want to turn into Pearl Jam, he had seen the kind of money they were pulling in.

Also, Eitzel knew that Warners and Virgin would not keep faith with the band forever. They would be allowed one near-miss, but the next album had to be a financial success.

"Reprise didn't really put too much pressure on us," Dan Pearson insists, "But it was a two-album deal with options so we knew if it didn't sell a little better ... There was that thing: 'That last record was really great you guys, but it didn't really sell anything.' So we were trying to do something more commercial."

Whatever their apprehensions, for the next album, AMC were going to look towards the pop mainstream.

As with *Mercury*, the first thing they had to do was appoint a producer. Bruce Kaphan knew what he wanted.

"I was lobbying very heavily with the band that we should record the album ourselves, much like we did *Everclear*. That was the album that got people interested in us."

While Eitzel believed that Kaphan "did a great job" on *Everclear*, he felt that because Bruce was now formally in the band, they should have a producer who was an "outside influence – another pair of ears."

The recording budget was $250,000, so AMC could afford to hire anyone they wanted. But the band and their management were wary of simply recruiting another big name.

To the pedal steel player's horror, instead of suggesting that Kaphan and the band produced the album themselves, Wally recommended Joe Chicarelli, who remixed *Everclear*. Eitzel and the other band members accepted the logic, but Kaphan, who had hated Chicarelli's mixing on that record, was incensed. As far as he could see, this was a case of nepotism that was not in the band's interests.

"It was a nightmare," Kaphan remembers. "I could not believe that it was happening – it was impossible to understand."

Joe Chicarelli, on the other hand, was delighted. He had kept in touch with Eitzel and some of the other band members, and seen AMC live whenever he had the opportunity. He thought he understood what the band was all about and was keen to work with them,

"I told them I thought there was a way to do the twisted, broken thing that they do normally, in a way that would appeal to more people... without diluting it or kowtowing to radio."

This was exactly what the band wanted. They recruited Chicarelli for a fee of $40,000 plus 2 points on sales and in January 1994 they began two weeks of intense pre-production. The rehearsals went well, and AMC came away with good demo arrangements of Eitzel's new material.

"Wish the World Away," and "The Revolving Door" were both earmarked early on as possible singles, and Chicarelli considered one other track especially promising.

"The demo they made at the rehearsal room of Gena Rowlands ["What Holds the World Together"] was brilliant," Chicarelli remembers. "It was so breathtaking and emotional."

AMC then relocated to a $2,000 dollar a day recording studio for the actual recording of the album. The Warners executives left the band alone at this stage, and showed few outward signs of anxiety about the commercial potential of

AMC's new material, but it was obvious that at these rates, they would expect to sell significant quantities of whatever the band produced. They would be pleased to know that from the off AMC had made it clear to Joe Chicarelli that they wanted to do something more pop, with a bit more of a groove. Also, in his writing, Eitzel was consciously avoiding the plaintive major 7th chords that had characterised his songs to date, and he had set nearly all of the new songs in 4/4 time. This emphasis of a more straightforward time signature was crucial. Eitzel normally favoured 3/4 time, but as Tim Mooney notes, "Rock people will tell you that there have been very few hit songs in waltz time."

For the first two months of recording, everything went fairly well. Chicarelli insisted Tim Mooney played to a click track, and tended to require more takes than the band felt necessary, but on the whole the basic tracks were put down with a minimum of heartache, and everyone liked the way they sounded. But, when it came to finishing everything off, a series of disputes broke out that would permanently damage the band.

As the recording costs mounted, the difficulties involved in getting some of the more radio-friendly tracks to realise their potential caused tension between Eitzel and Chicarelli. Also Eitzel became increasingly frustrated by the band's refusal to play his songs the way he wanted. Finally, having been frozen out by Mitchell Froom on *Mercury*, Bruce Kaphan was determined to play a larger role on this album. Even if he couldn't produce the sessions, he was adamant he would have input, and as he felt he could do the job better than Chicarelli, this would inevitably bring more conflict.

Bruce Kaphan was wrongly credited with mixing the final version of "The Thorn in My Side is Gone," but this was one of the first songs on which he fell out with Chicarelli.

Kaphan had suggested a different approach to the song,

"I wanted to record Mark's voice and guitar as a live performance in his living room, in his house in San Francisco with the doors open, just to get a kind of lazy afternoon feel." Kaphan also wanted a string quartet playing live at the same time, but Chicarelli would not countenance it. After a number of attempts in the studio with various overdubs, they did end up at Eitzel's house, but Chicarelli insisted they record in the basement instead, which Kaphan believes made the track sound too "claustrophobic."

The main source of dispute between artist and producer came towards the end of the initial recording process. Chicarelli was convinced that Eitzel kept drifting slightly out of tune. Eitzel thought the vocals sounded fine, so it drove him to distraction when the producer made him sing things like the bridge in "What Holds The World Together" over and over again. But some other songs were even worse.

"For 'In the Shadow of the Valley'," Eitzel explains, "I did twenty vocal techniques in a row to be pieced together, and Joe decided that we had the wrong microphone. But he didn't say that. He said: 'It's just not working – you're not singing it right.' I was like 'Joe, this is how I sing it'. So we changed the mike and I had to do it another thirty times another day."

Chicarelli maintains that Eitzel pushed him to get a vocal sound that was "really upfront and intimate. He wanted to sing really softly." As producer, he just felt that if the vocals were to be so much to the foreground, they had to be perfect. As Eitzel hated having effects on his vocals, Chicarelli's options were limited, but he was convinced that more depth was needed than just Eitzel's naked voice. He did try some delay and reverb, but Eitzel hated it. and Chicarelli didn't feel it sounded right.

Finally, Chicarelli picked up an old "Ursa Major Space Station" analogue effects box in a local pawn shop, which he felt solved the problem.

"It has a funny, canny sound," he explains. "Something about it with Mark's voice really worked. It filled out his voice without sounding too much like effects."

But the arguments over vocals didn't stop. Chicarelli still felt Eitzel needed to tighten his pitch up on certain songs. Eitzel couldn't hear where he was out of tune and was horrified to find Chicarelli spending hours harmonising his vocals.

"Joe didn't understand how I could sing out of tune and be happy with it!" he would tell Jack Rabid. "You know, this was my eighth or ninth album, and I know how I want to be in a studio and I know what I want to hear now. And I don't want things to be perfect, I want them to be really emotive."

As time went on, Eitzel began to see Chicarelli as more and more of an inter-ference.

"For 'What Holds the World Together'," he claims, "I changed the middle bridge, I wrote that bit about the 'light changing green, green like your fear....' And in the end I had to really fight Joe to let me change the lyrics to the middle eight, he'd say 'These new lyrics are not as good, the song has lost its quality now, the song isn't the same now, it's no good'." For once Eitzel stuck to his guns, insisting he would sing the words he wanted to sing. But this was Chicarelli's favourite song on the album, and he would repeatedly clash with Eitzel as they tried in vain to recapture the magic of the rehearsal demo.

In an argument over which vocal take to use, Eitzel eventually caved into Chicarelli just to placate the producer. He then watched in astonishment as the frazzled producer started shouting furiously, "Yeah, Fuck you! Fuck you! I told you that version was the best. Fuck you!"

"It was insane," Eitzel complains. "On 'Wish the World Away' it took two days to get a fuzz guitar sound. Joe did not like my guitar sound. Vudi and I were going to do the track live, and we both had our amps set up the way we like. In my headphones, I could hear Joe changing my guitar to the complete opposite of how it sounded. I said to Joe, 'Did you change it?' Joe says, 'Yeah, well it wasn't working with Vudi's guitar.' I said, 'Just make it my amp sound. Do you mind?'"

"'Wish The World Away' was difficult," Chicarelli concedes, "Because there was a feeling that this could be a single, but that it had to made unique and hon-est enough for the band – they didn't want it to sound like the generic alternative pop song of the time. I remember spending a little extra time, trying to come up with something that would give it their signature as opposed to sounding like some band out of Seattle."

Though they did have disagreements during the basic recording, it was during the overdubs and mixing that things really deteriorated. Chicarelli was searching for the final touches that would transform the basic tracks into radio material with hit potential.

"You can craft a basic performance in a matter of minutes," he explains. "But then it can take you days to come up with the one or two little finishing elements that make the whole thing pay off melodically... That can be very tense, because you spend all this time agonising over tiny little parts."

But though necessary, this process was not an exact science. It involved trying lots of different things and seeing which fitted. As Chicarelli continued experimenting, the band got more and more frustrated – especially as Joe wasn't great at explaining to them exactly what he was looking for.

"All those overdub sessions," Tim Mooney sighs. "I couldn't bear to go to them any more. It was just days of looking for what other overdubs we could put on these songs and not because they needed them. It just got out of hand."

As the studio costs spiralled upwards, the arguments became fiercer and more frequent. Eitzel claims Chicarelli gradually lost the plot, and ended up telling the engineers to just close their eyes and push buttons at random, "Because I don't really know what I am looking for."

Chicarelli maintains that if he had said something like this, it would have been in a joking manner, but he does acknowledge that things got out of control. If he hadn't loved Eitzel's music so much, he might have found it easier to maintain a sense of balance.

"Somewhere during the course of the record, perhaps we all got a little too precious," he admits. "We were making something bigger than it needed be. Adding a little overdub here and a little overdub there."

In the process, some of the spontaneity of the original takes was lost. Also, in his quest for a more pop feel, Chicarelli reduced the presence of Vudi's quirky but inspirational guitar playing. Vudi's guitar sound was such an integral part of American Music Club that without it the music lost a lot of its heart. Chicarelli is adamant this wasn't a conscious decision.

"For 'Can You Help Me,' we wanted a groove-based guitar part," he explains. "And Vudi had a hard time coming up with it. Then Bruce just picked up the guitar and came up with an idea that was great."

"Can You Help Me" was one of Eitzel's most promising demos: it had a rock groove, a strong chorus and a beautiful melody. In its solo acoustic incarnation, it was one of the songwriter's finest moments. But the process of recording it brought back to the surface all of Eitzel's problems with band collaborations.

"My 4-track arrangement is the best version of that song," he would later insist. "In the demo the bass line does the same thing as my chords. The guitar does the same thing as my chords – we all do the same thing together, and no fills – just a simple drum part. Dumb, right? But the biggest problem with American Music Club was that they didn't know how to play simple songs. They would always say, 'Simple songs are the hardest to play.' They are musicians – I am a songwriter. It's a different thing...

"With this particular song, I wanted to hear this very simple song, and the band were like, 'Well, we're not going to play your parts.' I'd say, 'Well, I worked on the bass part for hours, and you won't play it.' I'd hear, 'No, you did that. That's your thing. If you come in here and give us this stuff, it's insulting'."

With this track and others, Eitzel maintains that he tried to put his foot down. He wanted to make a more straightforward pop album, and tried to get the band to play simple parts, but they would not do it. They rejected his arrangements. But, considering Vudi, Kaphan, Pearson and Mooney were all extremely talented and creative musicians, whose distinctive and original input had for years helped realise the full potential of Eitzel's songs, it was not surprising that they would not accept this new approach.

Working with Chicarelli, Eitzel would tell Jack Rabid, "Basically brought to a crisis the whole American Music Club; it brought into relief the fact that we were a democracy, and that a democracy doesn't work in a band."

"Without Tom Mallon being there and being a total dictator to all of us," Eitzel later reflected, "It was a disaster, because there were five people all wanting their own thing."

If the overdubs were problematic, the mixing process was a nightmare. All of the problems and disputes reached their apotheosis when it came to finishing "Wish the World Away."

By this stage, Eitzel realised that the album was going significantly over budget, and that these increased costs were coming out of his own royalties. To his mind, many of the overdub sessions were a waste of time and money. When Chicarelli took four days – at $2,000 a day – to come up with four separate mixes of the song, none of which Chicarelli or Eitzel liked, the singer reached the end of his tether.

"On that song," Eitzel told Rabid, "Chicarelli hated the original demo; he said it sounded like garage-rock, and we were like, "So?" Because he heard the "hit" there, he tried to make it into hit-rock, which to him translates to Pat Benatar. And so he would spend like two days working on a fuzz tone sound for a guitar. Two days!" As the disputes became more savage, Chicarelli twice threatened to quit, but each time Eitzel asked him to stay. The singer resolved to make things work, though inwardly he continued to seethe. (As an odd footnote, Jack Rabid had recently made a record that Chicarelli had also produced. Rabid found Chicarelli a joy to work with; and, when the album went over budget, the producer took this increase out of his own fee.)

In an attempt to break the deadlock on "Wish The World Away" Bob Clearmountain and then Tom Lord Alge were recruited at $5,000 a time, to come up with alternative mixes of the song.

Clearmountain was a serious heavyweight who had remixed parts of Springsteen's *Born In The USA*, Journey's *Raised On Radio* and Crowded House's *Woodface*. No matter how much anyone said they weren't looking for hit singles, recruiting Clearmountain was a clear sign that the record company wanted results.

But, for all his track record, Clearmountain's mixes were quickly scrapped. It was yet more money down the drain. The band were happier with Tom Lord-Alge's mix which would be used as AMC's next single, but Eitzel still found it difficult working with him,

"I went to Tom and I said 'I'm not sure about the reverb.' Tom was watching a baseball game on TV, and without looking away from the screen, he said, 'OK, which one? I got a reverb on the first two lines on the first part of the song. I got more reverbs on the bridge. I got different kinds of reverb on the chorus, and I got another reverb ... OK, you tell me which one you don't like, alright.' I said, 'I just want it to sound cool.' Tom turned to the engineer and said, 'Cool, he wants it cool.' And they both laughed in my face."

"I wanted that song to be a dumb little garage rock song," Eitzel later reflected. "The demo is brilliant. $325,000 later 'Wish the World Away' became ... the meaning of the song really reflected how we felt after we made that record."

All of the problems between band and producer reached a climax when Chicarelli played AMC the initial rough mixes.

"I hated them," Eitzel recalls with vehemence. "Danny went through the roof, and I thought they sucked – they were really bass heavy, and to me sounded phoney. Vudi and Tim said they were great, while we were freaking out."

Vudi and Tim Mooney had no idea what the problem was, and thought Eitzel was crazy. He insisted they were terrible but decided to be diplomatic in order to keep the peace. Then Chicarelli overheard Eitzel bitching about the mixes and another row broke out.

"Joe finally confronted us," Eitzel explains. "Because he knew something was up, and I should have said, 'You know, I just hate it. If the final mixes sound like this, we can't continue. I was too wimpy, I should have said 'You're fired right now.' But I didn't, I went along with it, I said, 'I love you Joe, I think you're really talented...' – mostly because Tim and Vudi were so into the status quo – so into keeping the thing going. Me and Bruce – especially Bruce – felt that the record was fucked – that it sounded like shit!"

Considering Kaphan thought he should have been allowed to produce the album, it's not surprising he didn't like the mixes. For all the complaints, Warners executives like Michael Ostin were pleased with what they heard. It would have been impossible for Chicarelli to please everybody. The fact that Vudi and Tim liked the mixes, while Eitzel, Pearson and Kaphan felt he had ruined their album, shows what he was up against. Chicarelli's weakness was that he didn't draw Eitzel into the mixing process early enough. For all Eitzel's genius he was used to disowning his records and blaming their faults on others, whether Mallon, Froom or someone else. Now that the heat was on, Chicarelli was lining himself up as an easy fall guy.

As Chicarelli struggled to complete the mixes, the pressure did get to him, and he found it more and more difficult to discuss ideas with Eitzel without losing his cool.

"I'd go down to the sessions," Wally Brill remembers, "And Bruce would be sitting outside with Mark, saying, 'Did you hear what he did to X, Y and Z?' Bruce and Mark would be acting as though they were not involved, and as if someone was doing something to them. How can the producer do any creative work, when the artist prefers to sit outside the studio bitching about him for trying to do his job?

"I knew the songs were great, and I wanted the record to be good, and I knew Mark wanted the record to be good. I just wanted Mark to take responsibility, and I kept saying to him, 'If you don't think it's the right thing, then what is the right thing? What do you want to have as the right thing?'

"I'd go to them, 'Well, why don't you say something to Joe?' Mark goes, 'I do, but he won't listen.'

"In these situations I'd come in and ask Vudi, 'Vudi, How bad is it?' And Vudi would go, 'It's pretty bad, but you know…'

"I had the impression from Vudi that communication would have been possible, but finally Joe would explode and they would get into terrible rows, and it appeared that there was no way that Mark would be able to get a record that he could listen to if Joe mixed it."

Whether Wally's words sank in or not, about this time Eitzel did finally accept that he had to take control of the situation. Maybe he still believed the album could be a hit if it was finished and mixed properly, or perhaps he sensed that this would be the last American Music Club record and so wanted to get it right. With years of resentment at the way his songs had been arranged by others, he resolved to have his say. But by now things had got so acrimonious that Chicarelli was no longer listening. As Eitzel fought for more input, Chicarelli kept sending the band out of the studio, saying he just needed more time to fix the problems. He just needed another hour, or another three hours, or another day. All the while, the costs continued to escalate.

"I went to Joe," Eitzel says, "And told him, 'Joe, we've got to end this process. We're $50,000 over budget.' And he said, 'You don't care about your art do you? This is your future. This is who you are, and you don't care.' I'd say, 'Joe we are $50,000 over budget – money that is coming out of my pocket – and we're not making any difference to anything. We should just stop."

"I'd been working on the record for a long time," Chicarelli concedes, "And I think I got too close to it."

Eitzel sacked his producer the next day, but that only solved part of the problem. He and the band were still at loggerheads about how the album should sound. With all his patience long since exhausted, Eitzel got Wally to hire an engineer, banished the rest of the band from the control room, and proceeded to mix the album himself.

In the circumstances, drastic action was necessary, but this severely alienated the other members of AMC. Tim Mooney shrugged and left Eitzel to get on with it, but Bruce Kaphan couldn't believe that he wasn't going to have a say in the completion of the album, and went home resolving to quit the band. Dan Pearson was no happier.

"I just gave up…." He says. "No one was listening to me, so I just felt 'Fuck you guys, just do whatever you want!'"

Jim Scott who would later produce Whiskeytown – alt-country pioneers and in some ways inheritors of the AMC mantle – was brought in as engineer, and Eitzel got to work. But Vudi also stuck around. So the two members of AMC whose ideas of how this record should sound were the furthest apart, were left to argue the toss over every last detail.

"I'd come in and say, 'Right, let's make the best of this shit'." Eitzel recalls, "And Vudi would come in and go, 'I need a goth thing'.

"Even mixing B-sides for the single releases was a problem. I was mixing the B-sides in the studio with the engineer, and I'd been working with him for hours, when Vudi came in, listened for a while and then said, 'This really sucks! It really sucks! It's shit!' And the engineer didn't really know how to deal with that. He'd react and say, 'What do we do?' I'd say, 'Well, we've been at this for five hours, but what do you want?' He'd say, 'I think we should do it like... I don't know, but it has to be like a goth thing – a real Bauhaus goth thing. But, disco. A real disco goth Bauhaus thing.' And I'd get back, and find that there was no snare drum in the mix. But the snare is on the other microphones, so it just sounds like the snare is turned down. And there's this huge ocean of reverb everywhere. So I'd sit there and try and work with that, as opposed to what I'd been going towards, which was a very simple, honest, no reverb, mix with just the guitars up."

Vudi decided that they needed to do two separate mixes of the entire album: an Eitzel and a Vudi mix. Then they could decide which one to use. But, Vudi didn't seem to grasp the cost of this exercise. Every agonising step of this final mixing process seemed like another nail in AMC's coffin. It was a case study for Eitzel on why he should become a solo artist. When the whole thing was finished, he told the band, "If this album doesn't sell a million copies, I am leaving."

After the record was finally completed, AMC had time for a brief period of rest before the whole circus began once again. First off they had to film videos for the next batch of singles. They also started playing a few low-key live dates in preparation for the full UK and US tour that would tie in with the new album's Autumn release.

In the meantime an AMC cover of "Goodbye to Love" appeared on the well-received Carpenters tribute album, *If I Were A Carpenter*. The track had been recorded during the Chicarelli sessions, and Joe had again insisted that Eitzel's vocals were out of tune. By then Eitzel didn't care, he went to meet the project's executive producer and told him,

"You know what? This track is not going on the record, because I am not going to re-sing it. I'm sorry! It is done. If you don't like it, take it off the record." The executive decided to keep the track, and it was one of the highlights of a humourous and warmly affectionate album that also featured Cracker, Sonic Youth, Sheryl Crow and The Cranberries.

In April, AMC supported Smashing Pumpkins at the Fillmore Auditorium, where they didn't get a soundcheck because the headliners were "flying in from somewhere" at the last minute. As tickets were $30 there were no actual AMC fans in the audience and bad memories of the Pearl Jam shows still lingered.

"We thought because it was Smashing Fucking Pumpkins, we should play some of our rockier songs to win over the audience," Eitzel explains. "But, yes, the audience still hated us."

Bruce Kaphan quit the band that night. He liked the quieter, acoustic and ambient aspects of the American Music Club sound, but felt that at many of their recent shows they had been rocking out to much.

"I have no desire to be in a rock band," he would say.

But Kaphan's resignation had been coming for a while. It wasn't just a perceived change of musical direction. He had been unhappy during the recording of the last two albums, and was sick of working with the "wrong producers". He resented Wally's approach to management and felt no one listened to what he said anyway.

Also, Kaphan simply didn't enjoy going on tour and was tired of playing the "rock toilets" of the USA. Live performance was a problem for Kaphan as his equipment was cumbersome, difficult to set up, and not easily tuned. Even now the band could afford a road crew none of them knew how to deal with his pedal steel. Support slots were a nightmare, as he had to set up and dismantle his own gear in a particular hurry, and play without having soundchecked anything properly.

Kaphan would later collaborate with Eitzel again. But for now, he started carving out a lucrative living as an engineer and session musician, working with The Black Crowes, David Byrne and later REM.

AMC did not replace Kaphan. Ever since Tim Mooney had joined the band, they had felt that this was the final line-up. Kaphan's pedal steel had been a huge part of AMC's live sound, and the band were now torn about which direction to move in. Eitzel favoured the band's acoustic work, and was tired of romping through "Bad Liquor" just for the sake of it, whereas other members thought maybe a return to their more rock 'n' roll roots might be a good thing – especially in the post-grunge climate where hard rock was all the rage.

AMC's first outings without Bruce were a few semi "secret" San Francisco bar shows. In June at The Thirsty Swede, the band were a drunken mess, but by the end of July when they played The Bottom of the Hill and then returned to The Thirsty Swede, things were much better. The post-Kaphan arrangements were more stripped down, but the sound was still immensely powerful. But, opinion within the band was very much divided. Pearson felt this approach was giving the band a new lease of life,

"When we first started playing as a four piece again, without Bruce as orchestral conductor, it rocked like the early days." He remembers. "I liked it."

Eitzel however, hated it and took an extreme view of his band's prospects,

"When Bruce quit because of all the bullshit, it was obvious that we couldn't play live. Vudi doesn't play rhythm guitar, I don't play rhythm guitar, Bruce held it all together. He was the cement. And when he left, AMC left. AMC was over."

In spite of Eitzel's pessimism, the band continued to prepare for a full European and US tour. Then in August, he came to London to do interviews and prepare the ground for the new album. He also lined up a sold-out solo acoustic show at the Shaw Theatre, in London's shabby Kings Cross district. Eitzel hadn't done many solo shows in the last year, and he was having difficulty preparing for his set:

"I was in the dressing room beforehand," his agent Mick Griffiths remembers, "And Mark was so nervous. He was sitting there with the tour manager trying to relearn some of the old songs, because he hadn't played them on his own in some time."

When show time came around, Eitzel was still not ready, and although he entered to very warm applause, for the first three songs he was clumsy and ill at ease – his fingers like lead – they just wouldn't go where he wanted them to go. Indeed he fluffed the intro to the first song three times.

Then, as he tersely tuned up for the fourth song, a mobile phone went off in the audience. It broke the ice, Eitzel smiled, visibly relaxed, and introduced "Can You Help Me." It blew the audience away. Any murmuring stopped, and the crowd were carried away by a searing acoustic performance that reclaimed the song from the Chicarelli sessions. All Eitzel's previous nervousness and self-consciousness had completely evaporated.

Afterwards a baby cried and Eitzel said that it was his alter ego. While he tuned up, he demonstrated the crowd surfing he witnessed during the Pearl Jam tour. These comic asides, as Sharon O'Connell tellingly pointed out, "Are Eitzel's way of saying that although these songs mean the world to him, they also mean nothing at all."

After "I've Been A Mess," Eitzel told the crowd, "Here's where I roll things up into one big happy bundle," and paused as if to enjoy the moment. Then, wrestling uneasily with his guitar, he asked the audience if they were familiar with the work of John Cassavetes. Cassavetes was a celebrated US independent film-maker, married to the actress Gena Rowlands, who starred in many of his best known films. During the making of his final film *Love Streams*, it was clear that Cassavetes' alchoholism had got far worse; to all intents and purposes, he was drinking himself to death. Eitzel watched this film with someone he was romantically involved with, he told the audience, and couldn't stop thinking about the relationship between the actress and her husband. Every turn of Gena's head, every smile and every look and gesture, seemed to encapsulate her love for Cassavetes who as well as directing also co-starred in the film. In turn, Cassavetes' direction appeared to radiate his love for Rowlands. The more Eitzel watched, the more he was convinced that he would never have that degree of love with the person he was with. He referred repeatedly to several scenes where Gena Rowlands (playing the character Sarah) and John Cassavetes (playing the character of writer and drunk, Robert Harman) stare at each other in a way that steps out of the movie and into real life.

As the audience sat in an awed silence, Eitzel then performed a breathtaking version of "What Holds the World Together." Featuring the chorus line,

"What holds the world together / Is the wind that blows through Gena Rowlands hair," this was one of Eitzel's greatest ever songs, and the performance was achingly honest. Coming after his long introduction, the effect was indescribably moving.

As a coda to Eitzel's tale, in Autumn 1996 Gena Rowlands came to London to take part in a promotional interview and question and answer session to promote her son Nick Cassavetes' new film, *Unhook The Stars*, in which she starred. Rock journalist Nick Johnstone attended with the intention of passing her a tape of the song. After the interview Johnstone seized his chance,

"I called out, 'Have you heard of a songwriter from San Francisco called Mark Eitzel who wrote a beautiful song about you called 'What Holds The World Together?'

"She looked surprised at the question and then answered that, yes, she had heard of both him and the song. I asked her if she had heard the song and she said 'No' but that she would like to. I told her that the words were very pretty and that the chorus went, *"The world is held together / by the wind that blows through Gena Rowlands' hair."* She smiled sweetly as only Gena Rowlands can and said, 'Stop it, you're going to make me cry.' When she asked how I knew of the song I told her that I had seen a concert where Mark premiered the song and introduced it as being about the beautiful loving looks that she and her late husband exchanged throughout their final movie together, *Love Streams*. She got tears in her eyes and had the nicest look on her face. I then said that I had a copy of the song in my pocket and that I would throw it up to her on stage and she said, again surprised, 'Alright' and got up from her chair... She stood on the edge of the stage and posed like a baseball player which got laughs and then I threw the cassette which fell short and hit the front of the stage, busting from its case. Someone handed it to her and she smiled and said 'Thank you'."

When Eitzel heard the story he was delighted. As this book goes to press, Eitzel has still not met Gena Rowlands, but he does have her phone number. Out walking on a street in Seattle, a cousin of Gena's approached him,

"Oh My God, Mark Eitzel! Gena loves that song." The cousin passed him Gena's telephone number and invited him to give her a call, "Gena will make you spaghetti..."

Back at the Shaw Theatre, Vudi – having given up his seat to a ticketless fan – ended up backstage, and joined Mark on electric guitar backing for the last couple of songs. It was a fitting finish to one of Eitzel's finest shows. As the audience shuffled out, journalist Caitlin Moran still had tears in her eyes. The reviews were predictably astonishing.

A short while after the show, Dan Pearson and Tim Mooney joined Eitzel and Vudi in London. After a low-key warm-up gig in Colchester, the band set off to play the Reading festival acoustic tent.

It was the band's first show in the UK since Kaphan's departure, and it seemed like they missed him. Last time AMC played the festival, they had been the highlight of the weekend, this time as they powered through rough, rocked-up versions of their louder songs, nothing would go right. The band seemed like they had been drinking far too much, and their playing was ramshackle and belligerent. Eitzel appeared really unhappy, and there was real tension among the band.

"It was just so angry." Allan Jones, who was backstage, remembers. "And it is difficult to say where the anger was pointed at."

Some songs stopped and started; others just collapsed. Classic AMC anthems like "Outside This Bar," were barely recognisable as they merged into the general noise. Eitzel was clearly rattled, and everything sounded too loud and simplistic. Without Kaphan's mesmeric pedal steel, the sound raged with frustration. It was a mess.

"It was like [without Bruce] we were just another indie sloppy rock band, not realising what we were doing," Dan Pearson remembers sadly.

"It felt like they were sacrificing everything they were good at," Allan Jones says, "So that Eitzel could put on this tortured display: I'm not happy here, so no one is going to be happy, and the audience is not going to be happy. So we're not going to play anything they know or like, or if we do play something they know, it will be in a version that no one will recognise."

"We thought it went really badly!" Mooney reflects. "It was very out of control. Everyone came off stage and we said, 'Oh My God, that was horrible!'"

Booker Mick Griffiths thought the show was dreadful, and was worried that AMC had decided to try and emulate Pearl Jam.

"I think the band wanted to rock out a bit more," he muses. "And I think Mark was too nice to argue. So, he just went along with it to keep them happy, but in his heart he didn't want that to be the case... you could feel the tension on stage and it came to a head at Reading. Mark's beautiful songs were being given a harder treatment, and it just didn't work."

Tim Mooney denies vehemently that the band was trying to attract Pearl Jam's audience, and claims the dates with that band had the opposite effect. But, something was wrong. After the show, a teary-eyed Eitzel discussed with Griffiths how bad it had been, but he wouldn't talk to the band. Later he would remember someone telling him,

"The first time you play the Reading festival is on your way up; the second time you play is on your way down." Now Eitzel realised, "That was so true."

Chapter Twelve
I'll Be Gone

"Spiritually it couldn't work for me anymore ... it was like soaking in a bathtub that had become cold, and there's nothing to do but get out."

Mark Eitzel

"I haven't expounded any ideas at all. You know, it's more like just the same idea. It's like urinating the same piss with different smells. I'm the Armitage Shanks of songwriting."

Mark Eitzel

"There are always more ties you can sever."

("Mission Rock")

On 11th September 1994, AMC released "Wish the World Away" as their new single. While it was difficult to see where all the recording budget had gone, sounding as it did like a garage classic, "WTWA" was a much more convincing stab at a rock single than either "Rise" or "Keep Me Around." Both Warners and Virgin made every effort to get the song on the radio and in an effort to nudge "WTWA" into the charts in the first week, Virgin put out a cassette single, a limited edition seven inch single and two versions of the CD single. Each format had different B-sides and there was also a collector's box that left room for two more CDs of the next single.

On the other side of the ocean, Warners commissioned the band's most expensive video to date. Though its potency declined towards the end of the '90s, video was still a hugely powerful tool, and a low-key, smoky, black and white video of AMC playing in a lowlife bar, drinking and looking enigmatic, might just have done the trick. There was a big market for the Kerouac/Bukowski vein of booze-soaked introspection.

Instead, AMC chose to mercilessly satirise themselves and the whole rock video culture. Set on a sun-drenched golden beach, the video opens with gorgeous pneumatic Baywatch babes in bathing costumes playing volleyball with muscle bound lifeguards. Every so often one of them reaches into the drinks cooler for a cherryade style drink labelled American Music Club. When the camera finally pans to the band, they are dressed from head to toe in black and grey, and look even paler and more fed up than usual. Huddled under a parasol taking shelter from the sun, they run through the song sporting permanent frowns. In a few even more bizarre touches, the video also features band members fully clothed pretending to take part in a variety of watersports, filmed in front of an obvious "blue-screen" moving backdrop. Dan Pearson is windsurfing, Vudi surfs and Eitzel, most bizarrely of all, is water-skiing.

To some followers of the band, the video was the single most self-destructive act AMC ever committed, but the band thought it was great fun.

"We like it a lot," Eitzel would say with a smile. "Our vision was realised."

Tim Mooney though, while proud of how funny the self-parody came out, was aware of the problem. "There was the question," he acknowledges, "'Was it a good idea for a video?' There was always a tendency with AMC to make fun of itself. If you know the band, it's funny, but ..." In the end the video was shown on television only once.

"It was a joke at MTV's expense that unfortunately they got," Eitzel would reflect. But at a cost approaching $100,000, it was a rather expensive joke. When the single failed to chart in the US and peaked at 46 in the UK, few people within the AMC camp were heard laughing.

American Music Club's next album was released on 25th September 1994. Like a throwback to an earlier AMC era, it was called *San Francisco*. When asked by Lauren Axelrod if the title signified that this album was a tribute to their hometown, Dan Pearson replied:

"I wouldn't say a tribute. I wanted to call the album '4,000 days of shame,' that's how long the band has been together."

"If you live somewhere, then you write about it," was all Eitzel would say.

With a colourful *Everclear*-style Jean Lowe painting for its sleeve and a title reminiscent of *California*, *San Francisco* appeared to be an attempt to reclaim some of the ground lost on *Mercury*. In spite of all the problems in the recording studio, the album was a triumph. At 14 songs, it is maybe slightly too long, but the finest ten tracks would make one of AMC's greatest albums. A pop sheen has been added, and more obvious chords and time signatures adopted, but this is no mainstream cop out and the twisted edges of American Music Club's unique musical vision are clearly present. Vudi's guitar may be used more sparingly than in the Mallon era, but when it appears, it is inventive and ferocious. As on *Everclear*, Kaphan's eerie pedal steel holds all the disparate elements together.

For all the overdubs and remixes, songs like "Can You Help Me," "Broke My Promise" and "What Holds The World Together" showcase a band still at a creative peak. The music may be weird, occasionally dissonant, and extremely jagged, but it is packed with hooks and melodies, and in places almost danceable.

While *Mercury* was written with a certain amount of artistic detachment, the new album places Eitzel back in his adopted hometown, the last city on earth, sending out dark dispatches from his own world. Though written in snatched intervals between extended spells on the music industry treadmill, these are some of Eitzel's most remarkable and accomplished songs. And, in spite of his previous attempts at avoiding the confessional format, *San Francisco* is his most personal work since *United Kingdom*.

On the album's opener, "Fearless" – in part inspired by Peter Weir's film of the same name about the emotional problems encountered by plane crash survivors – Eitzel returns to one of the immensely personal themes that has dominated his work since *California*,

> *Lost again,...*
> *Am I found by your hands*
> *My home is in your hands.*

Back on familiar territory, Eitzel is restless, weary and far from home, hoping for redemption in a love he barely believes in. While "Fearless" partly echoes the sentiments of "Last Harbor" and "Heaven of Your Hands," its most telling image is new: *"A stubborn heart can stay broken forever."*

It marks another turn of the screw: rather than simply searching for redemptive love, he and his various protagonists are looking for a way to be able to accept love when it comes along. It is this extra level that makes the songs on *San Francisco* somehow bleaker, in that even if they find what they are looking for, they will probably not recognise or value it.

Whereas previously Eitzel's main protagonist was *"shuffling through people like cards"* without finding anyone to take his *"losing hand,"* now he's stuck in a *"revolving door,"* with a *"cold, cold heart that never opens and never tires."*

It's a terrifyingly forceful image that encapsulates so much of his life and defines the album; no matter how many new doors open – whether lovers, musicians, record companies or whatever – somehow, Eitzel always manages to bring things back to where he started. It was as if he could sense that the major label era was coming to an end for American Music Club, leaving the band back where they started, and though happy with his lover and coming to terms with his sexuality, he still feels drawn back to his first love, Kathleen. In "I Broke My Promise" he addresses her publicly for the first time in years, and it is heartbreaking.

> *I broke my promise, that I wouldn't write another song about you,*
> *I guess I lied, but after twelve years I still love you...*
> *I've missed you so long...*

The *"I'm glad you went back,"* refrain refers to real events. Kathleen had developed quite serious drug problems, and Eitzel and some friends had sent her away to Atlanta to get help. Eitzel was hopeful and optimistic that she would find a new beginning away from *San Francisco*, though she ended up being hospitalised with endocartis.

As if in tribute to his ill fated love for Kathleen, the only pure images of love on *San Francisco* are equally doomed – whether between Gena Rowlands and her dying husband, or the tragic lover in "The Thorn in My Side" who swears *"I'll never leave you"* from beyond the grave.

The powerlessness at the centre of the revolving door image gives this album a spirit of desperation made most explicit on "Can You Help Me." The narrator can feel time pass and knows that "loving is the only thing" that is going to get him by, but he can't seem to embrace it. Even his old stand-by response of walking away no longer helps.

> *I tried to run away but I was frozen in place*
> *My body was made of sawdust and my heart just split*
> *My old friend rigor mortis started to breathe in my face*
> *The air started to drain out of my spirit.*
> *Help me, Can you help me...*

Coming in the middle of such a buoyant and uplifting anthem, the cry for help is even more startling. With its shuffling and slightly funky rhythm, "Can You Help Me" seemed clearly to have radio potential, but to everyone's surprise it got no airplay whatsoever. Years later a fan ventures to Eitzel that maybe the problem was the main lyric. The song builds and builds in a groovy laid back way, up to a big rock chorus, the fan explains, but at that point instead of "I love you," "Don't leave," "I miss you" or some other big rock chorus staple, the words "Can you help me" jolt people back. It's not a line people will want to empathise with. Eitzel just laughs and says,

"Yeah – I love that! That's my favourite shit!"

The end of the tether desperation embodied in "Can You Help Me" recurs on *San Francisco* in song after song. In "Shadow of the Valley" the protagonist's nights are all sleepless and he is "weary" and tired of people. On "I Broke My Promise" he looks around and sees nothing in his town to delight him.

> *The California sun always shines*
> *But San Francisco is a cold place*
> *To have a run of bad luck*
> *People like to shine their little flashlights in your face...*
> *The blue blue sky is made of butchers' knives*
> *And everybody you meet is wearing some stupid disguise.*

While "Shadow of the Valley"'s ennui is mirrored by the song's dirge-like pace and tune, underneath "Wish the World Away"'s noisy glorious garage rock there lurks Eitzel's most despairing outburst. As the guitars grind out an uplifting anthem, Eitzel wails,

> *Where's the message in the bottle*
> *Where's the miracle in the pills*
> *Where's the nurse with the needle*
> *Where's all of my free will*
> *Count down backwards from 10 and everything's OK*
> *You can wish the world away.*

For those looking in Eitzel's lyrics for clues to his state of mind, this was disconcerting listening. Unsurprisingly considering this subject matter, in spite of its more uplifting sound, *San Francisco* would be another album that would be criticised for being depressing – a charge that Eitzel found increasingly annoying.

"This whole idea of depressing music is bullshit," Eitzel would say. "Now you have a whole generation making music with nothing but a smirk on their faces. They're laughing at the idea of being alive. For me, music has always been something that got me through, got me over. I love music for that reason..."

When years earlier, Tom Mallon described AMC's music as more like "blues" than rock, he hit on the key to the sadness at the heart of Eitzel's work. There is a combination of resignation, despair and defiance in his songs that is only really seen in blues music. It would be wrong to dismiss him as a modern angst ridden miserabilist, wallowing in his own unimportant woes. Eitzel's themes of dislocation, madness, death and aching loneliness, though rare in modern rock 'n' roll, were staples of the early blues.

From "Western Sky" and "Last Harbor" to *San Francisco*'s closing valediction, "I'll Be Gone," Eitzel is haunted by an indefinable ache and an intangible hungry emptiness similar to Robert Johnson's "low down shaking chill." He may be a white, middle class Californian, but Eitzel is singing about the same things as Johnson, Blind Blake and Muddy Waters.

"I don't see my songs as negative at all," Eitzel would reflect. "I think tears are more beautiful than people laughing. Laughter is a really ugly thing."

As if to reinforce his own words, the two humourous songs on *San Francisco* – "Hello Amsterdam," the story of a particularly chaotic AMC show at the Milkweg, and "How Many Six Packs Does It Take To Screw In a Light" – are Eitzel's least successful and attractive. Though underneath its one joke chorus, "How Many Six Packs"'s hides a very dark heart. Later he would bemoan the fact that he copped out on the lines: *"And a manic depression that just wouldn't go away / If I was empty inside no bullet would ever reach me."*

After a studio argument with the band, Eitzel switched the last line to the rather odd, *"Like Sam Peckinpah with a bunch of poisoned Ivy."*

One final footnote to the album was the back cover photograph of an old man. His name was Rojo or Redman.

"He is a local guy that has himself painted all red," Eitzel would explain.

"He only wears red, and his apartment is painted all red. The bushes in his backyard are also painted red. He writes folk art poetry that sometimes is scarily anti-white people... He is redman and he's crazy... He sits at the end of the bar in the Latin American Club and he screams at the whole bar all night."

San Francisco was another American Music Club album to receive almost universal critical acclaim. Some reviewers noticed a more commercial strain of AMC, but no one felt the band had compromised their art for the marketplace.

In *Time Out*, Peter Paphides noted, "Eitzel has realised that playing a little pop music once in a while doesn't necessarily make you Wet Wet Wet." Keith Cameron saw no fundamental difference in the band, and added that while he kept expecting AMC to make their "pop sell out" album, this was not it. Instead, Cameron concluded, *San Francisco* was "Another wondrous American Music Club album."

But when *San Francisco* entered the UK chart at number 72, and then dropped out after one week, it appeared the game was up. The album failed even to chart in the US. The critical acclaim made no impression. In the beginning rave reviews were the thing that kept AMC going. The press got them noticed and held out the promise of success. Now that they were singularly failing to achieve this success, the irony was becoming unbearable. There are only so many years you can go on hearing everyone say that your band is going to be huge... soon.

In spite of all the money spent on remixes, "Wish the World Away," had failed to become a hit single. AMC were still complete strangers to radio play, and now their album was dying a very quick death.

"When we were making *San Francisco*," Eitzel reflects, "When selling records was the thing that mattered, the press attention we'd had so far didn't matter. And the press that *San Francisco* got didn't matter, because when all that is over, you think, 'Where is our hit record?' 'Did we make it?' And *San Francisco* definitely failed."

If *San Francisco* had been the band's first album on a major label, it is arguable that it might have been strong enough to break them. But AMC had already been launched, and now the media and retail outlets were onto the next thing. Their longstanding admirers in the press would still praise them to the rafters, but the album didn't have anything like the initial profile enjoyed by *Mercury*.

At the time, arguments such as this were purely academic. All that mattered was that American Music Club's seventh album was yet another commercial failure. Morale amongst the band could not have been lower. As they prepared for their October UK tour at a New York gig shared with St Etienne and Grant Lee Buffalo, it was immediately apparent that the tension visible during their Reading Festival show was still present.

Eitzel hated the four-piece band arrangements, and was sick of playing rock songs – especially "Bad Liquor." He was also playing electric guitar on this tour, and his inability to work out the right levels for his amplifier, and his sloppy time-keeping was driving the rest of the band mad.

"He would get so fast and out of control that it would screw everything up," Mark Terrill recalls. "The problem was how the other people in the band could diplomatically rein him in, without having him feel that they were infringing on his artistic ability. This was the source of a lot of ongoing friction." To make matters worse, in order to perform the quiet music he loved, Eitzel was playing more and more solo acoustic shows.

When they arrived in the UK, even after the huge push both their major label albums had been given, the band could not fail to notice that the venues they were playing were nearly identical in size and profile to those of their last two tours.

AMC's first UK appearance was an MTV live special where they romped through AC/DC's "Highway to Hell" with tongues firmly in cheek. During the performance, Eitzel noticed two members of Foreigner in the studio audience who were clearly not amused.

The tour opened with a reasonable performance in Newcastle. Vudi was delighted to be playing the home town of The Animals, who he would praise as the "gnarliest band in the UK."

The next night in Manchester, Dan Pearson decided to quit, but his threat wasn't taken seriously. Vudi felt the band were starting to hit their stride, but Eitzel appeared extremely unhappy. When it came to the final encore, "Bad Liquor" he began the song, and then after a few seconds just tossed his guitar on the ground and left the stage. His facial expression said, what is the point? The band just shuffled off after him.

In Glasgow, the intense rock delivery seemed to work, and though Eitzel broke virtually every one of his guitar strings, the show was the best of the tour to date.

In Birmingham, the tour driver bought the band four inflatable Mr Blobby dolls to lighten the offstage atmosphere. Mr B was a plastic and unrealistic pink and yellow spotted character made famous on the Noel Edmond's Television show. The only words he could utter were "Blobby, Blobby."

"Blobby seems to have become something of a mascot on this tour, for better or for worse," Tim Mooney told *The Guardian* in a brief AMC tour diary feature. "Our lives are in his hands. All hail Blobby!"

A Blobby doll would sit at the front of Mooney's drum riser for the rest of the tour.

They set off later that day for Leeds, with a Chopin CD Eitzel picked up in the flea market, playing at full volume. When they checked into the Leeds Marriott, Pearson could not help but note, "The swanky rooms are a wry irony on our non-existence in the charts."

That night marked the tour nadir. Eitzel's voice was gone, and nothing was in tune. The audience didn't know what was wrong; applause was hesitant and a number of people left.

By Bristol, the relations within the band had clearly deteriorated. They rarely exchanged glances, and did not speak to each other or smile. As they continued to romp through rock versions of "Bad Liquor" and "Somewhere" Eitzel repeatedly made sarcastic jokes about Pearl Jam.

The previous time AMC played London was a triumphant sold-out show at The Astoria. This time they were at The Forum, but of the 1,800 tickets, only 1,500 had been sold. To make matters worse, Virgin had bought 300 of these, and only 100 of their guests bothered to show up.

"It should have sold out at that stage in their career," booking agent Mick Griffiths notes. "Another album down the line, and more good press."

In spite of the positive reviews that followed, it was not a good show. The playing was chaotic and much of the nuance of the songs was lost. A low point was "Firefly" where fuzz electric guitar in place of pedal steel sounded terrible. Eitzel trashed his electric guitar and would regularly drop down on one knee, head thrown back in mockery of rock lead guitarists the world over. At one point, determined to make a joke of the whole thing, he even performed two songs with a My Little Pony doll stuck through the flies of his trousers. Eitzel's whole performance was a return to the tortured, self-destructive madness of the early US shows. At such an important show, it was enough to make you cry.

"Trying to rock it up was probably not the best thing for us," Tim Mooney reflects. "That European tour was a lot of that – being a louder band, and it did not work a lot of the time. I'm not sure why we were rocking.... Perhaps out of frustration."

Towards the end of the show, Eitzel told the crowd, "This is the last time we'll ever be here. We are going to be dropped by Virgin." As Pearson appeared to flinch, and Mooney almost imperceptibly shrugged, Eitzel thanked all the staff at Virgin Records and muttered something about this being his last show.

But AMC had not been dropped. Orla Lee from their A&R department remembers choking, thinking "Why is he saying this? Why is he saying this?"

But, Eitzel knew his agent hated the band's new live sound, and was concerned that Virgin had given up on the band as a result of their poor chart showing. Maybe Eitzel sensed what was coming, and just wanted to hasten the inevitable.

Backstage, the atmosphere was funereal. Each AMC member was in a different corner, and all of them left at different times. Fans were looking for some kind of confirmation from Mark, Dan or Vudi that it was not all over. But all the talk was of units, loss of record company confidence and the like.

Mick Griffiths was so appalled by the performance that he left the venue before the show finished. Eitzel was convinced the agent was about to drop the band.

"I was so annoyed with them," Griffiths remembers. "They were doing everything wrong. It was a really important gig and they were trying to be a rock band, and there was no rapport with the audience. It felt like the last death throes."

AMC's next big show was the prestigious Les Incorruptibles French festival – an annual showcase for new cutting edge musical talent.

"French audiences are really into passion, and heartfelt music," Mick Griffiths, who booked the show, muses. "The French market is made for a band like AMC." But the band's new post-grunge full-frontal rock assault did not hit the mark. A few songs in and AMC were dying a death.

Griffiths had told Eitzel before the show that if he did "Last Harbor" solo, he would have the audience in his hand. When the band finished their rough and ready set, Eitzel returned with his acoustic guitar and did play a drawn out and highly emotional "Last Harbor." When he finished, the audience went wild. But it was too little too late. If AMC had played a whole set of their more soulful acoustic songs that night, Griffiths believes, it might have been a turning point for the band in France. But that show would be AMC's last in Europe.

On their return home, AMC prepared for an extended US tour. If the UK and European shows were problematic, the US dates would be a nightmare.

First of all, some of the band members decided something had to be done about Eitzel's onstage guitar playing. His lack of interest in playing in time had long been a problem for AMC's rhythm section, and this had recently become more and more of an issue for Pearson and Mooney.

They had previously agreed not to replace Bruce Kaphan, but now it seemed like a new musician might be the only answer.

"We were trying to rehearse without Bruce," Eitzel remembers. "I play guitar expressionistically – I speed up and slow down a lot – and Danny would say,

'We gotta take the guitar away from Eitzel, I can't play with him.' The band needed a good rhythm guitarist to hold things together.

"One of the guitarists had to be real sturdy," Mooney explains. As Dan Pearson was a great rhythm player, it made sense for him to switch from bass permanently. Accordingly, Pearson set out to recruit a replacement bassist.

Eitzel resented being told he couldn't play electric guitar on stage – it was just another example of him not being in control of his own music – and refused to get involved,

"It was all Dan's decision. I said, 'I don't want to know, if you want to bring someone else in that's your decision, I'm not going to approve it or disapprove it'."

Eventually Pearson found someone he liked, Dana Schecter from the band Torture. Dana promptly gave up her scholarship, dropped out of college and sold her apartment in order to go on tour with American Music Club. They had time for one rehearsal before the first date in Palo Alto on 14th November.

The show seemed fine to outsiders. Eitzel mostly just sang, and played very little guitar. But for the band it just wasn't working. Dana's ill-fated spell with American Music Club only lasted one night. Pearson fired her the next morning.

"I don't know if it was so bad," Mooney ponders, "But it just didn't have the right feeling. In a lot of ways, the sound of AMC was a big part Danny – his feel. So it was hard not to have him on bass. It wasn't a bad show, it just didn't feel good and the tour was starting, so we had to make a decision right then. Danny didn't feel right not playing bass, and it didn't feel quite as good to us."

Not surprisingly Dana was extremely disappointed.

"She was crying, it was awful," Eitzel remembers. "That was another nail in the coffin."

Pearson would say later only that, "It was a bad idea."

Even with Dan Pearson back on bass, the tour would not run smoothly.

"It was not good," Mark Terrill remembers. "Eitzel was going through the motions. Also we had a very good English crew that we used on the continent, and for some of the previous US tours. But Wally was wary that they didn't have work permits, so he got some other US guy, who used to be in a local punk rock band, and he was terrible. Plus, this guy played on some of the songs, which was very strange. So he'd come out, set up the amps, tune the guitars, and then he'd go off, come back later with an acoustic guitar and do a few songs, then go off again and do the whole road thing. His idea was to be a rock star and not a road-ie. This did not fit in with Eitzel's plans, and they ended up not speaking to each other. Eitzel insisted on doing his own tuning, setting up his own gear, and doing all the things he wasn't supposed to do – while not speaking to the guy who was supposed to be helping him – and then let that guy come on stage and interfere with his whole musical trip."

It was as if Eitzel was just completely past caring. A few days later, backstage in Sacramento after one of their better recent shows, Eitzel confided in a friend that he was going to do a solo album. He wanted to make a jazz-oriented album because the songs that he was writing like "Sacred Heart" and "When My Plane Finally Comes Down" just didn't work out with AMC.

The US shows followed so quickly on the heels of their European trip, that it seemed like they were stuck on one neverending tour. While some of the dates – like the Sacramento show – went really well, most of the performances displayed more signs of internal tension. AMC were still having problems making up for Kaphan's absence, and Eitzel was getting ever more fed up with playing rock songs. In turn, the other band members were getting so fed up with Eitzel that during his solo acoustic spots, they would talk so loudly just off stage that it would distract him. The entire band was also aware that the tour was a pointless exercise. AMC's album had bombed, they weren't making any money from the shows, and they weren't breaking any new ground.

"It became a hard place to be in," Tim Mooney reflects. "Not being able to jump up a peg. Especially in America, you'd go back to the same rock club in Columbus or Minneapolis. It was good to see the people you know there, and good to play. But it started to feel like you're doing the exact same thing over."

As the end of the year approached, it seemed likely that these were the band's final days. On the second of two nights at New York's Knitting Factory, Eitzel told the audience, "This is the last time you're ever going to hear these songs by us."

After a 27th December appearance on the nationally syndicated John Stewart show television show, the following day the band played their last ever show at Slims in San Francisco.

That night the tension was so tangible you could touch it. When the band's arrival on stage was greeted with slightly premature cries of "Happy New Year," Eitzel yelled simply, "Fuck you!" Throughout the gig, Tim Mooney looked like he was about to jump over the drum kit and strangle Eitzel. Though he would say later that he was just watching Eitzel in order to keep time with him.

Dan Pearson would say that it was "No different from any other gig," but he would add, "It could always have been the last show ever."

But, this time it really was. As others revelled in the festive season, Eitzel spent December 1994 at the end of his tether – worn out and feeling fenced into a corner, drowning under the despair so vividly portrayed on *San Francisco*.

His personal life and his career had reached a hiatus. He loved his partner but knew he would never feel for this lover what he had felt for Kathleen – though there was no question of going back to her. He also knew that AMC were the greatest band of musicians he could ever play with. And they were more like family than friends now. Yet he knew that the group had run its course – the issues tearing up AMC had become insurmountable.

Eitzel was tired of having other people rearrange his songs. During the sessions for the last album, the band had even insisted he changed a number of his lyrics. Also, they were rejecting some of his new material as not being right for the band.

Eitzel was also sick of singing in front of a loud rock band. He didn't think the band worked without Kaphan, and he was missing the pedal steel player's creative input. Kaphan was Eitzel's major ally in that he was equally dedicated to hard work, whereas Eitzel always felt the other members would rather just hang out than actually rehearse or record. Kaphan was the only one who shared his musical vision. As far as he could see, Vudi wanted the band to become the new

Jesus and Mary Chain, while Pearson wanted them to sound like the Carter Family.

Eitzel had also had enough of trying to have hit records – feeling under pressure from outsiders to be the band's cash cow or the hen that lays the golden eggs – and just wanted to write his own songs in his own way. He was exhausted by the tour and still recovering from the painful and bitter *San Francisco* recording sessions – a process which seemed even worse now that album had flopped so resoundingly. Eitzel also felt he was always looking out for the band, and bending over backwards to keep everyone happy. Deep down he even still felt that American Music Club was Vudi's band. Because Vudi formed AMC, and Vudi was older than him, Eitzel always believed he should defer to him.

But Eitzel was the public face of the band, and felt all the pressure of being a leader, without having any of the control that usually came with such a role. Even a simple task like getting some photographs shot was a major headache.

"To do a photo session," he explains, "'I'd say, 'I want it simple: headshots; high contrast' – that way you look good, everybody looks intense. Vudi would be saying, 'We need trees, atmosphere, we need to bring several outfits.' Danny would say, 'I'm only available for an hour, on Thursday,' and then Tim would say, 'I don't care. As long as I can smoke.' It was always bad. No one agreed on anything: total contrarians – nothing was ever easy."

Also, now that the album had failed to sell, money pressures were intensifying. Because a small fortune had been spent on the two Warners records, the band were not due any royalties. When the dust settled on *San Francisco*, AMC were in debt to Warners and Virgin for approximately 1.5 million dollars. This intensified Eitzel's resentment at the way he felt Wally and Ross were mismanaging the band. As the only money due to AMC was from publishing, the other band members were becoming even more alienated by Eitzel taking the lion's share. Now they knew how song publishing worked, they wanted to record some of their own songs, but Eitzel refused.

In December AMC's publishing deal was renewed and a large tranche of money was due. The previous year, because none of the band had any money, Eitzel paid the others' taxes – a sum of $35,000. Now all the other members were due to get some publishing income, Eitzel approached them,

"I said 'You know what, you can pay me back the money for your taxes.' And they were not into this. But I thought, 'I'm not your fucking Dad'."

As the New Year dawned, Eitzel decided he could not face another year like the last. Though he and Wally had been getting on much better lately, Eitzel still blamed his manager for the Chicarelli debacle, and felt Wally was taking too big a cut of the band's ever decreasing income. He decided his first act of the New Year would be to sack his management. Next he would break-up with his long time lover, and then give the band an ultimatum, after which, if they didn't accept, he would sack them too. He didn't have any role models in mind when it came to a solo career, and was very aware that once a band splits, the individuals rarely do as well on their own. But, Eitzel didn't know what else to do. More than anything else, he needed a clean slate.

The entire band had been angry to arrive home from their last tour without having made any money. Faced with a bill from Ross and Wally for 15% of their tour income, they had to find the commission from their own pockets. Eitzel also felt Wally's expenses on the UK leg were way too high. In a year from which AMC had very little to show, the management had invoiced the band some $90,000. In spite of all of these issues, the rest of the band didn't feel that Wally and Ross were that bad. Mooney liked both of them, and Vudi was positively keen to keep them on. When Eitzel insisted he would quit if they weren't sacked, he got his way, but it did further damage to the band.

Though the management contract was for six years, it also featured a heavily punitive "sunset clause" which gave them a share of AMC's and Eitzel's income way beyond that period. When Eitzel sacked them, he paid a fortune in legal fees to extricate himself from this clause. He claims Wally and Ross wanted $600,000, but eventually settled at $60,000.

"But it was worth going broke to get rid of them," he maintains.

As for Wally and Ross, it was a complete shock. "Mark has never expressed dissatisfaction to me," Wally insists.

"And, it seems so schizophrenic to me, because before I went to England, we were the closest we'd ever been.... I have never been told by Mark Eitzel that I was fired. I only saw it on paper, and it was devastating."

Wally maintains a huge admiration for the band, and especially Mark Eitzel's talent. "My only regret," he would say four years later, "Is that I'm not working with Mark and that the band is not together." But Wally would add defiantly, "What's happened since we stopped managing American Music Club?"

In the short term, while they hadn't backed the sacking, the rest of the band did feel some sense of relief. At least the squabbling between Eitzel and Wally was no longer their problem. But the difficulties weren't over yet. Next, Eitzel called a band meeting and told them that he would only continue if AMC ceased to be a democracy and he was given complete control. Eitzel would choose the producers and the studios. He would determine the song arrangements. He would decide which shows they would play and he would even choose the artwork on the albums.

Mooney and Pearson didn't like Eitzel's ideas but were reluctant to let go of the band, and agreed to the terms. Vudi was more hostile, and though the band as a whole accepted the new regime, it became instantly apparent that the plans were unworkable. Eitzel then quit the band.

"I didn't want to break up the band," he maintains. "But I couldn't figure out a way where we could carry on. I wrote that fucking *San Francisco* album to be the pop record. And I didn't want to be in a situation where I had to write corny pop songs. Verse, chorus, verse, chorus, bridge, verse, chorus. Songs like "Wild Sea," these rambling lyric driven songs, they wouldn't accept – half way through they'd say, 'Where's the change?' I'd say, 'It just grew.' I didn't feel how we'd grow musically. I didn't feel that I could write songs musically any more. I could with Danny, and I could with Bruce now, but Vudi was the genius of the group – the wild card. And I didn't see how I could work with Danny and Bruce and go over Vudi's head."

The other members could barely believe Eitzel's decision. He had threatened to quit so many times over the years, but they never thought it would actually happen.

"We were like a family," Pearson explains. "It was devastating to lose that family...." Pearson promptly packed up and moved to Montana.

"I felt sad. I loved that band," Mooney agrees. But Vudi took it worst of all. "He was much more tied up with it," Mooney explains. "That was his life!"

Eitzel split up with his lover shortly afterwards. Now he had cut all of his ties. He no longer had a band, management or a relationship. He was utterly free to do whatever he wanted. But the upheaval left him severely depressed, and he stayed in bed for much of the following three months.

Because they had sacked their management, and it was now not on anyone's priority list, nobody initially told Warners or Virgin that the band had broken up. There were no announcements, and the record companies continued with their release schedules.

Accordingly, on 12th March 1995, Virgin released "Can You Help Me" as AMC's second single off *San Francisco*. It was by far the band's best and most commercial sounding single to date. But compared to "Wish the World Away" the record company's promotion was desultory. The single came out as a one-format CD only, with just a few cheap looking flyposters to advertise its arrival. The music weeklies made it single of the week, but it didn't matter. "Can You Help Me" spent one week in the UK top 100 at number 91.

Shortly afterwards, Virgin dropped the band.

"It was an incredibly difficult decision," their spokesperson told *Melody Maker*. "But the option came up and we decided not to exercise it. We got the most fantastic support from the press, but commercially, it just didn't translate into the sort of sales that we were all hoping for."

Shortly afterwards, Warners released "Hello Amsterdam" as the title track of a six song EP. In addition to an alternative take of "The Thorn in my Side," a cover of "On A Clear Day You Can See Forever" which would point the way forward for Eitzel's solo career, and a weak Vudi composition, "Elbow Deep," the EP featured Eitzel's most successful venture into the world of humorous songwriting, "The President's Test for Physical Fitness." The song did not have an easy genesis.

"Danny had a real problem with this song," Eitzel explains. "Originally it was about a journalist in Amsterdam. Me and Vudi had a big fight with this guy in an interview. We were talking about pop music, and he was saying, 'Dylan is great art – he is Rembrandt, he is...' and we were like, 'No! No! It's pop music. It's worthless. It's trash. And he said, 'Oh, you are hating yourselves, you are ass-holes because you will not admit that you are artists.' I said, 'Yeah, we're ass-holes. That's it! We're assholes and we make trash. We make pop music: dispos-able diapers for the bourgeoisie.' He was like, 'OK, fuck you!' So I wrote this whole song about this journalist. And Danny said, 'Oh yeah. The world really needs to hear a song about a welterweight rock star complaining about being interviewed.' And he was kind of right.

"So I changed it all to be about this other incident with me and Vudi."

Eitzel would tell Jack Rabid that the band were also worried that the song's criticism of journalists might have made the press less keen to interview the band.

"But the point was not about interviews, it was about arrogant pre-conceptions of what music is all about. That's what the song is. It's like the President's Test for Physical Fitness; it's a test I can't pass."

Eitzel changed the subject matter to cover an incident where he and Vudi met:

"A band in the Bay Area – a heavy metal band who got very big by playing very quiet, acoustic music. I won't tell, you can guess easily enough! You know in the '80s, the only way a heavy metal band could get a big hit was to get close and personal, and sing a song about their feelings and shit? That song is a true story. Me and Vudi were at Black Market Music – this great guitar store in San Francisco… And these guys walked in, and they were from this famous band. It's like, (in mock dumb rock-ish voice) 'Alright, man. Cool! Yeah, you know, I'm fuckin' at night and my fuckin' wife won't put out...' It was awful. This whole sort of macho thing. Me and Vudi were like, 'Ewwhhhh!' (laughs)"

Eitzel admits that he made up the bit about them telling him he should join a health club, but the rest of it was accurate. The guy behind the counter said to the band,

"'Hey, do you want to meet Vudi and Mark from American Music Club?'" Eitzel remembers. "And the guy goes, (again mockingly) 'Oh yeah, alright, um, American, um, Music Club. Alright, cool man. What sort of music do you play?' That lyric was true. And we just said, 'Um, don't worry about it.'

"It was lucky that happened, because it's about exactly the same kind of thing: arrogant rock assholes, and they exist all over the world. Fill in whoever you like!"

For those who can't follow the clues – the band were heavy metal band Tesla who hit the big time with their unplugged album *Five Man Acoustic Jam*.

A few weeks later the press were given notice that American Music Club had broken up, and ran short obituaries bemoaning the band's failure to break-through. After nearly ten years, the adventure was over. Wally Brill would say Eitzel's bleak songs were simply out of step with the times.

"When Joy Division and The Smiths and all that kind of stuff was thriving," he argued, "Britain was a very different place. 25% of the population were unemployed and there was no money anywhere. Whereas all the people I meet now who are young go to parties, take lots of drugs and have got more money than ever before. And they're having a wonderful time. They do not want someone singing about 'The Thorn in my Side is Gone.' They really don't care. It is the wrong time for Mark."

But Wally's view does not explain how Radiohead's miserabilism or Manic Street Preachers' nihilism could have taken those bands to such heights. But then unlike the wasted glamourous self-loathing of Richey, Eitzel's bleak outlook was less dramatic and less attractive. AMC were older, less photogenic and more honest.

"We were this shambling crowd of balding men," Eitzel would reflect. "Glum without being beautiful. Is there anything worse?"

One more speculative argument for why AMC never made that all important commercial breakthrough, is that underneath all the bluster and talk of making pop records and trying for a hit, Mark Eitzel simply didn't want to reach the level of success he was being primed for. Perhaps he didn't want to be raised up for fear of later being knocked down. The level of exposure the band had after the *Rolling Stone* acclaim may have scared him. Eitzel felt the pressures that came with AMC's major label status more acutely than the other band members. While he wanted some kind of financial security, maybe Eitzel just wanted to be left alone to write songs. It is the only thing he ever wanted to do.

Chapter Thirteen

Living, Dying And Being Saved

"I remember people telling me, 'Keep the name. We'll just get new musicians and it's still American Music Club.' It's not. It's a very unique thing. It was a great, great band, but it's over."

Mark Eitzel

"Devoted fans? I don't care anymore. I can't live because I have devoted fans. I know a lot of people will listen to this album and go, 'Oh God, how come you don't just make *California* again?' So, why don't I make another *California*? I tell them get me another set of folks and then kill them, then I'll write *California* again. I'm going to write songs until I die, and I know the hardest core fan won't be there when I'm 50 and if they are I'll feel sorry for them."

Mark Eitzel

From January to early March 1995, Eitzel barely left his Bernal Heights home. He knew he'd made the right decisions as far as his lover, his management and his band were concerned, but he was still depressed, and didn't know what to do next.

Towards the end of March, his friend Bob Mould, formerly of Hüsker Dü and Sugar, dragged Eitzel out to play as his support act for shows in Philadelphia and in New York. The Philadelphia show went especially well, and helped Eitzel get some confidence back.

As he contemplated his own future, Eitzel realised he had to sort out his recording contract situation. As he was now without a manager, this was something he would have to do on his own – though he would rely heavily on his lawyer, Eric Greenspan.

When Virgin dropped AMC they chose not to pick up a solo option on Eitzel, which considering the band were now in debt to the label for a million dollars was a good thing. But, Eitzel still had friends and admirers at Virgin and after negotiations, the label agreed to re-sign him to a fresh contract. This effectively wiped his debt from the slate, and Virgin even paid Eitzel a new signing on advance of $72,000 which went towards his settlement with Wally and Ross.

In the US, Eitzel and AMC were still signed to Warners Reprise. Eitzel was keen to stay with the Warners group, but felt Reprise boss, Howie Klein, was not supportive. He considered that if Klein could sign a band called The Armageddon Dildos, he could hardly understand what Eitzel's music was about. Eitzel persuaded Warners to allow him to transfer from subsidiary label Reprise on to the Warners label. Warners also allowed Eitzel to leave his $750,000 debt with Reprise. If American Music Club ever reformed, they would still be signed to Reprise and owe the label this money, but until then the debt was frozen.

For a while Eitzel spent more time in meetings than writing and in conversation with Michael Goldberg, he worried that all these business negotiations might have affected his personality,

"It was hard work," he confided. "It kills you. It turns you into this sort of media savvy guy. You become like, 'Hey Joe, how you doing? Let's talk about this. Yeah, send me a fax. Doll, great. Hey have you heard about...'?"

Still, it was worth it. After the new round of negotiations, Eitzel was still signed to the same record companies as American Music Club, but no longer had any huge burden of debt hanging around his neck. His next album would be a fresh start in every respect.

Now that he was no longer tied to a band, Eitzel was keen to pursue a new musical direction. "When we made *San Francisco*," he explained,

"We made such an attempt to make rock songs just so we could play them live and it really made me kinda crazy. So I went out of my way not to write rock songs. There are more kinds of music than rock. I've been listening to lots of jazz recently ..."

Eitzel had first got hooked on jazz during the *Mercury* sessions. Tchad Blake used to bring in an old phonogram to the studio, and would play his Billy Holiday and Fats Waller 78s for the band. Eitzel taped many of these records and grew to love them, especially Waller's "Smoke Dreams of You." The meandering, irregular songs he had been writing since AMC's last album bore more resemblance to jazz than the rock music he was determined to put behind him.

Towards the summer, Eitzel's writing was briefly interrupted to follow up on a somewhat unlikely collaboration with Everything But The Girl. Formed in 1982 by Hull University sweethearts Tracey Thorn and Ben Watt, Everything But The Girl had in the early part of 1995 re-invented themselves when a Todd Terry trip-hop remix of their song "Missing" became a huge hit on both sides of the Atlantic, taking their *Amplified Heart* album to the higher reaches of the charts. They were now preparing for the follow-up album, *Walking Wounded*, which would almost inevitably be one of the big albums of 1996 and which would also come out on Virgin Records. Ironically, Warners had dropped the band after they delivered "Missing".

Both Ben and Tracey were long-term admirers of Eitzel's and for a while EBTG would include a version of "Firefly" in their live set. "I first heard AMC in a record shop," Watt recalls.

"I was going up to the checkout with a CD in my hand (I forget which CD now) and as I approached, the opening bars of track one side one of *Everclear* came on in the store. (I didn't know what it was at the time). I got to the check-out thirty seconds into the song and I said: 'I don't actually want this CD in my hand, I want whatever is playing now, and so I walked out with my first AMC record. I got home and played the opening track to Tracey and she stood still with her mouth open in the kitchen until it finished."

In the summer of 1994, when Watt and Thorn were expressing their enthusiasm for AMC to their manager Jasmine Daines, they discovered that she was also a good friend of Wally Brill's. Pretty soon talk turned to the possibility of the two acts working together. Eitzel wrote "When My Plane Finally Goes Down" as a tentative collaboration, and Wally sent Ben and Tracey tickets for Eitzel's Shaw Theatre solo show, where he played the song live for the first time in the UK.

After the gig, which Ben described as, "One of his brilliant teetering-on-the-brink-of-glory-or-failure solo shows," Ben and Tracey were introduced to Eitzel.

"It wasn't a particularly fruitful meeting," Ben would remember. "Two minutes on a fire escape." Nonetheless, Wally who was present claims that it was an "instant lovefest" between them.

Shortly after the show, Eitzel handed Wally a tape of "When My Plane Finally Goes Down" to pass on to Ben and Tracey. They loved it, and resolved to try and do something with it at a later date.

When they came to consider how they wanted their *Walking Wounded* album to sound, inspired by the success of the "Missing" remix, Ben and Tracey started looking for new musical colours and textures. As well as beats, filters and new vocal treatments, one new idea was for a vocal collaboration with Tracey by someone other than Ben. Immediately they thought of Eitzel. "[So] we approached Mark for a collaboration that might be included on [the album]," Ben explains.

"It was early days, but we recorded a half-finished version of 'When My Plane,' lifting Mark's voice off the whispered acoustic demo he provided, and dropping it into a new arrangement of breakbeats and acoustic guitars we'd put together, along with Tracey's freshly recorded voice – like a duet. Mark heard it and liked it, but wanted to re-record his voice. He came round to our house some weeks later – we had a small studio set up in the basement. It was a good day's recording, but by then we were deep into recording the rest of *Walking Wounded* and it struck us then that 'When My Plane' just didn't seem to fit the album's approach anymore. It wasn't bad, it just didn't seem to sit with the rest of the album, which had become so centred around Tracey's lone voice with no vocal adornment or additional backing vocals. Reluctant to junk the song entirely, we then thought about perhaps submitting it for a film soundtrack instead, but it was pointed out that I had naively used three huge uncleared samples to make up the texture of the backing track. It became obvious that to proceed we'd have to change the whole arrangement too. I tried a new approach but my heart wasn't in it. In the end, the weight of all these problems dragged the track down, and it remains unfinished and unreleased."

There was also one other further complication with the proposed collaboration which touched a raw nerve with Eitzel and that would have serious ramifications for his relationship with his record company. "I wrote 'When My Plane…' for EBTG," he confirms,

"But Wally told them, and not me, that if I recorded that song, then I would give them half the songwriting credits. So I flew to London, and Ben rearranged the song, and it was great. Ben had repeated the chorus and added a musical bridge. I did a duet with Tracey and it was beautiful. At the end of the session, Ben said two things. He said, 'So when you do your version on your record, you're not going to use this arrangement, right.' I said, 'No.' He said, 'OK.' [honestly, I did like his arrangement, but it wasn't my arrangement] Then he said, 'And you've no problem splitting the songwriting credits. Because Wally said that was fine.' I said, 'Well, Wally never mentioned it to me, but I guess it's OK'." [It transpired that Ben was expecting a 50:50 split]

Eitzel really liked Ben and Tracey. He knew their next album would be successful and that it would be a good move for him, but songwriting credits was his one sacrosanct subject. Even though he didn't hold any gripe with Ben, he was determined he would not give half the publishing away for a song which he felt he had written.

"I was a fool really, but I was really upset, I have a thing about songwriting. I think that if you're an artist you should get paid. Regardless of anything else, payment signifies respect. So I went to the head of Virgin's A&R, and said 'I don't think the track is going to make it on the EBTG record, because they think I'm going to give them songwriting credit, and I'm not. Virgin's view was, 'Well, we've got this one artist who sells no records, and we've got this other artist that are going to have the biggest album of the year, so…' Money talks and bullshit walks. So I think that's why I [later] got dropped as a solo artist. I came across as insane. Virgin were like, 'You come to me and say that you don't want a track on the EBTG album, because, because…why?'

"What Ben did to the song, did make it sound like a different song," Eitzel concedes.

"He added samples and trip hop beats. I'm not dissing them at all. They treated me so well, and at this time with real kid gloves, they were fine with the fact I wanted a different share. I told them in the end they could have 40%. Then I found a week later that the track was not on their record. They said it was because they used a Miles Davis sample, and they couldn't get clearance on it. And I believe them. But Virgin's view by now was 'The kid's an asshole.' I really blew it."

Eitzel had also hoped Ben Watt might help produce his next album, but Watt found himself tied up completing and promoting his book. In order to show that there were no hard feelings, and because both Ben and Tracey did really like and admire Eitzel, they invited him to fill the support slot on their forthcoming US tour. Eitzel accepted, and then returned to his own project.

Eitzel spent the tail end of the summer working at home – writing piano parts for his new songs using Macintosh software, aided by Bruce Kaphan. He wanted to keep guitar to a minimum on the album, keen to move away from any vestiges of indie-rock or grunge.

"I really didn't want it to sound like a lo-fi album," he recalls. "I wanted it to sound like a classical, classic record."

In September Eitzel made a brief trip to the UK to play a solo gig at the Garage Upstairs in North London. As well as a few old AMC classics, Eitzel previewed most of his forthcoming album, including an amazing take on "Southend On Sea" performed with a beer mat in between his guitar strings – dampening them to a primitive percussive sound. Afterwards he told fans they would give up on him when they heard the solo album, "You're gonna hate it."

On his return he assembled a band that included Kaphan, old AMC cohort Dan Pearson on upright bass, and Simone White of the Disposable Heroes of Hiphoprisy on drums. Determined to arrange the songs more simply, Eitzel kept rehearsals to a relative minimum, before relocating to the studio where for the first time, he was completely in charge. The musicians would all play exactly what he wanted them to play.

The songs Eitzel wrote for his first solo album were much less straightforward than those on *San Francisco*. Instead of verse, verse, chorus, verse, his new material was more like prose and the more irregular structures fitted well with the breezy Chet Baker sound he envisaged. Eitzel was also listening to a lot of John Coltrane and lined up a trumpet player for the recording sessions who he thought sounded like the legendary saxophonist. Unfortunately, when the trumpet player arrived, his lips were all broken and he couldn't play. In desperation Eitzel's engineer Mark Needham suggested he hire session legend and screen composer, Mark Isham.

Isham flew in and did six songs in one day. He charged triple-scale, so Eitzel wanted to get as much work out of him as quickly as possible. Lacking any expert knowledge, Eitzel instructed Isham to play like Miles Davis on some tracks and like Chet Baker on others, but this didn't always produce the desired effect.

"Sometimes it's too Kenny G for my taste," Eitzel reflected. "But that's okay too. I don't care. At times we were in the other room going, 'God, it's Herb Alpert and the Tijuana Brass!' But I like that." It was, after all, what his father used to listen to on the old family record player.

But, after Isham had gone Eitzel decided he wasn't happy with a lot of the trumpet parts. There was no budget for Isham to redo his contribution, so Eitzel had Needham recompose the solos on a sampler. There was only so much Needham could do however, and many of the trumpet parts Eitzel had originally envisioned, like a coda on "Cleopatra Jones" were left off the record – though the band would play them live on the forthcoming tour.

For the drums, Eitzel had originally wanted R&B veteran Al Jackson. He loved Jackson's simple style which did the job without drawing attention to itself – a refreshing antidote to the intellectual approach of his own former band. When he discovered Jackson had sadly died in the mid-'70s, he decided to use drum loops to create a similar soul groove. His plan was to get Dan Pearson to play eight bars of drums and then throw it into a pro tools Macintosh program. But when he met Simone White he immediately liked him, and also thought it would be good to have a drummer for the tour.

"Simone basically jazzed everything up," Eitzel would say.

For his own vocals, Eitzel was trying to sing in the laid back style of Jimmy Scott – a process he began during the *Mercury* sessions. Eitzel now kept all of Scott's recent Reprise albums in his car. When he described what he liked about the singer's style to an internet magazine, it is easy to see why Eitzel was drawn to him.

"He's changing reality. That's what a great singer does. He walks onstage, and you see this dwarf walk out, and once he opens his mouth, he could be the love object of your dreams. He's lifting you musically, and there's nothing better on this earth."

During the *Mercury* sessions, Mitchell Froom also showed Eitzel how jazz singers like Scott would always stay slightly after the beat, his first solo album would see him adopting it as the norm.

The album was finished in the middle of October; the entire recording and mixing process had taken three weeks, compared to three months for *San Francisco.*

On 11th November, after a couple of weeks of rehearsals with two new musicians, Eitzel joined the first night of the Everything But the Girl tour at San Francisco's 1,500-seat Warfield Theatre. There was very little overlap between AMC and EBTG fans, and a support act – especially a quiet acoustic act – was merely an inconvenience to the audience who were here for trip hop.

Eitzel didn't get a hostile reaction, the crowd were merely indifferent and would talk throughout his performance before politely applauding the end of each song. Sitting down, with his head bowed, Eitzel played a 30 minute set which included a lot of as yet unreleased songs such as "Cleopatra Jones." The stage was darkened, and Eitzel rarely looked at the audience. He was clearly uncomfortable.

At least if they'd hated him, he could have reacted against that. To be ignored was the worst cut of all. Eitzel also felt relations with Ben and Tracey got off to a bad start. He explains that on the first day, they approached him, and said, "'We don't want to share the tourbus with you.' I had no intention or expectation of this. It never crossed my fucking mind that I would travel in their tourbus. I didn't want to."

To make matters worse, Eitzel had signed up in anticipation of a tour of theatres, but due to popular demand, EBTG had now added a series of larger standing venues.

After San Francisco, the tour made its way down to Los Angeles and then on to Texas and Atlanta, and while some of the seated shows went well, most nights were absolute torture for Eitzel.

"Mark called me a lot during that tour," Kathleen Burns remembered. "And he would say 'I go out there and they don't want to see me, they just want to see EBTG.'"

Kathleen saw the Atlanta date and felt it went reasonably well. She felt the crowd liked Eitzel and especially enjoyed the songs he performed with Ben

Watt. But Eitzel was used to being the centre of attention and hated anything less.

The format of the shows did not help the unadvertised support act. Shortly after the doors opened, Ben Watt would come out and DJ for an hour. Then just when the crowd were warmed up and expecting EBTG to get started Eitzel would appear and slow things down. By the time EBTG took the stage, the support act had been completely forgotten.

After creating a huge stink, Eitzel eventually got Warners to poster his support slots, but by then, the tour was more than halfway through and as it was already sold out, it made little difference.

"Being the support act is never easy," Ben Watt reflects. "Especially when you are a solo artist. Non-committed audiences impatiently waiting for the main act are commonplace. I've been through it myself. Mark had very mixed success with our audiences. On good nights, with an interested patient audience at a seated venue (I remember the Spreckels auditorium in San Diego in particular) Mark had the crowd eating out of his hand, and he would soar in response to their appreciation. I would watch from the wings and want to be him. On bad nights (of which I suppose there were more, and I am thinking in particular of gigs in Florida and Texas and the mid-west) I was ashamed of our crowd for their lack of respect and occasional aggression."

As the tour dragged on, Eitzel came to hate EBTG's audience for their indifference, and his reactions to the crowd brought him into conflict with Ben and Tracey.

"The audience were the biggest bunch of fascistic yuppie assholes," Eitzel recalls with visible anger. "They should have a swastika on the foreheads that is a Lexus symbol."

But he does realise that he made matters worse for himself with his own erratic behaviour. "I behaved like a total lunatic," he admits.

"I would do a 15-minute set, and they'd be talking so loudly I couldn't hear myself, and no one would applaud the song. They'd just keep talking. I'd do another song, and they'd still be talking. I'd think, 'Why am I doing this?'

Nonetheless, at the end of his set every night, no matter how loud and rude the audience were, Eitzel would sign off by saying, "Thank you, you're wonderful, goodnight..."

"I'm far too polite for my own good," he sighs. "I should have said 'Shut the fuck up! I hope you all die!' I should have done that, but I didn't, I had too much respect for EBTG. I mean, their bass player was Danny Thompson! [Legendary session player and hero to Vudi's Farmers all those years ago] I thought, 'I'm not going to be an asshole in front of Danny Thompson! So, I'd just do my 17 minute set and then get the fuck off, and Ben and Tracey would be saying, 'Mark, come on, we've got 20 minutes until we play a 40-minute set, and the audience is just standing there.' I'd go, 'Fine. I don't care. Fire me!' They'd go, 'No. We love you. You're great, whatever.' And, they'd always pay me, and be nice, and they kind of laughed about it, but I could tell they were kind of pissed [off]. So I kind of drove them crazy. I mean, I am nuts on stage, and after I get off stage I'm in a state... I'm a nutcase, really. I can understand why they didn't want to produce my record."

After the EBTG tour came to its inexorable end there did appear one ray of light. Eitzel had been without a manager since sacking Wally and Ross that January. To begin with, he had enjoyed taking control of every aspect of his career, but for a while he had been in search of new management. He needed someone else to take control of the business side, so he could concentrate on writing songs.

"I need to be out of my mind to write," he explains. "When I talk to business people, I can be business-like. Great! But that is not the mood you want to be in when you're writing weird songs."

Eitzel's lawyer Eric Greenspan introduced him to Janet Billig, who together with John Silva, used to manage Nirvana, The Lemonheads and Smashing Pumpkins. Towards the end of Nirvana's career, she was the only one who could deal with Kurt Cobain. When Kurt died she was so devastated that she gave up management, and joined Atlantic Records where she became president, but now was keen to get back into the management business. She'd seen Eitzel play the Knitting Factory a few times and when she heard he was on the look-out for a new deal, she had Greenspan send her a tape of *60 Watt*, which she thought was a beautiful record. "So I called her up and we arranged a breakfast meeting," Eitzel remembers.

"She turned up in a Def Leppard tour jacket, and was like a total attitude rock chick. She sat down, a waiter came, she said, [Eitzel adopts New York 'rock chick' accent] 'We want two fruit bowls and two cappuccinos, and we're fine'."

Eitzel immediately warmed to Janet's up-front attitude as she explained that she was starting up from scratch and that this was the first time she'd run her own business. She also said that if he signed with her, it would be on a hand-shake basis – no contracts. She said that her cut would be 15% without expenses or 17.5% with, adding that as she only flew first-class, he'd be better off going for the 17.5% deal.

Shortly after she became Eitzel's manager, Janet put Eitzel in touch with a film maker who was looking for soundtrack music. The film-maker asked him to, "Write a song that replaces 'Sugar Mountain' by Neil Young." Eitzel was already a fan of Young's. He listened to "Sugar Mountain" a few times and decided it was one of the "greatest songs of teenage memories I've heard in my life."

Eitzel spent two intense weeks working on the song that would become "If I Had A Gun" and the experience affected him deeply. "I started thinking about all my wonderful teenage memories," he explains.

"I don't have memories of going to the circus, and sitting in a bleacher, and going out with girls. I don't have memories like that at all. My memories are very dark.... So I thought of my first specific childhood memory, and wrote about it. But [I knew] it would never make the movie, so I didn't submit it, and I stopped calling them. But I got a song out of it.

"But it was good, because suddenly, after *60 Watt* and after that whole bullshit yuppy-assed Everything But the Girl thing, I was writing songs again that meant something to me. It was a wake-up call: write something deep and dark about yourself! That's what's great about Neil Young, because all of his songs have that kind of vibe to them. Even in the funky assed-songs, there's an overwhelming presence of Neil Young. I'd lost that with *60 Watt* and *San Francisco*."

Eitzel actually owns six guns he inherited from his father, including a Luger and a Colt 45, but he explains that, "My sister won't let me have them, because she thinks I'll shoot myself."

While Eitzel decided to hang on to "If I Had A Gun," he did write another six songs for the film that would be called *No Easy Way*. He also drafted in Bruce Kaphan who added another ten instrumental pieces. They recorded the material together in Hyde Street Studios in the Tenderloin.

While Eitzel enjoyed the new discipline of writing for the screen, he did find it quite trying at times. To start with the film maker told Eitzel there were to be no strings or guitars.

"Then they'd tell me things like, 'We want more Miles Davis'," he explains, "And I'd go, 'Well go find him, because if you find him, dig him up'."

In the end, the project ground to a halt due to a shortage of funds. No release date is presently scheduled.

Eitzel's first solo album *60 Watt Silver Lining* finally arrived in the stores on 31st March, 1996. Musically, he had achieved what he set out to do with the record. The sound is laidback and warm. The mellow piano, haunting melodic trumpet playing and softly murmured vocals conjure the spirit of Chet Baker on *Let's Get Lost*.

The songs are memorable and melodic. "Mission Rock," "Cleopatra Jones," and "Everything is Beautiful" were as strong as his best from the AMC era.

Lyrically, *60 Watt*'s subject matter of broken hearts and bar rooms is reminiscent of much of Eitzel's back catalogue, in particular *Everclear,* though these songs are written from a more sober perspective. The narrator who sits in Specs and the Mission Rock bar is decidedly sober, perhaps even hung over. Fittingly for an album that was written for the most part after Eitzel left his lover and his band, the album feels like a reflective aftermath. Eitzel had written some very dark songs during the upheavals of 1995, but he was keen to show Warners that he could make a "light" record.

But, though it may be warm and breezy in its musical tone, and light on the lyrical surface, at the heart of *60 Watt*'s songs lies a bleak realisation. Eitzel had recently read Primo Levi's harrowing accounts of life in the Nazi concentration camps *If This Is A Man* and *The Drowned and The Saved*. Eitzel was so moved by Levi's work that he incorporated the author's name into his email address and enclosed excerpts from his writing with the US promo for *60 Watt*.

"There comes to light the existence of two particularly well differentiated categories among men," Levi wrote of life in the death camps, "the saved and the drowned. Other pairs of opposites (the good and the bad, the wise and the foolish, the cowards and the courageous, the unlucky and the fortunate) are considerably less distinct, they seem less essential, and above all they allow for more numerous and complex intermediary graduations."

The oceanic imagery that runs through *60 Watt* maintains the focus on these two classifications of people. Whether admiring the seascape from a bar, or contemplating a plane crash – metaphorical or otherwise – or even at a tacky English seaside resort, water surrounds the protagonists of these songs. The repetitive chords and meandering rhythms even conjure the ebb and flow of the sea. Previously in Eitzel's songs, those in search of redemption were "lost" now they are drowning – whether in depression, drink or drug dependency. As they search for ways to stop themselves from sinking, the drowning sometimes becomes even more inevitable.

Eitzel would describe *60 Watt* as a "Tribute to San Francisco" but it was really a tribute to the seascape beyond the city. The album's finest moment is "Mission Rock Resort," a conversation between Eitzel and a friend set in San Francisco's Mission Rock bar – a favourite haunt of the singer's which also had one of the best views of the ocean.

"It's like the edge of the world," he would say.

Musically, it is a sequel to "An Apology for an Accident" and it remains Eitzel's favourite song on the album.

What fascinated Eitzel most about Levi's observations on concentration camp inmates, was how even in the most dire of circumstances, some of the inmates would still wash, clean and try to go through the motions of being human, while some just let themselves go, shuffling around in rags. While Levi's comments were based on very extreme circumstances, Eitzel could see they held a wider application.

The friend Eitzel talks to in the Mission Rock bar had been a heroin addict, but had sworn off drugs after contracting an infection which temporarily hospitalised her. He was now horrified to discover that she was back on heroin.

As he sits there offering words of consolation to someone who is not even sure if she cleaned a syringe needle before injecting herself, he realises that some people cannot be saved whatever you do. All talk is useless. It just makes the speaker feel clever.

> *If I could talk you out of it, I would.*
> *If I could beat it out of you, I would*
> *But all I can do is follow stupidly behind*
> *And watch you walk to the ocean in your mind.*

Three months later his friend was still on heroin, and nearly died. Like Levi, Eitzel makes no moral judgement. This is simply an observation, though one which was made more resonant to him now that Kathleen Burns was back in rehab again, seemingly unable to kick her drug problems.

When asked about the song, Eitzel told a journalist, "I just want to write about living and dying and being saved." The words could apply to the whole album.

In "Some Bartenders Have The Gift of the Pardon" – a short story or one-scene play in the tradition of Eugene O'Neill or Tennessee Williams, Eitzel tells the story of Kent, the barman at North Beach bar Specs, which he describes as a "Museum to help the shipwrecked remember that the near-drowned grow quiet."

Kent died after taking heroin for the first time, but Eitzel describes this demise in vivid tones reminiscent of Levi.

> *Seems one night he was having a hard time falling asleep*
> *And found himself in an accidental shipwreck*
> *Dreaming he was still at the bar counting sheep*

And the cold ocean threw its chains around his neck.

On "Always Turn Away" Eitzel even makes the ocean appear like a scene from a mausoleum, *"There are pools across the tidal plain that look / like white sheets draped across a vacuum."* Finally "Wild Sea" is a blow by blow account of some sort of drowning. Eitzel would tell a fan that this was "Basically just a story of the ocean," but this could only be true in the widest possible sense. The song's distracted protagonist is pulled back into *"wild sea that moans and boils filled with old ghosts..."*

> *Welcome to the laws of decay the song of Darwin and dismay*
> *The wild sea rises higher*
> *Heavier it rushes down on him...*

While all the while the piano chords sound like waves. Eitzel would say later that the song came from "smoking pot on Big Sur." Eitzel tried to get AMC to play "Wild Sea," but they never took to it.

The recurring imagery of the sea gives much of the album a dreamy feel, amplified by the sparseness of detail on some songs. Eitzel would say he didn't want Kent's widow to recognise the story in "Some Bartenders," or the victim of a brutal rape and assault to see his experiences turned into song in "Aspirin."

But, just as Eitzel was moving away from rock song conventions, he was also keen to try new lyrical approaches, and was experimenting with writing that was far less transparent.

"I don't like narrative," Eitzel explained to an internet fanzine. "I like implausible images, I like things that make no sense, that resonate. It is not narrative."

This change in emphasis would mean it was impossible to determine the subject matter of a song like "Aspirin" unless you already knew.

While Eitzel's friend, Kent and the victims of the "Wild Sea" and the events in "Aspirin" were drowned in different ways, "Cleopatra Jones" is one of life's survivors – sad eyed and sweet, but able to take care of herself, *"Always kind to strangers, But you know enough never to look back..."*

Eitzel went to a gay bar with his lesbian neighbours, and got talking to this big woman in a Cleopatra shirt. He eventually got dragged away by his friends who told him not to talk to her, because she was a "faghag on drugs." Eitzel thought she was great and wrote the song as a tribute to "this strong black woman in a gay bar."

For all the talk of drowning and salvation, there are moments of humour on *60 Watt*. "Sacred Heart" is a fairly light hearted and rambling tale of Eitzel as a "worthless tourist" in a foreign city on tour with AMC. "Southend on Sea" is Eitzel's most successful attempt to date to play an edgy situation for laughs. "I went on vacation with my then-lover," Eitzel explained to a journalist,

"And we had a really bad time, It's basically about my love affair with England, and how I like trashy working-class English things. And the person I was with didn't.

"The day I got back to London I was really bummed and I saw a newspaper and it said 'Two Shot Dead By Shotgun at Southend on Sea.' That made total sense: the vibe I got was heat, and any minute now the heat was going to kill you."

But the tacky seaside scenes combined with a shuffling rhythm and Eitzel's histrionic delivery keep the song's black humour to the foreground.

Considering Eitzel has always stressed he is a songwriter more than a singer, and that he left American Music Club in part because they rejected or were unable to play his new songs, it is odd that *60 Watt Silver Lining* is the first album he has written to feature a cover version. It opens with a beautiful take on Goffin and King's "No Easy Way Down."

"I think I included it because of my whole experience with AMC," he would explain. "Because all the talk was that we were going to be the next big thing, and then we weren't."

It immediately sets out the album's stall as a comedown after the party – a farewell to his old cohorts and an apprehensive contemplation of a low-key future as a solo artist.

"No Easy Way Down" was made famous by Barbara Streisand. But, though Eitzel had friends who loved Streisand and had been to see her live a few times – and in fact even wrote "Saved" in the hope that she would record it – he claims to "Really hate Barbara Streisand and all that bullshit."

His version was based on Dusty Springfield's performance.

"A friend of mine gave me a cassette with a selection of songs to give to some-one else," he explains, "And I never gave it to them. I put the tape on in the car and it is the first song on the second side, and I thought 'Fuck, I can sing that song.' *The Dusty in Memphis* version is beautiful."

In typical style, Eitzel would maintain it was better than anything he could ever write.

Like the cover version that begins *60 Watt*, the album's closing song, "Everything is Beautiful" also has a separate tone from the record's other materi-al. In fact it was written as part of a musical adaptation of Peter Handke's book *Left Handed Woman*. So far it is the only song from that project to officially sur-face.

Eitzel's first solo album was eagerly anticipated by the press and on its arrival the critics who loved AMC were quick to praise his new direction. *Spin* maga-zine's Ann Powers compared *60 Watt* to the book *Leaving Las Vegas*, and deemed "Mission Rock Resort," "Cleopatra Jones," and "Some Bartenders," to be "as good as AMC got." *Melody Maker*'s Nick Johnstone waxed lyrical across the best part of a page comparing Eitzel to Carver and Bukoswki. *The Guardian* considered it "impressive and evocative" and *Time Out* even felt "Southend On Sea" might be Eitzel's "first hit single."

But it was Stephanie Zacharek in *The Boston Phoenix* who described Eitzel's solo debut most vividly. "Like a stone whose color fluctuates with the light," she wrote, "*60 Watt Silver Lining* took on a different cast with every listening."

Even the *NME* found something to praise, but Tommy Udo's description of the record as "a fine collection of middle-aged, middle-class balding white bloke blues," did not help Eitzel's fragile self-esteem. He was aware that his new direc-tion might be seen as a cliched retirement from rock 'n' roll. When a friend rein-forced this view, Eitzel started to regret the overtly jazz sound.

"I was talking to an old friend," Eitzel explains, "And I told him that I wrote every single note on the record except for some of the bass parts. I wrote it all on a computer at home, and I worked for months on it. I felt I had to prove something. I had no management, and I had to hire Danny and Brúce to play on it. I had to prove to Virgin and Warners that I could make a big AMC sounding record, without management and without a producer, because I didn't want to use a producer. I talked along these lines for a while, saying that I was really making new ground and then my friend said, 'Mark, all you did was make your mid-career jazz record. That's what every songwriter does.' And it was fair enough, I think, because it was kind of that.

"Warners wanted me to make anything I wanted, Virgin wanted a quiet acoustic record that was dark and weird. Both record companies were really disappointed with *60 Watt*, because it was so middle-of-the-road jazz. I just wanted to make a classic record. I was a fool – I was trying to make a Chet Baker record – I became a middle-aged man making that record. I like it in retrospect, there are some good things on it. But I spent too much money and I worked too hard, and I didn't have to. I was writing a jazz record and I didn't know anything about jazz."

When *60 Watt* peaked at number 111 on the British charts, and failed to make any impression in the US, it reinforced Eitzel's view that the album was a failed experiment. As he prepared a new band for a short promotional trip in Europe, it appeared as futile an exercise as the *San Francisco* tour. Worse still, this time he would not have his old friends for morale support. Eitzel felt he couldn't afford Dan Pearson, Kaphan or Simone White for the dates. Pearson in particular was waiting for the call, but it never came. Eitzel recruited a new band from scratch.

Eitzel didn't really know these young musicians, and they for the most part were intimidated by his manner – with the exception of Mark Capelle who played trumpet and keyboard. Capelle would even play both instruments at the same time, and his most "out there" solos would bring a smile to Eitzel's face on a generally smile-free series of shows.

The new drummer felt aggrieved from the start. Eitzel wouldn't let him play his soft-funk tapes on the bus, and also made him drop one of his favourite cymbals from his kit. The singer reasoned that as he was paying the band, they should at least try and sound like he wanted.

Even setting aside misgivings about his band, Eitzel had little confidence that the new jazz material would work in a live context. He was also convinced that after *60 Watt*'s poor commercial showing, he was about to be dropped by Virgin for the second time. By the time he reached London for the first of two shows at the Bloomsbury Theatre, his nerves were severely frayed. When at the first soundcheck the bass in the monitors was so loud that the stage was literally shaking, he started to resign himself to another disaster. He couldn't hear himself sing, or think. He instructed the bass player to take his instrument out of the monitor and to rely on the bass amp, but the soundcheck did not augur well. As he left the stage he caught a glimpse of his booking agent, Mick Griffiths at the back of the hall, just shaking his head.

And it was not alright on the night. During the first show, Eitzel kept stopping mid-song to address people in the audience, but instead of his usual amicable reciprocal banter he criticised things he'd overheard members in the front rows say. His banter with the crowd was awkward and angry rather than funny and self-deprecating.

He was clearly not happy with the other musicians and repeatedly looked daggers at them. When the bassist kept inching his instrument up in the mix, Eitzel banished the entire band from the stage. There were isolated moments of pure beauty when Eitzel's voice mingled with Capelle's piano and trumpet, but mainly Eitzel's new musical experiment was dying a death. As he prepared for another number, someone in the crowd shouted, "Where's Vudi?" Then everything stopped.

Suddenly the singer looked lost and frightened. The question seemed to sum up so many of the doubts that were going through his mind.

"I almost cried!" he remembers. "I thought, 'Fuck you! You don't even know what I did to be here? Yeah, where is fucking Vudi?'"

Eitzel started to wonder why the hell AMC weren't with him. And, why the hell was it going so badly? What was the point anyway?

After a few more halfhearted attempts, Eitzel just gave up, threw his guitar down on the floor mid-song and walked off stage. Moments later he returned in a different outfit, played one song and walked straight out of the venue, onto the tube and back to the Columbia Hotel. That night he refused to take calls from anyone. Alone in his room, it was a long night.

Somehow, Eitzel managed to pick himself up the next day, and played a more professional show. He apologised for the previous night, and generally pulled through. Nonetheless, it was clear that all was far from well. After the show, Mick Griffiths, Spike Hyde and another ten or so friends and supporters went downstairs to see Eitzel in his dressing room. He passed them on the stairs, muttered, "See you all later, bye" and then disappeared.

Eitzel's apprehensions about Griffiths proved well founded. His agent didn't think the jazz format worked, and shortly afterwards he and Eitzel parted company. Things with Virgin were no better. They had earmarked "Southend On Sea" for a single release, but the album had stiffed so resoundingly, that they decided there was no point in throwing good money after bad. As his mismatched four-piece headed off to do some US dates, it appeared that Eitzel's career was reaching a new nadir. In the end, the US shows were much better – the band had got used to each other, and Eitzel was getting more comfortable with the new material. But the venues he was playing were pretty small, and he still didn't feel that the tour was achieving anything.

Then, halfway through his schedule, Eitzel got a call asking him if he wanted to join Everything But The Girl for the second leg of their tour.

"I did the first tour and then I told everyone that I wouldn't do another one again as long as I lived," Eitzel remembers. But his agent told him he should do the next leg. When Eitzel asked why, his agent replied, "Well, it's going to be the biggest tour of the year, and you're not exactly getting any other offers."

Against all his better judgement, Eitzel was persuaded. "I wanted to bring that album to a lot more people, and I thought that Everything But The Girl tour would do it."

Eitzel regretted his decision almost instantly. He knew the second EBTG tour would be no different from the first. As he prepared for the shows with a pair of solo dates at the Seattle Crocodile Café, he felt tired, frustrated and apprehensive about his future.

Chapter Fourteen

Call Me A Cussardly Fuck

"You have to realise that Mark is always a bit at the end of his tether – he's an end of his tether kind of guy."

Peter Buck

Mark Eitzel: "I have a real idea of what I want to do now… "
Interviewer: "What is that?"
Mark Eitzel: "'What is that?' I don't know."

When Eitzel arrived at Seattle's Crocodile Café and prepared to start setting up his gear, it crossed his mind that REM's guitarist, Peter Buck, might be in the audience that night. After all the club was owned by Buck's wife, Stephanie. Oddly, considering they moved in similar circles for a while, Eitzel and Buck had never met, though Vudi had taken a dislike to Buck years before in Hamburg, when at an REM show, he deemed the guitar player too much of a Rock Star.

Oblivious to Vudi's initial disdain, Buck had been a fan of American Music Club since the days of *The Restless Stranger*. He was delighted Eitzel was playing his wife's venue, and attended both nights. Afterwards, Buck approached Eitzel to tell him how much he'd enjoyed the show, and within minutes they were arguing about Leni Riefenstahl.

"I said he should see this documentary movie about her life that was out on video," Eitzel remembers.

"I said he should see it because it was interesting – a 'Must see.' He said, 'I don't need that in my head – I don't need someone telling me why they weren't evil, when they really were.' I said, 'You have to understand what evil is.'" Buck replied that he didn't need to know about a woman who raised fascism to an art form.

Later Buck introduced Eitzel to Stipe, ["I said, 'Whoooa, hi!'"] and then Buck, his wife, Eitzel and Greg Dulli of the Afghan Whigs sat talking and drinking till the early hours.

After a while the conversation turned to San Francisco and in particular its restaurants. Eitzel told Buck that next time he was in the city, he should call up and he would take him out for dinner. Buck assured him he would and they left it at that.

When Eitzel woke the next day, nursing a slight hangover, it was time to join the next stage of the Everything But The Girl tour, and just as he expected, it was worse than before. To begin with at least, he tried to put on a full set.

"We did a show in Boston," he shudders, "where we played all the songs as best we could, and nobody listened. Nobody! The whole thing was, there'd be a secretary here talking to a secretary there, saying very loudly, 'I don't believe what she wore at work, it was amazing, she had gel in her hair, and it looked stupid.' And I was doing 'Gena Rowlands'."

Pretty soon, the audience's mixture of indifference and hostility had Eitzel back playing aggressive 17-minute sets.

"And it was awful. The heckling was amazing! In Cleveland for instance, I said, 'This song is about a freak, and a lot of you people wouldn't know what that's all about, because you're all yuppies.' And this guy started shouting, 'Yeah! You're a freak! You're a freak.' And during my next three songs, they were all linking arms and dancing in a circle, and singing another song."

At one show, the promoter even came out and apologised for Eitzel's performance.

By the time the tour got to New York, Eitzel's every word and gesture was aimed at communicating to the audience how much he hated them.

"Every song was as fast as possible." He explains. "'Mission Rock' became a total 'Fuck you' to the audience – a total 'Fuck you'. Though, everything was a total 'Fuck you.' And this crowd would shout at me, 'Why are you doing this, if you hate us so much?' And I said, 'I don't hate you. FUCK YOU!' And actually, the crowd in New York like that, but it was terrible really.

"In New York, the promoter at the Avalon gave us an extra 100 bucks, because he said, 'I've never seen an audience that rude in my life'."

"I thought that because they were friends and because I liked their album, I thought I could do well, but I should have never done that tour. Much as I love Everything But The Girl, touring with them for two months devastated me."

For all Eitzel's complaints, his attitude to the small number of his fans who actually tracked him down and coughed up the $25 to see his short support set, was even more bizarre.

"There were always five or six AMC fans and I would always try really hard to piss them off," he told a journalist shortly afterwards. When asked why, Eitzel replied, "Oh I don't know, call me a cussardly fuck."

Eitzel's experiences on the tour definitely brought out his more misanthropic side. Previously, he was a firm believer in the healing power of music. During the *Engine* and *California* eras, he would insist that it didn't matter if AMC's albums sold in big quantities, as long as the music they were making was good, and as long as it helped people in some way. Live shows in particular were about communication with the audience. Now this had all changed.

"After touring with Everything But the Girl,... I guess you could say I had a nervous breakdown," Eitzel confesses. "Now I just hate people in the audience so much that I ignore them and I just try and get through it without anything getting in the way of my professionalism. I just don't deal with the audience any more.

"I just want to write music and not have to worry about my future. I couldn't give a shit if I'm recognised in the street, I couldn't give a shit if people like me, like my music or it means something to them. I really don't care.

"[That tour] also taught me that if I'd stayed in American Music Club, I could have had a future...It was the biggest wake-up call for me regarding my future. It dispelled any feelings that I might have had about being a successful musician. It taught me that in America and in the world, I am a thing that people least want to hear – that my pretentious little songs of quiet self-loathing were exactly the wrong thing for people. They didn't care about them. Subtlety, art and poetry were things that 99% of the population couldn't give a shit about. I'll never be in the mass market, because I really care about those things. Even today writing my really MOR song, the first line is 'We wandered through the bombed out downtown.' It's a very MOR pop song, but that is not a great line for a [hit]. I like that kind of music, but I can't help but write the stuff that I have to say."

Eitzel has always refused to sugar his pill. "A lot of my life has been spent wandering around downtown at night in different cities going 'Wow' because American downtowns are bombed out, but they're beautiful. I'd do this as a revenge against the suburban American culture which has become so fascistic. America should have been bombed [literally] or invaded – they should have learned that you have to pay for freedom. You can't [just] eat and watch TV, and go to work, have a nice car and house.... There is a price.... You get freedom to do art, to learn new things. You don't get freedom to consume more. Americans are really lost, and get more and more evil as years go by."

For all Eitzel's convictions that his poor reception from Everything But The Girl's new trip hop convert crowd meant he was finished, he was simply a slightly inappropriate support act. As his comments about American Music Club illustrate, his reactions were very much linked to his own insecurities about the path his career and life in general was taking. If his own solo tour could not convince him that what he was doing was worthwhile, it is unlikely that some other band's audience would.

"I think Mark was running away from things on those tours," Ben Watt would reflect. "Away from AMC, away from San Francisco, away from things in the past perhaps. it meant he was committed to the task but vulnerable – a classic Eitzel state of mind, you might say. He wanted to be loved by a new audience and on paper we looked like a likely home. Maybe he expected too much, and our audience weren't as sympathetic as he'd hoped. I remember one night he said how he was sick of playing to pissed-up crowds in smoky ballrooms like he did with AMC, and was looking forward to attentive sit-down audiences who would embrace the subtleties and lyrics in his songs. Ironically we were in transition at the point he joined us – trying to move in the opposite direction to a certain extent. I think had Mark joined us on our acoustic tour of 1994 rather than our dance-hall tours of 1995 and 1996, he would have enjoyed himself much more."

When pressed as to why he thought Eitzel joined the second leg of the tour, Ben Watt would offer, "Because, in spite of many things, I think Mark finds inspiration in hope and struggle. Maybe we all do."

For all the difficulties, Watt remains hopeful that an EBTG-Eitzel collaboration may happen in the future, "He is still one of the greatest singers and songwriters I've known."

When the EBTG tour finished in New York, Eitzel decided to stay there for the rest of the summer. His new manager Janet was based there and Eitzel was keen to take a longer break from San Francisco.

During his *60 Watt* tour, Janet had dragged Eitzel to see alternative country pioneer Jay Farrar's new band, Son Volt. It would reinforce his desire to move away from the sound of his first solo album. "I was so blown away," he remembers. "I just said to myself, 'I want to do that. Why do I want to keep dragging this jazz crap out?'"

Eitzel celebrated the end of his touring commitment by buying a new guitar. In the following weeks, in between late night drinking sessions with Kid Congo Powers and various members of Lush, he wrote about twenty songs. The new material was very much guitar based and far bleaker than his previous album. It was a move toward the dark acoustic record that Virgin had wanted him to make in the first place. But it was too late. Virgin had not liked *60 Watt*, and were unimpressed with its poor sales. They decided they had spent enough money on Mark Eitzel and dropped him for the second time.

Coming so close to the soul destroying EBTG tour, this was a bitter blow. But, with moral support from Janet Billig, he threw himself further into writing his next record. He was still signed to Warners in the US but they were not yet ready for another album. As Eitzel was so keen to put his new material out, Warners allowed him one low-key record with Gerard Cosloy's Matador label.

Envisaging this album as a low-budget solo acoustic album, Eitzel initially planned to record it on a DAT player in a series of motels on a trip to the Grand Canyon. He was concerned that his life was getting too comfortable and that this might take the edge off his writing. Alone in a motel room, he would have less distractions. "I've bought a house and a car," he explained, "I'm not out in the street like I should be. I think that's why I keep travelling, because I want to write. I can't really write in my nice little house, with a washer-dryer and all mod cons, a nice big bath tub, and a VCR. I've got all this bullshit that I never had before. Four years ago, I didn't have anything – no car, no colour TV, I lived in a tiny little cubby hole, paying 75 dollars a month. Then at one strike, I got a house, a car, a VCR, a computer. I got all this stuff, and it's insane. And it really keeps you from working the way I want to work.

"All the best songs I've ever written have been when I've been alone – when I haven't been talking to anybody. I wrote "Western Sky" and "Blue And Grey Shirt" in a little log cabin, when I hadn't spoken to anyone in two weeks."

For all his monastic intentions, Eitzel was beginning to enjoy hanging out in New York and decided to record his album in Manhattan with Kid Congo instead. He realised on balance that he didn't want to spent weeks alone on the road and felt he might not get much actual work done that way.

Before he could get started, Eitzel made a short trip back to San Francisco to check up on his house and play a couple of West Coast shows with Bob Mould. He then got a call from Peter Buck. It was nearly four months since they'd met in Seattle. The REM guitarist was in San Francisco on a brief vacation and decided to take Eitzel up on his offer of dinner. Eitzel was playing a solo show that night, so Buck went to the gig, and then afterwards the two musicians retired to Brunos restaurant. Fortunately for Eitzel, Buck insisted on picking up the tab.

During the meal, Eitzel broached the idea of some kind of musical collaboration. Buck had enjoyed side projects with Warren Zevon and The Troggs in the past and keen to fill in time in between REM albums, he leapt at the chance. He told Eitzel he'd bring a bass and mandolin down and add some parts to Eitzel's demos.

Two weeks later Buck was back in San Francisco with his wife and kids. He rented a hotel suite, and told Eitzel, "Well Wednesday is off, I have Monday, Tuesday, Thursday and maybe Friday."

The project couldn't have come at a better time for Eitzel. His ego had taken a series of batterings since AMC had broken up and his morale was at a low ebb.

"I needed something that would inspire me," he told Nick Johnstone.

"And when Peter came around, I thought, 'I don't really know who the fuck this guy is, but he seems fine, and he's great to have a drink with. He's intelligent and we agree on the same things,' so it was liberating."

Buck arrived at Bernal Heights that Monday, expecting to work on parts for Eitzel's new album, only to discover that the amp on Eitzel's 8-track home studio had broken. So while Eitzel checked over the recording equipment, Buck picked up the other man's guitar, sat down at the kitchen table, and started strumming. The guitar was in the open G tuning with a C added, that Eitzel uses for songwriting, and Buck initially found it a bit of a struggle. But to Eitzel's ears, as Buck wrestled with the unfamiliar tuning, he started to come up with some really fresh guitar parts, and while initially reluctant to give Buck the song that was germinating in his mind, Eitzel gradually decided to join in.

"Peter was playing, and I thought what he was playing was good enough for me, and so I ended up singing the first thing that came into my head. I taped it on a portable DAT player, and that became the song 'Lower East Side Tourist'" – a song prompted by the recent suicide of Lush's drummer Chris Acland.

The collaboration gelled immediately, and they got through three songs that first afternoon. "On the poppy ones like 'In Your Life'," Buck muses, "I assumed he'd just go, 'I don't do that kind of stuff.' But it was great; he came up with stuff right away."

The next day they got through four more songs, and on the third day five. The prodigious work-rate was more amazing considering they were not even working all day. Buck would go to Mark's at 1pm each day and they'd finish at 5.30pm. Buck would then spend some time with his kids, and later they'd meet up for dinner.

The creative process of doing the tracks was a completely new experience for both men. Theirs was an equal collaboration along fixed lines, Buck writing the music, and Eitzel the lyrics and vocal melodies. Buck had music for about four songs already written, and the rest he improvised on the spot. He would play his guitar lines while Eitzel would leaf through his journal looking for inspiration. While Buck maintains he's not good at reading Mark's handwriting, he was aware that Mark wasn't just reading fully realised songs or poems out to his music. Eitzel's journal was full of notes and half formed ideas that he was very quickly transforming into songs – far more quickly than anyone Buck had ever worked with before.

Once Eitzel had consulted his notes for a few moments, says Buck, "He'd just start coming up with words on the spot... It was the most spontaneous I've ever worked. He was so willing to just start singing... Michael [Stipe] would occasionally come up with something in five minutes, but normally it was a lot longer. Lyrics would go through hundreds of rewrites."

Instead of massaging and shaping, Eitzel would record every single rehearsal with Buck, and then take the lyrics and cut and paste them according to which verse he liked. Buck insisted that he didn't go back to the songs afterwards and change any of the lyrics.

Buck's songs adopted conventional verse-chorus-verse structures. They were exactly the kind of thing Eitzel had been trying to move away from since *San Francisco* but he still found the experience refreshing. Even if he did occasionally question his writing partner's approach:

"I do remember a conversation I had with Peter, where I said, 'Do we have to repeat this chorus so many times? Is it really necessary?' He just said, 'Try it. Try it. And you tell me later if it's bad, and if it's bad, we won't do it.' And it did make a pop sense that I like – I had just never done it before."

Because Eitzel found Peter such a grounding influence, he was willing to take certain things on trust. Also because it was an equal two-way collaboration, Eitzel didn't feel any of the pressure of the AMC or *60 Watt* sessions.

After three days, Eitzel and Buck had got together the verses, choruses and middle eights for eleven new songs. At that stage they had no firm plans for the material, other than Eitzel possibly putting a few of the songs on his next album. But when Buck and Eitzel listened back to the DAT tapes at the end of the three days, they got more excited. To their ears, the songs did sound fully formed; the guitar parts, chord progressions, vocal melodies and lyrics were all strong. Eitzel especially felt that they should take the project further. "The very last night," he remembers, "We went to dinner, and I said, 'You know Peter, we should document these songs somehow. We should book a studio – just you and me and maybe a drummer'." Buck immediately agreed, and suggested Tuatara – an instrumental group he'd recently been working with – as the musicians.

A few days later, Eitzel returned to New York to record his second solo album. In addition to his friend King Congo, Eitzel's band for the project included Sonic Youth drummer Steve Shelley and Yo La Tengo bassist James McNew. (Eitzel would return Congo's favour by adding vocals to Congo's album *Abnormals Anonymous*.) Eitzel's album would be called *Caught In A Trap And I Can't Back Out 'cause I Love You Too Much, Baby*, from the Elvis song "Suspicious Minds" which kept running through Eitzel's mind during the Everything But The Girl tour.

"When Elvis sings it," Eitzel explains, "It's such a dark thing…. Because Elvis *was* so caught in a trap. On that tour, I *was* Elvis."

Eitzel's budget for the album was $5,000, so he did not have much studio time. But, his experience of working with Peter Buck had persuaded him that it was possible to record quickly and spontaneously.

By now Eitzel had decided against the originally planned acoustic format. He recorded eight songs with his newly assembled combo, putting his Gibson Chet Atkins guitar through Lee Renaldo's guitar amplifier. Eitzel told the band what he wanted them to play and they played it. The process was quick and simple – everything was done live except for the vocals – and he was initially happy with the results. But, at the end of the session, Eitzel decided he didn't like four of the songs, so he wrote seven more in a furious brainstorm. By then he didn't have enough money or studio time left to do any more recording with the band, so the rest of the album ended up acoustic.

When the sessions were finished, Eitzel was reluctant to go back to San Francisco. Keen to play another UK date to make up for the mixed Bloomsbury shows, he lined up another low-key date at London's Garage Upstairs. When the gig approached, the venue pointed out that Buffalo Tom's singer, Bill Jankowitz, was playing a solo acoustic show at the London Borderline on the same night. They were concerned that this might take away part of Eitzel's audience, so a plot was hatched for Eitzel to support Jankowitz at the Borderline, while Jankowitz would open for Eitzel two miles to the North. The artists could then make their way to their own headline slots in the interval. Without Mick Griffiths on board, nobody seemed to realise that Eitzel could have sold the tiny North London venue out many times over. It was an ill-conceived plan that was even worse in execution. The two artists had little in common except they were Americans playing solo acoustic shows.

"I wanted to do one good show in London to repay for the awful shows that I did," Eitzel recalls. "Then it became this other thing – that me and Bill Jankowitz were good friends, two songwriters together – but that was bullshit! Because I'm not a big fan of Bill Jankowitz at all. I think Bill is a sweet kid and I think his songs are good, but they don't interest me at all.

"For me to open for him at the Borderline was humiliating. I agreed to it because my agent and my manager convinced me it was a good idea. But it was bullshit, and I did not get paid for that Borderline show.

"I fucking hated the Garage show. I didn't want to be there. I wanted to do the best show I could, but I was still so angry from the Borderline show. I mean, I get off the Borderline, I get on the tube – I don't take cabs, I can't afford them – I get to the Garage and I start setting up. The only vocal mike they have smells of puke, so I say 'I'm not using that.' I get back on the tube, I go back to my hotel, get my own mike, get another tube, and get back to the Garage. And I'm glad I did it because the mike sounded good and it saved the show.

"Also, I walked in and it was half full when it was supposed to be sold out. I went up to the club owner and told him it was only half full. He insisted it was sold out. But I knew someone was lying, because I'd seen a bunch of shows here and it was packed. So – I was not a happy man."

As Eitzel walked on to the small stage, he kicked his stool out of the way and appeared forlorn and intense as he worked his way through a short and bitter set. When three girls at the back repeatedly shouted for Jankowitz to return, Eitzel seemed to lose control. From then on the set just steadily collapsed. It was his worst ever show on British soil.

"Those girls were heckling me from the back all night long," he remembers, "And they were singing really loud during my song. So I asked them to get up on stage and sing. So they got up and they were like Spice Girls, singing 'We Love Bill Jankowitz, We Love Bill Jankowitz.' And I suppose it was kind of funny, but then all my fans were shouting, 'Get off the stage you fucking bitches.'

"It was really bad. It kind of summed up my career. Because I don't have a pretty face, I have no success. Because I don't have a pretty face, people think I have no talent.

"Bill's a good-looking guy, and plays rock music. He's cute. Good luck to him, but that was the defining moment of the last four years of my life... I'm an ugly man."

While the Garage shows were pretty erratic in many ways, Eitzel previewed a number of the *Caught* songs, "Goodbye," "Go Away," and most striking of all, "If I Had A Gun." The material was far more rough-hewn than AMC or *60 Watt*, but it had an intensity that boded well for the future. Eitzel's next step was to fly to Seattle to record his collaboration with Peter Buck.

As well as Tuatara, Buck had also booked engineer Ed Brooks who had worked on REM's multi-platinum *Automatic For The People*. In the week leading up to the studio sessions he contacted Warner Brothers, the record company he shared with Eitzel, to tell them about the project – mainly with a view to ensuring that they would pick up the $8,000 studio tab. "The record company were fine about it," he remembers. "I think they just thought, let's humour the guy."

Sensing possible commercial potential, Warners also insisted to Eitzel that this putative session would form his next album. This immediately cast a shadow over the project for him, because his initial hopes of the recording session were not that high,

"I thought, well if we've got a week to record eleven songs, we might actually end up with three that are any good – because I work slowly."

But, in spite of his disappointment with Warners' pushiness, Eitzel went into the studio in a philosophical mood, thinking, "We'll see. If we don't end up with anything, then we don't."

Buck too had some initial apprehensions:

"Once I'd booked the musicians and the studio and the engineer, when I finally came to listen to the songs again, I was really worried that they might not be as good as I remembered. But once I heard them again, I knew they were good and fully formed."

In keeping with the spontaneous genesis of the material, the band rehearsed for one day, and then recorded the album in a week – mixing it in another. Eitzel was also aware that Buck – for whom money was not a critical factor at the time – was looking out for Eitzel's well being.

"I could have spent $100,000 on my last record," he explains. "I don't get that money, that's the recording budget, and I can spend up to that amount. The trouble is, if I spend that amount, an accountant will look at it and I'll get dropped. That's why Virgin dropped me. Peter was aware of all of this, and so we spent nothing on that record."

Once they were in the studio, the makeshift collaboration had to come up with a name. "I wanted it to be a Mark Eitzel and Peter Buck record," Eitzel recalls. "He said, 'No'."

Buck had good reasons for his stance: "I said to him, you're just starting out solo, you've made one record as Mark Eitzel, if this is under a different name, it will only confuse people. Also, he sang on the record and he wrote all the lyrics, so it was really a Mark Eitzel album."

Buck later elaborated the point to *Rolling Stone*: "I think his voice is so distinctive, I don't think there's any point in making up a name for a band and sticking it on there just for the sake of having a name. It will be good if it can help him out a little bit."

Eitzel enjoyed recording with Buck and Tuatara. He considered them to be "Really good live players, and sensitive." Compared to the tensions of AMC records with Mallon, Froom and Chicarelli, the atmosphere here was relaxed. From time to time, Buck would just stop everyone and say something like, "You know what? I think we should all get margaritas." Eitzel was used to suffering for his art, and this was actually fun.

In the studio, Eitzel and Buck tried to stay pretty true to their original DAT recordings. "Free of Harm" was the only song that was materially changed. Originally it was going to be a very quiet piece with acoustic guitar and maybe even flugelhorn. But, in the studio Barrett Martin came up with a more pop drum pattern and Buck switched to electric guitar accordingly.

When they completed the Bernal Heights compositions, Buck and Eitzel had eleven songs. Buck in particular was convinced that there should be at least twelve tracks on the album, so Eitzel proposed "Live or Die," a song he'd written on his own about a week before the recording.

Throughout the recording session, Eitzel tended to defer to Buck when it came to arrangements. "None of this was done my way at all," he would typically explain.

"In the studio, I didn't really have any say. I don't speak the language of musicians. I prevaricate, and waffle, and say things like, 'I want it darker,' and I was surrounded by musicians who were better than me. The creative thing I did was to shut the fuck up. And it was Peter's band!"

Now that Eitzel finally had complete freedom, it seems like a bizarre move to throw it all away, by taking part in a collaboration where he was only the lyric writer and singer – leaving the music, guitar parts, production and everything else to someone he barely knew.

But Eitzel had just come out of making a record where he was in complete control – For *Caught In A Trap...* he'd written all of the songs and chosen the musicians and the studio. Now he found the lack of control refreshing. While a lot of what they did in the studio was not done the way Eitzel would have chosen to do it, there was very little done that he could disapprove of. The fact that someone else was in charge was also strangely liberating.

"If I had more control," he explained to Nick Johnstone, "I wouldn't have been able to say a lot of the things that I said in the songs. There are really few collaborators that I have ever worked with where I could make stuff up on the spot. There are things that I like on this album, that I couldn't have said otherwise."

Of working so quickly, Eitzel would say later, "It helped me a lot – in ways I can't even describe. It helped me to see songs in a much clearer light. Peter's philosophy with me was. 'If it's not done in the first take, it's never going to be done'."

It was a million miles away from the "Wish The World Away" re-remix debacle. Ironically, Buck later described to Eitzel the laborious process that REM would go through to make an album – recording everything to Macintosh computer software, and adjusting individual tracks through Pro-Tools software.

When the sessions were completed Eitzel took a week's vacation with Buck and his family at their Hawaii holiday home. He was happy with the work they'd done and enjoyed the break. Finally, for the first time since the Everything But The Girl tour, Eitzel felt relaxed and at ease.

Chapter Fifteen

We Were American Music Club

"I'm sick of being ostracised by boys and scene goddesses and scenemeisters from their little scenes because they think, (whiney accent) 'REM is bad! Pop is bad!'"

Courtney Love, 1998

As soon as Eitzel got back from Hawaii, he packed up some personal belongings, rented out his house and headed across the length of the US to New York. He enjoyed the prospect of settling in a new city where he wasn't burdened down by the need to be the Mark Eitzel of local myth.

It was ironic that just as he was leaving behind a city that was known as the gay capital of the world, Eitzel found his own sexuality coming under increasing scrutiny. Gay magazine *The Advocate* was keen to do a profile, but Eitzel was initially reluctant. He felt the subject had no bearing on his work. "It's not an issue," he would say.

"I'm a musician. An artist's work is pretty separate from what they are. You have to judge them on their work."

Later that Spring an interview with Bill Crandle appeared in *BAM* magazine, where Eitzel expounded further on this theme.

"People expect too much of an artist. They expect me to be my songs. Like my kind of sexuality, for instance. I don't even want to analyse it. I guess I'm a fag now after all these years, but people expect me to write about only that issue. And I won't. I was in love with a woman for many, many years – I guess I'm bi. I don't even want to be part of that whole scene."

When Crandle asked him if he was worried that people might start reading his music from a gay perspective, Eitzel was quick and firm in his response, "Well, they better not, because I don't know if I am. How can you write from a gay perspective when you're writing love songs for women? And I really feel that I do that."

"*Out* magazine wanted to do a story on me," Eitzel later explained. "And I said sure, as long as the focus is on my music. And the guy said 'No, that's not what we want.' So I said forget it. Look, when I write songs, I try to be as non-specific as a fiction writer... Whether people are gay or straight, black or white, everybody has essentially the same soul. I really believe that."

When Eitzel finally did *The Advocate* interview, he revealed a deep ambivalence about being publicly gay, which may partly explain why he wanted to move to a new city.

"The gay people who like me aren't particularly vocal or obvious. They're kind of shy. They think that if they talk to me, I'm going to want to sleep with them, and that scares them to death... If I were going to be this incredibly out person in San Francisco, I'd have all these political boys coming to my shows wanting me to be their poster child. I won't do that."

Eitzel also told *Genre* magazine that he found it difficult fitting in with mainstream gay culture. "I'm terrified of the bars," he confessed, "Because I never see women. It's like this locker-room jock scenario. It's just stupid."

Now that Eitzel was living on the East coast, he named the new album *West*. Eitzel would say that at the time he was, "Looking for a totally fresh start, in every way. And this album reflects it."

Certainly the music is very different from anything he had recorded before. There were virtually none of Eitzel's quirky open tunings and weird chords. Similarly, the songs in the main had very conventional structures and were simple and up-tempo. Choruses were short, catchy and frequently repeated. Buck's trademark guitar playing is immediately recognisable throughout and "In Your Life" and "Free of Harm" sound like great REM singles. In fact Buck had made a demo of "In Your Life" for REM's last album, but they never got round to it.

Eitzel's voice occasionally sounds ill at ease without the comfort of his own favourite chords but his singing is generally as good as it has ever been.

Part of *West*'s freshness came from Eitzel's willingness to relinquish control in the studio. With Buck as a stabilising influence, Eitzel didn't feel that he had anything to prove – he just went in and sang the songs.

"Peter was the daddy, the boss," he reflects.

"And I suppose he is a bit of a father figure to me. I love people who ground me and he is so grounded – the man is all perspective".

Buck's presence certainly contributed to the more optimistic tone discernible on some of the new compositions. "Then It Really Happens" is about finally getting what you've spent your whole life waiting for, while "Fresh Screwdriver" features the telling line, *"I forgot there was such a thing/ As good people left."*

Ignoring these shafts of light, Eitzel would say the album was, "about memories and death." Eitzel's comments on Buck as father figure are fascinating as at least two songs on *West* feature memories inextricably linked with his own father.

On "Stunned and Frozen" Eitzel reflects on a disastrous show – falling from grace like a trapeze artist plummeting to the ground. In the song's third verse he muses, *"If I get sick like an animal giving up the ghost / With thoughts of*

Christmas and Burl Ives," bringing to mind his sister's comments on Eitzel senior – "He would play Burl Ives at Christmas." On "Old Photographs" Eitzel is literally leafing through the old family album, pausing over snaps from Singapore and portraits of ships that his father was so fond of.

Perhaps because of the spontaneous germination of the material, there is no overall consistency of mood or subject matter on this album. Moving from song to song is like flitting through the pages of Eitzel's journal from which they quickly emanated. While this helps explain *West*'s breezy freshness, it also points to the album's most obvious flaw.

Eitzel is not a fast worker. He has often taken long periods of time to hone his strongest material. *West* is packed with powerful images and compelling couplets, but unlike say, "Western Sky," "I've Been a Mess," or "Last Harbor," there are few songs on the album that could not have benefited from the appliance of more craft. Normally Eitzel's songs would go through multiple redrafts; here Buck insisted he stick to draft one. The most fully-formed lyric on the album is "Live or Die," the song he wrote on his own a week before recording.

West was certainly a successful project – a classy and enjoyable record. If it had been allowed to appear as a low-key spontaneous experiment credited to "Eitzel and Buck" it would have been difficult to criticise. Who else after all could come up with such strong material in such an impossibly short period of time?

But as Warners rightly saw Buck's involvement as a chance to finally bring Eitzel to a bigger audience, *West* would mark his highest profile since the days of *Mercury*. For critics and fans wrestling to get a handle on what was not an obvious record for either Buck or Eitzel, the temptation would be to compare it to each artist's best work and find it wanting. On the whole though, the critics were kinder than Eitzel's fans.

Mojo concluded, "Eitzel's plainspoken tales of entropy have never been more fun to listen to." *Q*'s Martin Aston gave the album four stars out of five, feeling that *"West* is the potential breakthrough that his industry sponsors have been praying for."

Rolling Stone concluded another four-star review with the belief that this was the album that would make most people care for Mark Eitzel.

But among Eitzel's long-term admirers there was also plenty of critical dissent.

Melody Maker concluded , "I realise [now] that this is a Tuatura record with a guest vocalist. Make no mistake, this is NOT a Mark Eitzel record, it's a Peter Buck project."

Andrew Mueller was one of Eitzel's most ardent supporters in the media, but writing in *Time Out*, he found the album, "Curiously underwhelming."

Comparing the new offering to *Songs of Love Live*, he mused, "Possibly this is due to the fact that visions as singular as Eitzel's tend to be diluted rather than augmented by outside collaborators."

Like a number of writers, Mueller concluded that *West* was a "Pretty poor advertisement for the abilities of its two creators."

Curious as to what his fans were making of the new album, Eitzel lurked briefly on a newsgroup dedicated entirely to his own work – firefly@fragment.com. He admitted this was "the most narcissistic things I could possibly do," before quickly de-subscribing due to the amount of criticism of his work with Buck.

The harsh words about *West* would further alienate Eitzel from his fans. Not only did he hate to be criticised, he was also fiercely loyal. He saw the negative response as an affront on a friend who had only tried to help him. He would defend his collaborator at every opportunity.

"[Peter Buck] is just a really, really genuinely nice guy," Eitzel would maintain. "All he wanted to do was make music, because REM don't play a lot."

While fans and critics were still trying to absorb *West*, indeed one reviewer saw the process as akin to trying to grasp a wetfish wriggling in his hands, Buck and Eitzel embarked on a promotional tour. This was never part of the original plan, but Buck had enjoyed the atmosphere in the studio, wanted to help Eitzel and was keen to do some shows – REM had no touring plans for the rest of the year.

The tour was called The Magnificent Seven vs the United States and involved sets by Tuatara without Eitzel as well as the Buck-Eitzel band. In a particularly shrewd move, Buck had Eitzel invite Dan Pearson along as a supportive and comforting presence for the singer. Pearson wouldn't be there for the early shows, but when he joined up with the tour, Buck liked him immediately and the bassist fitted easily into the band.

Pearson had recently put his own band together with Tim Mooney. Called Clodhopper, they played bluegrass-tinged country rock. Of Eitzel's other former cohorts, Vudi meanwhile had returned from a spell with Michael Gira's Swans and was also putting a new band together. Bruce Kaphan in the meantime was touring with David Byrne's band, although he did join The Magnificent Seven for a few dates when schedules allowed.

Buck and Eitzel's shows began on 1st May at the Crocodile Café in Seattle. They spent the rest of May touring the US. Because Buck wrote most of *West*'s guitar parts using conventional chords, as opposed to the open tuning patterns Eitzel normally employs, the singer couldn't play guitar on the new tracks live. Buck tried to explain the chords down the phone to him, but Eitzel could not get a handle on them. In a way this was a blessing for Barrett Martin, who found it difficult to deal with Eitzel's erratic timekeeping. For Martin, the fewer times Eitzel picked up a guitar, the better.

The shows were well received and Eitzel seemed far more relaxed than he had been for years. He didn't stop songs in mid-flow and was rarely distracted by the audience. Buck was helping him come to terms with his post-Everything But The Girl wariness of live shows. "I'd say to Mark," Buck remembers,

"'Look, it doesn't matter that not everyone in the whole hall is listening. OK there are people at the back talking, but the people at the front are hanging on your every word, and I'm behind you with the rest of the band, and if you let things go because of a few people, you'll be letting us down'. And I think it helped a bit."

Dan Pearson agrees, "We shared a room for the whole tour and Mark was fine. He was in the best spirits I've ever seen."

In June, the band played three low-key gigs in Ireland without Buck before meeting up with him in London. The Irish shows were not just warm-ups.

Eitzel's reputation was steadily growing in a country where songwriting is highly valued. *Hot Press* magazine trailed his Dublin show as gig of the fortnight.

A couple of days later Peter Buck checked into London's Mayfair Intercontinental and prepared for a full media onslaught. Round the corner Eitzel and Pearson settled into a hotel Eitzel would describe simply as a "fucking piss-hole." But the disparity did not cause any tension. Eitzel was grateful that Buck had come all the way to the UK to help push the record. Buck was one of the most generous people he'd ever met, and he was after all, paying his own way. The tour would cost the REM man in the region of $40,000 out of his own pocket.

On 18th June, after a hectic schedule of press interviews, Buck, Eitzel, Pearson and Barrett Martin played a short set at the Virgin Megastore on Oxford Street. The band looked relaxed, and the place was packed. Though he looked embarrassed at times, Eitzel sang with real conviction. But, unable to pretend the event was anything other than a marketing ploy, Eitzel came immediately clean:

"We're playing here so that you buy our new record," he explained. He then belched and added, "the next track should close the sale." A beautiful new take on "Old Photographs" followed.

As the set finished, Buck and Eitzel hurried to a cordoned off area to sign copies of *West*. Meanwhile, Dan Pearson stepped up to the microphone and said, "We were American Music Club."

That night the band were at the Islington Union Chapel – an amazing multi-tiered gothic church in North London. The show was advertised as The Mark Eitzel Ordeal.

The band started the show as a three-piece. Eitzel, Pearson on a majestic imposing upright double bass and Barrett Martin on vibes and drums worked through beautiful, stripped-down versions of "What Holds The World Together," "An Apology For An Accident" and "Mission Rock Resort." Only on "Last Harbor" did the inappropriateness of the new arrangements jar.

"I used to have the best band in the world," Eitzel told the crowd at one point. "But no-one liked us, no-one bought the records, so..."

As the audience noisily disagreed, Eitzel added, "Yeah, you lot bought the records, but you know ...". He told the audience he would reform AMC if someone will only give him $1 million.

"Hang on," he added, "Make that $5 million: a million each." And his makeshift band launched into "Western Sky."

Buck then joined the band for refreshing versions of nearly all of the *West* material. His grounding presence allowed Eitzel to let rip and by the time they get to "Old Photographs" Eitzel was down on one knee, without a guitar to restrain him, lost in the passion of his singing.

Before the next song, someone at the back yelled a request for "Live or Die", at which point someone closer to the stage countered from the shadows, "No, none of that shit." .

It was an odd exchange. Eitzel's hardcore fans would rather publicly insult him than listen in silence to another song from his much maligned collaboration. The heckle took some of the wind out of the singer's sails, but by the time of the final encore, "I've Been a Mess," he was back at full tilt.

After one verse he ripped out the mike lead, staggered to the front of the stage and sang the rest of the song unamplified. It was an Eitzel trademark that many of the assembled REM fans were simply not expecting. The church went absolutely silent. Dan Pearson stepped back onto the stage and maintaining a permanently furrowed brow, tugged the lead gently from his upright bass and started to quietly caress its strings. His playing was loud enough to give Eitzel's singing some backing, without disturbing his mood. Eitzel's pleasure at the understated support was tangible. Then in the words of *Melody Maker*'s Victoria Seagal, "Mark Eitzel walks to the front of the stage, throws back his head and sings. And, suddenly, everything becomes clear."

Later Eitzel would enthuse over the venue and its acoustics, "If I could play the Union Chapel and draw that many people without Peter Buck there, it would be the best show of my life. It would be the defining show. I'd do a two-hour set of all my songs, with no PA. Just the moment!

"I could walk out into the crowd and sit on beautiful boys and beautiful girls laps. And I could make this totally funny and beautiful thing. It would be great. But I can't draw that many people without Peter Buck!"

The next day Eitzel finally got to play the John Peel show – performing a short acoustic set with Buck. Afterwards the band flew back to the US. As the dust settled, Eitzel found himself getting increasingly irritated by the bitchy response of some fans and critics. "I read one review of the album and a show," he remembers,

"And it was called 'Buck Off.' ... I didn't think this was going to be the record, and I did not intend to do 300 interviews – the promo stuff really bugged me, and I did it purely and simply because Peter is a friend. It did pass through my mind that it would be a more commercial record, and that it might sell more because Peter was there. That more than passed through my mind. I thought, 'Great!'

"And I was really proud of the songs. I think later people will look back on it, and think that it is such a good record. But I didn't really think it was going to sell many copies. The songs were still too dark."

For Eitzel, the album's relative lack of success provoked mixed feelings. No sooner was he back in the spotlight, than he wanted to be out of it again – left alone just to write his own songs and follow his muse.

"Peter is a total professional. Being with Peter, you know why REM are where they are. The man is a complete dynamo. He always wants to work, and to be popular, and a rock star. That is all he wants. It's not all I want though.

"I guess I have this unfortunate spiritual feeling that my songs change the world... So when I see successful things, I see that success can limit an artist as much as anything else. I'd love the money though."

In the end, Eitzel was philosophical about the collaboration, telling a reporter

"I don't have any money, so it's hard for me to get really good players. Peter brought in people to play, they basically decided what would happen and everything they played was beautiful. I can't tell you how pleasant this all was. It's usually pretty difficult for me to find people to work with. With Peter, though, what he does is instantly recognisable – he's in REM, for fuck's sake – so I just run with that. I always write dark and quiet songs and he writes these big, jangly choruses. I can't do that. If I was going to write "Walk Like An Egyptian," it would be a funeral song. We make a perfect match."

Eitzel and Buck worked on another seven songs later that summer, though as yet there are no plans to release them. Pressed for a last word on his work with Eitzel, Buck would reflect:

"It was a great pleasure and a great experience, but above all, everything you've heard about Mark Eitzel is not true. It's all an act. He's never had a drink, he's not melancholy and he's not gay."

In the next couple of months Eitzel did a few US live shows with another grounding influence, singer Jill Sobule, before taking part in two quite different side-projects. On 30th August in a darkened Hollywood soundstage, he previewed his score for a new musical film adaptation of Peter Handke's *The Left Handed Woman*, in front of an intimate gathering of filmmakers and fans, with just a goateed xylophonist for musical accompaniment.

The film tells the story of a woman who divorces her husband, quits her job, and realising all the men in her life are too needy, casts herself away from everyone she knows.

"I wanted to write a soundtrack that was not the normal corny bullshit," Eitzel would reflect. "I really don't like musicals. The only way I can get through a musical is if I smoke a huge joint."

Eitzel's point was borne out by recent research watching Madonna in *Evita*, "Three puffs and I could not walk. Hallucinatory pot! We sat down in the front row, with a huge screen. And you know what? I loved it. I cried throughout the whole thing! I kept getting this idea, that when people sing, that is their souls singing. And I thought, 'I can do this a thousand times better than Andrew Lloyd Fucking Webber.' I loved it, but it was really bad."

Although the Handke project had not started shooting yet, the cast had been recruited and actresses Ann Magnuson and Grace Zabriskie joined Eitzel at the premier to sing some of their characters' pieces. The film will also feature Billy Zane and is scheduled for a 1999 release. "It's really different from anything I've ever written before," Eitzel explains.

"It uses songs to describe what's in the people's hearts as opposed to songs that just move the plot around, and the songs I've written are pretty surreal."

In September, Eitzel was back in New York taking part in a *CMJ* spoken word night at the Knitting Factory, along with the likes of Elliott Smith, Lori Carson, Foetus' Jim Thirlwell, and Kurt Reighley. While some of the performers remained po-faced throughout, Eitzel managed to regularly reduce the audience to hysterical laughter.

"I only started writing poems a couple of weeks ago," he began. "And I'm really bad at it." He then introduced his first piece as "Crappy poem #1," read the first line and then said, "I hate poetry." When he finally finished the poem, somebody shouted, "That poem rocked." Eitzel replied, 'Leave me alone. I just want a drink'. He then read one more poem, "For Ralph Reed on the Death of Allen Ginsberg."

When Eitzel was later asked about the likelihood of him doing a poetry record, he laughed and explained that he could barely get his songs released, never mind anything else. He then returned to his day job with a short solo acoustic tour that would take in parts of the US untouched by the Magnificent Seven shows.

To help cover some of the touring costs, Eitzel pressed up 500 copies of a CD of outtakes from *Caught in A Trap* – together with a couple of home DAT recordings and some songs recorded with Bruce Kaphan for a project provisionally titled "What Happened to the Future?" His alternative working title was "I Don't Know Anything, Parts 1-10." Kaphan and Eitzel worked on the material in the Summer of 1997.

"It's something I'm doing without any expectations of anyone having it," Eitzel would say at the time. "It's on a sampler, so it's sampled stuff, but I don't want to do another Portishead thing. There's enough fucking Portishead rip-offs already."

The project sampled a famous soundtrack of space music, but Eitzel will not say which one for fear of having to pay up.

He titled the CD *Lover's Leap USA* and drew each CD cover by hand himself – varying the design radically from sleeve to sleeve. Eitzel would refer to the material as "patriotic songs about logging."

Once the CDs were pressed, Eitzel decided it was a mistake to include the first two home demos. On his DIY artwork, he named both songs "Skip to Track 3" adding at the bottom of the tracklisting, "The first two songs are really awful."

"They're not good songs," he insists. "They are not good recordings of those songs – I was being vain and arrogant putting them on."

In actual fact, though the recording was rudimentary, they were two of the CD's strongest tracks. Considering *Lover's Leap* consists entirely of rejected material, most of which was never finished, it is consistently strong. The highlights were two songs that Eitzel included in his live repertoire during the Autumn '97 tour and for shows in the following year: "Steve I Always Knew" and "Leave Her Alone." Both songs marked distinct departures for the writer.

"Steve" was Eitzel's only gender-specific love song to a man. It begins with a night of sex and crystal meth and goes on to document a long relationship's decline. "Leave Her Alone" was a protest against Eitzel's sister's treatment by her right-wing brother-in-law. It was partly an attack on the anti-abortionist lobby, America's so-called moral majority, and partly a tribute to Renee. It was also Eitzel's first foray into political songwriting. Over time he and Renee had become close again. Eitzel got on well with her husband too, and would spend a lot of time at their house. Sharing the same sense of humour and liberal political affiliations, Eitzel and Renee could now relax in each other's company.

While the *Lover's Leap* jaunt had a low profile, taking in mainly smaller venues, Eitzel felt the gigs went well and enjoyed being on the road on his own. "I did two shows at McCabe's guitar shop in LA," he recalls, "And the first night was the best show in my whole life. Then there was a show in a church hall in Nashville, where the PA was really bad. The guy had all this reverb on the vocal, and I watched the opening act, and you couldn't hear a word they said. The guy behind the board didn't know how to turn on the monitors, so I did a whole song and a half without any monitors. Then I got off the stage, moved down into the audience, parked down on a stool and did the rest of the show acoustically. I'd do all the shows that way if I could."

Shortly after the shows, Eitzel was back in New York. The first thing he did was attend a Belle and Sebastian gig where he bumped into Joe Chicarelli for the first time since the *San Francisco* sessions. Since the *60 Watt* tour, Eitzel had criticised his former producer at every possible opportunity – including one particularly damning extended rant in Jack Rabid's *The Big Take Over* magazine.

"I was really high," Eitzel remembers. "In every way. I was high because I love that record [*If You're Feeling Sinister*] and because I was a big fan, and because I was so drunk that I could barely stand up. I was actually being visited by the Holy Spirit. I am not kidding – I really felt God was talking to me ... It wasn't really to do with Belle and Sebastian, because they are like teenagers, but the moment was just so wonderful! We were in the second oldest synagogue in America, and it was beautiful. And I was really happy to be there. It was the most sold out show in New York, and it took my agent all day to get me in, and it was joyous.

"Then Joe Chicarelli came up from behind me, and poked me down here [the small of his back] and I was like, 'Aargh!' I am not a touchy feely kind of person anyway. I went, 'What? Oh no! Not you!' And I really screamed it at him. Then I went, 'Joe, I want to tell you something. I'm sorry about the things I said about you in the press. He said, 'Yeah, I know. It's bad.' I said, 'I know. I'm sorry. It was unprofessional, I shouldn't have done it. I mean, I meant it, but I shouldn't have done it.' He accepted the apology, and I was sorry... Then I said to Joe, 'So you like Belle and Sebastian?' and he goes. 'Yeah, they're great.' And I said to him: 'Keep your fucking hands off them! Don't you dare!'"

About this time Eitzel was considering working with Kentucky band The Rachels. Rumours of a collaboration with Kevin Shields of My Bloody Valentine were also bandied about – though only one short track, an instrumental with an Eitzel spoken word contribution entitled provisionally "Incidental One" was ever recorded. After his work with Buck and Kid Congo, as well as his soundtrack work and his poetry, it appeared that Eitzel was willing to accept any offer that came his way. Some observers would say he needed to be more discerning, but then what did he have to lose? Without a band, Eitzel was enjoying his freedom.

In December Eitzel left his side-projects behind for a while in order to play a solo acoustic show at London's Rheingold Club. The gig was scheduled to build Eitzel's media profile in anticipation of the release of *Caught In A Trap* ... early the following year. Admission was by invitation. Scattered amongst the press and hardcore fans were former House of Love man Guy Chadwick and The Divine Comedy's Neil Hannon.

Eitzel was playing to a group of committed converts, but he appeared angry and on edge. As he ran through an old AMC favourite, he forgot the words and looked to the audience for assistance. A fan at the front helped him, and he continued the song with a smile on his face, clearly enjoying the rapport. Seconds later, he stumbled again and a girl near the back shouted out a line. The prompting continued, but Eitzel was frowning now, and wanted to get on with the song, though later in between verses he looked at the first lyric prompter for approval of his ability to remember the balance of the words. The fan rather jokily pointed out that he had got one of the lines wrong, and Eitzel frowned, cursed his prompter and left the stage. The inadvertently offending fan, sat at the front of the stage, looking shocked and hurt. The audience was stunned, and began to chatter nervously. Then before you know it, Eitzel hopped from behind a curtain and continued the song at exactly the point he had left off, as if nothing had happened.

But there was still an undercurrent of anger and there was another skirmish to come. When a bespectacled fan near the front called for a song off *Lover's Leap*, Eitzel turned on him and scathingly said, "Oh you've got that have you?" with bitter sarcasm. Eitzel then denigrated both the song and the request. The fan looked shocked, protesting "I just really like the song, man, I understand it." It was a moving and poignant moment, and Eitzel, with heavy irony, grudgingly agreed to play it later. But he didn't.

After the show the fan sits on his own at a table, hugging a drink with a strange expression on his face. He came to see his favourite artist, pleased to be on the guest list and to get such a great seat at the front. Now he appeared unsure as to how this experience could fit into his admiration for Eitzel. He was clearly one of the most devoted fans there. His whole night was centred on the show, while most of the audience were checking Eitzel out on their way somewhere else. He just wanted Eitzel to realise how much he loved his work. Would he go home and play Eitzel's records anyway, rejoicing in the music while trying to forget the humiliation, or would he bracket it away in some part of his mind, justifying his hero's behaviour under the grounds that that is how tortured artists are bound to behave?

Previously Eitzel stood out among performers as someone who would never ignore his audience or try and put them down. In interviews he would stress how reciprocal the relationship between artist and performer was. Ever since those ill-fated support slots, Eitzel's attitude to his most fervent supporters had become at best ambivalent. But then his contempt for his fans was nothing compared to his own self-loathing.

Eitzel had obviously hardened his outer skin. But the saddest thing of all was that one of the greatest songwriters of the 1980s and 1990s had travelled all the way from San Francisco only to play some kitsch little London bar in front of the same old faces when he should have been a household name.

Still as the audience made their way out of the Rheingold, Eitzel was euphoric. He knew it was a good show and was high from performing his new material to a truly enthusiastic audience. If *Caught In A Trap* doesn't bring some breakthrough, maybe the next one will. Or the next...

Chapter Sixteen

A Fire That Can't Be Put Out

Interviewer: "How long do you see yourself doing music? I mean, is there a point where you can't do it anymore, you get too old or...?"
Mark Eitzel: "Yeah, I'm sure there will be a point like that. When I come back with a name like the American Music Starship."

"It may sound egotistical, but I think I'll be a late discovery. I think people will see the clarity and simplicity in my work and appreciate it for those qualities."

Charles Bukowski 1974

"Mark knows he'll be writing songs for the next 20 years, and being a songwriter is not such a bad life, you get to write and stay at home. And if your records are available and you tour the right way you can make a living."

Peter Buck, 1998

"You make this clear vision happen. You make this clear moment happen, and that doesn't always happen, and even when you create this thing, it is like a glass of water that you will not drink.

"The great thing about songwriting is... the latest song I wrote is this incredibly craven, corny, adult contemporary pop song. It's awful, but I'm insanely proud of it and I felt really high this afternoon, because I'd created this very clear and direct thing – I'd gotten through my own bullshit to make such a thing so other people could understand. But I also know that I did it in a clever enough way to make it entertaining for a while, rather than for a minute."

On 7th January 1998, in a small San Francisco bar a former member of American Music Club was playing a short solo set. He sat with a banjo on his knee and worked his way through the haunting story of a family funeral, "1,000

Days Of Shame." His singing had never sounded better – his name was Dan Pearson.

A week later Mark Eitzel sat in a London bar and ran his hand across his furrowed brow. A journalist had just asked him if he thought his new album would be a success. "I don't think anybody is going to buy this record," he sighed.

"It's too dark and all the reviews are going to say the same thing – that it's 'very bitter', or 'a nightmare of melancholy', and even if they are very poetic about it, people are going to go, 'Well I don't want that in my fucking house.'"

Eitzel was back living out of hotel rooms again. He made a short trip back to San Francisco to put his furniture in storage and was now back on the promotional treadmill. He was doing some European solo dates to showcase his new material while once again baring his soul to the press. He was armed just with an acoustic guitar, but was already telling journalists that he wanted to form a group again. He had lined up a bassist and DJ to fill out his sound.

"I want it to be really intense and hard-edged," he told Joel Selvin. "I'm sick of being a folksinger."

Mark Eitzel's second solo album, snappily titled *Caught In a Trap and I Can't Back Out 'Cause I Love You Too Much, Baby* came out on Matador Records on 20th January 1998. For the first time since *California* and *United Kingdom*, Eitzel had recorded an album of the stripped down folk-blues-country amalgam that had prefigured the now burgeoning Alternative Country/No Depression scene led by Uncle Tupelo, Son Volt, Wilco, Whiskeytown and a host of others.

Indeed Whiskeytown's Ryan Adams told writer Nick Johnstone, "Mark Eitzel? I love him. I love the *Engine* record, when that came out I played it over and over. It's amazing. Adams explained that his aim was never to play "country-rock." He just wanted to emulate AMC. "American Music Club would push the parameters," he added. "That's what I wanted to do."

On this mainly acoustic offering, Eitzel appeared hellbent on producing the bleakest album imaginable. The album's sound was relentlessly stripped down and no concession whatsoever was made to the marketplace. Either Eitzel had given up hope of ever being heard on the radio, or he needed to get a resolutely non-commercial work out of his system.

"I've tried my hardest to be part of the marketplace," Eitzel would explain.

"I do every interview that I'm asked to do more or less politely, I do everything that's asked of me. I try really hard. I just can't write commercial songs to save my precious little life."

With hindsight, Eitzel's keenness to acquiesce on *West* to all of Peter Buck's pop impulses, can be seen partly as a response to this bleak album which he had recorded only weeks before in New York.

Caught begins with a peculiarly vicious tirade on a discarded lover, "Are You the Trash." Devoid of humour or compassion, bitterly misanthropic and with a two-note vocal melody, it paves the way for the dark collection that follows.

Eitzel's anguish at the break-up of his band, his resentment at his commercial failure and his devastation after the Everything But the Girl tour all helped forge this album's dismal and sombre mood, though initially he would give little away about its subject matter. "All the songs are about sex," he would explain elliptically, "Except the second one that's about food."

But neither sex nor food are particularly evident on *Caught*. Instead, world-weariness, resignation and misanthropy predominate. On "Are You the Trash," Eitzel intones, *"Evil gets what it wants."* On "Auctioneer Songs" *"People are nails on the chalkboard."* During "Xmas Lights Spin" this bitterness almost becomes self-parody as Eitzel sings, *"St Nicholas left your toys at the bar / St Nicholas the wolves see right through you."*

On "Goodbye" Eitzel neatly sums up the state of mind that runs through the album, *"It's all been said and done / The who's and the why's and the what's / Now I'm tired to the bone."*

But the songwriter doesn't exclude himself from his apparent loathing of life and humanity. He is a *"solitary ghost... a goldmine in reverse."*

But *Caught*'s problem was not simply the bleakness of its sound and subject matter. What really lets it down is a defiant reluctance to tease out the melodies lurking within six of the songs written in Eitzel's furious eleventh-hour writing session. Though the performances were consummate, the writing had a rushed air.

Tim Mooney would say of Eitzel's *Mercury* demos, "There would always be all these open tunings, so we'd have to look very carefully to find the melodic elements and the rhythmic structure of the song, so they wouldn't all sound the same."

It was a process that would have benefited some of *Caught*'s first few tracks. Eitzel has said that he finds melody the hardest part of the songwriting process. He was also becoming more interested in non-musical writing, feeling more of an affinity with American writers and film-makers than with other musicians or songwriters. On the initial batch of *Caught*'s solo songs, Eitzel is really just intoning verse over intricate acoustic guitar backing. The songs are not fully developed.

The recent live favourite "If I Had a Gun," was one of the album's highlights, but it could not compete with an earlier version planned as the B-side for Virgin's aborted "Southend On Sea" single. With breezier acoustic guitar and delicate piano from Mark Capelle the earlier version inherited some of the spirit of its inspiration, Neil Young's "Sugar Mountain." Eitzel's vocals strained in the slow understated style of Paul Buchanan, and when Capelle's trumpet joined the piano, guitar and soft percussion for an aching coda it was an Eitzel solo high-point. The *Caught* version featured a wonderful finger-picked guitar pattern, but was far more malevolent and claustrophobic.

In that *Caught* was for the most part a return to bleak, heartwrenching, solo acoustic music, it was perceived by Eitzel's hardcore fans as a return to form. Many of his long-term supporters in the media saw it as his best work in years.

"It's great stuff, yet again," Andrew Mueller raved in *Time Out*. Andrew Smith in *The Times* also felt Eitzel was back on the right track:

"The truth is that Eitzel, whose wit and wistfulness has often been mistaken for morbidity, has been inconsistent in recent years, ever since Virgin Records tried to turn him into a bona fide pop star. Now back with an independent label, and backed by a terrific band, he seems to have hit form again.... An unexpected treat."

But other less hardcore supporters in the media were repelled by the album's dark, unrelenting bleakness.

Mojo's Martin Aston summed the album up as, "An outpouring of acoustic misery blues to shame all-comers... One wonders why, if he can find poetry in his soul, he can't express one iota of hope."

Stuart Bailie in the *NME* similarly yearned, "for some relief" from the album's relentless mood. In truth, *Caught...* was an album Eitzel had to make at that time.

"The press likes me," he explained, "but then they write things like, 'This devastating, dark journey through despair, through the torpid tides of morbidity...' Nobody wants to buy that. So nobody buys my records, and nobody's going to play them on the radio because the radio sucks. So I gave up trying to make pop records."

Giving no ground to the public, *Caught* proved to the songwriter that he didn't have to please anyone other than himself. If he didn't feel like making an album accessible, so be it. The darker and bleaker it was, the better.

But there were still many flashes of Eitzel's genius in evidence. At least five of the eleven tracks could bear comparison with his best work. "Go Away" in particular shared the sprawling build to aching climax of "Apology for an Accident" and "Mission Rock Resort." Its lyrics too were among Eitzel's most striking, as he mulled over his never-ending feelings for Kathleen. He had written "Free of Harm" about her for the *West* album, and confessed on the internet, "I want her back in my life." "Go Away" is more vivid, crafted and ambiguous than that collaboration,

> *The butcher shop in the air is heavy with all the choice cuts.*
> *Columbus God of hope twists a knife in your guts*
> *All you talk about is how disappointed you are...*
> *I just wanted to fill your soul with light and free us both from the Ohio day*
> *But my touch just made you draw farther and farther away."*

The band tracks, "Goodbye," "Queen of No-one" and "Cold Light of Day," were also immeasurably more convincing than the acoustic material. And, if "Attico 18" didn't have the catchiest vocal melody, it featured a mesmeric acoustic guitar figure reminiscent of incidental music from a '60s revisionist Western – the wry and hopeful soundtrack to a time already past.

Caught would win Eitzel no new fans whatsoever, but it cleared the decks to allow him to make an album that perhaps would. As he embarked on a short tour to promote his new record, Eitzel was already thinking about the next one, which would have a completely different tone.

"I wrote a whole album where everything is completely hopeful and upbeat," he told The Divine Comedy's Neil Hannon, in a *CMJ*-sponsored interview.

"I'm really happy. And this album that's like a year old comes out and all the reviews are like 'Oh shit... who wrote these,' and it's like, No! No! No! My next album is going to be this incredibly pop thing."

Later Eitzel would claim his next project would be a double album on one CD. He was writing lots of new material and wanted to release it all. "The first half will be a total pop record," he explained. "Only two songs will be less than 90 bpm." Then after five minutes of traffic noise, there would be another ten songs of a far darker and slower nature. Eitzel's working title for the project was, "I'm Not Afraid of Rain Clouds, I'm Not Afraid of Rain, I'm Gonna Live Forever."

During the latter half of February, Eitzel travelled around the British Isles with just his guitar and a few boxes of *Lover's Leap* – though he would only allow fans to buy the CDs if he was in a good mood!

"I'd love to be in a band again, but I can't afford it anymore," he admitted at the time.

"But because I'm a major label artist people think I have all this money, so if I get a band together, band members think I can give them $500 each per week. But without tour support from the label, I don't have $500 to give anybody."

Even though he was still on his own, Eitzel's performances during this tour were completely reinvigorated and he garnered his best live reviews in years. He then headed off on a short jaunt across mainland Europe, before returning to the US for more low-key dates. This leg would bring Eitzel to San Francisco's Great American Music Hall on the 13th of April. He then had a couple of rest days before heading up to play Stephanie Buck's Crocodile Café in Seattle. When he found out Dan Pearson and Tim Mooney's new band Clodhopper would be playing old AMC haunt The Hotel Utah on the 15th April, he offered his services as support act. He would even bring Bruce Kaphan along for some additional backing.

Clodhopper's line-up was completed with former Wade member Joe Goldring and Tim Bierman on guitar. After a year of sporadic shows and rehearsals, they had just released their debut album, *Red's Recovery Room,* and were now trying to raise their profile. Tinged with country and bluegrass influences, *Red's* is a promising debut album. It mixes early American folk music, with a guitar sound and sensibility not dissimilar to mid-period AMC. The material is mostly written by Pearson – though there are also a couple of traditional folk songs. Highpoints are the beautiful laidback folk-blues shuffle of "Café Jolie," "1,000 Days of Shame," the title track and a new arrangement of Pearson's old AMC B-side, "Walking Tune." Then there is "Goodnight Nobody" – a wonderful Neil Young-style country rock ballad where Pearson's vocals reach new heights.

The album was recorded in three days. Regardless of budgetary constraints, Pearson and Mooney appeared to have taken away the same lesson as Eitzel from the prolonged agony of the *San Francisco* debacle.

"I learnt from having my own studio," Mooney acknowledges, "That you don't need three months."

Bruce Kaphan dropped in to help with a couple of *Red's* tracks, and on one song, "Cecil," Vudi plays virtually inaudible accordion.

Like American Music Club, Clodhopper's problem so far has been getting people to hear them. The banjo and bluegrass element was also perhaps too strong for them to fit neatly into the rising Alt-country boom.

Eitzel's offer to support his former band-mates could no doubt have helped Clodhopper sell a few more tickets to their Hotel Utah show, but he was keen to downplay his appearance. Both he and Pearson resisted the promoter's attempts to bill the show as an American Music Club reunion and Eitzel wasn't mentioned in any publicity. In the end, the venue was only two-thirds full.

When Eitzel and Kaphan took to the stage, their faces were barely discernible through lights dimmed to a dark red glow. After two new Eitzel compositions, "If They Dismiss You" and "Highway 40" they moved into "What Holds The World Together."

At which point Pearson, who was sitting on the floor to one side of the stage, got up, plugged in his bass, and played along. It just felt right, he would say afterwards. Eitzel then invited Tim Mooney up to join in. The drummer accepted and the four-piece ran through a short emotional set of AMC classics.

Eitzel appeared really happy throughout, while Mooney didn't know whether to laugh or cry.

"It's funny to play a song as the drummer," he would say of that night's performance of "Why Won't You Stay," "And actually be choked up as you're playing it!"

There was only one person stopping the show from being a full-scale reunion of American Music Club's most successful line-up. Vudi arrived at the Hotel Utah just as Pearson strapped on his bass guitar. He sat at the bar throughout the show, but in spite of repeated cries from the audience, refused to join his old colleagues. Later he would claim he couldn't remember any of those old songs.

After the show all four participants seemed to have enjoyed the temporary get together.

"It was fun," Mooney enthuses. "The magic of the band was still there and that felt real good – we knew what to do."

A few days after the reunion show Eitzel went round to Mooney's home studio and the two musicians recorded a couple of demos. It was an enjoyable experience and pretty soon the drummer found himself mulling over the possibility of AMC working together again.

"For me it's always good to work with Mark, because I love his work...but I don't know what kind of record we would make... I don't know if there is a place for it to go."

About this time, Tim Mooney's home studio would bring him into contact with another old AMC cohort, when Tom Mallon stopped by to do some tapes. In spite of all the problems, Mallon remained on reasonable terms with most of American Music Club.

"I think he just got fed up," Mooney reflects.

"Tom had a lot to do with how those records sound and they are Tom's records too. There is a lot of frustration there – he worked a lot of hours making those records sound the way they do."

While Mallon was working round at Mooney's home, Eitzel started to record the initial tracks for his new album at Bruce Kaphan's place. In January Eitzel had been talking about moving to a monastery, or maybe settling in London for a while. Now he was back in San Francisco; having rented out his house, he was living in a basement box room without "toilet privileges."

But it was good to be home again. Eitzel felt buoyed up by the AMC reunion and was looking forward to working with Kaphan on his new songs. Then tragedy struck.

Eitzel got word that Kathleen Burns had died of an overdose. Even though she had been persistently troubled by drugs problems and had been in and out of hospital for years, this was still a huge shock. Kathleen was the one woman Eitzel would claim to have ever really loved. She was the subject of so many of his greatest songs, and since *San Francisco* she had been in his mind more and more. Above all, she was Eitzel's closest friend. Her death would be something that it would take Eitzel a long time to come to terms with.

For now, he would throw himself back into his writing, but it was clear to onlookers that Eitzel would never be quite the same again. Those around him feared he might go to pieces but, initially at least, he appeared to cope with the tragedy amazingly well. But no one knew what was going on inside him. One of the things that Eitzel had found especially moving in Primo Levi's work was the author's huge guilt at having survived The Holocaust when so many hadn't. Now Eitzel would almost certainly be tortured by guilt concerning Kathleen, for failing to do more to help her and above all for surviving her.

***

While Eitzel continued working on his next record, he appeared in a cameo role on Mitchell Froom's solo album, *Dopamine*. A pompous and pretentious affair, Froom's debut was partially redeemed by a wonderful Eitzel vocal on the track, "Watery Eyes." In every other respect *Dopamine* was simply a series of production gimmicks waiting for some songs. In a way the album formed an epilogue to AMC's *Mercury* experiences. It made plain the fact that Froom had always wanted to make his own record with Eitzel singing over the top.

At about the same time, Wally Brill was back the in public arena with a new recording project: ancient yiddish chants set to an Enigma-style dance beat. Unlike similar treatments featuring Native American Indians and Tibetan Monks, it did not take off.

Eitzel's first live show since Kathleen's death was in New York City's Central Park as part of the extended Newport Folk Festival. It was a warm sunny afternoon and Eitzel played a short set with Kaphan and a drummer. As well as a few AMC favourites, he gave an outing to some startling new songs, but gave away little clue to his overall mood, or how he was dealing with his recent tragedy. And, there was more bad news to come.

In September, Eitzel was dropped by Warners. Waronker and Ostin were long gone and Eitzel had few supporters in the label's new corporate regime. Warners had finally begun a low-key programme of American Music Club reissues with *Engine* and *The Restless Stranger*. Now it appeared that this process would stop, leaving *California* and *United Kingdom* still impossible to find in the shops.

On 9th December, Eitzel was back in London, playing the second of two nights at The Twelve Bar Club – a tiny 16th Century barn on the edge of Soho. For the most part he was in good spirits and his set of predominantly new material was well received by a capacity audience.

Highlights among the new songs – named here by first or repeated chorus lines – are the rambunctious, up-tempo "It's The End of the World As We Know It"-style romp, "Proclaim Your Joy," the anthemic "Highway 40," and an aching paean to Kathleen, "I'd Give Anything (To Be With You)."

When did you decide
That the chill would never leave your bones?...
Have you lost so much that none of your tiny wishes can find a toe-
hold...
But if it weren't for you my life would have been spent alone
I'd give anything to be where you are
I'd give anything to be where you are right now.

At about 11 O'Clock, Eitzel asked the audience for requests, "But I won't play 'Firefly'," he insists, "I'm sick of that."

Someone at the back shouted for "Kathleen." Eitzel looked pained and said, "Okay that's it. That's what this whole fucking life is about." As people made comments about San Francisco, Eitzel replied sternly, "No, she's from Cleveland... she *was* from Cleveland."

"You know," he continued, "I'll probably never be with another woman again, because, I was with the only woman who was all women to me." The performance was breathtaking, and the last two lines were new.

When no one cares for you
You're made of straw.
You're living on borrowed time,
You can't do nothing right,
And you can't commit a crime.
Your love Kathleen, is for someone
That I swear, I could have been...
You're a fire that can't be put out,
Water that has to fall.

*** *** ***

Shortly after the December acoustic shows Eitzel announced that he was putting a band together again. The idea was to play with Vudi in Clovis de la Foret, and Vudi was to join Eitzel in his new band. A number of joke names for the new project were bandied about, including Mark Eitzel's Full Release and Eitzel's Superhits International.

When Eitzel's group played their first shows in January 1999, his new material was reborn with a fresh vigour. While many of his new songs were great in their solo acoustic format, they could still have benefited from more work to fully bring out their melodic potential. In their embryonic state, some of the new songs had a tendency to sound similar to each other. Now, with just a few slight changes and the addition of drums, guitar and keyboard, the new songs sound as dynamic as anything Eitzel has written. After a number of different cul de sacs, Eitzel was back doing what he is so good at: writing wonderful songs and performing them with a band. It appears like Eitzel's next album will be the one that his fans have been waiting for since American Music Club disbanded. Maybe everything is going to turn out fine.

In January 1999, when asked what he wanted to do in the rest of the year, Eitzel replied, "To be with Kathleen."

Chapter Seventeen

It Happened One Night

"At the Astoria, it did feel like it was fitting into place. That show was one of the best parts of our lives. It felt like we had arrived."

Dan Pearson

"It did feel great to sell The Astoria out. That was the biggest we were ever going to get, and I knew it."

Mark Eitzel

Interviewer: "That night at the Astoria you really won the crowd over."
Eitzel: "Well, then we lost them again."

It is a sunny afternoon in September 1998. Dan Pearson pulls up outside Tim Mooney's apartment. Once he has picked the drummer up Pearson will drive the van down to a rehearsal studio. The two musicians will then load up their equipment and set off for Seattle – their band Clodhopper have a high profile gig there and are expecting plenty of press.

Pearson and Mooney leave San Francisco and head up Highway 5. The rest of the band are making their own way to the venue. For 1,000 miles it will be just the two of them. The scenery is spectacular, and as they drive across a breathtaking landscape, Pearson remarks how compared to the days of AMC, this was a short trip.

Across town in the Black Market Music guitar shop, owned by Lisa Davis' husband, Mark Pankler is showing a customer a vintage Gibson Les Paul. Later that evening he will rehearse with his new band, Clovis de La Foret for a prestigious slot supporting Nick Cave at the Great American Music Hall. It will be only their second gig. This band will play Vudi's most experimental music since The Farmers.

Across the Bay, Bruce Kaphan tinkers away in his home studio. Enjoying a break from his more lucrative session work, he is working on material for Eitzel's forthcoming album and thinks it is the best thing he has done in years.

On the opposite end of the same continent, Mark Eitzel sits in a characterless hotel, a cup of hot coffee on the dresser and an acoustic guitar resting on his knees. He has a notebook in front of him, and writes in it furiously, in between sips of his drink. After a few more minutes, he pauses, looks back at what he has written and stops. He runs tentatively through the song on his acoustic guitar in a low murmur, not wanting to disturb the other residents. It reminds him of being back in his parents' home, many years ago, where he would practise his guitar as quietly as possible, so as not to have his mother shout up the stairs that he shouldn't be wasting his time like that.

When he finishes the song, he puts the guitar down, picks up his jacket, goes outside and closes the door gently behind him. The look on his face is the diametric opposite of a rictus of pain. He feels happy.

"I'm never going to quit writing songs. How could I? It's a question of whether the songs quit me, I'm not going to leave them. It's what I do."

***

On a rainy morning in October 1998, I open an envelope from the US. Inside there is a tape, some photos, and a brief note:

"I am writing this while making some archival tape of AMC, mostly Eitzel demos he would slip me. I remember, I remember, I remember, I forget...

"Lending him my 4-track so he could record stuff at home because we were always so fucking poor.

"So it's '98, Kathleen finally overdosed. Mark got dropped from Warners. Listening back to Eitzel's demos, repeating lines, I remember maybe 15 years ago talking with Jeannie (a woman in the original AMC) and her telling me he's writing the same song over and over and over. All the turmoil of our ordeal was only the spirit of compromise? How can we present this so people will listen? I don't know. I do know that all the cast had their own ideas, their own agendas...

All I know is that I had a family called American Music Club."

Dan Pearson, 29 September 1998

***

Afterword

A few years earlier on a cool Spring Sunday night in London, American Music Club are about to finish a UK tour with their biggest headlining show to date. Tonight they are at The Astoria on the Charing Cross Road, a venue that can hold 1,600.

Throughout the tour, some of the AMC party have voiced concerns that maybe they might not fill this show. Then it would be an anticlimactic finale, which would detract from what they had already achieved.

But, it is OK. Virgin have fly-posted, advertised and pushed the *Mercury* record and the Astoria show through every media source available. The sign above the doors says, "Tonight American Music Club: Sold Out." And even at 7.00 pm there is a real buzz of excitement inside and outside the venue. For the first time at an American Music Club show in the UK, there are a significant number of ticket touts gathered outside in designer sportswear barking, "Buy or sell all spares."

Earlier, the band have run through a soundcheck in a far more professional manner than usual. They have also spent an inordinately long time planning the setlist. Now, backstage, they are quiet. The atmosphere in the band's dressing room gradually evolves into apprehension and gloom, as all the while, Mark Terrill continues to juggle a number of ringing phones, keeping one eye on the constantly whirring fax.

Inside the slightly run-down venue, amongst the gathering press there is a general feeling of vindication: after three or four years of support it feels like it has come good. Writers from traditional AMC champions such as *Melody Maker* jostle shoulders with reviewers from *The Times, The Guardian* and *The Independent. Time Out*, London's hip entertainment bible has plugged this as the show of the fortnight.

Former AMC publicist Spike Hyde is conscious that, "The groundwork has been done..." Amongst the new record company, there was a feeling that everything is coming together.

At 7.45pm, The Cranberries come on and play a tightly controlled set of tuneful indie rock. One year later Dolores O'Riordan will be an international media babe. Her band will sell 8 million albums in the US and Dolores' wedding will be the cover story for *Hello* magazine. The Cranberries are destined to become millionaires. After the Irish quartet disappear backstage and into a different stratosphere from the headlining band, the bar area starts to clear as people jockey to get nearer the stage.

At 9.00pm *Rolling Stone*'s songwriter of the year 1991, Mark Eitzel, walks onstage in an ill-fitting pin-stripe suit carrying a white semi-acoustic guitar. There is no sign of the other band members. Eitzel's face is a mixture of nervousness and downright fear. After some initial cheers, an unnerving total and absolute silence takes over. The press have talked, cajoled, harangued and begged this capacity crowd here tonight, and now the non-partisan members of the audience wait for AMC to deliver. It is highly likely that at least 800 people here have never seen the band live before. Meanwhile, the believers are just praying that nothing goes wrong.

Mark Terrill remembers the pre-show nerves,

"They knew that this would be the decisive thing: they had to do it right, so there was a lot of pressure. In a way they can act well when it comes to it. There doesn't need to be a lot of discussion. They all knew intuitively what they were up against, without having to discuss it much."

The anticipation is tangible – this is not just another gig. Eitzel is aware this is the big moment. Various members of the crowd shout encouragement and wise cracks. He laughs when someone at the front mentions the previous night's fiasco:

"No, we will not play Sheffield again." Then he starts to pluck the guitar delicately and a crisp sound hovers in the air. The PA and the acoustics are perfect. Haunting arpeggios, wash over the audience like a warm balm. The song will later be called "The Thorn In Your Side is Gone." The crowd listens in total silence.

"It was incredibly quiet," Terrill remembers. "I have never heard that many people together in one place be that quiet."

Dan Pearson agrees, "You could hear a pin drop."

When the song ends, there is a moment's pause … and then the crowd nervously react – the haphazard applause genuinely reflecting the fact that the audience are stunned by Eitzel's intensity rather than unappreciative. The band wander on nervously smiling. They have never played to such a silent and respectful audience before. As Mark Terrill explains,

"They'd been a bar band for all these years – playing in noisy clubs, and trying to win the people over. And if it failed, they'd do something crazy. Here they could do neither. It was strange."

"It is just a good feeling," Tim Mooney would reflect. "To know that everyone was there to see you. And we thought, 'Okay, we can really play!'"

The band then work their way through a stunning performance of their best material. For once they are doing the right thing. After "Thorn" comes "Laughing Stock," "If I Had a Hammer," "I've Been A Mess," "Ex-Girlfriend" and "Nightwatchman." Each song is more intense and cathartic than the last.

As the performance develops, the new *Mercury* songs are reborn with a frightening belligerence, but instead of the flailing, spitting, twisted chaos of old, Eitzel's intensity is contained. He is more like a caged panther than the usual baited angry bear. "Gratitude Walks" again features exquisite backing vocals from Pearson, and along with "Johnny Mathis' Feet," proves to any doubters that *Mercury* featured some of Eitzel's best writing.

Then the band is into "Western Sky". Acoustic guitar notes weave across Kaphan's haunting pedal steel set to a delicate Mooney drum shuffle. Vudi's playing is piercingly understated while Eitzel croons one of his life-time best vocal performances.

Then the band leave Eitzel alone on the stage, re-tuning his guitar for "Last Harbor." Halfway into the first verse, he pauses, "What do you want me to do?"

A hail of different requests pours out of the front reaches of the audience. Then one voice shouts, "What do you want to do?"

"I want to sit at the bar and have a few drinks," the singer replies, then peers out to survey the packed and reverent crowd, "You know, this is so nice that you all showed up and I guess this is like our big triumph."

He fiddles with the tuning heads of his guitar, shuffles back and forward, takes in the size of the venue, and says: "Well, it's all downhill from here – that is true."

Years later, in a small pub on the edge of Soho, with a third pint of lager in his hand, Eitzel would reflect: "As soon as I said that thing at the Astoria, I could feel all around me, all those mathematical straws breaking, ... as soon as I said it on stage."

***

> *The only thing that held me together in the good old days,*
> *was a wish... That I could wish the world away...*
> *You can wish the world away.*

Mark Eitzel, Wish The World Away.

Appendices

Appendix 1 – Discography

(Serial numbers relate to UK releases unless stated otherwise)

American Music Club: Albums and EPS

The Restless Stranger – Grifter FR001 US 1985 / Reissue CD Warners 9 46675-2 US, 1998 with extra tracks *.
"Room Above the Club," "$1,000,000 Song," "Away Down My Street," "Yvonne Gets Dumped," "Mr Lucky," "Point Of Desire," "Goodbye Reprise #54," "Tell Yourself," "When Your Love Is Gone," "Heavenly Smile," "Broken Glass," "Hold On To Your Love," "Restless Stranger,"* "How Low,"* "I'm In Heaven Now,"*

Engine – LP Frontier 1023 US 1987 / CD Zippo ZONG CD 020 UK 1990 / Reissue CD Warners 9 46671-2 US, 1998 with extra tracks*
"Big Night," "Outside This Bar," "At My Mercy," "Gary's Song," "Nightwatchman," "Clouds," "Electric Light," "Mom's TV," "Art of Love," "Asleep," "This Year," "Away Down My Street (Live),"* "Art of Love (Rock 'n Roll Version)"* "Shut Down (Live)."*

California – LP/CD Demon FIEND 134 UK, 1988
"Firefly," "Somewhere," "Laughing Stock," "Lonely," "Pale and Skinny Girl," "Blue and Grey Shirt," "Bad Liquor," "Now You're Defeated," "Jenny," "Western Sky," "Highway 5," "Last Harbor."

United Kingdom – LP /CD Demon FIEND 151 UK, 1989
"Here They Roll Down," "Dreamers of the Dream," "Never Mind," "United Kingdom," "Dream is Gone," "Heaven of Your Hands," "Kathleen," "The Hula Maiden," "Animal Pen."

United Kingdom and California – on one CD Demon FIEND CD 151 UK,
1990 Includes all tracks from each album.

Everclear – Alias A105, 1990
"Why Won't You Stay," "Rise," "Miracle on 8th Street," "Ex-Girlfriend," "Crabwalk," "The Confidential Agent," "Sick of Food," "The Dead Part of You," "Royal Café," "What The Pillar Of Salt Held Up," "Jesus' Hands."

Mercury – Virgin Records CDV 2708, 1993
"Gratitude Walks," "If I Had A Hammer," "Challenger," "I've Been A Mess," "Hollywood 4-5-92," "What God Said to Godzilla When His Name Wasn't Found in the Book of Life," "Keep Me Around," "Dallas, Airports, Bodybags," "Apology for an Accident," "Over and Done," "Johnny Mathis' Feet," "The Hopes and Dreams of Heaven's 10,000 Whores," "More Hopes and Dreams," "Will You Find Me."

San Francisco – Virgin Records CDV 2752, 1994
"Fearless," "It's your Birthday," "Can You Help Me?" "Love Doesn't Belong to Anyone," "Wish the World Away," "How Many Six Packs Does it Take to Screw in a Light?" "Cape Canvaral," "Hello Amsterdam," "The Revolving Door," "In the Shadow of the Valley," "What Holds the World Together," "I Broke My Promise," "The Thorn in my Side is Gone," "I'll Be Gone."
NB Vinyl LP also features "I Just Took My Two Sleeping Pills and Now I'm Life A Bridegroom Standing at the Altar,"
US Reprise CD features hidden tracks at the end of the album, "Fearless (Reprise)," and "California Dreamin'"

Hello Amsterdam – Reprise 9 45862-2, 1995
"Hello…," "I Just Took My Two Sleeping Pills and Now I'm Like a Bridegroom Standing at the Altar," "The President's Test For Physical Fitness," "On A Clear Day You Can See Forever," "The Thorn in My Side is Gone (Alternative Version)" "Elbow Deep."

Singles

"Rise," CD single Alias A014-D, 1991

"Rise," "Chanel #5," "The Right Thing," "Crabwalk."

"Johnny Mathis' Feet," CD single, Virgin VSCDG 1445, 1993

"Johnny...," "Will You Find Me (Ahuja Mix," "The Hopes and Dreams of Heaven's 10,000 Whores (Home Demo)," "Apology For an Accident (Home Demo),"

"Johnny Mathis' Feet," CD single, Virgin VSCDT 1445, 1993

"Johnny...," "Amyl Nitrate Dreams of Pat Robertson," "What God Said to Godzilla When His Name Wasn't Found in the Book of Life (Home Demo)," "Dallas, Airports, Bodybags (Home Demo),"

"Johnny Mathis' Feet," Cassette single Virgin VC 1445, 1993

"Johnny...," "Will You Find Me (Ajuha Mix)," "Amyl Nitrate Dreams of Pat Robertson," "Hopes and Dreams of Heaven's 10,000 Whores (Home demo)"

"Keep Me Around," CD single Virgin VSCDG 1464, 1993

"Keep...," "In My Role As The Most Hated Singer In The Local Underground Music Scene," "Memo From Aquatic Park," "Walking Tune."

"Keep Me Around," Cassette single Virgin VC 1464, 1993

"Keep...," "In My Role As The Most Hated Singer In The Local Underground Music Scene," "Challenger (home demo)," "Memo From Bernal Heights."

"Wish The World Away," CD Single Virgin VSCDT 1512, 1994

"Wish...," "I Just Took My Two Sleeping Pills and Now I'm Life A Bridegroom Standing at the Altar," "The Revolving Door (Original Band Demo)."

"Wish The World Away," CD Single Virgin VSCDT 1512X, 1994

"Wish... (Original Band Demo)," "The President's Test For Physical Fitness," "Cape Canaveral."

"Wish The World Away," Cassette single Virgin VSC1512.
"Wish...," "I Just Took..."

"Can You Help Me," CD Single Virgin VSCDT 1523, 1995

"Can...," "The Thorn in My Side is Gone (Alternative Version)," "California Dreamin'."

Compilations

Acoustic Music Project Alias A009 US
features United Kingdom version of "Dreamers of the Dream."

Human Music double album Homestead HMS 100 US, 1988
CD reissue HMS 100-2 features previously unreleased track, "I'm In Heaven Now."

Volume 6, CD free with magazine, 6VCD6 BMG / Worlds End,
features AMC previously unreleased track, "Love Connection NYC."

No Alternative CD Compilation BMG 18737-2, 1993
features AMC previously unreleased track, "All Your Jeans Were Too Tight."

Signed, Sealed and Delivered 1 Virgin CD sampler VV SAM 22, 1994
features Mercury version of "Challenger,"

If I Were A Carpenter A&M 540 258-2, 1994
Carpenters Tribute album features AMC version of "Goodbye To Love."

Americanism Nectar Masters NTMCD 509
features California version of "Firefly."

Promos

Engine / Flying Colour sampler cassette, Frontier, 1987
"Outside This Bar," "Gary's Song," "Clouds," "Electric Light." b/w 4 Flying Colour tracks

Over and Done Reprise PRO-CD-6066, 1993
"Over and Done," "Nightwatchman," "Outside This Bar," "Bad Liquor," "Highway 5," "Rise," "Why Won't You Stay," "Sick of Food," "The Dead Part of You," "Chanel #5," "The Hopes and Dreams of Heaven's 10,000 Whores (Demo)" "If I Had a Hammer (Demo)," "Challenger (Demo)" Tracks interspersed with interviews.

Johnny Mathis' Feet Plus Live Tracks Reprise, 2 CDs PRO-CD-6527, 1993
CD 1, "Johnny Mathis' Feet." CD 2, Live at Slim's San Francisco, June 15th, 1993, "Outside This Bar," "Challenger," "Western Sky," "Johnny Mathis' Feet, " "I've Been a Mess," "Nightwatchman," "Bad Liquor," "Hula Maiden," "Pale Skinny Girl," "Somewhere."

"Keep Me Around," Virgin Records 12" One sided VSTDJ 1464, 1993
"Keep Me Around."

"Over and Done," Reprise PRO-CD-6263, 1993
"Over and Done," "In My Role As The Most Hated Singer In The Local Underground Music Scene," "The Amyl Nitrate Dreams of Pat Robertson."

I'll Be Gone, Reprise PRO CD 7416, 1994
"I'll Be Gone," "I Just Took My Two Sleeping Pills…," "The President's Test For Physical Fitness," "On A Clear Day," "The Thorn in my Side is Gone," "Elbow Deep."

Miscellaneous

Breakfast Without Meat fanzine free flexi features previously unreleased "Crystal Always Knows," circa, 1990.

Mark Eitzel solo albums and EPs

Mean Mark Eitzel Gets Fat – cassette only release, 1981
"Swing Low," "You Can Be Beautiful," "Hold On To Your Love," "I Speak French," "A Tall Black Lady," "Keep This Dance For Me," "Shadow of My Name."

Songs of Love (Live At The Borderline 17.1.91) FIEND CD 213, 1991
"Firefly," "Chanel No. 5," "Western Sky," "Blue and Grey Shirt," "Gary's Song," "Outside This Bar," "Room Above the Club," "Last Harbour," "Kathleen," "Crabwalk," "Jenny," "Take Courage," "Nothing Can Bring Me Down."

60 Watt Silver Lining – Virgin Records CDV 2798, 1996
"No Easy Way Down," "Sacred Heart," "Always Turn Away," "Saved," "Cleopatra Jones," "When My Plane Finally Goes Down," "Mission Rock Resort," "Wild Sea," "Aspirin," "Some Bartenders Have The Gift of the Pardon," Southend on Sea," "Everything is Beautiful."

West – Warner Brothers CD 9 46602-2, 1997
"If You Have To Ask," "Free of Charge," "Helium," "Stunned and Frozen," "Then it Really Happens," "In Your Life," "Lower Eastside Tourist," "Three Inches of Wall," "Move Myself Ahead," "Old Photographs," "Fresh Screwdriver," "Live or Die."

Lovers Leap USA – Self-released ME 1001, 1997
"Skip to Track 3," "Skip Over to Track 3," "Dream in Your Heart," "Lost My Humor," "How Will You Face Yourself in Sleep," "Lost and Lonely," "Pay it Back," " Leave Her Alone," "Steve I Always Knew," "Nice Nice Nice," "Your Glass Jaw," "What Good is Love," "Sun Smog Seahorse."

Caught in a Trap And I Can't Get Out 'Cause I Love You Too Much Baby Matador Records OLE179-2, 1998

"Are You the Trash," "Xmas Lights Spin," "Auctioneer's Song," "White Rosary," "If I Had A Gun," "Goodbye," "Queen of Noone," "Cold Light of Day," "Go Away," "Attico 18," "Sun Smog Seahorse."

Singles

"Take Courage," 7" single, Matador Records, 1991 #OLE –016-7

"On The Emblematic Use of Jewlery as a Metaphor for the Disolution of Our hopes and Dreams," b/w "The Ecstatic Epiphany: A Celebration of Youth and Beauty Past, Present and Future."

Cover versions

"Frog Princess" – Divine Comedy, Setanta CD single features "Johnny Mathis Feet."

Grand World – Cool For August, Warners CD 9 46105-2 features "Big Night" (Eitzel and Kaphan also contribute to the song.

Other projects featuring members of AMC

Pre-AMC, Tim appeared on a number of records by SF band, Sleepers. Bruce played and engineered on a host of recordings, and Dan Pearson made a number of obscure singles with The Ironics. To list all of the records in which Tom Mallon was involved would require a whole book in itself. This discography is by no means exhaustive or definitive.

The Cowboys (featuring Mark Eitzel)

"Teenage Life," single b/w "Supermarket," Tet Offensive Records TOR-1 US, 1980

The Naked Skinnies (featuring Mark Eitzel)

"All My Life," single b/w "This Is The Beautiful Life," Naked House Records 103457 US, 1981

The Farmers (featuring Vudi)

Packed In An Urban Area. EP, BFM Records, 1982

Tragic Tales of Life, EP, BFM Records, 1983

Toiling Midgets (Mark 1 featuring Tim Mooney)

Sea of Unrest album (re-issued 1994 on CD Fist Puppet Records #16)

Toiling Midgets (Mark 2 Featuring Mark Eitzel and Tim Mooney. Other band members Craig Gray, Paul Hood, Karl J Goldring, produced Tom Mallon, with contributions from Lisa Davis on bass and Carla Fabrizio on cello)

"Golden Frog," 7" single, Matador, 1992

"Golden Frog," b/w "Mr Foster's Shoes"

"Faux Pony," 3 track CD single, Hut CD 25, 1993

"Faux Pony," "Golden Frog," "Mr Foster's Shoes."

Son (Matador OLE 030-1) US, 1992; (Hut) UK, 1993

"Faux Pony," "Fabric," "Slaughter on Sumner Street," "Mr Foster's Shoes," "Process Words," "Clinging Fire / Clams," "Third Chair," "Listen," "Chains."

Clodhopper (featuring Dan Pearson and Tim Mooney)

Red's Recovery Room (My Own Planet Records) cat 637543001425, 1998

"Dinah," "Walking Tune," "1,000 Days of Shame," "Café Jolie," "Goodnight Nobody," "Red's Recovery Room," Chrystalline," "Cecil," "Thomas Hart Benton," "900 Miles," "Moonshine," "Little Match Girl."

(Anyone who has trouble purchasing this US only recording should consult the following website: www.imusic.com/labels/myownplanet. Or write to p.o. box 95921 sea wa 98145, USA)

Dan Pearson solo

San Francisco Song Cycle OWR-0245-2 Compilation CD features Dan Pearson solo acoustic live recording of "1,000 Days of Shame."

The Wannabe Texans (featuring Brad Johnson)

Alcohol Is A Cheap Perfume, Snat Records, 1990

Virginia Dare (featuring Brad Johnson)

Six Songs, Vinyl EP, Nuf Said Records (Nuf Said Velocity Ribs, PO Box 591075, SF, CA 94159), 1993

Gone Again, Vinyl EP, Nuf Said Records, 1994

Virginia Dare, CD, Brinkman Records, 1994 (Includes material from above two Eps)

Baby Got Away, CD, Absolutely Kosher Records, 1998

Congo Norvell

Abnormals Anonymous, 1997 (features Mark Eitzel on vocals and backing vocals)

Mitchell Froom

Dopamine, Atlantic Records, 1998 (Eitzel sings and shares writing credits on one track, "Old Watery Eyes.")

Appendix 2 – Bibliography

All Music Guide to Rock – Michael Erliner et al, Miller Freeman, 1997 (in particular Jason Ankeny's section on Red House Painters)

Beneath A Diamond Sky – Barney Hoskyns, Bloomsbury, 1997

Hank: The Life of Charles Bukowski – Neeli Chernovski, Random House, 1991

Expensive Habits: The Dark Side of the Music Industry by Simon Garfield, Faber and Faber, 1986

Hardcore California – Peter Belsito and Bob Davis, Last Gasp, 1983

Hitmen – Fredric Dannen, Muller, 1990

The Hustler – Walter Tevis, Michael Joseph, 1960

Hymn to Her – Karen O'Brien, Virago, 1995

If This Is A Man – Primo Levi, Penguin Books, 1979

Nick Drake: The Biography – Patrick Humphries, Bloomsbury, 1997

Nightbeat – Mikal Gilmore, Picador, 1998

Route 666 On the Road to Nirvana – Gina Arnold, Picador

"Surrealism and the practice of writing" by John Lechte from Writing the Sacred Ed Caroline Bailey, Routledge, 1995

The Sex Revolts – Simon Reynolds and Joy Press, Serpents Tail, 1995

Appendix 3 – Sources and Acknowledgements

Acknowledgements
Thanks to all those who agreed to be interviewed:

Mark Eitzel, especially for giving so much of his time; Brad Johnson, Bruce Kaphan, Tim Mooney; Dan Pearson, Lisa Davis-Romanov, Peter Buck, Mark Kozelek, James Manniello, Mark Terrill, whose help was absolutely invaluable, Lisa Fancher, for help also truly beyond the call, Joe Chicarelli, Ben Watt, Renee Eitzel, The late Kathleen Burns, Jenny Gonzalvez, Phil Nicholls, Spike and Lisa Hyde, Mick Griffiths, Wally Brill, Orla Lee and Kelly Pyke at Virgin, Allan Jones, Steve Granados, Andrew Smith, Nick Johnstone and Pat McCarthy at St Mary's College.

Thanks also go to:
Vudi for informal assistance, and help in tracking down elusive characters.

Karen O'Brien, without whose encouragement I would have almost certainly given up. Nick Johnstone deserves another special mention for help truly beyond the call. James Manniello, without whose contribution this book would be considerably lighter. He is *the* expert on AMC dates and shows. Much of the specialist eye-witness knowledge derives from or was verified by James, Anthony Kyle Monday and Chris Metzler, who was particularly helpful with live shows.

Janet Billig at Manage This for helping the project off the ground, and David Newgarden from the same company for assistance along the way. Ella and Jasmine at JFD Management for arranging the interview with Ben Watt.

A huge debt is due to the photographers whose work appears in this book. Without the kindness and generosity of Phil Nicholls, Tom Erikson and Steve Gullick in waiving photo reproduction fees, the photo section of the book would be practically non-existent.

More thanks due to Mark Terrill, Dan Pearson and Lisa Fancher for allowing the use of personal photos. Thanks also to Jay Blakesberg for the cover shot.

Thanks also to Kieron Perry, Paul Austin, William Britt, Gina Arnold, Chris Stults, Paul Murphy and anyone else at firefly@fragment.com whose thoughts and words I have drawn on consciously or otherwise.

Mick and Dave at SAF Publishing for taking on a project that was not prima facie profitable, and Mick in particular for turning a sow's ear into something somewhat silkier.

Mike, Caroline, Paula and Linda at Helter Skelter, for words of encouragement, and patience with callers wondering how come the book wasn't out yet.

Pete Burton for input on controversial issues.

Finally, thanks also to those who have accompanied me on various AMC treks around the country, especially Strobes, Warlock, Doug of Douges (WK I) and Tantor the Mighty.

Sources:
The bulk of the material in this book is based on interviews I conducted between October 1997 and September 1998 with the people listed above.

The manuscript underwent a number of drafts, and in addition to the wonderful chaps at SAF, it bears the huge imprint of creative input from Karen O'Brien. I am also forever indebted to Nick Johnstone for a number of unpublished article, source tapes, and generally inspirational "rants", many of which are incorporated into the text in a number of disguises. Nick and Michael O'Connell of Helter Skelter, also reviewed different parts of the draft manuscript, and helped translate it into English.

Others who read drafts of the book and who offered invaluable input are Michael Barry of the Mission Rock Site, Anthony Kyle Monday, Sylvie Simmons, Peter Doggett and David Essery.

I should point out here that the first segment of the final chapter is a part fictionalisation, and some of the information in this section is conjectural, although based on real events.

James Maniello provided me with most of the information about the *United Kingdom* shows. All the otherwise uncredited information about US shows comes directly or indirectly from James.

In addition to my own primary research, I did draw on many secondary sources. And I have quoted so liberally from reviews, both of records and shows, because in a sense AMC and Eitzel's success really only happened in the print media. And the dichotomy between the lack of commercial progress and the rave reviews can only be appreciated by regularly referring to the press.

The following secondary sources were particularly helpful.

"Suffer Time," By Andrew Smith, *Melody Maker*, 26 October 1991 (Andrew's work together with that of Allan Jones, forms not only the best writing on Eitzel and AMC, but also probably helped their cause in the UK more than any other press.)

Partially unpublished Mark Eitzel interview by Nick Johnstone, April 1997

"Death Of A Band" by Jack Rabid *The Big Take-Over*, Issue No. 40

"Sober as a Judge," by Jon Storey and Jud Cost Bucketful of Brains Sept/Oct 1991

"Wishing the World Away with the American Music Club" – Michael Goldberg *Addicted to Noise* internet zine

Michael Barry's unnofficial Mark Eitzel website, Mission Rock:
http:\\www.2extreme.net\missionrock

Other articles I have referred to are as follows:

"The Locals" by Cary Tennis, *The Ward Report*

The Restless Stranger LP review by Kevin Berger *The Ward Report*, 3 February 1986

"Spins: What's in the Grooves" By Jackson Brian Griffith 1985

"Independent Showcases Bands" By Cary Tennis, *Calendar* magazine 16-30 November 1987

Engine album review by Alex Abey *The California Aggie*, 18 November, 1987

Engine album review by Jack O'Neill *NME* 20 February 1988

Engine album review by David Rothon, *Melody Maker*, 20 February 1988

"Ace of Clubs" By Ralph Traitor, *Sounds*, 1988

"The Song Remains the Thing: Tom Mallon Interview" by Alan Di Perna, *Music and Sound Output*, February 1988

"On The Run" by George Paaswell, *Jet Lag* magazine

I-Beam, 2/2/87 live review by "CT," *Calendar* magazine,

"AMC In the Land of Fruits and Vegetables" by Todd Stadtman, *Calendar* Magazine, 1988

"American Music Club: Perhaps The Most Ignored Great American Band" by Seana Baruth, 1988

California album review by Edwin Pouncey, *NME,* January 1988

California album review by Karen Schoemer, *Spin* 1989

California album review by Allan Jones, *Melody Maker* 28 January 1988

"Psycho Thrill" By Simon Reynolds in *Melody Maker*, 4 February 1988

Scary is Beautiful by Duncan Strauss, *Musician,* June 1989

American Music Club by Amy Gelman, *Your Flesh*, Spring 89

"Club Class," By Ralph Traitor, *Sounds,* March 1989

Mean Fiddler live review by Roy Wilkinson, *Sounds* 8 April 1989

"Dark Stars" Mean Fiddler live review by Allan Jones, *Melody Maker*, 8 April 1989

American Music Club interview by Darren Crook, *Offbeat* magazine, April 1989

American Music Club by Jon Storey, *Bucketful of Brains,* Issue 29, April/ May 1989

"One in a Thousand." By Evelyn McDonnell, *Village Voice,* May 9, 1989

"Canned Laughter," Mean Fiddler review by Keith Cameron, *Sounds* October 1989

"The American Dream," Mean Fiddler review by Andrew Smith, *Melody Maker*, October 1989

"Trial and Terror," by Andrew Smith, *Melody Maker*, 21 October 1989

Mark Eitzel interview by Steve Connell, *Puncture* Magazine No. 18, 1989

"Kingdom Come," United Kingdom album review by Bob Stanley, *Melody Maker*, 28 October 1989

United Kingdom album review by David Cavanagh, *Sounds,* 28 October, 1989

American Music Club By Andrea Freedman, *Option* magazine, 1989

"US Empathy" Mean Fiddler review by Simon Williams, *NME,* 4 November 1989

"Eitzel's Ebb" By Simon Williams, *NME,* 2 December 1989

"Symphony in D: American Music Club live at the I-Beam San Francisco" by Everett True, *Melody Maker,* March 1990

Engine (reissued) album review by Allan Jones, *Melody Maker*, October 1990

Engine (reissued) album review by Ralph Traitor, *Sounds,* October 1990

"Dark Side of the Loon" Mark Eitzel interview by Bob Stanley, *Melody Maker*, 26 January 1991

Mark Eitzel at the Borderline live review by Andrew Smith, *Melody Maker*, 26 January 1991

Mark Eitzel at the Borderline live review by Bobby Surf, *NME,* 26 January 1991

Songs of Love Live album review by Everett True, *Melody Maker*, April 1991

Songs of Love Live album review by Edwin Pouncey, *NME*, April 1991

Songs of Love Live album review by Jeremy Clarke, *Q,* April 1991

Songs of Love Live album review by Max Bell, *Vox,* April 1991

"Love is the Drug," By Nick Griffiths, *Select* 1991

Eitzel Towers, Mean Fiddler review, *NME* by Jim Arundel

Reading Festival live review, by Karen Ablaze, *Ablaze* fanzine

"Death Row" *Everclear* review by Allan Jones, *Melody Maker.* 19 October 1991

"Eitzel Towers High," *Everclear* review by Keith Cameron, *NME*, 19 October, 1991

Everclear album review by Graham Linehan, *Select*, November 1991

Everclear album review by Martin Aston, *Q*, December 1991

"Frown Time is Over," By Caren Myers, *Melody Maker*, 1 February 1992

"Beers, Tears and Fears," ULU live review by Paul Mathur, 8 February 1992

"Sullen Impact" by Laura Lee Davies, *Time Out* 8 February 1992

"Wishing the World Away with the American Music Club" – Michael Goldberg *Addicted to Noise* internet zine

"Nice songs, shame about the hair" *Daily Telegraph*, 24 March 1993

"Cosmic Nihalism: An American Music Club Retrospective" From the excellent fanzine, *Hearsay* Issue 8 Winter 94/95 various writers

Son by Toiling Midgets album review by Everett True, *Melody Maker*, 23 January 1993

Mark Eitzel solo, Camden Falcon, live review by Keith Cameron, *NME* 13 February 1993

Mark Eitzel solo, Camden Falcon, live review by Peter Paphides, *Melody Maker*, 13 February 1993

"Wary of shedding the tears of a clown," by Robert Yates, *The Observer* 21/3/93

"Join Our Club,"by Keith Cameron, *NME* 13 March 1993

"Club for Zeroes," by Andrew Mueller, *Melody Maker*, 27 March 1993

Mercury album review by John Mulvey, *Melody Maker*, March 1993

Mercury Album review by Paul Mathur, *MM*, March 1993

Mercury Album review by Andy Gill, *Q*, April 1993

Mercury Album review by Ann Scanlon, *Vox*, April 1993

Mercury Album review by David Cavanagh, *Select,* April 1993

Mercury Album review by Ross Fortune, *Time Out*, April 1993

Leeds Duchess of York, live review by Dele Fadele. *NME*, 3 April 1993

Manchester University live review by Andrew Smith, *Melody Maker*, 3 April 1993

Astoria live review by John Mulholland, *The Guardian*, 6 April 1993

"Mercury Reverence" by David Cox, *Lime Lizard*, April 1993

American Music Club by David Cavanagh, *Volume* April 1993

"Long Distance Call" by David M Yaffe, *Village Voice*, June 1993

"Sung From the Heart," By Emma Forrest, *The Times*, 19 September 1993

"How Many Six Packs Does It Take To Screw in a Light?" By Wendy L. Yee, *Ruta 66*, November 1994

Shaw Theatre Live review by Alan Jackson, *The Times*

Shaw Theatre Live review by John Robinson, *NME*

Shaw Theatre Live review by Sharon O'Connell, *MM* 20 August 1994

"I'm An Ant" By Caitlin Moran, *MM*, 3 September 1994

San Francisco album review by Chris Roberts, *Melody Maker* 10 September 1994

San Francisco album review by Keith Cameron, *NME* 10 September 1994

"New York City Alive With Sound" by Richard Haw, 29 September 1994

"Son of Frankenstein" by David Atkinson, *Heaven Up Here* fanzine

"Mood Swings" by Julene Snyder *SF Bay Guardian*

San Francisco album review by Peter Paphides, *Time Out,* October 1994

"On The Road: American Music Club," Tour diary, *The Guardian*, 21 October 1994

London Forum live review by Bidisha, *NME*, 26 October 1994

London Forum live review by Michael Bonner, *Melody Maker,* 26 October 1994

"Eitzelating" by Ignatius Carmichael, *Sun Zoom Spark* November 1994

"The Complete Useless Loser," Michael Goldberg *Addicted to Noise* internet zine 1996

"Headaches and Heartaches, *San Francisco Bay Guardian*, 17 January 1996

"It's Kind of Like … An Interview With Bruce Kaphan," By Anthony Kyle Monday published on the internet.

"Mope Springs Eternal" By Allison Stewart *Strobe* magazine 1996

"Godlike Genius Or What" By Caitlin Moran, *The Times*, 24 March 1996

60 Watt Silver Lining album review by Ann Powers, *Spin* April 1996

60 Watt Silver Lining album review by Peter Paphides, *Time Out*, April 1996

60 Watt Silver Lining album review, *The Guardian*, April 1996

60 Watt Silver Lining album review by Nick Johnstone, *Melody Maker*, April 1996

"It's A Small World After All" by d.n.l *Pop Culture Press*, Issue 38

"Mark Eitzel faces the world without American Music Club," by Rob O'Connor, *BAM* 3 August, 1996

"Home Again," By Greg Heller, *San Francisco Chronicle*, 6 October, 1996

"Gospel According to Mark," By Scott Carlson, *The Minnesota Daily Online*

'Unsentimental Journey' by Barry Walters *The Advocate*, Feb 97

"Way Out West," by Aidin Vaziri, *Rolling Stone*, 1 May, 1997

"Under a Western Sky: Mark Eit

"The Good News is Worrisome," by Jane Ganahl, *San Francisco Examiner*, 6 May, 1997

"Under a Western Sky" By Bill Crandall, *BAM* magazine, 2 May 1997

"West" – Bob Gulla *Guitar* July 1997

'Eitzel's soul,' by Jennie Punter *Toronto Star*

Dan Pearson interview by Lauren Axelrod, Published on the internet

Untitled Mark Eitzel interview by Mike Agate, *Comes With A Smile* fanzine issue #2 – January 1998

Caught review by Stuart Baillie, *NME* 31 January 1998

Caught review by Tony Naylor, *MM* 31 January 1998

Caught review by Andrew Mueller, *Time Out* 7-14, Jan 1998

Dingwalls live review by Carl Bigelow, *NME,*7 March 1998

"Mark Eitzel's Heartstoppers," By Emmanuel Tellier, *Les Inrockuptibles*, April 1998 (Translated to English and posted to *Firefly* newsgroup by Jonathan Takagi, 16 April 1998)

Appendix 4

The 10 Greatest Tracks by American Music Club & Mark Eitzel – A Personal Selection

1   "Western Sky," AMC *California*

2   "What Holds The World Together," AMC *San Francisco*

3   "Last Harbor," Mark Eitzel *Songs of Love Live*

4   "Heaven of Your Hands," AMC *United Kingdom*

5   "Ex-Girlfriend," AMC *Everclear*

6   "Pale Skinny Girl," AMC *California*

7   "An Apology For An Accident," AMC *Mercury*

8   "Chanel No 5," Mark Eitzel *Songs of Love Live*

9   "I've Been A Mess," AMC *Mercury*

10   "Mission Rock," Mark Eitzel *60 Watt Silver Lining*

A selection of the best less well known songs including AMC members

1   "Mrs Wright," Eitzel home demo not released

2   "Mrs Foster's Shoes," Toiling Midgets (non album cello version) on Hut CD single

3   "If I Had a Gun," Mark Eitzel solo (With Mark Capelle) demo

4   "Goodbye To Love," AMC, *If I Was a Carpenter* tribute compilation album

5   "This is The Beautiful Night," The Naked Skinnies, "All My Life," single B-side

6   "Green Borders," The Farmers, Tragic Tales of Life

7   "California Dreaming," AMC cover, B-side to "Can You Help Me"

8   "1,000 Days of Shame," Dan Pearson solo live, San Francisco Song Cycle

9   "Memo From Aquatic Park," AMC Vudi composition, B-side to "Keep Me Around."

10   "Café Jolie," Clodhopper from the album *Red's Recovery Room*

Coming Soon From Helter Skelter

Waiting for the Man: The Story of Drugs and Popular Music
by Harry Shapiro
Due in April 320 pages, ISBN 1 900924 08 0   Price: £12.99

First published in 1988, this is the definitive study of the extravagant, if sombre, association between drugs and popular music. Shapiro tells in detail the stories of the most famous heroes - Charlie Parker, Jimi Hendrix, Jim Morrison, Keith Moon, Sid Vicious - and examines the relationship between two billion-dollar industries. Fully revised, and including over 100 pages of new material covering the rise of Ecstasy and dance music; rap music and "crack" cocaine, and the return of the wasted junky rock star that came with the Seattle grunge scene. Featured artists in these new sections include Shaun Ryder, Tupac Shakur and Kurt Cobain.

Solo: A Biography of Sandy Denny by Pamela Winters
Due in May. 256 pages,   ISBN 1 900924 11 0   Price: £12.99

Sandy Denny became famous as the distinctive singer Fairport Convention, and later with Fotheringay, as well as releasing four highly acclaimed solo albums. Melody Maker voted her best female singer in 1970 and 1971. But like many of the great musical artists of the seventies, she took refuge in drink and drugs. Sandy Denny died 20 years ago in mysterious circumstances, and this is the first ever Biography. US music journalist Pam Winters has had unprecedented access to Sandy's personal papers. She has interviewed at length all those who were close to her, to produce an illuminating portrait of one of the great English singers.

Coming Soon From SAF Publishing

An American Band - The Story of Grand Funk Railroad by Billy James
ISBN: 0946 719 26 8   224 pages (illustrated) UK £12.95

Grand Funk Railroad were one of the biggest grossing US rock 'n' roll acts of the seventies - they sold millions of records and played to sold out arenas the world over and were often cited as the loudest rock and roll band in the world. An American Band charts Grand Funk's meteoric rise to fame. The mixture of management hype, rock 'n' rolling and political beliefs, might seem naïve by today's standards, but their mammoth success as the 'people's band' has rarely been equalled since. Recently reformed and playing arenas in the States, this is a fascinating look at one of the hardest rocking bands of the seventies.

TEDDY BOYS DON'T KNIT - The Story of Viv Stanshall and the Bonzo
Dog Doo-Dah Band   by Chris Welch   ISBN: 09467119 27 6

Viv Stanshall was one of pop music's true eccentrics. During the sixties he fronted one of Britain's funniest and most surreal musical outfits, The Bonzo Dog Doo Dah Band. However, Stanshall's life was one of extreme highs and lows, varying from playing pranks with The Who's Keith Moon to depression, alcoholism, and his final sad demise in a house fire. Former Melody Maker editor Chris Welch is a long-time Stanshall afficianado and recounts his incredible life story - a man who on the one hand could write lyrics for Steve Winwood, whilst on the other accused of attempting to murder his wife.

New Titles From SAF Publishing

Wish The World Away - Mark Eitzel and the American Music Club
by Sean Body   ISBN: 0 946719 20 9
192 pages (illustrated) UK £11.95

Mark Eitzel's songs are poignant, highly personal tales, encapsulating a sense of loss and loathing, but often tinged with a bitter twist of drink-fuelled humour. Through his solo work and that of his former band American Music Club, Eitzel has been responsible for some of the most individual and memorable records of recent years. Through unrestricted access to Eitzel, former band members, associates and friends, Sean Body has written a fascinating biography which portrays an artist tortured by demons, yet redeemed by the aching beauty of his songs.

LUNAR NOTES - Zoot Horn Rollo's Captain Beefheart Experience
by Bill Harkleroad with Billy James   ISBN: 0 946719 217
160 pages (illustrated) - UK £11.95

Bill Harkleroad joined Captain Beefheart's Magic Band at a crucial time in their development. Beefheart rechristened Harkleroad as Zoot Horn Rollo and they embarked on recording one of the classic rock albums of all time - *Trout Mask Replica* - a work of unequalled daring and inventiveness. Further LPs, *Lick My Decals Off Baby* and *Clear Spot*, highlighted Zoot's skilled guitar playing and what a truly innovative band they were. For the first time we get the insider's story of what it was like to record, play and live with an eccentric genius such as Beefheart.

Meet The Residents - America's Most Eccentric Band! by Ian Shirley
ISBN: 0946 719 12 8   200 pages (illustrated) UK £11.95
Fully updated and now available again!

An outsider's view of The Residents' operations, exposing a world where nothing is as it seems. It is a fascinating tale of the musical anarchy and cartoon wackiness that has driven this unique bunch of artistic maverics forward.

"This is the nearest to an official history you are ever likely to get, slyly abetted by the bug-eyed beans from Venus themselves". **Vox**

"Few enthusiasts will want to put this book down once they start reading".
Record Collector

Digital Gothic - A Critical Discography Of Tangerine Dream
by Paul Stump   ISBN: 0946 719 18 7
160 pages (illustrated) UK £9.95

In this critical discography, music journalist Paul Stump picks his way through a veritable minefield of releases, determining both the explosive and those which fail to ignite. For the very first time Tangerine Dream's mammoth output is placed within an ordered perspective.

"It focuses fascinatingly on the pre-soporific roots of the group and their place in a cool electronic lineage which traces right up to Detroit techno". **Mojo**

"A stimulating companion to the group's music". **The Wire**

No More Mr. Nice Guy - The Inside Story of the Alice Cooper Group
by original guitarist Michael Bruce and Billy James
ISBN: 0946 719 17 9   **160 pages (illustrated). UK £9.95**
Michael Bruce opens the lid on his years with the platinum selling group,
revealing the truth behind the publicity stunts, the dead babies, the drinking,
the executions and, of course, the rock 'n' roll.
*"I'm Eighteen changed Alice Cooper from the group that destroyed chickens to
the group that destroyed stadiums".* **Village Voice.**
*"It might even be argued that the band defined what it meant to be a role
ridden seventies teenager".* **Rolling Stone**

Wire - Everybody Loves a History by Kevin Eden
ISBN: 0946 719 07 1
192 pages (illustrated). UK £9.95
A fascinating look at one of punk's most endearing and enduring bands,
including interviews with all band members. A self-analysis of the complex
motivations which have often seen the various members cross the boundaries
between music and art.
"Any band or their fans could feel well served by a book like Eden's". **Vox**
*"Eden delivers a sharp portrayal of the punk industry's behaviour, influence
and morality".* **Q magazine**

TAPE DELAY by Charles Neal
ISBN: 0946 719 02 0
256 pages (illustrated). UK £11.95
Marc Almond, Cabaret Voltaire, Nick Cave, Chris & Cosey, Coil, Foetus,
Neubauten, Non, The Fall, The The, Lydia Lunch, New Order, Psychic TV, Rollins,
Sonic Youth, Swans, Test Department and many more...
*"A virtual Who's Who of people who've done the most to drag music out of
commercial confinement".* **NME**
"Intriguing and interesting". **Q magazine**

Dark Entries - Bauhaus and Beyond by Ian Shirley
ISBN: 0946 719 13 6
200 pages (illustrated). UK £11.95
The full gothic rise and fall of Bauhaus, including offshoot projects Love and
Rockets, Tones on Tail, Daniel Ash, David J and Peter Murphy. Ian Shirley unravels
the uncompromising story of four individuals who have consistently confounded
their detractors by turning up the unexpected.
*"A brilliant trench-to-toilet missive of who did what, where and when. It works
brilliantly".* **Alternative Press**
"Solidly researched account of goth-tinged glam". **Top Magazine**

Available Now From SAF Publishing

The One and Only: Peter Perrett - Homme Fatale by Nina Antonia
ISBN: 0946 719 16 0
224 pages (illustrated). UK £11.95

An extraordinary journey through crime, punishment and the decadent times of The Only Ones. Includes interviews with Perrett and all ex-band members.
"Antonia gets everyone's co-operation and never loses her perspective on Perrett".
Mojo
"Antonia is the ideal chronicler of Perrett's rise and fall. From his time as drug dealer, to the smack sojourn in The Only Ones, Perrett's tale is one of self-abuse and staggering selfishness". **Select**

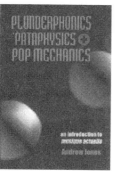

Plunderphonics, 'Pataphysics and Pop Mechanics by Andrew Jones
ISBN: 0946 719 15 2
256 pages (illustrated) UK £12.95

Chris Cutler, Fred Frith, Henry Threadgill, Ferdinand Richard, Amy Denio, Lindsay Cooper, John Oswald, John Zorn, The Residents and many more...
"The talent assembled between Jones's covers would be interesting under any rubric. Thought provoking and stimulating". **Mojo**
"Jones's book is perhaps the first study of the growth of these techniques within the avant-garde. Packed with fascinating interviews and written with wit and insight". **Q magazine**

Kraftwerk - Man, Machine and Music by Pascal Bussy
ISBN: 0946 719 09 8
200 pages (illustrated). UK £11.95

Uniquely definitive account of Kraftwerk's history, delving beyond their publicity shunning exterior to reveal the full story behind one of the most influential bands in the history of rock music. Based on interviews with Ralf Hutter, Florian Schneider, Karl Bartos, Emil Schult and many more.
"Bussy engagingly explains why they are one of the few groups who've actually changed how music sounds". **Q magazine**
"I doubt this book will ever be bettered". **Vox**

Wrong Movements - A Robert Wyatt History by Mike King
ISBN: 0946 719 10 1
160 pages (illustrated). UK £14.95

A sumptuous and detailed journey through Robert Wyatt's 30 year career with Soft Machine, Matching Mole and as a highly respected solo artist. Packed with previously unpublished archive material and rare photos. Commentary from Wyatt himself, Hugh Hopper, Mike Ratledge, Daevid Allen, Kevin Ayers & more.
"King's careful chronology and Wyatt's supreme modesty produce a marvellously unhysterical, oddly haunting book". **Q magazine**
"Low key, likeable and lefty. Like the man himself". **iD magazine**

Available Now From Helter Skelter Publishing

Bob Dylan by Anthony Scaduto 1-900924-00-5 £11.95
The first and best biography of Dylan.

"Scaduto's 1971 book was the pioneering portrait of this legendarily elusive artist. Now in a welcome reprint it's a real treat to read the still-classic Bobography".
Paul Du Noyer, Q***

"Superb on the Greenwich Village scene, insightful on the meaning of John Wesley Harding ... it's still perhaps the best book ever written on Dylan".

**A Journey Through America With The Rolling Stones
by Robert Greenfield   1-900924-01-3 £12.00**
Definitive insider's account of the Stones' legendary 1972 US tour.

"Greenfield is afforded extraordinary access to the band... drugs... groupies. In all, it's a graphic if headache inducing document of strange days indeed".
Tom Doyle, Q**

"Sure, I was completely mad. I go crazy."
Mick Jagger

**Back To The Beach - A Brian Wilson and the Beach Boys Reader
edited by Kingley Abbott 1-900924-02-1 £12.99**
A collection of the best articles about Brian and the band, together with a number of previously unpublished pieces and some specially commissioned work. Features Nick Kent, David Leaf, Timothy White and others with a foreword by Brian.
"A detailed study and comprehensive overview of the BB's lives and music. Most impressively Abbott manages to appeal to both die-hard fans and rather less obsessive newcomers." **Time Out**
"Rivetting!" ****** **Q Magazine**

**Born In The USA - Bruce Springsteen and the American Tradition
by Jim Cullen 1-900924-05-6 £9.99**

The first major study of Bruce Springsteen's that looks at his music in the context of his blue collar roots, and his place in American culture

"Cullen has written an excellent treatise expressing exactly how and why Springsteen translated his uneducated hicktown American-ness into music and stories that touched hearts and souls all around the world." **Q****
"This is a provocative look at one of America's cultural icons." **Newsweek**

Available Now From Helter Skelter Publishing

Like The Night -
Bob Dylan and the Road to the Manchester Free Trade Hall.
ISBN: 1 900924 07 2   192 pages (illustrated). UK £12.00
The full history and background to the show that would become Bob Dylan's latest album, the most famous bootleg in history, now The Bootleg Series vols 4 and 5.
"When Dylan went electric, he both alienated the audience that had championed him and changed the face of rock music.
Lee's enjoyable and atmospheric reconstruction of this phase of Dylan's career is essential reading." **Uncut Magazine**
"CP Lee was there, but the point is that he can put you there too". **Greil Marcus**

XTC - The Exclusive Authorised Story Behind the Music
by XTC and Neville Farmer
ISBN: 1 900924 03 X   306 pages (illustrated). UK £12.00
Co-written by one of the most popular - and usually reclusive - cult bands of all time, this book is timed to coincide with their long-awaited new album.
"A cheerful celebration of the minutiae surrounding XTC's music with the band's musical passion intact. It's essentially a band-driven project for the fans, high in setting-the-record-straight anecdotes. The personality of Partridge dominates this book as it does XTC's music. Superbright, funny, commanding." **MOJO**

GET BACK: The Beatles' Let It Be Disaster
by Doug Sulphy and Ray Schweighhardt
ISBN: 1 900924 12 9   256 pages   UK £12.99
A detailed document of the group's breakdown seen through the prism of the Get Back recording sessions. Instead of making the planned new album, the greatest band in the world were falling apart.
"One of the most poignant Beatles books ever." **Patrick Humphries, MOJO**
"Monumental... Fascinating and revealing" **Goldmine**

If you find difficulty obtaining any title, all Helter Skelter, Firefly and SAF books are stocked by, and are available mail order from:
Helter Skelter Bookshop, 4 Denmark Street, London WC2H 8LL Tel: 0171 836 1151 Fax: 0171 240 9880.

Available From Firefly Publishing

an association between Helter Skelter and SAF Publishing

Poison Heart - Surviving The Ramones by Dee Dee Ramone and Veronica Kofman   ISBN: 0946 719 19 5
192 pages (illustrated). UK £11.95
A crushingly honest account of his life as a junkie and a Ramone.
"One of THE great rock and roll books...this is the true, awesome voice of The Ramones". **Q magazine** *****
"His story - knee deep in sex, drugs and rock and roll - is too incedent packed to be anything less than gripping". **Mojo**
"A powerful work that is both confessional and exorcising" **Time Out.**

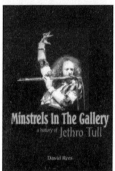

Minstrels In The Gallery - A History of Jethro Tull by David Rees
ISBN: 0 946719 22 5   224 pages (illustrated) - UK £12.99
At Last! To coincide with their 30th anniversary, a full history of one of the most popular and inventive bands of the past three decades. Born out of the British blues boom, Jethro Tull sped to worldwide success and superstardom - the band were one of the biggest grossing acts of the seventies. With LPs like *Aqualung,Thick As A Brick* and *Passion Play*, Anderson mutated from the wild-eyed tramp through flute wielding minstrel to the country squire of rock n' roll.
"Rees has interviewed all the key players and told the Tull tale with zest and candour. A fine read for Tull fans and non-believers alike." **MOJO**

DANCEMUSICSEXROMANCE - Prince: The First Decade by Per Nilsen   ISBN: 0946 719 23 3
256 pages approx (illustrated). UK £12.99
For many years Per Nilsen has been a foremost authority on Prince. In this in-depth study of the man and his music, he assesses the years prior to the change of name to a symbol - a period which many consider to be the most productive and musically satisfying. Through interview material with many ex-band members and friends Nilsen paints a portrait of Prince's reign as the most exciting black performer to emerge since James Brown. In this behind the scenes documentary we get to the heart and soul of a funk maestro.

All Helter Skelter, Firefly and SAF titles can be ordered direct from the world famous
Helter Skelter music bookstore which is situated at:

Helter Skelter,
4 Denmark Street, London WC2H 8LL
Tel: +44 (0) 171 836 1151   Fax: +44 (0) 171 240 9880.
Consult our website at: http://www.skelter.demon.co.uk

This store has the largest collection of music books anywhere in the world and can supply any in-print title by mail to
any part of the globe. For a mail order catalogue or for wholesaling enquiries, please contact us.